Fiat Cinquecento
Service and Repair Manual

Steve Rendle and Spencer Drayton

Models covered
All Fiat Cinquecento models including special/limited editions
899 cc (ohv) & 1108 cc (ohc) petrol engines

(3501 - 216 - 10AG2)

© Haynes Group Limited 2003

A book in the **Haynes Service and Repair Manual Series**

ISBN **978 0 85733 618 7**

British Library Cataloguing in Publication Data
A catalogue record for this book is available from the British Library.

Haynes Group Limited
Haynes North America, Inc

www.haynes.com

The manufacturer's authorised representative in the EU for product safety is:

HaynesPro BV
Stationsstraat 79 F, 3811MH Amersfoort, The Netherlands
gpsr@haynes.co.uk

Disclaimer

There are risks associated with automotive repairs. The ability to make repairs depends on the individual's skill, experience and proper tools. Individuals should act with due care and acknowledge and assume the risk of performing automotive repairs.

The purpose of this manual is to provide comprehensive, useful and accessible automotive repair information, to help you get the best value from your vehicle. However, this manual is not a substitute for a professional certified technician or mechanic.

This repair manual is produced by a third party and is not associated with an individual vehicle manufacturer. If there is any doubt or discrepancy between this manual and the owner's manual or the factory service manual, please refer to the factory service manual or seek assistance from a professional certified technician or mechanic.

Even though we have prepared this manual with extreme care and every attempt is made to ensure that the information in this manual is correct, neither the publisher nor the author can accept responsibility for loss, damage or injury caused by any errors in, or omissions from, the information given.

Contents

LIVING WITH YOUR FIAT CINQUECENTO

Roadside Repairs

Weekly Checks

MAINTENANCE

Routine Maintenance and Servicing

Contents

REPAIRS AND OVERHAUL

Engine and Associated Systems

Transmission

Brakes and suspension

Body equipment

Wiring diagrams

REFERENCE

Index

The Fiat Cinquecento range was launched in the UK in June 1993, initially with the well-proven 899 cc OHV engine used previously in over 3 million Fiat cars. In January 1995, the 1108 cc OHC-engined "Sporting" model was introduced, providing a sporty alternative to the smaller-engined models.

All models have front-wheel-drive, and share the same 3-door Hatchback body design, with the engine and 5-speed manual transmission mounted transversely at the front of the vehicle. The transmission is mounted on the left-hand side of the engine. All engines have single-point fuel injection, and a catalytic converter to reduce harmful exhaust emissions.

The front suspension is of fully-independent McPherson strut type, with lower arms and, on "Sporting" models, an anti-roll bar. The rear suspension is semi-independent, with a torsion beam axle, trailing arms, coil springs and separate telescopic shock absorbers. The suspension on "Sporting" models uses stiffer springs and revised shock absorbers to give a lower ride-height, and improved handling.

A good range of equipment is available across the model range, including central locking, electric windows, air conditioning, and a driver's airbag.

For the home mechanic, the Cinquecento is a straightforward vehicle to maintain and repair, since design features have been incorporated to reduce the actual cost of ownership to a minimum, and most of the items requiring frequent attention are easily accessible.

Fiat Cinquecento

Fiat Cinquecento Sporting

The Fiat Cinquecento Team

Haynes manuals are produced by dedicated and enthusiastic people working in close co-operation. The team responsible for the creation of this book included:

Authors	Steve Rendle Spencer Drayton
Sub-editor	Sophie Yar
Editor & Page Make-up	Steve Churchill
Workshop manager	Paul Buckland
Photo Scans	Steve Tanswell John Martin
Cover illustration & Line Art	Roger Healing
Wiring diagrams	Matthew Marke

We hope the book will help you to get the maximum enjoyment from your car. By carrying out routine maintenance as described you will ensure your car's reliability and preserve its resale value.

Your Fiat Cinquecento Manual

The aim of this manual is to help you get the best value from your vehicle. It can do so in several ways. It can help you decide what work must be done (even should you choose to get it done by a garage), provide information on routine maintenance and servicing, and give a logical course of action and diagnosis when random faults occur. However, it is hoped that you will use the manual by tackling the work yourself. On simpler jobs it may even be quicker than booking the car into a garage and going there twice, to leave and collect it. Perhaps most important, a lot of money can be saved by avoiding the costs a garage must charge to cover its labour and overheads.

The manual has drawings and descriptions to show the function of the various components so that their layout can be understood. Then the tasks are described and photographed in a clear step-by-step sequence.

References to the 'left' or 'right' are in the sense of a person in the driver's seat, facing forward.

Acknowledgements

Thanks are due to Draper Tools Limited, who provided some of the workshop tools, and to all those people at Sparkford who helped in the production of this manual.

We take great pride in the accuracy of information given in this manual, but vehicle manufacturers make alterations and design changes during the production run of a particular vehicle of which they do not inform us. No liability can be accepted by the authors or publishers for loss, damage or injury caused by any errors in, or omissions from, the information given.

Working on your car can be dangerous. This page shows just some of the potential risks and hazards, with the aim of creating a safety-conscious attitude.

General hazards

Scalding

• Don't remove the radiator or expansion tank cap while the engine is hot.
• Engine oil, automatic transmission fluid or power steering fluid may also be dangerously hot if the engine has recently been running.

Burning

• Beware of burns from the exhaust system and from any part of the engine. Brake discs and drums can also be extremely hot immediately after use.

Crushing

• When working under or near a raised vehicle, always supplement the jack with axle stands, or use drive-on ramps. *Never venture under a car which is only supported by a jack.*
• Take care if loosening or tightening high-torque nuts when the vehicle is on stands. Initial loosening and final tightening should be done with the wheels on the ground.

Fire

• Fuel is highly flammable; fuel vapour is explosive.
• Don't let fuel spill onto a hot engine.
• Do not smoke or allow naked lights (including pilot lights) anywhere near a vehicle being worked on. Also beware of creating sparks (electrically or by use of tools).
• Fuel vapour is heavier than air, so don't work on the fuel system with the vehicle over an inspection pit.
• Another cause of fire is an electrical overload or short-circuit. Take care when repairing or modifying the vehicle wiring.
• Keep a fire extinguisher handy, of a type suitable for use on fuel and electrical fires.

Electric shock

• Ignition HT voltage can be dangerous, especially to people with heart problems or a pacemaker. Don't work on or near the ignition system with the engine running or the ignition switched on.

• Mains voltage is also dangerous. Make sure that any mains-operated equipment is correctly earthed. Mains power points should be protected by a residual current device (RCD) circuit breaker.

Fume or gas intoxication

• Exhaust fumes are poisonous; they often contain carbon monoxide, which is rapidly fatal if inhaled. Never run the engine in a confined space such as a garage with the doors shut.
• Fuel vapour is also poisonous, as are the vapours from some cleaning solvents and paint thinners.

Poisonous or irritant substances

• Avoid skin contact with battery acid and with any fuel, fluid or lubricant, especially antifreeze, brake hydraulic fluid and Diesel fuel. Don't syphon them by mouth. If such a substance is swallowed or gets into the eyes, seek medical advice.
• Prolonged contact with used engine oil can cause skin cancer. Wear gloves or use a barrier cream if necessary. Change out of oil-soaked clothes and do not keep oily rags in your pocket.
• Air conditioning refrigerant forms a poisonous gas if exposed to a naked flame (including a cigarette). It can also cause skin burns on contact.

Asbestos

• Asbestos dust can cause cancer if inhaled or swallowed. Asbestos may be found in gaskets and in brake and clutch linings. When dealing with such components it is safest to assume that they contain asbestos.

Special hazards

Hydrofluoric acid

• This extremely corrosive acid is formed when certain types of synthetic rubber, found in some O-rings, oil seals, fuel hoses etc, are exposed to temperatures above 400°C. The rubber changes into a charred or sticky substance containing the acid. *Once formed, the acid remains dangerous for years. If it gets onto the skin, it may be necessary to amputate the limb concerned.*
• When dealing with a vehicle which has suffered a fire, or with components salvaged from such a vehicle, wear protective gloves and discard them after use.

The battery

• Batteries contain sulphuric acid, which attacks clothing, eyes and skin. Take care when topping-up or carrying the battery.
• The hydrogen gas given off by the battery is highly explosive. Never cause a spark or allow a naked light nearby. Be careful when connecting and disconnecting battery chargers or jump leads.

Air bags

• Air bags can cause injury if they go off accidentally. Take care when removing the steering wheel and/or facia. Special storage instructions may apply.

Diesel injection equipment

• Diesel injection pumps supply fuel at very high pressure. Take care when working on the fuel injectors and fuel pipes.

⚠️ *Warning: Never expose the hands, face or any other part of the body to injector spray; the fuel can penetrate the skin with potentially fatal results.*

Remember...

DO

• Do use eye protection when using power tools, and when working under the vehicle.

• Do wear gloves or use barrier cream to protect your hands when necessary.

• Do get someone to check periodically that all is well when working alone on the vehicle.

• Do keep loose clothing and long hair well out of the way of moving mechanical parts.

• Do remove rings, wristwatch etc, before working on the vehicle – especially the electrical system.

• Do ensure that any lifting or jacking equipment has a safe working load rating adequate for the job.

DON'T

• Don't attempt to lift a heavy component which may be beyond your capability – get assistance.

• Don't rush to finish a job, or take unverified short cuts.

• Don't use ill-fitting tools which may slip and cause injury.

• Don't leave tools or parts lying around where someone can trip over them. Mop up oil and fuel spills at once.

• Don't allow children or pets to play in or near a vehicle being worked on.

The following pages are intended to help in dealing with common roadside emergencies and breakdowns. You will find more detailed fault finding information at the back of the manual, and repair information in the main chapters.

If your car won't start and the starter motor doesn't turn

☐ Open the bonnet and make sure that the battery terminals are clean and tight.

☐ Switch on the headlights and try to start the engine. If the headlights go very dim when you're trying to start, the battery is probably flat. Get out of trouble by jump starting (see next page) using a friend's car.

If your car won't start even though the starter motor turns as normal

☐ Is there fuel in the tank?
☐ Is there moisture on electrical components under the bonnet? Switch off the ignition, then wipe off any obvious dampness with a dry cloth. Spray a water-repellent aerosol product (WD-40 or equivalent) on ignition and fuel system electrical connectors like those shown in the photos. Pay special attention to the ignition coil wiring connector and HT leads.

A Check the condition and security of the battery connections.

B Check that the spark plug HT leads are securely connected by pushing them onto the ignition coil.

C Check that the wiring connectors are securely connected to the ignition coil.

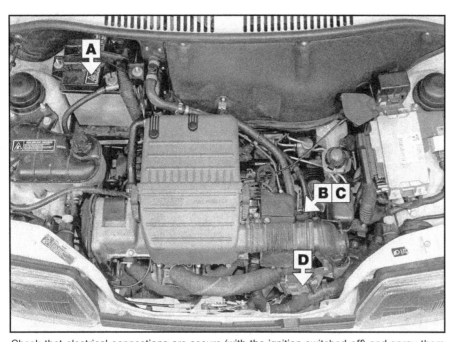

Check that electrical connections are secure (with the ignition switched off) and spray them with a water dispersant spray like WD40 if you suspect a problem due to damp

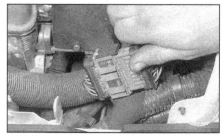

D Check that the two halves of the engine wiring harness connector are securely connected.

E Check that the inertia switch has not been activated (see Chapter 4 for further details).

HAYNES HiNT *Jump starting will get you out of trouble, but you must correct whatever made the battery go flat in the first place. There are three possibilities:*

1 *The battery has been drained by repeated attempts to start, or by leaving the lights on.*

2 *The charging system is not working properly (alternator drivebelt slack or broken, alternator wiring fault or alternator itself faulty).*

3 *The battery itself is at fault (electrolyte low, or battery worn out).*

When jump-starting a car using a booster battery, observe the following precautions:

✔ Before connecting the booster battery, make sure that the ignition is switched off.

✔ Ensure that all electrical equipment (lights, heater, wipers, etc) is switched off.

✔ Take note of any special precautions printed on the battery case.

✔ Make sure that the booster battery is the same voltage as the discharged one in the vehicle.

✔ If the battery is being jump-started from the battery in another vehicle, the two vehicles MUST NOT TOUCH each other.

✔ Make sure that the transmission is in neutral (or PARK, in the case of automatic transmission).

⚠ *Warning: Before attempting to jump-start a Cinquecento, the battery clamp must be removed, and the battery must be pulled forwards (see Chapter 5A). This is necessary to give enough room to connect the red jump lead to the battery positive terminal. Make sure that the red jump lead connector does not touch the body.*

1 Connect one end of the red jump lead to the positive (+) terminal of the flat battery

2 Connect the other end of the red lead to the positive (+) terminal of the booster battery.

3 Connect one end of the black jump lead to the negative (-) terminal of the booster battery

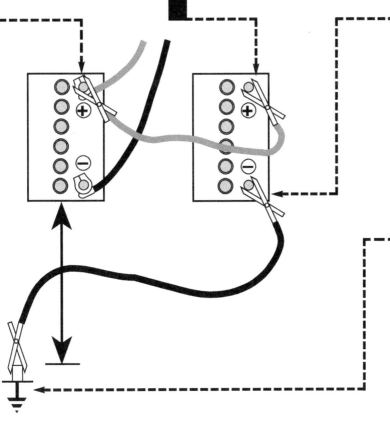

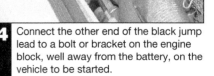

4 Connect the other end of the black jump lead to a bolt or bracket on the engine block, well away from the battery, on the vehicle to be started.

5 Make sure that the jump leads will not come into contact with the fan, drive-belts or other moving parts of the engine.

6 Start the engine using the booster battery and run it at idle speed. Switch on the lights, rear window demister and heater blower motor, then disconnect the jump leads in the reverse order of connection. Turn off the lights etc.

Wheel changing

Some of the details shown here will vary according to model. For instance, the location of the spare wheel and jack is not the same on all cars. However, the basic principles apply to all vehicles.

Warning: Do not change a wheel in a situation where you risk being hit by another vehicle. On busy roads, try to stop in a lay-by or a gateway. Be wary of passing traffic while changing the wheel - it is easy to become distracted by the job in hand.

Preparation

☐ When a puncture occurs, stop as soon as it is safe to do so.
☐ Park on firm level ground, if possible, and well out of the way of other traffic.
☐ Use hazard warning lights if necessary.

☐ If you have one, use a warning triangle to alert other drivers of your presence.

☐ Apply the handbrake and engage first or reverse gear.

☐ Chock the wheel diagonally opposite the one being removed – a couple of large stones will do for this.
☐ If the ground is soft, use a flat piece of wood to spread the load under the jack.

Changing the wheel

1 The jack and wheel brace are located inside the spare wheel, in a recess in the floor of the luggage compartment. Lift up the luggage compartment carpet panel, then release the elastic strap securing the tools to the spare wheel. The wheel brace and jack are clipped into a plastic holder. Unscrew the retainer and remove the spare wheel.

2 Where applicable, prise off the wheel trim from the wheel with the flat tyre and/or prise the covers from the wheel bolts, then loosen each wheel bolt by half a turn. Where anti-theft wheel bolts are used, a special adapter will be required.

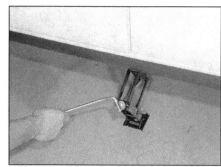

3 Locate the jack head below the reinforced jacking point nearest the wheel to be changed, and on firm ground (don't jack the car at any other point on the sill). Ensure that the lug on the jack head engages with the cut-out in the jacking point.

4 Turn the jack handle clockwise until the wheel is raised clear of the ground. Remove the bolts and lift the wheel clear, then fit the spare wheel. Refit the wheel bolts and tighten moderately with the wheel brace.

5 Lower the car to the ground, then finally tighten the wheel bolts in a diagonal sequence, and where applicable, fit the wheel trim. Note that the wheel bolts should be slackened and retightened to the specified torque at the earliest opportunity.

Finally...

☐ Remove the wheel chocks.

☐ Stow the jack and tools in the correct locations in the car.

☐ Check the tyre pressure on the wheel just fitted. If it is low, or if you don't have a pressure gauge with you, drive slowly to the nearest garage and inflate the tyre to the right pressure.

☐ Have the damaged tyre or wheel repaired as soon as possible.

Identifying leaks

Puddles on the garage floor or drive, or obvious wetness under the bonnet or underneath the car, suggest a leak that needs investigating. It can sometimes be difficult to decide where the leak is coming from, especially if the engine bay is very dirty already. Leaking oil or fluid can also be blown rearwards by the passage of air under the car, giving a false impression of where the problem lies.

 Warning: Most automotive oils and fluids are poisonous. Wash them off skin, and change out of contaminated clothing, without delay.

 The smell of a fluid leaking from the car may provide a clue to what's leaking. Some fluids are distinctively coloured. It may help to clean the car carefully and to park it over some clean paper overnight as an aid to locating the source of the leak.

Remember that some leaks may only occur while the engine is running.

Sump oil

Engine oil may leak from the drain plug...

Oil from filter

...or from the base of the oil filter.

Gearbox oil

Gearbox oil can leak from the seals at the inboard ends of the driveshafts.

Antifreeze

Leaking antifreeze often leaves a crystalline deposit like this.

Brake fluid

A leak occurring at a wheel is almost certainly brake fluid.

Power steering fluid

Power steering fluid may leak from the pipe connectors on the steering rack.

Towing

When all else fails, you may find yourself having to get a tow home – or of course you may be helping somebody else. Long-distance recovery should only be done by a garage or breakdown service. For shorter distances, DIY towing using another car is easy enough, but observe the following points:

☐ Use a proper tow-rope – they are not expensive. The vehicle being towed must display an 'ON TOW' sign in its rear window.
☐ Always turn the ignition key to the 'on' position when the vehicle is being towed, so that the steering lock is released, and that the direction indicator and brake lights will work.
☐ Only attach the tow-rope to the towing eyes provided.

☐ Before being towed, release the handbrake and select neutral on the transmission.
☐ Note that greater-than-usual pedal pressure will be required to operate the brakes, since the vacuum servo unit is only operational with the engine running.
☐ On models with power steering, greater-than-usual steering effort will also be required.
☐ The driver of the car being towed must keep the tow-rope taut at all times to avoid snatching.
☐ Make sure that both drivers know the route before setting off.
☐ Only drive at moderate speeds and keep the distance towed to a minimum. Drive smoothly and allow plenty of time for slowing down at junctions.

☐ On models with air conditioning, a screw-in front towing eye is provided. The towing eye is located with the jack and wheel brace in the luggage compartment (see "Wheel changing").
☐ To fit the screw-in-type towing eye, prise the cover from the slot under the left-hand headlight, then screw in the towing eye, clockwise as far as it will go. Tighten the towing eye with the wheel brace. A fixed rear towing eye is welded to the rear of the chassis.

⚠️ **Warning: To prevent damage to the catalytic converter, a vehicle must not be push-started, or started by towing, when the engine is at operating temperature. Use jump leads (see "Jump starting").**

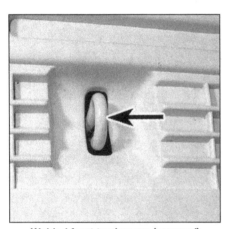

Welded front towing eye (arrowed)

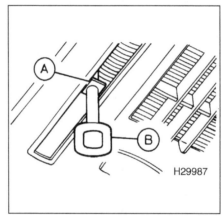

Screw-in type front towing eye

Screw towing eye A into bracket B

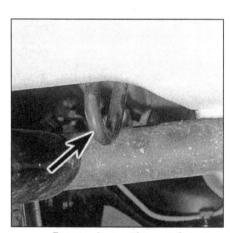

Rear towing eye (arrowed)

Introduction

There are some very simple checks which need only take a few minutes to carry out, but which could save you a lot of inconvenience and expense.

These "Weekly checks" require no great skill or special tools, and the small amount of time they take to perform could prove to be very well spent, for example;

☐ Keeping an eye on tyre condition and pressures, will not only help to stop them wearing out prematurely, but could also save your life.

☐ Many breakdowns are caused by electrical problems. Battery-related faults are particularly common, and a quick check on a regular basis will often prevent the majority of these.

☐ If your car develops a brake fluid leak, the first time you might know about it is when your brakes don't work properly. Checking the level regularly will give advance warning of this kind of problem.

☐ If the oil or coolant levels run low, the cost of repairing any engine damage will be far greater than fixing the leak, for example.

Underbonnet check points

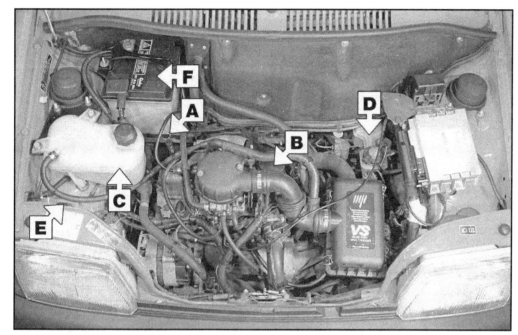

◀ OHV engine

A Engine oil level dipstick
B Engine oil filler cap
C Coolant reservoir (expansion tank)
D Brake fluid reservoir
E Washer fluid reservoir
F Battery

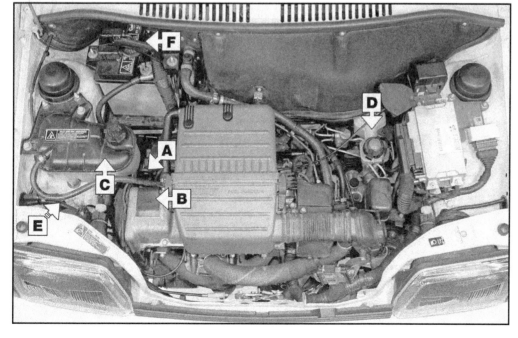

◀ OHC engine

A Engine oil level dipstick
B Engine oil filler cap
C Coolant reservoir (expansion tank)
D Brake fluid reservoir
E Washer fluid reservoir
F Battery

Engine oil level

Before you start
✔ Make sure that your car is on level ground.
✔ Check the oil level before the car is driven, or at least 5 minutes after the engine has been switched off.

 HAYNES HiNT *If the oil is checked immediately after driving the vehicle, some of the oil will remain in the upper engine components, resulting in an inaccurate reading on the dipstick!*

The correct oil
Modern engines place great demands on their oil. It is very important that the correct oil for your car is used (See "Lubricants, fluids and tyre pressures" on page 0•17).

Car Care
● If you have to add oil frequently, you should check whether you have any oil leaks. Place some clean paper under the car overnight, and check for stains in the morning. If there are no leaks, the engine may be burning oil.

● Always maintain the level between the upper and lower dipstick marks (see photo 3). If the level is too low severe engine damage may occur. Oil seal failure may result if the engine is overfilled by adding too much oil.

1 The dipstick is located in a tube at the right-hand corner of the engine next to the coolant reservoir (see "*Underbonnet Check Points*" on page 0•11 for exact location).

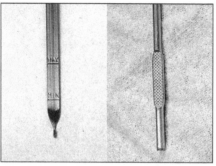

3 Note the oil level on the end of the dipstick, which should be between the upper ("MAX") mark and the lower ("MIN") mark, or in the cross-hatched area (depending on model)

2 Withdraw the dipstick. Using a clean rag or paper towel, wipe all the oil from the dipstick. Insert the clean dipstick into the tube as far as it will go, then withdraw it again.

4 Oil is added through the filler cap. Unscrew or unclip (as applicable) the filler cap, then top-up the level. A funnel may help to reduce spillage. Add the oil slowly, checking the level on the dipstick often. Don't overfill.

Coolant level

⚠️ **Warning: DO NOT attempt to remove the expansion tank pressure cap when the engine is hot, as there is a very great risk of scalding. Do not leave open containers of coolant about, as it is poisonous.**

Car Care
● With a sealed-type cooling system, adding coolant should not be necessary on a regular basis. If frequent topping-up is required, it is likely there is a leak. Check the radiator, all hoses and joint faces for signs of staining or wetness, and rectify as necessary.

● It is important that antifreeze is used in the cooling system all year round, not just during the winter months. Don't top-up with water alone, as the antifreeze will become too diluted.

1 The coolant level should be checked in the expansion tank, which is located on the right-hand side of the engine compartment. The expansion tank has "MAX" and "MIN" level markings. When the engine is cold, the level should be between the two marks. When the engine is hot, the level may rise slightly above the "MAX" mark.

2 If topping up is necessary, wait until the engine is cold, then turn the pressure cap on the expansion tank slowly anti-clockwise, and pause until any pressure remaining in the system is released. Unscrew the cap and lift off.

3 Add a mixture of water and antifreeze to the expansion tank, until the coolant is up to the "MAX" mark. Refit the cap, turning it clockwise as far as it will go until it is secure. Re-check that the cap is securely tightened once the engine is warm.

Brake fluid level

Warning:
● Brake fluid can harm your eyes and damage painted surfaces, so use extreme caution when handling and pouring it.
● Do not use fluid that has been standing open for some time, as it absorbs moisture from the air, which can cause a dangerous loss of braking effectiveness.

● Make sure that your car is on level ground.
● The fluid level in the reservoir will drop slightly as the brake pads wear down, but the fluid level must never be allowed to drop below the "MIN" mark.

Safety First!

● If the reservoir requires repeated topping-up this is an indication of a fluid leak somewhere in the system, which should be investigated immediately.

● If a leak is suspected, the car should not be driven until the braking system has been checked. Never take any risks where brakes are concerned.

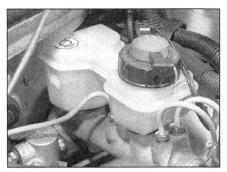

1 The reservoir is located at the rear left-hand side of the engine compartment. The fluid level must be sufficiently high to be able to flow between the two chambers in the reservoir (make sure that the car is parked on level ground when making the check).

3 Carefully add fluid, avoiding spilling it on surrounding paintwork. Use only the specified hydraulic fluid; mixing different types of fluid can cause damage to the system and/or a loss of braking effectiveness. Bear in mind that the level in the reservoir will rise slightly when the cap/float assembly is refitted. After filling to the correct level, refit the cap securely. Wipe off any spilt fluid.

2 If topping-up is necessary, first wipe the area around the filler cap with a clean rag, then hold the fluid level sensor wiring plug as the cap is unscrewed. When adding fluid, it's a good idea to inspect the reservoir. The system should be drained and refilled if dirt is seen in the fluid (see Chapter 9 for details).

4 Also check the operation of the low fluid level warning light. Switch on the ignition and ask an assistant to press the test button on top of the brake fluid reservoir cap; the brake fluid level/handbrake "on" warning light should come on. If not, the level switch, wiring or bulb may be faulty. If the warning light comes on and the fluid level is not low, check that the handbrake is not on.

Washer fluid level

Screenwash additives not only keep the winscreen clean during foul weather, they also prevent the washer system freezing in cold weather - which is when you are likely to need it most. Don't top up using plain water as the screenwash will become too diluted, and will freeze during cold weather. **On no account use coolant antifreeze in the washer system - this could discolour or damage paintwork.**

1 The windscreen/tailgate washer fluid reservoir filler is located at the front right-hand corner of the engine compartment, in front of the coolant reservoir. If topping-up is necessary, open the cap.

2 When topping-up the reservoir a screenwash additive should be added in the quantities recommended on the bottle.

Tyre condition and pressure

It is very important that tyres are in good condition, and at the correct pressure - having a tyre failure at any speed is highly dangerous. Tyre wear is influenced by driving style - harsh braking and acceleration, or fast cornering, will all produce more rapid tyre wear. As a general rule, the front tyres wear out faster than the rears. Interchanging the tyres from front to rear ("rotating" the tyres) may result in more even wear. However, if this is completely effective, you may have the expense of replacing all four tyres at once!

Remove any nails or stones embedded in the tread before they penetrate the tyre to cause deflation. If removal of a nail does reveal that the tyre has been punctured, refit the nail so that its point of penetration is marked. Then immediately change the wheel, and have the tyre repaired by a tyre dealer.

Regularly check the tyres for damage in the form of cuts or bulges, especially in the sidewalls. Periodically remove the wheels, and clean any dirt or mud from the inside and outside surfaces. Examine the wheel rims for signs of rusting, corrosion or other damage. Light alloy wheels are easily damaged by "kerbing" whilst parking; steel wheels may also become dented or buckled. A new wheel is very often the only way to overcome severe damage.

New tyres should be balanced when they are fitted, but it may become necessary to re-balance them as they wear, or if the balance weights fitted to the wheel rim should fall off. Unbalanced tyres will wear more quickly, as will the steering and suspension components. Wheel imbalance is normally signified by vibration, particularly at a certain speed (typically around 50 mph). If this vibration is felt only through the steering, then it is likely that just the front wheels need balancing. If, however, the vibration is felt through the whole car, the rear wheels could be out of balance. Wheel balancing should be carried out by a tyre dealer or garage.

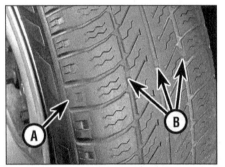

1 Tread Depth - visual check
   The original tyres have tread wear safety bands (B), which will appear when the tread depth reaches approximately 1.6 mm. The band positions are indicated by a triangular mark on the tyre sidewall (A).

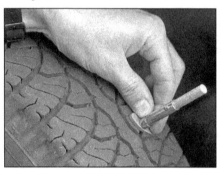

2 Tread Depth - manual check
   Alternatively, tread wear can be monitored with a simple, inexpensive device known as a tread depth indicator gauge.

3 Tyre Pressure Check
   Check the tyre pressures regularly with the tyres cold. Do not adjust the tyre pressures immediately after the vehicle has been used, or an inaccurate setting will result.

Tyre tread wear patterns

Shoulder Wear

Underinflation (wear on both sides)
Under-inflation will cause overheating of the tyre, because the tyre will flex too much, and the tread will not sit correctly on the road surface. This will cause a loss of grip and excessive wear, not to mention the danger of sudden tyre failure due to heat build-up.
Check and adjust pressures
Incorrect wheel camber (wear on one side)
Repair or renew suspension parts
Hard cornering
Reduce speed!

Centre Wear

Overinflation
Over-inflation will cause rapid wear of the centre part of the tyre tread, coupled with reduced grip, harsher ride, and the danger of shock damage occurring in the tyre casing.
Check and adjust pressures

If you sometimes have to inflate your car's tyres to the higher pressures specified for maximum load or sustained high speed, don't forget to reduce the pressures to normal afterwards.

Uneven Wear

Front tyres may wear unevenly as a result of wheel misalignment. Most tyre dealers and garages can check and adjust the wheel alignment (or "tracking") for a modest charge.
Incorrect camber or castor
Repair or renew suspension parts
Malfunctioning suspension
Repair or renew suspension parts
Unbalanced wheel
Balance tyres
Incorrect toe setting
Adjust front wheel alignment
Note: *The feathered edge of the tread which typifies toe wear is best checked by feel.*

Wiper blades

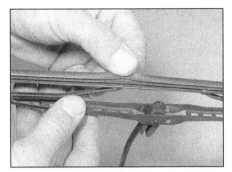

1 Check the condition of the wiper blades; if they are cracked or show any signs of deterioration, or if the glass swept area is smeared, renew them. For maximum clarity of vision, wiper blades should be renewed annually, as a matter of course.

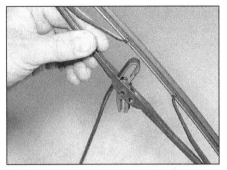

2 To remove a windscreen wiper blade, pull the arm fully away from the screen until it locks. Swivel the blade through 90°, then prise apart the securing lugs at the end of the mounting block, and slide the blade out of the hooked end of the arm.

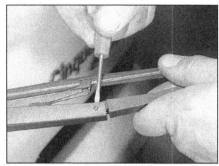

3 Don't forget to check the tailgate wiper blade as well. The blade can be removed by swivelling the blade through 90°, then prising the sides of the arm apart to release the blade.

Battery

Caution: *Before carrying out any work on the vehicle battery, read the precautions given in "Safety first" at the start of this manual.*

✔ Make sure that the battery tray is in good condition, and that the clamp is tight. Corrosion on the tray, retaining clamp and the battery itself can be removed with a solution of water and baking soda. Thoroughly rinse all cleaned areas with water. Any metal parts damaged by corrosion should be covered with a zinc-based primer, then painted.

✔ Periodically (approximately every three months), check the charge condition of the battery as described in Chapter 5A.

✔ If the battery is flat, and you need to jump start your vehicle, see *Roadside Repairs*.

1 The battery is located on the rear right-hand side of the engine compartment. Check the tightness of the battery cable clamps to ensure good electrical connections. You should not be able to move them. Also check each cable for cracks and frayed conductors.

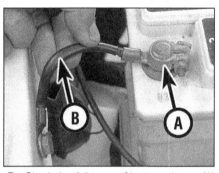

2 Check the tightness of battery clamps (A) to ensure good electrical connections. You should not be able to move them. Also check each cable (B) for cracks and frayed conductors.

Battery corrosion can be kept to a minimum by applying a layer of petroleum jelly to the clamps and terminals after they are reconnected.

3 If corrosion (white, fluffy deposits) is evident, remove the cables from the battery terminals, clean them with a small wire brush, then refit them. Automotive stores sell a tool for cleaning the battery post . . .

4 . . . as well as the battery cable clamps

Electrical systems

✔ Check all external lights and the horn. Refer to the appropriate Sections of Chapter 12 for details if any of the circuits are found to be inoperative.

✔ Visually check all accessible wiring connectors, harnesses and retaining clips for security, and for signs of chafing or damage.

 If you need to check your brake lights and indicators unaided, back up to a wall or garage door and operate the lights. The reflected light should show if they are working properly.

1 If a single indicator light, brake light or headlight has failed, it is likely that a bulb has blown and will need to be replaced. Refer to Chapter 12 for details. If both brake lights have failed, it is possible that the stoplight switch operated by the brake pedal has failed. Refer to Chapter 9 for details.

2 If more than one indicator light or headlight has failed, it is likely that either a fuse has blown or that there is a fault in the circuit (see *"Electrical fault finding"* in Chapter 12). The main fuses are mounted in a panel located at the lower driver's side of the facia under a cover. Pull the cover to release it from the facia. On models fitted with air conditioning, the air conditioning system fuses are located in an additional fusebox on the left-hand side of the engine compartment, and on certain models, additional engine-related fuses are located in a fusebox on the right-hand side of the engine compartment.

3 To replace a blown fuse, pull it out from the fusebox. Fit a new fuse of the same rating, available from car accessory shops. It is important that you find the reason that the fuse blew (see *"Electrical fault finding"* in Chapter 12).

Lubricants and fluids

Engine . . . . Multigrade engine oil, viscosity SAE 15W/40, to API SG and/or CCMC-G4

Cooling system . . . . Ethylene glycol-based antifreeze

Manual transmission . . . . SAE 80 W EP gear oil to API GL4 and/or MIL-L-2105

Braking system . . . . Hydraulic fluid to DOT 4

Choosing your engine oil

Engines need oil, not only to lubricate moving parts and minimise wear, but also to maximise power output and to improve fuel economy.

HOW ENGINE OIL WORKS

• Beating friction

Without oil, the moving surfaces inside your engine will rub together, heat up and melt, quickly causing the engine to seize. Engine oil creates a film which separates these moving parts, preventing wear and heat build-up.

• Cooling hot-spots

Temperatures inside the engine can exceed 1000° C. The engine oil circulates and acts as a coolant, transferring heat from the hot-spots to the sump.

• Cleaning the engine internally

Good quality engine oils clean the inside of your engine, collecting and dispersing combustion deposits and controlling them until they are trapped by the oil filter or flushed out at oil change.

OIL CARE - FOLLOW THE CODE

To handle and dispose of used engine oil safely, always:

0800 66 33 66
www.oilbankline.org.uk

• *Avoid skin contact with used engine oil. Repeated or prolonged contact can be harmful.*
• *Dispose of used oil and empty packs in a responsible manner in an authorised disposal site. Call 0800 663366 to find the one nearest to you. Never tip oil down drains or onto the ground.*

Tyre pressures

Note: *Pressures given here are a guide only, and apply to original-equipment tyres – the recommended pressures may vary if any other make or type of tyre is fitted; check with the vehicle handbook, or the tyre manufacturer or supplier for latest recommendations.*

	Front	Rear
Normal load		
145/70 R 13 and 155/65 R 13 tyres	2.0 bars (29 psi)	2.0 bars (29 psi)
165/55 R 13 tyres	2.1 bars (30 psi)	2.1 bars (30 psi)
Full load		
All models	2.2 bars (32 psi)	2.2 bars (32 psi)

Advanced driving

Many people see the words 'advanced driving' and believe that it won't interest them or that it is a style of driving beyond their own abilities. Nothing could be further from the truth. Advanced driving is straightforward safe, sensible driving - the sort of driving we should all do every time we get behind the wheel.

An average of 10 people are killed every day on UK roads and 870 more are injured, some seriously. Lives are ruined daily, usually because somebody did something stupid. Something like 95% of all accidents are due to human error, mostly driver failure. Sometimes we make genuine mistakes - everyone does. Sometimes we have lapses of concentration. Sometimes we deliberately take risks.

For many people, the process of 'learning to drive' doesn't go much further than learning how to pass the driving test because of a common belief that good drivers are made by 'experience'.

Learning to drive by 'experience' teaches three driving skills:

- ☐ Quick reactions. (Whoops, that was close!)
- ☐ Good handling skills. (Horn, swerve, brake, horn).
- ☐ Reliance on vehicle technology. (Great stuff this ABS, stop in no distance even in the wet...)

Drivers whose skills are 'experience based' generally have a lot of near misses and the odd accident. The results can be seen every day in our courts and our hospital casualty departments.

Advanced drivers have learnt to control the risks by controlling the position and speed of their vehicle. They avoid accidents and near misses, even if the drivers around them make mistakes.

The key skills of advanced driving are **concentration,** effective all-round **observation, anticipation** and **planning.** When **good vehicle handling** is added to

these skills, all driving situations can be approached and negotiated in a safe, methodical way, leaving nothing to chance.

Concentration means applying your mind to safe driving, completely excluding anything that's not relevant. Driving is usually the most dangerous activity that most of us undertake in our daily routines. It deserves our full attention.

Observation means not just looking, but seeing and seeking out the information found in the driving environment.

Anticipation means asking yourself what is happening, what you can reasonably expect to happen and what could happen unexpectedly. (One of the commonest words used in compiling accident reports is 'suddenly'.)

Planning is the link between seeing something and taking the appropriate action. For many drivers, planning is the missing link.

If you want to become a safer and more skilful driver and you want to enjoy your driving more, contact the Institute of Advanced Motorists at www.iam.org.uk, phone 0208 996 9600, or write to IAM House, 510 Chiswick High Road, London W4 5RG for an information pack.

Chapter 1
Routine maintenance and servicing

Contents

Degrees of difficulty

Easy, suitable for novice with little experience	**Fairly easy,** suitable for beginner with some experience	**Fairly difficult,** suitable for competent DIY mechanic	**Difficult,** suitable for experienced DIY mechanic	**Very difficult,** suitable for expert DIY or professional

Lubricants and fluids

Refer to *"Weekly checks"* on page 0•17

Capacities

	OHV engines	OHC engines
Engine oil (including filter)	3.75 litres	3.47 litres
Cooling system	4.8 litres	4.0 litres
Transmission	2.4 litres	2.4 litres
Washer fluid reservoir	1.8 litres	1.8 litres
Fuel tank	35.0 litres	35.0 litres

Engine

Valve clearances – OHC engine:
Inlet	0.40 ± 0.05 mm
Exhaust	0.50 ± 0.05 mm

Cooling system

Antifreeze mixture:
28% antifreeze	Protection down to -15°C
50% antifreeze	Protection down to -30°C

Note: *Refer to antifreeze manufacturer for latest recommendations.*

Fuel system

Engine idle speed:
OHV engine	850 ± 50 rpm
OHC engine	900 ± 50 rpm

Exhaust gas CO content (at tailpipe):
OHV engine	< 0.50 %
OHC engine	< 0.35 %

Ignition system

Spark plugs:	Type	Electrode gap
OHV engines:		
Up to October 1995	Bosch WR 7 D+X	1.1 mm
From November 1995	Bosch FR 8 D+	0.8 mm
OHC engines	Bosch FR 7 D+	0.9 mm

Clutch

Pedal travel:
OHC (Sporting) models	120 ± 5 mm
OHV models	110 ± 5 mm

Brakes

Friction material minimum thickness:
Front brake pads	1.5 mm
Rear brake shoes	1.5 mm

Torque wrench settings

	Nm	lbf ft
Alternator securing bolts	49	36
Exhaust manifold:		
OHV engine	20	15
OHC engine	28	21
Exhaust front pipe to manifold	18	13
Inlet manifold:		
OHV engine	20	15
OHC engine	28	21
Roadwheel bolts	86	63
Spark plugs	27	20
Transmission filler/level plug	25	18
Transmission drain plug	45	33

1 The maintenance intervals in this manual are provided with the assumption that you, not the dealer, will be carrying out the work. These are the minimum maintenance intervals recommended by us for vehicles driven daily. If you wish to keep your vehicle in peak condition at all times, you may wish to perform some of these procedures more often. We encourage frequent maintenance, because it enhances the efficiency, performance and resale value of your vehicle.
2 If the vehicle is driven in dusty areas, used to tow a trailer, or driven frequently at slow speeds (idling in traffic) or on short journeys, more frequent maintenance intervals are recommended.
3 When the vehicle is new, it should be serviced by a factory-authorised dealer service department, in order to preserve the factory warranty.

Every 250 miles or weekly
☐ Refer to "Weekly checks"

Every 9000 miles (15 000 km) or 12 months, whichever comes first
☐ Renew the engine oil and filter (Section 3)
☐ Check the front brake pads and discs for wear (Section 4)
☐ Check all components, pipes and hoses for fluid leaks (Section 5)
☐ Check the steering and suspension components for condition and security (Section 6)
☐ Check the condition of the driveshaft gaiters (Section 7)
☐ Check the exhaust gas emissions (Section 8)
☐ Check the engine idle speed (Section 9)
☐ Lubricate all hinges and locks (Section 10)
☐ Carry out a road test (Section 11)

Every 18 000 miles (30 000 km) or 2 years, whichever comes first
☐ Renew the air cleaner element (Section 12)
☐ Renew the spark plugs (Section 13)
☐ Check the condition of the spark plug HT leads (Section 14)
☐ Renew the fuel filter (Section 15)
☐ Check the condition and tension of the auxiliary drivebelt (Section 16)
☐ Check the clutch adjustment (Section 17)
☐ Check the tightness of the inlet and exhaust manifold bolts (Section 18)
☐ Check the valve clearances - OHC engine only (Section 19)
☐ Check the operation of the engine management system (Section 20)

Every 36 000 miles (60 000 km) or 2 years, whichever comes first
☐ Renew the coolant (Section 21)

Every 2 years, regardless of mileage
☐ Renew the brake fluid (Section 22)

Every 27 000 miles (45 000 km) or 3 years, whichever comes first
☐ Check the transmission oil level (Section 23)
☐ Check the fuel evaporative emission control system (Section 24)
☐ Check the operation of the oxygen sensor (Section 25)

Every 36 000 miles (60 000 km) or 4 years, whichever comes first
☐ Check the rear brake shoes and drums for wear (Section 26)
☐ Renew the timing belt (Section 27)

Every 54 000 miles (90 000 km) or 6 years, whichever comes first
☐ Check the condition of the crankcase ventilation system components (Section 28)

Every 72 000 miles (120 000 km)
☐ Renew the transmission oil (Section 29)

Underbonnet view of an OHV engine model

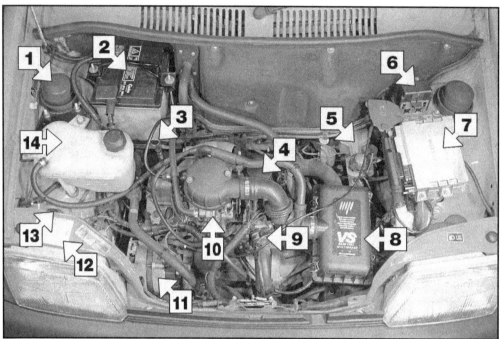

1 Suspension strut top mounting cover
2 Battery
3 Engine oil level dipstick
4 Engine oil filler cap
5 Brake fluid reservoir
6 Fusebox
7 Engine management ECU
8 Air cleaner
9 Thermostat housing
10 Throttle body
11 Alternator
12 VIN plate
13 Washer fluid reservoir location
14 Coolant reservoir (expansion tank)

Underbonnet view of an OHC engine "Sporting" model

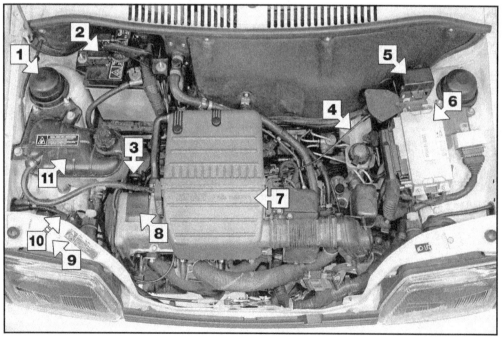

1 Suspension strut top mounting cover
2 Battery
3 Engine oil level dipstick
4 Brake fluid reservoir
5 Fusebox
6 Engine management ECU
7 Air cleaner
8 Engine oil filler cap
9 VIN plate
10 Washer fluid reservoir location
11 Coolant reservoir (expansion tank)

Front underbody view of an OHC engine "Sporting" model

1 Anti-roll bar
2 Front suspension lower arm
3 Brake caliper
4 Washer fluid reservoir
5 Radiator
6 Engine oil filter
7 Horn
8 Transmission
9 Driveshafts
10 Catalytic converter
11 Steering gear
12 Engine oil drain plug

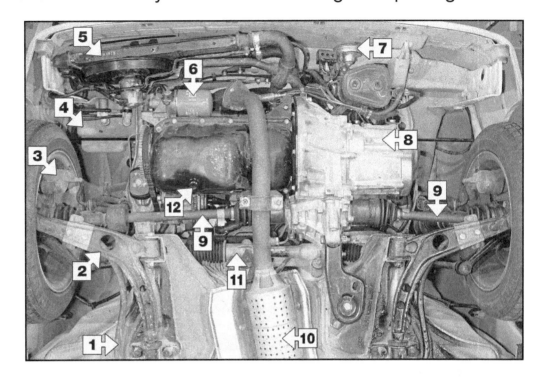

Rear underbody view

1 Handbrake cable
2 Rear suspension trailing arm
3 Rear shock absorber lower mounting
4 Exhaust expansion box
5 Spare wheel housing
6 Rear suspension crossmember
7 Fuel tank

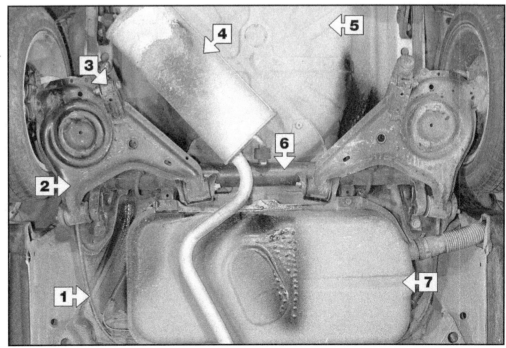

1 General information

This Chapter is designed to help the home mechanic maintain his/her vehicle for safety, economy, long life and peak performance.

The Chapter contains a master maintenance schedule, followed by Sections dealing specifically with each task in the schedule. Visual checks, adjustments, component renewal and other helpful items are included. Refer to the accompanying illustrations of the engine compartment and the underside of the vehicle for the locations of the various components.

Servicing your vehicle in accordance with the mileage/time maintenance schedule and the following Sections will provide a planned maintenance programme, which should result in a long and reliable service life. This is a comprehensive plan, so maintaining some items but not others at the specified service intervals, will not produce the same results.

As you service your vehicle, you will discover that many of the procedures can - and should - be grouped together, because of the particular procedure being performed, or because of the proximity of two otherwise-unrelated components to one another. For example, if the vehicle is raised for any reason, the exhaust can be inspected at the same time as the suspension and steering components.

The first step in this maintenance programme is to prepare yourself before the actual work begins. Read through all the Sections relevant to the work to be carried out, then make a list and gather all the parts and tools required. If a problem is encountered, seek advice from a parts specialist, or a dealer service department.

2 Intensive maintenance

1 If, from the time the vehicle is new, the routine maintenance schedule is followed closely, and frequent checks are made of fluid levels and high-wear items, as suggested throughout this manual, the engine will be kept in relatively good running condition, and the need for additional work will be minimised.
2 It is possible that there will be times when the engine is running poorly due to the lack of regular maintenance. This is even more likely if a used vehicle, which has not received regular and frequent maintenance checks, is purchased. In such cases, additional work may need to be carried out, outside of the regular maintenance intervals.
3 If engine wear is suspected, a compression test (refer to Chapter 2A or 2B, as applicable) will provide valuable information regarding the overall performance of the main internal components. Such a test can be used as a basis to decide on the extent of the work to be carried out. If, for example, a compression test indicates serious internal engine wear, conventional maintenance as described in this Chapter will not greatly improve the performance of the engine, and may prove a waste of time and money, unless extensive overhaul work is carried out first.
4 The following series of operations are those most often required to improve the performance of a generally poor-running engine:

Primary operations

a) Clean, inspect and test the battery (refer to "Weekly checks").
b) Check all the engine-related fluids (refer to "Weekly checks").
c) Check the condition and tension of the auxiliary drivebelt (Section 16).
d) Renew the spark plugs (Section 13).
e) Check the condition of the air cleaner element, and renew if necessary (Section 12).
f) Renew the fuel filter (Section 15).
g) Check the condition of all hoses, and check for fluid leaks (Section 5).
5 If the above operations do not prove fully effective, carry out the following secondary operations:

Secondary operations

All items listed under "Primary operations", plus the following:
a) Check the charging system (refer to Chapter 5A).
b) Check the ignition system (refer to Chapter 5B).
c) Check the fuel system (refer to Chapter 4).

Every 9000 miles or 12 months, whichever comes first

3 Engine oil and filter renewal

1 Frequent oil and filter changes are the most important preventative maintenance procedures which can be undertaken by the DIY owner. As engine oil ages, it becomes diluted and contaminated, which leads to premature engine wear.
2 Before starting this procedure, gather together all the necessary tools and materials. Also make sure that you have plenty of clean rags and newspapers handy, to mop up any spills. Ideally, the engine oil should be warm, as it will drain better, and more built-up sludge will be removed with it. Take care, however, not to touch the exhaust or any other hot parts of the engine when working under the vehicle. To avoid any possibility of scalding, and to protect yourself from possible skin irritants and other harmful contaminants in used engine oils, it is advisable to wear gloves when carrying out this work. Access to the underside of the vehicle will be greatly improved if it can be raised on a lift, driven onto ramps, or jacked up and supported on axle stands (see "Jacking and Vehicle Support"). Whichever method is chosen, make sure that the vehicle remains level, or if it is at an angle, that the drain plug is at the lowest point. Where necessary, remove the fasteners and lower the guard panel away from the underside of the engine.
3 Slacken the drain plug about half a turn; on some models, a square-section adapter may be needed to slacken the plug. Position the draining container under the drain plug, then remove the plug completely **(see illustrations)**.

> **HAYNES HINT** As the drain plug releases from the threads, move it away sharply, so that the stream of oil issuing from the sump runs into the container - not down your arm !

4 Recover the sealing ring from the drain plug (where fitted).
5 Allow some time for the old oil to drain, noting that it may be necessary to reposition the container as the oil flow slows to a trickle.

3.3a Slacken the drain plug about half a turn; on some models, a square-section adapter may be needed to slacken the plug

3.3b Position the draining container under the drain plug, then remove the plug completely

3.7a On OHC engines, the oil filter is mounted on a housing at the front of the engine

3.7b On all other models, the filter is on the rear of the cylinder block (viewed through right-hand wheel arch, with liner removed)

3.8 Unscrew the oil filter and remove it from the engine

6 After all the oil has drained, wipe off the drain plug with a clean rag, and fit a *new* sealing washer; don't reuse the old one - it will probably leak. Clean around the drain plug

3.9 Remove all oil, dirt and sludge from the filter sealing area on the engine using a clean rag

opening, then refit and tighten the plug.

7 Move the container into position under the oil filter. On OHC engines, the filter is mounted on a housing at the front of the engine. On all other models, the filter is located on the rear side of the cylinder block **(see illustrations)**.

8 Using an oil filter removal tool if necessary, slacken the filter initially, then unscrew it by hand the rest of the way **(see illustration)**. As the filter releases from the engine, minimise spillage by tipping the open end upwards. If any oil remains inside the filter, empty it into the container.

9 Use a clean rag to remove all oil, dirt and sludge from the filter sealing area on the engine **(see illustration)**. Check the old filter to make sure that the rubber sealing ring hasn't stuck to the engine. If it has, carefully remove it.

10 Apply a light coating of engine oil to the

sealing ring on the new filter, then screw it onto the engine. Tighten the filter firmly by hand only, but **do not** use any tools. If necessary, refit the splash guard under the engine **(see illustrations)**.

11 Remove the old oil and all tools from under the car, then lower the car to the ground (if applicable).

12 Remove the dipstick, then unscrew (or pull on OHC engines) the oil filler cap from the cylinder head cover. Fill the engine, using the correct grade and type of oil (see *"Lubricants and fluids"*). An oil can with a spout, or a funnel may help to reduce spillage. Pour in half the specified quantity of oil first, then wait a few minutes for the oil to fall to the sump. Continue adding oil a small quantity at a time until the level is between the lower and upper marks on the dipstick. Refit the filler cap **(see illustrations)**.

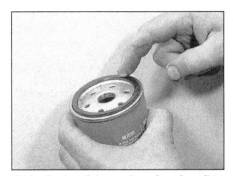

3.10a Apply a light coating of engine oil to the sealing ring on the new oil filter

3.10b Screw the new filter onto the engine by hand - don't use any tools to tighten it

3.12a Remove the dipstick . . .

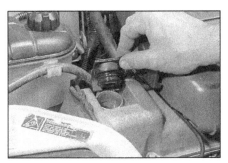

3.12b . . . then remove the oil filler cap from the cylinder head cover (OHC engine shown)

3.12c Fill the engine with the specified quantity and grade of oil; allow plenty of time for the oil to fall into the sump

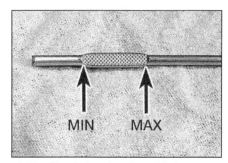

3.12d Check that the oil level is between the upper and lower markings on the dipstick (OHC engine shown)

13 Start the engine and run it for a few minutes; check for leaks around the oil filter seal and the sump drain plug. There may be a delay of a few seconds before the oil pressure warning light goes out when the engine is first started, as the oil circulates through the engine galleries and the new filter (where fitted) before the pressure builds up.

14 Switch off the engine, and wait a few minutes for the oil to settle in the sump once more. With the new oil circulated and the filter completely full, recheck the level on the dipstick, and add more oil as necessary.

15 Dispose of the used engine oil safely, with reference to "General Repair Procedures".

4 Front brake pad and disc wear check

1 Apply the handbrake, then jack up the front of the car and support it securely on axle stands (see "Jacking and Vehicle Support"). Remove the front roadwheels.

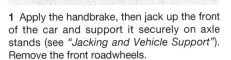
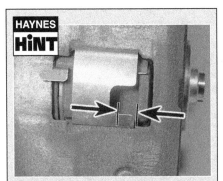

For a quick check, the thickness of the brake pad friction material can be measured through the aperture in the caliper body.

2 For a comprehensive check, the brake pads should be removed and cleaned. The operation of the caliper can then also be checked, and the condition of the brake disc itself can be fully examined on both sides. Refer to Chapter 9 for further information.

3 On completion refit the roadwheels, lower the car to the ground and tighten the wheel bolts to the specified torque setting.

5 Hose and fluid leak check

1 Visually inspect the engine joint faces, gaskets and seals for any signs of water or oil leaks. Pay particular attention to the areas around the cylinder head cover, cylinder head, oil filter and sump joint faces. Bear in mind that, over a period of time, some very slight seepage from these areas is to be expected - what you are really looking for is any

indication of a serious leak. Should a leak be found, renew the offending gasket or oil seal by referring to the appropriate Chapters in this manual.

2 Also check the security and condition of all the engine-related pipes and hoses, and all braking system pipes and hoses. Ensure that all cable ties or securing clips are in place, and in good condition. Clips which are broken or missing can lead to chafing of the hoses, pipes or wiring, which could cause more serious problems in the future.

3 Carefully check the radiator hoses and heater hoses along their entire length **(see illustration)**. Renew any hose which is cracked, swollen or deteriorated. Cracks will show up better if the hose is squeezed. Pay close attention to the hose clips that secure the hoses to the cooling system components. Hose clips can pinch and puncture hoses, resulting in cooling system leaks. If the crimped-type hose clips are used, it may be a good idea to replace them with standard worm-drive clips.

4 Inspect all the cooling system components (hoses, joint faces, etc) for leaks. Where any problems are found on system components, renew the component or gasket with reference to Chapter 3.

A leak in the cooling system will usually show up as white- or rust-coloured deposits on the area adjoining the leak.

6 With the vehicle raised, inspect the fuel tank and filler neck for punctures, cracks and other damage. The connection between the filler neck and tank is especially critical. Sometimes a rubber filler neck or connecting hose will leak due to loose retaining clamps or deteriorated rubber.

7 Carefully check all rubber hoses and metal fuel lines leading away from the fuel tank. Check for loose connections, deteriorated hoses, crimped lines, and other damage. Pay particular attention to the vent pipes and hoses, which often loop up around the filler neck and can become blocked or crimped. Follow the lines to the front of the vehicle, carefully inspecting them all the way. Renew damaged sections as necessary. Similarly, whilst the vehicle is raised, take the opportunity to inspect all underbody brake fluid pipes and hoses.

5.3 Checking a heater hose

8 From within the engine compartment, check the security of all fuel, vacuum and brake hose attachments and pipe unions, and inspect all hoses for kinks, chafing and deterioration.

6 Steering and suspension check

Front suspension and steering check

1 Raise the front of the vehicle, and securely support it on axle stands (see "Jacking and Vehicle Support").

2 Visually inspect the balljoint dust covers and the steering rack-and-pinion gaiters for splits, chafing or deterioration **(see illustration)**. Any wear of these components will cause loss of lubricant, together with dirt and water entry, resulting in rapid deterioration of the balljoints or steering gear.

3 Grasp the roadwheel at the 12 o'clock and 6 o'clock positions, and try to rock it **(see illustration)**. Very slight free play may be felt, but if the movement is appreciable, further investigation is necessary to determine the source. Continue rocking the wheel while an assistant depresses the footbrake. If the movement is now eliminated or significantly reduced, it is likely that the hub bearings are at fault. If the free play is still evident with the footbrake depressed, then there is wear in the suspension joints or mountings.

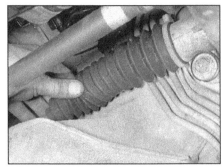

6.2 Inspect the steering gear gaiters for damage and deterioration

6.3 Grasp the roadwheel at the 12 o'clock and 6 o'clock positions, and try to rock it

4 Now grasp the wheel at the 9 o'clock and 3 o'clock positions, and try to rock it as before. Any movement felt now may again be caused by wear in the hub bearings or the steering track-rod balljoints. If the outer balljoint is worn, the visual movement will be obvious. If the inner joint is suspect, it can be felt by placing a hand over the rack-and-pinion rubber gaiter and gripping the track-rod. If the wheel is now rocked, movement will be felt at the inner joint if wear has taken place.

5 Using a large screwdriver or flat bar, check for wear in the suspension mounting bushes by levering between the relevant suspension component and its attachment point. Some movement is to be expected, as the mountings are made of rubber, but excessive wear should be obvious. Also check the condition of any visible rubber bushes, looking for splits, cracks or contamination of the rubber.

6 With the car standing on its wheels, have an assistant turn the steering wheel back and forth, about an eighth of a turn each way. There should be very little, if any, lost movement between the steering wheel and roadwheels. If this is not the case, closely observe the joints and mountings previously described. In addition, check the steering column universal joints for wear, and also check the rack-and-pinion steering gear itself.

Rear suspension check

7 Chock the front wheels, then jack up the rear of the vehicle and support securely on axle stands (see *"Jacking and Vehicle Support"*).

8 Working as described previously for the front suspension, check the rear hub bearings, the suspension bushes and the shock absorber mountings for wear.

Shock absorber check

9 Check for any signs of fluid leakage around the shock absorber body, or from the rubber seal around the piston rod. Should any fluid be noticed, the shock absorber is defective internally and should be renewed. **Note:** *Shock absorbers should always be renewed in pairs on the same axle.*

10 The efficiency of the shock absorber may be checked by bouncing the vehicle at each corner. Generally speaking, the body will

return to its normal position and stop after being depressed. If it rises and returns on a rebound, the shock absorber is probably suspect. Also examine the shock absorber upper and lower mountings for any signs of wear.

7 Driveshaft gaiter check

1 With the vehicle raised and securely supported on axle stands (see *"Jacking and Vehicle Support"*), turn the steering onto full lock then slowly rotate the roadwheel. Inspect the condition of the outer constant velocity (CV) joint rubber gaiters while squeezing the gaiters to open out the folds **(see illustration)**. Check for signs of cracking, splits or deterioration of the rubber which may allow the grease to escape and lead to water and grit entry into the joint. Also check the security and condition of the retaining clips. Repeat these checks on the inner CV joints. If any damage or deterioration is found, the gaiters should be renewed as described in Chapter 8.

2 At the same time check the general condition of the CV joints themselves by first holding the driveshaft and attempting to rotate the wheel. Repeat this check by holding the inner joint and attempting to rotate the driveshaft. Any appreciable movement indicates wear in the joints, wear in the driveshaft splines or loose driveshaft retaining nut.

8 Exhaust gas emissions check

General information

1 The air:fuel mixture is controlled directly by the Weber IAW engine management system (refer to Chapter 4 for greater detail). As a result, the idle exhaust gas CO content is not manually adjustable, without the aid of special test equipment.

2 However, experienced home mechanics equipped with an accurate tachometer and a calibrated exhaust gas analyser should be able to check the exhaust gas CO content, as described in the following sub-Section.

3 If the results of the test show that the CO content is different to that quoted in the Specifications, this indicates a fault within the fuel delivery, engine management or emission control systems (assuming the vehicle is otherwise in good mechanical order).

4 The engine management system wiring harness incorporates a diagnostic socket, which can only be used in conjunction with Fiat dedicated test equipment. The socket allows the engine management system to be electronically 'interrogated' to establish the presence of faults detected by the ECU.

7.1 Checking a driveshaft outer CV joint gaiter

5 Testing the Weber IAW system components individually, with standard workshop equipment, in an attempt to locate the fault by elimination is a time consuming operation that is unlikely to be fruitful (particularly if the fault occurs dynamically). It also carries a high risk of damage to the electronic control unit's internal components.

Exhaust gas CO content check

6 Take the vehicle on a short run to allow it to warm up to normal operating temperature. Allow it to idle and wait until the auxiliary cooling fan has cut in and out again, at least twice, before proceeding.

7 Switch on the CO meter and allow it to warm up and stabilise, in accordance with the manufacturer's instructions.

8 Insert the CO meter probe into the exhaust tailpipe. Connect a calibrated tachometer to the engine, again in accordance with the manufacturer's instructions.

9 Check the engine idle speed (see Section 9).

10 Ensure that all electrical and mechanical loads (such as headlights, heater blower motor, air conditioning) are switched off.

11 Raise the engine speed and maintain it at 2500-3000 rpm for at least two minutes. If the auxiliary cooling fan cuts in, wait until it cuts out again.

12 Check the reading on the CO meter, when the display has stabilised.

13 Repeat the test procedure to obtain an average figure, then compare your result with the figure given in the Specifications.

9 Engine idle speed check

1 Engine idle speed is controlled by the Weber IAW engine management system, and is achieved partly by an idle speed stepper motor, mounted on the side of the throttle body and partly by the ignition system, which gives fine control of the idle speed by altering the ignition timing (see Chapters 4 and 5B for greater detail). As such, manual adjustment of the idle speed is not possible.

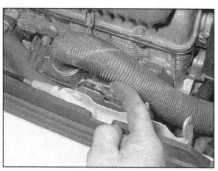

10.2 Applying grease to the bonnet lock

2 The engine idle speed can, however, be checked using a proprietary tachometer. Take the vehicle on a short run to allow it to warm up to normal operating temperature. Park and switch off the ignition, then connect the tachometer in accordance with the manufacturer's instructions.
3 Start the engine and allow it to idle for a few minutes, with all electrical equipment switched off. Check the engine idle speed without the cooling fan running.
4 The idle speed may vary as the reading is taken, due to the closed-loop nature of the idle speed control system, but it should be possible to obtain a good estimate reading.
5 Compare your reading with the figure listed in the Specifications. If the idle speed is too high, too low, or is erratic, there may be a fault within the engine management system.
6 The engine management system wiring harness incorporates a diagnostic socket, which can only be used in conjunction with Fiat dedicated test equipment. The socket allows the engine management system to be electronically 'interrogated', to determine whether the electronic control unit (ECU) has detected any system faults.
7 If your suspect that the engine management system may be faulty, have the vehicle assessed by a suitably-equipped Fiat dealer, or fuel injection specialist. Testing the Weber IAW system components individually, with standard workshop equipment, in an attempt to locate the fault by elimination is a

time consuming operation that is unlikely to be fruitful (particularly if the fault occurs dynamically). It also carries a high risk of damage to the electronic control unit's internal components.

10 Hinge and lock lubrication

1 Work around the vehicle and lubricate the hinges of the bonnet, doors and tailgate with a light machine oil.
2 Lightly lubricate the bonnet release mechanism and exposed section of the inner cable with a smear of grease **(see illustration)**.
3 Check carefully the security and operation of all hinges, latches and locks, adjusting them where required. Check the operation of the central locking system (if fitted).
4 Check the condition and operation of the tailgate struts, renewing them if either is leaking or no longer able to support the tailgate securely when raised.

11 Road test

Instruments and electrical equipment

1 Check the operation of all instruments and electrical equipment.
2 Make sure that all instruments read correctly, and switch on all electrical equipment in turn, to check that it functions properly.

Steering and suspension

3 Check for any abnormalities in the steering, suspension, handling or road "feel".
4 Drive the vehicle, and check that there are no unusual vibrations or noises.
5 Check that the steering feels positive, with no excessive "sloppiness", or roughness, and check for any suspension noises when cornering and driving over bumps.

Drivetrain

6 Check the performance of the engine, clutch, transmission and driveshafts.
7 Listen for any unusual noises from the engine, clutch and transmission.
8 Make sure that the engine runs smoothly when idling, and that there is no hesitation when accelerating.
9 Check that the clutch action is smooth and progressive, that the drive is taken up smoothly, and that the pedal travel is not excessive. Also listen for any noises when the clutch pedal is depressed.
10 Check that all gears can be engaged smoothly without noise, and that the gear lever action is not abnormally vague or "notchy".
11 Listen for a metallic clicking sound from the front of the vehicle, as the vehicle is driven slowly in a circle with the steering on full-lock. Carry out this check in both directions. If a clicking noise is heard, this indicates wear in a driveshaft joint (see Chapter 8).

Braking system

12 Make sure that the vehicle does not pull to one side when braking, and that the wheels do not lock prematurely when braking hard.
13 Check that there is no vibration through the steering when braking.
14 Check that the handbrake operates correctly, without excessive movement of the lever, and that it holds the vehicle stationary on a slope.
15 Test the operation of the brake servo unit as follows. Depress the footbrake four or five times to exhaust the vacuum, then start the engine. As the engine starts, there should be a noticeable "give" in the brake pedal as vacuum builds up. Allow the engine to run for at least two minutes, and then switch it off. If the brake pedal is now depressed again, it should be possible to detect a hiss from the servo as the pedal is depressed. After about four or five applications, no further hissing should be heard, and the pedal should feel considerably harder.

Every 18 000 miles or 2 years, whichever comes first

12.1 Release the clips at either side of the air cleaner casing

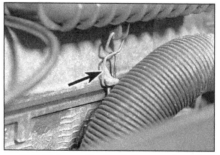

12.2 Release the hook (arrowed) and separate the front section of the air cleaner casing from the rear section

12 Air cleaner element renewal

Sporting models

1 Release the clips at either side of the air cleaner casing **(see illustration)**.
2 Release the hook, detach the front section of the air cleaner casing from the camshaft cover, then pull it forward and separate it from the rear section **(see illustration)**.
3 Lift the filter element from the air cleaner casing **(see illustration)**. Check that the

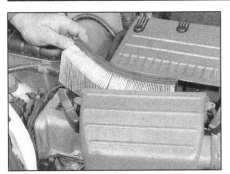

12.3 Lift out the filter element

12.7 Work around the edge of the air cleaner casing and release each of the metal spring clips

12.9 Lift the air cleaner cover and remove the filter element

replacement element is the same, before discarding the old one.

4 Remove any dirt or debris from the inside of the air cleaner casing, using a brush or rag.

5 Fit the new element in position in the air cleaner, pressing the rubber edging firmly into the recess in the air cleaner casing.

6 Refit the front section of the air cleaner to the rear section and fasten the two clips. Hook the lower front edge of the casing onto the spigot on the camshaft cover.

All other models

7 Work around the edge of the air cleaner casing and release each of the metal spring clips **(see illustration)**.

8 Lift the cover from the air cleaner casing - the air intake ducting can remain connected.

9 Lift the filter element from the air cleaner casing **(see illustration)**. Check that the

replacement element is the same, before discarding the old one.

10 Remove any dirt or debris from the inside of the air cleaner casing, using a brush or rag.

11 Fit the new element in position in the air cleaner, pressing the rubber edging firmly into the recess in the air cleaner casing.

12 Place the cover in position over the air cleaner casing and secure it in position with the metal spring clips.

13 Spark plug renewal

1 The correct functioning of the spark plugs is vital for the correct running and efficiency of the engine. It is essential that the plugs fitted are appropriate for the engine (a suitable type

is specified at the beginning of this Chapter). If the correct type is used and the engine is in good condition, the spark plugs should not need attention between scheduled replacement intervals. Spark plug cleaning is rarely necessary, and should not be attempted unless specialised equipment is available, as damage can easily be caused to the firing ends.

2 On Sporting models, the spark plugs are threaded into the rear of the cylinder head; access can be gained by removing the air cleaner casing - see Chapter 4 for details. On all other models, the spark plugs can be accessed from the front of the engine.

3 If the marks on the original-equipment spark plug (HT) leads cannot be seen, mark the leads "1" to "4", to correspond to the cylinder the lead serves; No 1 cylinder is at the right-hand (or timing belt/chain end) of the engine. Disconnect the HT leads from the spark plugs by gripping the end fitting, not the lead itself, otherwise the lead's internal connection may be fractured **(see illustrations)**.

4 It is advisable to remove the dirt from the spark plug recesses using a clean brush, vacuum cleaner or compressed air before removing the plugs, to prevent dirt dropping into the cylinders.

5 Unscrew the plugs using a spark plug spanner, suitable box spanner or a deep socket and extension bar **(see illustrations)**. Keep the socket aligned with the spark plug - if force is applied with the socket fitted at a slight angle, the ceramic insulator may be cracked or broken off. As each plug is removed, examine it as follows.

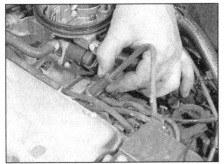

13.3a Disconnect the HT leads from the spark plugs by gripping the end fitting - not the lead itself (OHC engine shown)

13.3b Disconnecting the HT lead from a spark plug (OHV engine shown)

13.5a Unscrew the spark plugs from the engine . . .

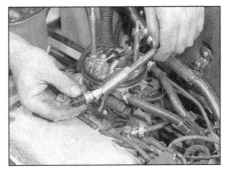

13.5b . . . and remove them from the socket (OHC engine shown)

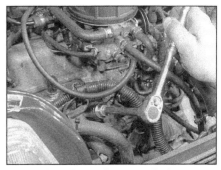

13.5c Removing a spark plug (OHV engine shown)

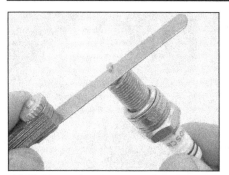

13.10 Measuring the spark plug electrode gap with a feeler blade

13.11 Adjusting the spark plug electrode gap using a proprietary tool

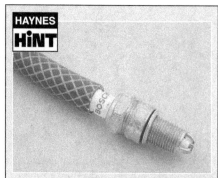

It is often very difficult to insert spark plugs into their holes without cross-threading them. To avoid this, fit a short length of 5/16" internal diameter rubber hose over the end of the spark plug. The flexible hose acts as a universal joint to help align the plug with the plug hole. Should the plug begin to cross-thread, the hose will slip on the spark plug preventing thread damage to the cylinder head.

6 Examination of the spark plugs will give a good indication of the condition of the engine. If the insulator nose of the spark plug is clean and white with no deposits, or has a 'glazed' appearance, this is indicative of a weak mixture.

7 If the tip and insulator nose are covered with powdered, black-looking deposits, then this is indicative that the mixture is too rich. Should the plug be black and oily, or have a thick coating of white crusty deposits, then it is possible that either the valve guides or piston rings are worn.

8 If the insulator nose is covered with light tan to greyish-brown deposits, then the mixture is correct and it is likely that the engine is in good condition.

9 The spark plug electrode gap is of considerable importance as, if it is too large or too small, the size of the spark and its efficiency will be seriously impaired. The gap should be set to the value given in the Specifications at the beginning of this Chapter.

10 To set the gap, measure it with a feeler blade, and then bend the outer plug electrode until the correct gap is achieved **(see illustration)**. The centre electrode should never be bent, as this may crack the insulator and cause plug failure, if nothing worse. If using feeler blades, the gap is correct when the appropriate-size blade is a firm sliding fit.

11 Special spark plug electrode gap adjusting tools are available from most motor accessory shops, or from some spark plug manufacturers **(see illustration)**. Read the manufacturer's information before gapping a

new set of plugs; some types of plugs have specially shaped electrodes which cannot be adjusted.

12 Before fitting the spark plugs, check that the threaded connector sleeves are tight, and that the plug exterior surfaces and threads are clean. It is very often difficult to insert spark plugs into their holes without cross-threading them. To avoid this possibility, fit a short length of hose over the end of the spark plug **(see Haynes Hint)**.

13 Remove the rubber hose (if used), and tighten the plug to the specified torque using the spark plug socket and a torque wrench. Refit the remaining plugs in the same way .

14 Connect the HT leads in the correct firing order, and refit any components removed for access.

14 Spark plug HT lead condition check

1 Label the HT leads from 1 to 4 to preserve the correct firing order; No 1 plug is at the right-hand (timing belt/chain) end of the engine (see Chapter 5B for details).

2 Disconnect the HT leads from the ignition coils and spark plugs one at a time **(see illustration)**. Clean each lead thoroughly and examine it along its entire length for signs of cracking, melting or chaffing. Examine the connection terminals at either end for signs of breakage and/or corrosion.

3 Renew any lead which shows signs of deterioration. If the engine is misfiring and you

suspect a faulty HT lead, try substituting a known good lead in its place.

4 On completion, refit the HT leads to the ignition coil and spark plugs in the correct order. Spray the HT leads with a proprietary water dispersant, but do not use an excessive amount, as this will attract dirt, which can trap moisture and may cause the lead insulation to break down in damp conditions.

15 Fuel filter renewal

⚠ *Warning: Observe the precautions listed in Chapter 4 before working on any component in the fuel system.*

Removal

1 The fuel filter is mounted in the fuel supply line, midway between the fuel tank and the engine compartment. Access is from the underside of the vehicle.

2 Refer to Chapter 4 and depressurise the fuel system. It is important to relieve all pressure in the fuel system before disconnecting a fuel line, as fuel may be ejected under pressure.

3 Disconnect the battery negative cable and position it away from the terminal.

4 With the vehicle parked on a level surface, select first gear and chock the front roadwheels. Raise the rear of the vehicle and support it securely on axle stands (see *"Jacking and Vehicle Support"*).

5 Remove the screw, then lower the filter together with its mounting bracket away from the underside of the vehicle. Undo the screw and release the filter cartridge from the retaining strap **(see illustrations)**.

14.2 Disconnect the HT leads from the ignition coils and spark plugs one at a time

15.5a Remove the screw, then lower the filter and its mounting bracket away from the underside of the vehicle

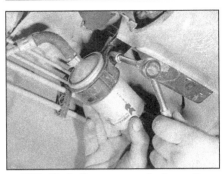

15.5b Undo the screw and release the filter cartridge from the retaining strap

6 Seal off the flexible fuel supply and delivery hoses on both sides of the filter using proprietary hose clamps.

Caution: Do not use G-clamps or mole grips as these may damage the hoses internally, causing them to rupture.

7 Slacken the hose clips and disconnect the fuel lines from either side of the filter unit. Be prepared for an amount of fuel loss; position a small container underneath the filter and pad the surrounding area with absorbent rags.

Refitting

8 Refitting is a reversal of removal, noting the following points:

(a) The arrow marking on the side of the filter unit casing must point in the direction of fuel flow (ie towards the engine) when fitted.

(b) Ensure that the filter retaining clip is correctly positioned over the anti-corrosion plastic sleeving, on the filter casing.

(c) Tighten the hose clips securely.

9 On completion, start the vehicle and check around the disturbed components for leaks. Note that the fuel pump has to purge the system of air, so the engine may take a little longer than usual to start.

16 Auxiliary drivebelt check and renewal

Checking

1 Park on level ground then jack up the front of the vehicle and support it securely on axle stands (see "*Jacking and Vehicle Support*"). Remove the right-hand front roadwheel.

2 Disconnect the battery negative cable and position it away from the terminal.

3 Extract the stud fixings and remove the screws, then lower the plastic liner away from the right-hand wheel arch.

4 Inspect the full length of the drivebelt for cracks and separation of the belt plies. It will be necessary to turn the engine (via a socket and wrench on the crankshaft pulley sprocket) in order to move the belt from the pulleys so that the belt can be inspected thoroughly - twist the belt between the pulleys so that both sides can be viewed. Also check for fraying, and glazing which gives the belt a shiny appearance. Check the pulleys for nicks, cracks, distortion and corrosion.

Removal

5 Slacken the alternator upper and lower mounting bolts, then pivot the top of the alternator towards the engine, to relieve the tension from the drivebelt (see illustrations).

Caution: It will be necessary to remove the TDC sensor from its mounting bracket to allow the auxiliary belt to pass over the pulley teeth; see Chapter 4 for greater detail. On OHV engines, DO NOT slacken or remove the sensor bracket-to-timing case screws, as the sensor alignment will be disturbed.

6 Uncouple the belt from the alternator and crankshaft pulleys (and coolant pump pulley on OHV engines) then remove it from the engine compartment (see illustration).

Refitting

7 Pass the drivebelt over the pulleys, ensuring that it sits squarely in the 'V' of each pulley. If the belt is difficult to fit over the last pulley, turn the crankshaft pulley using a socket and wrench, whilst pressing the belt over the rim of the pulley.

8 Lever the alternator away from the engine, to apply tension to the belt, then tighten the alternator securing bolts.

9 Check the tension of the belt by applying moderate thumb pressure mid-way along the run between the crankshaft and alternator pulleys (or crankshaft and coolant pump pulleys on OHV engines). It should be possible to deflect the belt by approximately 10 mm when it is correctly tensioned (see illustration).

10 If the belt tension is incorrect, slacken the alternator securing bolts and move the alternator towards, or away from the engine (as appropriate) to achieve the correct belt tension. On completion, tighten the alternator securing bolts to the specified torque wrench setting.

11 Re-check the belt tension after approximately 200 miles driving and adjust if necessary.

16.5a Slacken the alternator upper ...

16.5c Alternator mounting bolts (OHV engine shown)

16.5b ... and lower mounting bolts (OHC engine shown)

16.6 Remove the auxiliary drivebelt from the engine (OHC engine shown)

16.9 Check the tension of the belt at a point (arrowed) mid-way between the crankshaft and coolant pump pulleys (OHV engine shown)

17.2a With the clutch pedal in the rest position, measure the distance from the centre of the clutch pedal pad to the base of the steering wheel

17.2b Repeat the measurement with the clutch pedal fully depressed

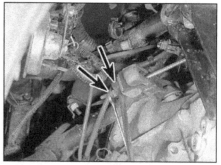

17.5 With a pair of spanners, counterhold the locknut whilst turning the adjuster nut (viewed through right-hand wheel arch, charcoal canister removed)

17 Clutch adjustment check

1 The clutch adjustment is checked by measuring the clutch pedal travel. If a new cable has been fitted, settle it in position by depressing the clutch pedal several times.
2 Ensure that there are no obstructions beneath the clutch pedal then measure the distance ('Distance 1') from the centre of the clutch pedal pad to the base of the steering wheel with the pedal in the at-rest position. Depress the clutch pedal fully to the floor, and measure the distance ('Distance 2') from the centre of the clutch pedal pad to the base of the steering wheel **(see illustrations)**.
3 Subtract the first measurement from the second ('Distance 2' minus 'Distance 1') to obtain the clutch pedal travel. If this is not with the range given in the Specifications at the start of this Chapter, adjust the clutch as follows.
4 The clutch cable is adjusted by means of an adjuster nut on the transmission end of the cable.
5 Working in the engine compartment, slacken the locknut from the end of the clutch cable **(see illustration)**. Adjust the position of the adjuster nut, then depress the clutch pedal several times and re-measure the clutch pedal travel. Repeat this procedure until the clutch pedal travel is as specified.

6 Once the adjuster nut is correctly positioned, and the pedal travel is correctly set, securely tighten the cable locknut.

18 Inlet and exhaust manifold bolt tightness check

1 If the car has been driven, allow the engine to cool before starting work. Jack up the front of the vehicle and support it securely on axle stands (see *"Jacking and Vehicle Support"*).
2 Using a correctly set torque wrench (see Specifications), check the tightness of the inlet manifold-to-cylinder head, exhaust manifold-to-cylinder head and exhaust pipe-to-exhaust manifold nut and bolts. Some of the nuts/bolts are accessible from underneath the engine compartment, but most are more easily accessed from above (see Chapter 2A or 2B for details, as applicable).
Caution: Do not be tempted to tighten the nuts/bolts beyond their recommended torque values 'just to be sure' - this could lead to failure of the nut/bolt/stud, and deformation or even breakage of the manifolds.

19 Valve clearance check (OHC engine only)

Refer to the information given in Chapter 2B.

20 Engine management system check

The vehicle's engine management system ECU has a built-in, self-diagnostic capability. It can monitor the system's sensors and actuators and is able to detect when they fail, even if the failure is temporary or intermittent. These faults are allocated a 'code' by the ECU and are stored in its memory.

Periodically, the ECU fault memory must be analysed and checked for stored fault codes. These can be used to identify components that have failed without the driver noticing, or may help to pinpoint problems that occur intermittently under conditions that are difficult to simulate in a workshop.

On some models, an engine management system warning lamp, mounted on the instrument panel is fitted. The ECU illuminates this lamp when it detects certain types of fault. After the fault has been rectified, the ECU fault code memory must be 'cleared', before the lamp will extinguish.

These operations must be carried out by a Fiat dealer, as access to specialist diagnostic equipment is required.

Every 36 000 miles or 2 years, whichever comes first

21 Coolant renewal

Cooling system draining

⚠️ *Warning: Wait until the engine is cold before starting this procedure. Do not allow anti-freeze to come in contact with your skin, or with the painted surfaces of the vehicle. Rinse off spills immediately with plenty of water. Never leave antifreeze lying around in an open container, or in a puddle in the driveway or on the garage floor. Children and pets are attracted by its sweet smell, but antifreeze can be fatal if ingested.*
1 With the engine completely cold, remove

the expansion tank filler cap. Turn the cap anti-clockwise, wait until any pressure remaining in the system is released, then unscrew it and lift it off. Where applicable, remove the coolant bleed screw(s) – see paragraph 17 – to assist draining.
2 Where applicable, remove the engine undershield, then position a suitable container beneath the radiator bottom hose, at the bottom left-hand corner of the radiator.

21.3 Disconnecting the radiator bottom hose

21.17a Radiator bleed screw location in radiator bleed pipe (arrowed)

21.17b Bleed screw location (arrowed) in heater hose

3 Slacken the hose clip, then disconnect the bottom hose from the radiator, with reference to Chapter 3 if necessary, and allow the coolant to drain into the container **(see illustration)**.

4 When the flow of coolant stops, reconnect the radiator bottom hose, and tighten the hose clip.

5 If the coolant has been drained for a reason other than renewal, then provided it is clean and less than two years old, it can be re-used, though this is not recommended.

Cooling system flushing

6 If coolant renewal has been neglected, or if the antifreeze mixture has become diluted, then in time, the cooling system may gradually lose efficiency, as the coolant passages become restricted due to rust, scale deposits and other sediment. The cooling system efficiency can be restored by flushing the system clean.

7 The radiator should be flushed independently of the engine, to avoid unnecessary contamination.

Radiator flushing

8 Disconnect the top and bottom hoses and any other relevant hoses from the radiator, with reference to Chapter 3.

9 Insert a garden hose into the radiator top inlet. Direct a flow of clean water through the radiator, and continue flushing until clean water emerges from the radiator bottom outlet.

10 If after a reasonable period, the water still does not run clear, the radiator can be flushed with a good proprietary cleaning agent. It is important that their manufacturer's instructions are followed carefully. If the contamination is particularly bad, insert the hose in the radiator bottom outlet, and reverse-flush the radiator.

Engine flushing

11 Remove the thermostat as described in Chapter 3.

12 With the bottom hoses disconnected from the radiator, insert a garden hose into the radiator bottom hose. Direct a clean flow of water through the engine, and continue flushing until clean water emerges from the thermostat housing location.

13 On completion of flushing, refit the thermostat and reconnect the hoses with reference to Chapter 3.

Cooling system filling

14 Before attempting to fill the cooling system, make sure that all hoses and clips are in good condition, and that the clips are tight. Note that an antifreeze mixture must be used all year round, to prevent corrosion of the engine components. Also check that the cylinder block drain plug is in place and tight.

15 Remove the expansion tank filler cap.

16 Place a container under the vehicle, below the expansion tank, to catch any coolant which may be spilt during the topping up procedure. Also place a wad of rag around the expansion tank.

17 Where applicable, if not already done, unscrew and remove the cooling system bleed screw(s). Some models may not have any bleed screws, while others may have a radiator bleed screw located at the end of the radiator bleed pipe (connected to the right-hand top corner of the radiator), in front of the coolant expansion tank. There may also be an additional bleed screw located in the upper heater hose at the engine compartment bulkhead on the left-hand side of the battery **(see illustrations)**. If no bleed screws are fitted, slacken the hose clip and disconnect the smaller heater hose from the thermostat housing.

18 Slowly pour coolant into the expansion tank until it emerges from the bleed screw hole(s), or the heater hose, as applicable, then refit and tighten the bleed screw(s), or reconnect the heater hose and tighten the hose clip **(see illustration)**.

19 Top up the coolant level until the level reaches the "MAX" mark on the side of the expansion tank, then refit and tighten the expansion tank filler cap securely.

20 Start the engine, and allow it to run until it reaches normal operating temperature (until the cooling fan cuts in and out).

21 Stop the engine, and allow it to cool, then re-check the coolant level with reference to *"Weekly checks"*. Top-up the level if necessary and refit the expansion tank filler cap.

Antifreeze mixture

22 The antifreeze should always be renewed at the specified intervals. This is necessary not only to maintain the antifreeze properties, but also to prevent corrosion which would otherwise occur as the corrosion inhibitors become progressively less effective.

23 Always use an ethylene-glycol based antifreeze which is suitable for use in mixed-metal cooling systems. Fiat recommend that a 50:50 mixture of water and antifreeze is used in the cooling system all year round.

24 Before adding antifreeze, the cooling system should be completely drained, preferably flushed, and all hoses checked for condition and security.

25 After filling with antifreeze, a label should be attached to the expansion tank, stating the type and concentration of antifreeze used, and the date installed. Any subsequent topping-up should be made with the same type and concentration of antifreeze.

Caution: Do not use engine antifreeze in the windscreen/tailgate washer system, as it will cause damage to the vehicle paintwork. A screenwash additive should be added to the washer system in the quantities stated on the bottle.

21.18 Pouring coolant into the expansion tank

Every 2 years, regardless of mileage

22 Brake fluid renewal

⚠️ *Warning: Brake hydraulic fluid can harm your eyes and damage painted surfaces, so use extreme caution when handling and pouring it. Do not use fluid that has been standing open for some time, as it absorbs moisture from the air. Excess moisture can cause a dangerous loss of braking effectiveness.*

1 The procedure is similar to that for the bleeding of the hydraulic system as described in Chapter 9 except that the brake fluid reservoir should be emptied by siphoning, using a clean poultry baster or similar before starting, and allowance should be made for the old fluid to be expelled when bleeding a section of the circuit.

2 Working as described in Chapter 9, open the first bleed screw in the sequence, and pump the brake pedal gently until nearly all the old fluid has been emptied from the master cylinder reservoir. Top-up to the "MAX" level with new fluid, and continue pumping until only the new fluid remains in the reservoir, and new fluid can be seen emerging from the bleed screw. Tighten the screw, and top the reservoir level up to the "MAX" level line.

3 Work through all the remaining bleed screws in the sequence until new fluid can be

 Old hydraulic fluid is invariably much darker in colour than the new, making it easy to distinguish the two.

seen at all of them. Be careful to keep the master cylinder reservoir topped-up to above the "MIN" level at all times, or air may enter the system and greatly increase the length of the task.

4 When the operation is complete, check that all bleed screws are securely tightened, and that their dust caps are refitted. Wash off all traces of spilt fluid, and recheck the master cylinder reservoir fluid level.

5 Check the operation of the brakes before taking the car on the road.

Every 27 000 miles or 3 years, whichever comes first

23 Transmission oil level check

1 Park the car on a level surface. The oil level must be checked before the car is driven, or at least 5 minutes after the engine has been switched off. If the oil is checked immediately after driving the car, some of the oil will remain distributed around the transmission components, resulting in an inaccurate level reading.

2 Wipe clean the area around the filler/level plug, which is situated on the front face of the transmission. Note that on models where an evaporative loss emission control system is fitted, the plug is partially obscured by the charcoal canister. Unscrew the plug and clean it; discard the sealing washer, where fitted (see illustrations).

3 The oil level should reach the lower edge of the filler/level hole. A certain amount of oil may have gathered behind the filler/level plug, and will trickle out when it is removed; this does **not** necessarily indicate that the level is correct. To ensure that a true level is

established, wait until the initial trickle has stopped, then add oil as necessary until a trickle of new oil can be seen emerging. The level will be correct when the flow ceases; use only good-quality oil of the specified type.

4 Filling the transmission with oil is an extremely awkward operation; above all, allow plenty of time for the oil level to settle properly before checking it (see illustration). If a large amount is added to the transmission, and a large amount flows out on checking the level, refit the filler/level plug and take the vehicle on a short journey so that the new oil is distributed fully around the transmission components, then recheck the level when it has settled again.

5 If the transmission has been overfilled so that oil flows out as soon as the filler/level plug is removed, check that the car is completely level (front-to-rear and side-to-side), and allow the surplus to drain off into a suitable container.

6 When the level is correct, fit a new sealing washer to the filler/level plug. Refit the plug, tightening it to the specified torque wrench setting and wash off any spilt oil.

24 Fuel evaporative emission control system check

1 The evaporative loss emission control system controls the release of fuel vapour from the fuel tank by directing the vapour back to the engine under certain engine operating conditions. It is important to check the condition of the components within the system, to ensure its correct operation.

2 Locate the charcoal canister, with is situated at the front left-hand corner of the engine compartment, in front of the transmission casing; see Chapter 4 for greater detail. Check the casing for signs of damage or corrosion.

3 Examine each vapour hose along its length and check for evidence of chaffing, splitting or other damage. Renew any section of hose which shows signs of deterioration.

4 The purge solenoid valve, mounted next to the charcoal canister, is controlled by the engine management system ECU. As the valve is only activated under certain engine

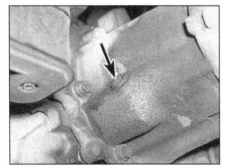

23.2a Transmission oil level/filler plug (arrowed) - model with OHV engine shown

23.2b Removing the transmission oil level/filler plug - Sporting model shown

23.4 If required, top up the transmission with the specified grade of oil

conditions, it is difficult to assess whether it is functional. The valve can be tested without having to remove it from the vehicle, using dedicated Fiat diagnostic equipment. If you suspect that the valve may be faulty, have the car examined by your Fiat dealer.

5 The remaining emission systems components (the multi-function valve mounted at the top of the fuel tank, and the safety valve, fitted in the breather hose adjacent to the fuel filler neck) are difficult to access without further dismantling and removal of surrounding components. Refer to Chapter 4 for further details.

25 Oxygen sensor operation check

1 The oxygen sensor is crucial to the correct operation of the fuel system. If it is faulty, the engine management system may supply the engine with too much or too little fuel, and this can lead to excessive exhaust emissions, poor performance and economy, catalytic converter failure and even engine damage.

2 Specialised diagnostic equipment is needed to test the operation of the sensor comprehensively; this check should therefore be carried out by a Fiat dealer.

Every 36 000 miles or 4 years, whichever comes first

26 Rear brake shoe and drum wear check

1 Check the front wheels, and select first gear, then jack up the rear of the vehicle and support securely on axle stands (see "*Jacking and Vehicle Support*"). Remove the rear roadwheels.

2 Check the thickness of the brake shoe friction material by looking through the hole provided in the drum **(see illustration)**. Turn the drum as necessary so that both shoes can be viewed.

3 For a comprehensive check, remove the rear brake drums (see Chapter 9), and check the brake shoes for signs of wear or contamination. At the same time, also inspect the wheel cylinders for signs of leakage, and the brake drum for signs of wear. Refer to the relevant Sections of Chapter 9 for further information.

27 Timing belt renewal

Refer to the information given in Chapter 2B.

26.2 Check the brake shoe lining thickness through the hole (arrowed) in the drum

Every 54 000 miles or 6 years, whichever comes first

28 Crankcase ventilation system component check

1 The crankcase ventilation system allows blow-by gases released from the engine oil to be drawn back into the engine and burnt, reducing the pollution that the gases cause.

2 A blocked crankcase ventilation system is not only damaging to the environment, but can cause the engine to leak, due to crankcase pressure build-up.

3 Examine each of the rubber crankcase ventilation hoses in turn. Look for signs of splitting, or damage caused by melting or abrasion. Leaks will show up as oily patches.

4 Check the area around the engine oil dipstick tube. If a lot of oil seems to be leaking from this point, the ventilation system could be blocked.

5 Slacken each of the clips and detach the hoses from their stubs. Look into the end of the hose - they can often become blocked by the white/brown sludge which forms when water vapour from the engine mixes with the oil.

6 On completion, reconnect each of the ventilation hoses and securely fasten the clips.

Every 72 000 miles (120 000 km)

29 Transmission oil renewal

1 This operation is much quicker and more efficient if the car is first taken on a journey of sufficient length to warm the engine/transmission up to normal operating temperature.

2 Park the car on level ground, switch off the ignition and apply the handbrake firmly. For improved access, jack up the front of the car and support it securely on axle stands (see "*Jacking and Vehicle Support*"). Note that the car must be level, to ensure accuracy, when refilling and checking the oil level.

3 Wipe clean the area around the filler/level plug, which is situated on the front face of the transmission casing - see Section 23 for details. Unscrew the plug and remove it.

4 Position a container under the drain plug, which is situated on the right-hand side of the transmission housing, directly below the driveshaft joint on models with OHV engines, or at the rear of the transmission casing on Sporting model engines.

5 Unscrew the drain plug and allow the oil to drain into the container **(see illustrations)**. If the oil is hot, take precautions against scalding. Clean both the filler/level and the drain plugs, being especially careful to wipe any metallic

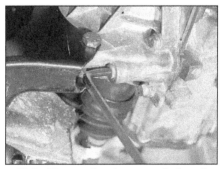

29.5a Unscrewing the transmission oil drain plug - Sporting model shown

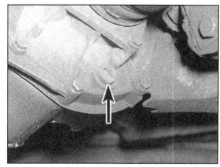

29.5b Transmission oil drain plug (arrowed) - model with OHV engine shown

particles off the magnetic inserts. Discard the original sealing washers; they should be renewed whenever they are disturbed.

6 When the oil has finished draining, clean the drain plug threads and those of the transmission casing, fit a new sealing washer and refit the drain plug, tightening it to the specified torque setting. It the car was raised for the draining operation, now lower it to the ground.

7 Refilling the transmission is an extremely awkward operation. Above all, allow plenty of time for the oil level to settle properly before checking it. Note that the car must be parked on flat level ground when checking the oil level.

8 Refill the transmission via the filler/level plug hole with the exact amount of the specified type of oil then check the oil level as described in Section 23. When the level is correct, refit the filler/level plug with a new sealing washer (where fitted) and tighten it to the specified torque. **Note:** *If the correct amount was poured into the transmission and a large amount flows out on checking the level, refit the filler or filler/level plug and take the car on a short journey so that the new oil is distributed fully around the transmission components, then check the level again on your return.*

Chapter 2 Part A:
OHV engine in-car repair procedures

Contents

Degrees of difficulty

Easy, suitable for novice with little experience	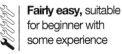	Fairly easy, suitable for beginner with some experience		Fairly difficult, suitable for competent DIY mechanic		Difficult, suitable for experienced DIY mechanic		Very difficult, suitable for expert DIY or professional	

Specifications

General

Engine code	1170 A1.046
Capacity	899 cc
Nominal bore	65.0 mm
Stroke	67.7 mm
Compression ratio	8.8 : 1
Max power output	29 kW (EEC) @ 5500 rpm
Max torque developed	65 Nm (EEC) @ 3000 rpm
Firing order	1 - 3 - 4 - 2
No 1 cylinder location	At timing chain (right hand) end of engine

Torque wrench settings

	Nm	lbf ft
Alternator mounting bolts	45	33
Camshaft sprocket bolt	50	37
Crankshaft pulley nut	100	74
Cylinder head bolts		
Stage 1	30	22
Stage 2	Angle tighten through 90°	
Stage 3	Angle tighten through a further 90°	
Flywheel	45	33
Flywheel lower cover plate bolts	10	7
Front (left hand) engine mounting, bracket-to-transmission casing	25	18
Front (left hand) engine mounting, through bolt-to-nut	50	37
Front (left hand) engine mounting, flange-to-bodyshell	25	18
Rear engine mounting, bracket-to-differential casing (M12 bolts)	85	63
Rear engine mounting, bracket-to-differential casing (M10 bolts)	70	52
Rear engine mounting, flange-to-bodyshell	25	18
Rear engine mounting, through bolt-to-nut	50	37
Right hand engine mounting, through bolt-to-nut	50	37
Right hand engine mounting, flange-to-bodyshell	25	18
Rocker cover	8	6
Rocker shaft pedestal nuts	40	30
Roadwheel bolts	86	63
Sump	10	7
Timing chain casing bolts	8	6

1 General information

Using this Chapter

Chapter 2 is divided into three Parts; A, B and C. Repair operations that can be carried out with the engine in the vehicle are described in Parts A (OHV engines) and B (OHC engines). Part C covers the removal of the engine/transmission as a unit, and describes the engine dismantling and overhaul procedures.

In Parts A and B, the assumption is made that the engine is installed in the vehicle, with all ancillaries connected. If the engine has been removed for overhaul, the preliminary dismantling information which precedes each operation may be ignored.

Engine description

The engine is a water-cooled, overhead valve (OHV), in-line four-cylinder unit, with a cast iron cylinder block and aluminium-alloy cylinder head. The engine is mounted transversely at the front of the vehicle, with the transmission bolted to the left-hand side of the engine.

The cylinder head houses the inlet and exhaust valves, which are closed by single coil springs, and which run in guides pressed into the cylinder head. The valves are operated by rocker arms mounted on a single rocker shaft. Hydraulic tappets integrated into the rocker arms eliminate the need for valve clearance adjustment.

The camshaft is mounted in the cylinder block and is driven from the crankshaft by a duplex chain. The camshaft operates the rocker arms via pushrods, which run vertically inside the cylinder block.

The crankshaft is supported by three main bearings, and endfloat is controlled by a thrust bearing fitted to the upper section of the centre main bearing.

Engine coolant is circulated by a pump, driven by the auxiliary belt. For details of the cooling system, refer to Chapter 3.

Lubricant is circulated under pressure by an oil pump, which is gear-driven from the end of the camshaft. Oil is drawn from the sump through a strainer, and then forced through an externally-mounted, replaceable screw-on filter. From there, it is distributed to the cylinder head, where it lubricates the rocker shaft, arms and hydraulic tappets, and also to the crankcase, where it lubricates the main bearings, connecting rod big and small-ends, gudgeon pins and cylinder bores.

Repair operations possible with the engine in the car

The following work can be carried out with the engine in the car:

a) Auxiliary drivebelt - removal and refitting
b) Cylinder head rocker cover - removal and refitting
c) Cylinder head rocker gear - removal and refitting
d) Hydraulic tappets - removal and refitting
e) Coolant pump - removal and refitting (see Chapter 3)
f) Pushrods - removal and refitting
g) Crankshaft oil seals - renewal
h) Crankshaft sprocket - removal and refitting
i) Timing chain, sprockets and tensioner - removal and refitting
j) Cylinder head - removal and refitting*
k) Engine mountings - inspection and renewal
l) Oil pump and pickup assembly - removal and refitting
m) Sump
n) Flywheel

*Cylinder head dismantling procedures are detailed in Chapter 2C.

Note: It is possible to remove the pistons and connecting rods (after removing the cylinder head and sump) without removing the engine. However, this is not recommended. Work of this nature is more easily and thoroughly completed with the engine on the bench, as described in Chapter 2C.

2 Cylinder compression test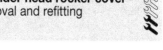

1 When engine performance is down, or if misfiring occurs which cannot be attributed to the ignition or fuel systems, a compression test can provide diagnostic clues as to the engine's condition. If the test is performed regularly, it can give warning of trouble before any other symptoms become apparent.

2 The engine must be fully warmed-up to normal operating temperature, the battery must be fully charged, and all the spark plugs must be removed (see Chapter 1). The aid of an assistant will also be required.

3 Disable the ignition system by disconnecting the LT supply to the ignition coils.

4 Fit a compression tester to the No 1 cylinder spark plug hole - the type of tester which screws into a spark plug thread is preferable.

5 Have the assistant hold the throttle wide open, and crank the engine on the starter motor; after one or two revolutions, the compression pressure should build up to a maximum figure, and then stabilise. Record the highest reading obtained.

6 Repeat the test on the remaining cylinders, recording the pressure in each.

7 All cylinders should produce very similar pressures; any excessive difference indicates the existence of a fault. Note that the compression should build up quickly in a healthy engine; low compression on the first stroke, followed by gradually increasing pressure on successive strokes, indicates worn piston rings. A low compression reading on the first stroke, which does not build up during successive strokes, indicates leaking valves or a blown head gasket (a cracked head could also be the cause).

8 If the pressure in any cylinder is very low, carry out the following test to isolate the cause. Introduce a teaspoonful of clean oil into that cylinder through its spark plug hole and repeat the test.

9 If the addition of oil temporarily improves the compression pressure, this indicates that bore or piston wear is responsible for the pressure loss. No improvement suggests that leaking or burnt valves, or a blown head gasket, may be to blame.

10 A low reading from two adjacent cylinders is almost certainly due to the head gasket having blown between them; the presence of coolant in the engine oil will confirm this.

11 If one cylinder is about 20 percent lower than the others and the engine has a slightly rough idle, a worn camshaft lobe could be the cause.

12 On completion of the test, refit the spark plugs and reconnect the ignition HT coil lead.

3 Cylinder head rocker cover - removal and refitting

Removal

1 Disconnect the battery negative cable and position it away from the terminal.

2 With reference to Chapter 4, carry out the following:
(a) Slacken the clips and detach the air inlet ducting from the collector box, at the top of the throttle body.
(b) Remove the throttle body from the cylinder head cover flange.

3 Refer to Chapter 5B and remove the ignition coils from the end of the rocker cover.

4 Disconnect the breather hose from the port on the rocker cover.

5 Where applicable, unbolt the engine oil dipstick support bracket from the rear of the rocker cover.

6 Disconnect the vacuum servo hose from the throttle body flange, with reference to Chapter 9.

7 Work around the outer edge of the rocker cover and progressively slacken and remove the securing screws. Note the position of any support washers and remove them from the cover **(see illustration)**.

3.7 Rocker cover bolt support washers (arrowed)

8 Lift the rocker cover away from the cylinder head **(see illustration)**. If it sticks, do not attempt to lever it off - instead free it by working around the cover and tapping it lightly with a soft-faced mallet.

Refitting

9 Clean the cylinder head and rocker cover mating surfaces thoroughly, removing all traces of the old gasket material. Check the cover signs of distortion, which may cause oil leakage.

10 Locate a new gasket on the cylinder head and make sure it is correctly seated.

11 Lower the cover onto the gasket, making sure the gasket is not displaced.

12 Insert the rocker cover securing screws and tighten them progressively to the specified torque.

13 Reconnect the breather hose to the port on the rocker cover.

14 Reconnect the vacuum servo hose to the port at the base of the throttle body flange.

15 Refit the dipstick tube support bracket to the rocker cover and tighten the bolt securely.

16 Refit the ignition coils with reference to Chapter 5B.

17 Refit the throttle body and air cleaner ducting with reference to Chapter 4.

18 Reconnect the battery negative cable.

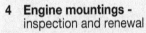

4 Engine mountings -
inspection and renewal

Inspection

1 Jack up the front of the vehicle and support on axle stands (see "*Jacking and vehicle support*").

2 Check the mounting rubbers to see if they are cracked, hardened or separated from the metal at any point; renew the mounting if any such damage or deterioration is evident.

3 Check that all the mountings fasteners are securely tightened; use a torque wrench to check if possible.

4 Using a large screwdriver or a crowbar, check for wear in the mounting by carefully levering against it to check for free play. Where this is not possible enlist the aid of an assistant to move the engine/transmission back and forth, or from side to side, while you watch the mounting. While some free play is to be expected even from new components, excessive wear should be obvious. If excessive free play is found, check first that the fasteners are correctly secured, then renew any worn components as described below.

Right-hand mounting

5 Raise the front of the vehicle and support on axle stands (see "*Jacking and vehicle support*").

6 Place a trolley jack beneath the right-hand side of the engine, with a block of wood on

3.8 Lift the rocker cover away from the cylinder head

the jack head. Raise the jack until it is just supporting the weight of the engine.

7 Working underneath the car, slacken and withdraw the two bolts securing the engine mounting to the bodywork.

8 Lower the engine slightly, then unscrew the nut and withdraw the through-bolt from the centre of the engine mounting. Lift off the mounting rubbers and washers, and renew as necessary.

9 Locate the new mounting on the bracket, insert the through-bolt and tighten to the specified torque.

10 Raise the engine using the jack and line up the engine mounting plate bracket with the bodywork. Refit the two securing bolts and tighten them to the specified torque.

Rear mounting

11 Raise the vehicle and support on axle stands (see "*Jacking and vehicle support*").

12 Working beneath the vehicle, unscrew the bolts securing the rear engine mounting to the underbody.

13 Temporarily support the weight of the engine/transmission using a trolley jack.

14 Unbolt the rear mounting assembly from the transmission and withdraw from under the vehicle.

15 Unscrew the bolt and separate the bracket from the mounting.

16 Fitting the new mounting is a reversal of the removal procedure.

Left-hand mounting

17 Raise the front of the vehicle and support on axle stands (see "*Jacking and vehicle support*").

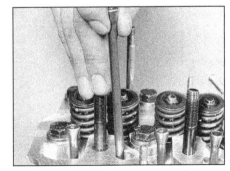

5.4 Withdrawing a pushrod

18 Place a trolley jack beneath the transmission, with a block of wood on the jack head. Raise the jack until it is supporting the weight of the engine/transmission assembly.

19 Unscrew the bolts securing the left-hand mounting to the body.

20 Unscrew the nut securing the mounting to the transmission bracket and recover the washers.

21 Lower the transmission sufficiently to remove the mounting from the transmission bracket.

22 Locate the new mounting in the transmission bracket and refit the nut and washers. Tighten the nut to the specified torque.

23 Raise the engine and refit the mounting-to-body bolts. Tighten the bolts to the specified torque.

24 Remove the trolley jack and lower the vehicle to the ground.

---

5 Rocker gear -
removal, inspection and refitting

Removal

1 Refer to Section 3 and remove the rocker cover.

2 Unscrew the rocker pedestal securing nuts progressively, to prevent damage to the rocker shaft.

3 Recover the spring washers, then ease the rocker assembly away from the cylinder head studs. Place the assembly on a work surface; do not turn it upside down as oil will leak from the hydraulic tappets.

4 Withdraw the pushrods from their bores, keeping them in the correct order to aid correct refitting **(see illustration)**. This can be achieved by pushing the rods through a numbered piece of card.

Inspection

5 To dismantle the rocker shaft assembly, remove the circlip from the end of the shaft, then withdraw the washers from the shaft, making a careful note of their order of fitment.

6 Slide off the rocker arms, the support pedestals and coil springs from the shaft, but take great care to keep them in their original order of fitting **(see illustration)**. Make a note the orientation of the rocker arms with respect to the rocker shaft to aid correct refitting later.

7 Remove the hydraulic tappets from the rocker arms as described in Section 6.

8 Clean the rocker assembly components thoroughly. Check that the oil lubrication holes in the rocker shaft are completely clear.

9 Check the ball-ended rocker shaft adjuster screws for evidence of excessive wear and scoring. Check the rocker arms bushes for excessive wear by temporarily sliding a rocker arm onto the rocker shaft and trying to twist it.

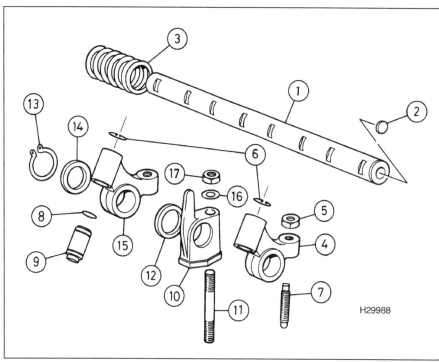

5.6 Rocker gear components

1 Rocker shaft	5 Lock nut	9 Hydraulic tappet	14 Thrust washer
2 Plug	6 Circlip	10 Pedestal	15 Rocker arm
3 Coil spring	7 Adjuster	11 Stud	16 Washer
4 Rocker arm	screw	12 Washer	17 Nut
	8 Shim	13 Circlip	

A large amount of lateral movement indicates a worn bush; bush renewal is not straightforward and should be entrusted to a Fiat dealer or engine reconditioning specialist.

Refitting

10 Lubricate the pushrods with clean engine oil and slide them into their respective bores. Ensure that they are refitted to the correct bores, as noted during removal, or accelerated wear will occur.

11 Refit the hydraulic tappets to the rocker arms with reference to Section 6.

12 Apply clean engine oil to the rocker shaft prior to reassembling. Reassemble the components in the reverse order of dismantling. Ensure that the rocker shaft is fitted through the rocker arm bushes the right way round, so that the oilways in the shaft and arms line up. The end of the rocker shaft which has the circlip fitted to it should face the transmission end of the engine. This is essential for the correct lubrication of the cylinder head components.

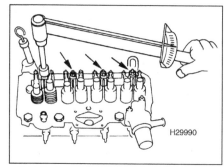

5.14 Refit the rocker shaft pedestal nuts and tighten them to the specified torque

13 Refit the rocker shaft assembly onto the cylinder head studs. As it is fitted, ensure that the rocker adjuster screws engage with the cups at the tops of the corresponding pushrods. Also ensure that the ends of the hydraulic tappets bear squarely on the ends of the valve stems.

14 Fully slacken all the rocker arm adjuster screws. Refit the rocker shaft pedestal retaining washers and nuts, then tighten them progressively to the specified torque wrench setting (see illustration).

15 Adjust the hydraulic tappet preload as described in Section 7.

16 On completion, refit the rocker cover as described in Section 3.

6 Hydraulic tappets - removal and refitting

Removal

1 With reference to Section 5, remove the rocker gear from the cylinder head, then remove the rocker arms from the rocker shaft.

2 At the top of the rocker arm, remove the circlip using circlip pliers and lift out the shim, noting which way around it is fitted (see illustrations).

3 Withdraw the hydraulic tappet from the rocker arm and place it the right way up on a work surface. If the tappet is to be re-used, do not turn it upside down as this will cause the oil to leak out.

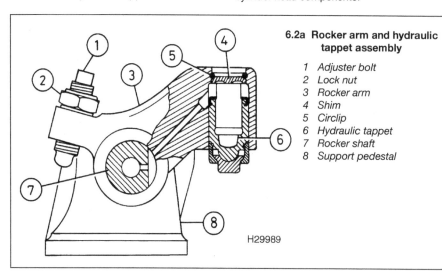

6.2a Rocker arm and hydraulic tappet assembly

1 Adjuster bolt
2 Lock nut
3 Rocker arm
4 Shim
5 Circlip
6 Hydraulic tappet
7 Rocker shaft
8 Support pedestal

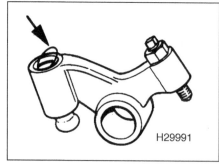

6.2b Extract the circlip (arrowed), remove the shim and lift the hydraulic tappet from the rocker arm

Refitting

4 Slide the tappet into the rocker arm, so that the piston faces upwards. The tappet should slide freely in the rocker arm without resistance.

5 If a new tappet is being fitted, or if the oil has leaked from the existing tappet, pour a small quantity of clean engine oil into the space above the tappet piston.

6 Fit the shim over the tappet piston, ensuring that it is the right way (as noted during removal). Fit the circlip into the groove in the rocker arm, to retain the shim and tappet.

7 Repeat the above procedure for the remaining tappets. Refit the rocker arms to the rocker shaft, then refit the assembly to the cylinder head as described in Section 5.

7 Hydraulic tappets - preload adjustment

General information

1 The following procedure ensures the correct operation of the hydraulic tappets. It is not a routine maintenance operation, but must be carried out after disturbing the cylinder head and/or rocker gear components, regardless of whether any of the components were renewed. Failure to do so will result in noisy tappet operation, reduced engine performance and ultimately increased rocker gear wear.

Caution: The heads of the rocker arm adjuster bolt are specially shaped; the use of a FIAT adjusting tool is recommended, to avoid the possibility of damaging the bolts.

Adjustment

2 Remove the rocker cover as described in Section 3. Set the engine to TDC on cylinder No 1, as described In Section 8.

3 At the first valve on cylinder No 1, slacken the adjuster screw locknut, then fully slacken the adjuster screw so that there is no preload on the hydraulic tappet.

4 Position the rocker arm so that the bottom of the hydraulic tappet is just touching the end of the valve stem. Hold the rocker arm in this position, then turn the adjuster screw clockwise, until the end of the adjuster screw just touches the top of the pushrod. Check that there is now no clearance between the components by gently trying to rock the rocker arm.

5 Turn the adjuster screw through a further **one and a quarter** turns, to pre-load the hydraulic tappet. Hold the adjuster screw still in this position, then tighten the locknut securely **(see illustration)**.

6 Repeat the above procedure for the second valve on cylinder No 1.

7 Bring the engine to TDC on the next cylinder, with reference to Section 8, and

repeat the above procedure. Continue until the preload has been adjusted on all eight hydraulic tappets.

8 On completion, refit the rocker cover as described in Section 3.

8 Location of TDC on cylinder No 1

1 Top dead centre (TDC) is the highest point of the cylinder that each piston reaches as the crankshaft turns. Each piston reaches its TDC position at the end of its compression stroke, and then again at the end of its exhaust stroke. For the purpose of engine timing, TDC at the end of the compression stroke for No 1 piston is used. On the engine covered in this Chapter, No 1 cylinder is at the timing chain end of the engine. Proceed as follows.

2 Ensure that the ignition is switched off. Disconnect the HT leads from the spark plugs, then unscrew and remove the plugs as described in Chapter 1.

3 Apply the handbrake, then jack up the front of the vehicle and support it on axle stands (see *"Jacking and Vehicle Support"*). Remove the right hand front roadwheel, then slacken and withdraw the screws and lift out the plastic wheel arch liner.

4 Turn the engine over by hand (using a spanner on the crankshaft pulley) to the point where the timing mark on the crankshaft pulley aligns with the TDC ('I') mark on the timing cover **(see illustration)**. As the pulley mark nears the timing mark, the No 1 piston is simultaneously approaching the top of its cylinder. To ensure that it is on its compression stroke, place a finger over the No 1 cylinder plug hole, and feel to ensure that air pressure exits from the cylinder as the piston reaches the top of its stroke.

5 A further check to ensure that the piston is on its compression stroke can be made by

7.5 Turning a rocker arm adjuster bolt, using a FIAT special tool, to set the hydraulic tappet pre-load

removing the rocker cover (see Section 3) and observing the movement of the valves and rockers.

6 With the TDC timing marks on the crankshaft pulley and timing cover are in alignment, rock the crankshaft back and forth a few degrees each side of this position, and observe the action of the valves and rockers for No 1 cylinder. When No 1 piston is at the TDC position, the inlet and exhaust valve of No 1 cylinder will be fully closed, but the corresponding valves of No 4 cylinder will be seen to rock open and closed.

7 If the inlet and exhaust valves of No 1 cylinder are seen to rock whilst those of No 4 cylinder are shut, then cylinder No 1 is on its exhaust stroke; the crankshaft will need to be turned through one full rotation to bring No 1 piston up to the top of its cylinder on the compression stroke.

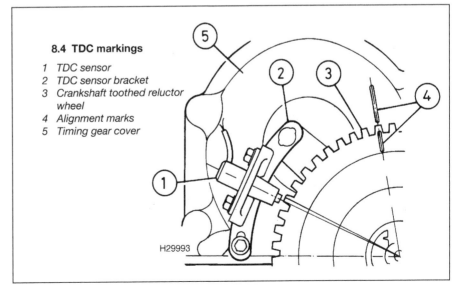

8.4 TDC markings

1 TDC sensor
2 TDC sensor bracket
3 Crankshaft toothed reluctor wheel
4 Alignment marks
5 Timing gear cover

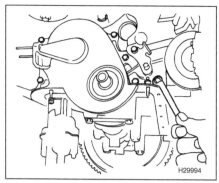

9.8 Progressively slacken and remove the timing gear cover securing screws

8 Once No 1 cylinder has been positioned at TDC on the compression stroke, TDC for any of the other cylinders can then be located by rotating the crankshaft clockwise (in its normal direction of rotation), 180° at a time, and following the firing order (see *Specifications*).

9 On completion, refit the wheel arch liner and roadwheel, lower the vehicle to the ground and tighten the roadwheel bolts to the specified torque setting.

10 Refit the spark plugs (see Chapter 1) and reconnect the HT leads.

9 Timing chain, sprockets and tensioner - removal and refitting

Removal

1 Drain the engine oil, as described in Chapter 1. Raise the front of the vehicle and support it securely on axle stands (see "*Jacking and Vehicle Support*").

2 Remove the auxiliary drivebelt as described in Chapter 1.

3 Working underneath the car, slacken and withdraw the securing screws and remove the flywheel cover plate from the bottom of the transmission bellhousing.

4 Insert a large screwdriver, or cold chisel, between the bellhousing and the flywheel ring gear to lock the flywheel in position and prevent the crankshaft from rotating.

9.13 Slide the camshaft and crankshaft sprocket together with the timing chain away from the engine

9.10 Crankshaft and camshaft sprocket timing marks aligned (arrowed)

5 Ensure that the flywheel is locked, then undo the securing nut and remove the crankshaft sprocket and recover the Woodruff key.

6 With reference to Chapter 4, remove the securing screws and withdraw the RPM/TDC sensor from its mounting bracket on the front of the timing gear casing.

Caution: Do not unbolt the bracket from the timing gear casing - its position is set with precision during manufacture and is very difficult to re-align once disturbed.

7 Refer to Section 13 and remove the sump. Note that the timing gear casing can be removed without removing the sump, but it is unlikely that the sump gasket will seal adequately again on the lower edge of the timing gear casing, once it has been disturbed.

8 Work around the outside of the timing gear cover and progressively unscrew the securing screws **(see illustration)**. Remove the two nuts from the studs at the lower edge of the casing. Note that these nuts also secure the right hand end of the sump.

9 Carefully prise the timing gear casing away from the engine block and recover the gasket.

10 Clean off the faces of the camshaft and crankshaft sprockets and locate the timing marks stamped into the surface of each sprocket. Temporarily remove the flywheel locking tool and turn the engine, using a socket and wrench on the crankshaft sprocket nut, until the two marks are directly opposite each other **(see illustration)**. Refit the flywheel locking tool.

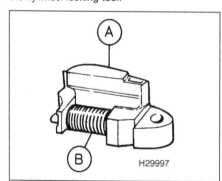

9.15 Check the tensioner rubber pad (A) and coil spring (B) for signs of wear

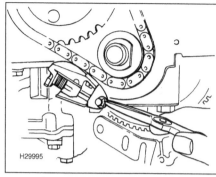

9.11a Remove the circlip . . .

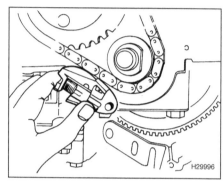

9.11b . . . and lift off the timing chain tensioner

11 Remove the circlip and then pull the timing chain tensioner from its mounting stud **(see illustrations)**.

12 With the flywheel still locked in position, unbolt the camshaft sprocket securing bolt and recover the spacer.

13 Slide the camshaft sprocket, together with the crankshaft sprocket and timing chain away from the engine **(see illustration)**. Recover the dowel from the camshaft sprocket and the Woodruff key from the crankshaft nose.

Note: *With the timing chain and sprockets removed, ensure that the flywheel remains locked (to prevent the engine from rotating) so that the valve timing is preserved.*

14 Inspect the timing gear components for evidence of wear or damage. If any component shows signs of deterioration, the timing chain and both sprockets must be renewed as a complete set. Interchanging old and new components will lead to accelerated wear and early failure.

15 Inspect the tensioner for signs of wear; in particular check the condition of the rubber pad and coil spring **(see illustration)**. Renew the tensioner if it shows signs of deterioration.

Refitting

16 Remove all traces of sealant from the timing chain casing and crankcase mating surfaces.

17 Fit a new crankshaft front oil seal to the timing gear casing, with reference to Section 11.

18 Engage the timing chain with the teeth of the camshaft and crankshaft sprockets, such that the sprocket timing marks are aligned (as described during removal).

19 Place the dowel in the slot in the crankshaft nose, and fit the dowel into the drilling in the camshaft end face.

20 Slide the sprockets, together with the timing chain, onto the crankshaft and camshaft. Engage the Woodruff key with the cutout in the crankshaft sprocket and the dowel with the hole in the camshaft sprocket. Check that the sprocket timing marks are correctly aligned.

21 Fit the camshaft sprocket spacer followed by the securing bolt, then tighten the bolt to the specified torque.

22 Compress the timing chain tensioner against its spring tension, then slide it onto its mounting stud and refit the circlip. Release the tensioner spring and allow it to tension the timing chain.

23 Place a new gasket in position on the crankcase then refit the timing gear casing. Insert the securing screws and tighten them to the specified torque.

24 Refit the sump with reference to Section 13.

25 Refit the crankshaft pulley and tighten the securing nut to the specified torque. Remove the locking tool, then refit the flywheel protection plate.

26 Refit the RPM/TDC sensor and tighten the retaining screws securely.

27 Refer to Chapter 1 and refit the auxiliary drivebelt.

10 Cylinder head - removal and refitting

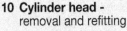

Removal

1 Disconnect the battery negative cable and position it away from the terminal.

2 Refer to Chapter 3 and drain the cooling system.

3 Unplug the wiring from the coolant temperature sensor. Label the connector to aid correct refitting later.

4 Slacken the clips and disconnect the radiator top hose and the two smaller-bore coolant hoses from the ports on the thermostat housing.

5 Disconnect the warm air hose from the top of the exhaust manifold collector duct.

6 Remove the spark plugs with reference to Chapter 1.

7 Raise the front of the car and rest it securely on axle stands (see "*Jacking and Vehicle Support*"). Working underneath the front of the car, unbolt the exhaust system front pipe from the exhaust manifold.

8 Refer to Section 3 and remove the cylinder head rocker cover.

9 Remove the rocker gear and pushrods from the cylinder head as described in Section 5.

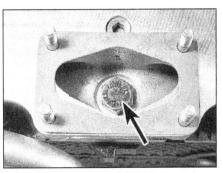

10.10 Cylinder head bolt (arrowed) beneath throttle body

10 Progressively unscrew the cylinder bolts (half a turn at a time), following the tightening sequence in reverse **(refer to illustration 10.25)**. When the bolts are no longer under tension, they can be unscrewed and withdrawn by hand. Do not forget the bolt inside the inlet manifold, exposed by the removal of the throttle body **(see illustration)**.

11 Lift the cylinder head from the engine block. If it sticks, try to free it by grasping the inlet and exhaust manifolds and gently rocking the head from side to side. Do not lever between the cylinder head and engine block as this could easily damage the mating surfaces, leading to leakage.

12 Place the cylinder head on a work surface, then recover the gasket from the engine block. Note that the gasket must always be renewed, whenever the cylinder head is discovered. Keep the new gasket in its packaging until you are ready to use it - the gasket material begins to harden, once it is exposed to the air.

13 According to the manufacturer, the cylinder head retaining bolts may be re-used up to four times. They should be marked accordingly with a punch or dab of paint each time they are re-used. If there is any doubt as to how many times the bolts have been used, they should be renewed as a precaution.

14 If necessary, remove the two dowel pins from the cylinder block.

15 To dismantle/overhaul the cylinder head, refer to Part C of this Chapter. It is standard practice for the cylinder head to be decarbonised and the valves to be reground whenever the head is removed.

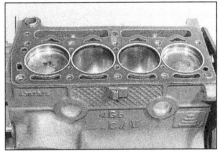

10.22 Ensure that the cylinder head gasket is correctly aligned with the coolant passages and oil galleries

Preparation for refitting

16 The mating faces of the cylinder head and cylinder block must be perfectly clean before refitting the head. Use a hard plastic or wood scraper to remove all traces of gasket and carbon; also clean the piston crowns. Take particular care during the cleaning operations, as aluminium alloy is easily damaged. Also, make sure that the carbon is not allowed to enter the oil and water passages - this is particularly important for the lubrication system, as carbon could block the oil supply to the engine's components.

17 Using adhesive tape and paper, seal the water, oil and bolt holes in the cylinder block.

> **HAYNES HiNT** *To prevent carbon entering the gap between the pistons and bores, smear a little grease in the gap. After cleaning each piston, use a small brush to remove all traces of grease and carbon from the gap, then wipe away the remainder with a clean rag.*

18 Check the mating surfaces of the cylinder block and the cylinder head for nicks, deep scratches and other damage. If slight, they may be removed carefully with a file, but if excessive, machining may be the only alternative to renewal.

19 If warpage of the cylinder head gasket surface is suspected, use a straight-edge to check it for distortion. Refer to Part C of this Chapter if necessary.

20 Clean the threads of the cylinder head bolts, (or fit new ones, as applicable) and clean out the bolt holes in the block as thoroughly as possible. Screwing a bolt into a blind, fluid-filled hole could otherwise cause the block to fracture, through hydraulic pressure.

Refitting

21 Make sure that the two dowel pins are correctly located in the cylinder block.

22 Check that the new cylinder head gasket is the same type as the original, and that the "TOP" (or "ALTO") marking is facing upwards. Locate the new cylinder head gasket onto the top face of the cylinder block and over the dowels. Ensure that it is correctly aligned with the coolant passages and oilways **(see illustration)**.

23 Lower the cylinder head carefully into position on the engine block, ensuring that the locating dowels engage correctly with the cylinder head.

24 Ensure that the cylinder head bolt threads are totally clean, then dip the bolts and their washers in clean engine oil and allow them to drain for thirty minutes. Insert the bolts through the cylinder head carefully (do not drop them into their holes) and hand-tighten them.

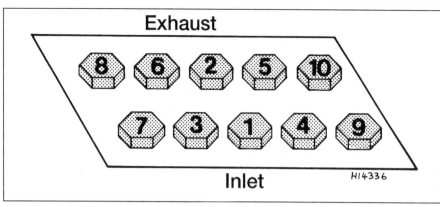

Exhaust

8 6 2 5 10

7 3 1 4 9

Inlet

H14336

10.25 Cylinder head bolt tightening sequence

25 Tightening of the cylinder head bolts must be done in three stages, and in the correct sequence **(see illustration)**. First tighten all of the bolts in the sequence shown to the Stage 1 torque setting. When the first stage tightening is completed on all of the bolts, further tighten them to the Stage 2 angle setting (in sequence). When all of the bolts are tightened to the Stage 2 setting, further tighten each bolt through the Stage 3 angle setting (in sequence) to complete the operation. Where possible, use an angle-tightening setting gauge attachment tool for accurate tightening of stages two and three.

26 Refit the pushrods and rocker gear, with reference to Section 5. Adjust the hydraulic tappet pre-load as described in Section 7.

27 Refit the rocker cover as described in Section 3.

28 The remainder of the refitting procedure is a reversal of the removal process. Tighten all fastenings to their specified torque setting (where given). Refer to Chapter 4 for details on reconnecting the fuel system and exhaust system components. Ensure that all coolant, fuel, vacuum and electrical connections are securely made.

29 On completion, refill the cooling system and top-up the engine oil (see Chapter 1 and *"Weekly Checks"*). When the engine is restarted, check for any sign of fuel, oil and/or coolant leakage from the various cylinder head joints.

12.4 Unscrew and remove the mounting bolts, then lift off the flywheel

11 Crankshaft oil seals - renewal

Front (right-hand side) oil seal

1 The front oil seal is located in the timing gear cover, on the front of the crankshaft, carry out the following preliminary operations:
(a) Remove the auxiliary drivebelt as described in Chapter 1.
(b) Remove the crankshaft pulley and timing chain casing, as described at the beginning of Section 9.

2 Place the timing chain casing on a work surface, across two block of wood, with the outer surface facing downwards.

3 Drive out the old oil seal using a punch and mallet. The punch should be inserted through the splining on the inner surface of the oil seal housing.

4 Clean the mating surfaces of the oil seal housing and the crankshaft. To prevent damage to the new oil seal as it is being fitted, wrap some self-adhesive tape around the end of the crankshaft and lightly oil it.

5 Dip the new oil seal in clean engine oil, then offer it up to the timing chain casing, making sure that the sealing lip faces inwards.

6 Drive the oil seal squarely into the casing, using a suitable tubular drift (such as a large socket, or a section of metal pipe). Avoid damage to the seal by using a drift that bears only on the hard outer surface of the seal, and not on the softer sealing lip.

7 Place a new gasket in position on the crankcase, then refit the timing chain casing to the engine (as described in Section 9), passing the oil seal over the end of the crankshaft. Ensure that the seal remains seated squarely in its housing.

8 Refit the crankshaft sprocket (Section 9) and the auxiliary drivebelt (Chapter 1).

Rear (left-hand side) oil seal

Note: *The following paragraphs describe renewal of the rear oil seal leaving the housing in position. Refer to Chapter 2C for details of removing the housing.*

9 Remove the flywheel as described in Section 12.

10 Using a suitable hooked instrument, remove the oil seal from the rear oil seal housing taking care not to damage the surface of the crankshaft.

11 Clean the seating in the housing and the surface of the crankshaft. Check the crankshaft for burrs which may damage the oil seal lip of the new seal, and if necessary use a fine file to remove them.

12 Dip the new seal in clean engine oil and carefully locate it over the crankshaft rear flange making sure that it is the correct way round.

13 Drive the oil seal into its housing, keeping it square to prevent distortion. A circular drift of the same diameter as the seal may not be readily available. Instead, work around the circumference of the seal and progressively tap it into the housing using a length of wooden dowel and a mallet. Avoid damage to the seal by ensuring that the dowel bears only on the hard outer surface of the seal, and not on the softer inner sealing lip.

14 Refit the flywheel with reference to Section 12.

12 Flywheel - removal, inspection and refitting

Removal

1 Set the engine to TDC on cylinder No 1, as described in Section 8.

2 The flywheel must be held stationary while the bolts are loosened.

> **HAYNES HINT** *A home-made locking tool may be fabricated from a piece of scrap metal and used to lock the ring gear.*

3 Bolt the tool to one of the transmission bellhousing mounting holes.

4 Unscrew and remove the mounting bolts then lift off the flywheel **(see illustration)**. Note the TDC marking on the front face of the flywheel.

Inspection

5 If the flywheel's clutch mating surface is deeply scored, cracked or otherwise damaged, the flywheel must be renewed. However, it may be possible to have it surface-ground; seek the advice of a FIAT dealer or engine reconditioning specialist.

6 If the ring gear is badly worn or has missing teeth, the flywheel should be renewed. Renewal of the ring gear requires access to specialised workshop equipment and should be entrusted to a Fiat dealer.

Refitting

7 Clean the mating surfaces of the flywheel/driveplate and crankshaft. Remove any

13.9 Refitting the sump to the crankcase (shown with engine removed for clarity)

remaining locking compound from the threads of the crankshaft holes, using the correct-size tap, if available.

HAYNES HiNT *If a suitable tap is not available, cut two slots down the threads of one of the old bolts with a hacksaw, and use the bolt to remove the locking compound from the threads.*

8 If the new retaining bolts are not supplied with their threads already pre-coated, apply a suitable thread-locking compound to the threads of each bolt.
9 With the engine still set at TDC on cylinder No 1, offer up the flywheel to the crankshaft, using the TDC alignment mark on the front face of the flywheel. Fit the new retaining bolts and tighten them by hand initially.
10 Lock the flywheel using the method employed on dismantling, and tighten the retaining bolts to the specified torque.
11 Refit the clutch as described in Chapter 6.

12 Refit the transmission as described in Chapter 7.

13 Sump - removal and refitting

Removal

1 Disconnect the battery negative cable and position it away from the terminal.
2 Working underneath the front of the car, slacken and remove the screws and lower the sump protection panel away from the underside of the engine compartment.
3 Refer to Chapter 1 and drain the engine oil.
4 Undo the bolts and remove the flywheel protection plate from the bottom of the transmission bellhousing.
5 Work around the edge of the sump and progressively slacken the nuts and bolts that secure the sump to the bottom of the crankcase. Recover the load spreader washers.
6 Carefully lower the sump away from the engine. If it sticks, strike the side of the sump with the palm of your hand - do not use excessive force as this may deform the sump. Recover the sump sealing gasket.

Refitting

7 Ensure that the sealing surfaces of the sump and the crankcase are both completely clean. If the gasket broke as the sump was removed, ensure that all pieces are removed.
8 Press a new seal into the ridge at the outer edge of the sump. Ensure that the perforations line up with the sump mounting bolt holes.

9 Lift the sump up to the crankcase and insert the retaining screws together with the spreader washers **(see illustration)**. Fit the retaining nuts to the studs, then work around the edge of the sump and progressively tighten the nuts and bolts to the specified torque setting.
10 Refit the flywheel cover plate to the bottom of the bellhousing, and the sump protection plate to the underside of the engine compartment.
11 Lower the vehicle to the ground and fill the engine with oil (see Chapter 1). Check for oil leakage around the edge of the sump, after running the engine for a few minutes.

14 Oil pump - removal and refitting

Removal

1 Refer to Section 13 and remove the sump.
2 Slacken and remove the securing bolts and lower the pump and its housing away from the engine **(see illustrations)**. Remove the gasket and discard it - a new one must be used on refitting.
3 Details of oil pump overhaul and inspection are given in Chapter 2B.

Refitting

4 Refitting is a reversal of removal. Use a new oil pump housing-to-crankcase gasket and ensure that the oil pump shaft pinion engages correctly with the camshaft drive gear **(see illustration)**. Tighten the oil pump housing bolts securely.

14.2a Slacken and remove the securing bolts . . .

14.2b . . . and remove the pump and its housing from the engine

14.4 New oil pump housing gasket correctly fitted

Notes

Chapter 2 Part B:
OHC engine in-car repair procedures

Contents

Degrees of difficulty

| **Easy,** suitable for novice with little experience | | **Fairly easy,** suitable for beginner with some experience | | **Fairly difficult,** suitable for competent DIY mechanic | | **Difficult,** suitable for experienced DIY mechanic | | **Very difficult,** suitable for expert DIY or professional | |

Specifications

General

Engine code	176.B2.000
Capacity	1108 cc
Nominal bore	70.0 mm
Stroke	72.0 mm
Compression ratio	9.6:1
Max power output	40 kW (EEC) @ 5500 rpm
Max torque developed	86 Nm (EEC) @ 3250 rpm
Firing order	1 - 3 - 4 - 2
No 1 cylinder location	Timing belt (right-hand) end of engine
Timing belt tension	see Text

Valve clearances

Inlet	0.40 ± 0.05 mm
Exhaust	0.50 ± 0.05 mm

Lubrication system

Oil pump type	Bi-rotor driven from front of crankshaft
Outer rotor-to-housing clearance	0.080 to 0.186 mm
Axial clearance	0.025 to 0.056 mm

Torque wrench settings

	Nm	lbf ft
Camshaft caps:		
M8 x 1.25	20	15
M8	10	7
Camshaft cover	8	6
Camshaft sprocket	70	52
Crankshaft pulley bolt	100	74
Cylinder head:		
Stage 1	30	22
Stage 2	Angle-tighten through 90°	
Stage 3	Angle-tighten through a further 90°	
Engine mounting bolt:		
M10 x 1.25	59	44
M8	25	19
Engine mounting nut (M10 x 1.25)	59	44
Flywheel	44	32
Roadwheel bolts	86	63
Sump	10	7
Timing belt tensioner	28	21

1 General information

Using this Chapter

Chapter 2 is divided into three Parts; A, B and C. Repair operations that can be carried out with the engine in the vehicle are described in Parts A (OHV engines) and B (OHC engines). Part C covers the removal of the engine/transmission as a unit, and describes the engine dismantling and overhaul procedures.

In Parts A and B, the assumption is made that the engine is installed in the vehicle, with all ancillaries connected. If the engine has been removed for overhaul, the preliminary dismantling information which precedes each operation may be ignored.

Engine description

The engines are water-cooled, single overhead camshaft, in-line four-cylinder units, with cast iron cylinder blocks and aluminium-alloy cylinder heads. All are mounted transversely at the front of the vehicle, with the transmission bolted to the left-hand side of the engine.

The cylinder head carries the camshaft which is driven by a toothed timing belt and runs in three bearings. It also houses the inlet and exhaust valves, which are closed by single coil springs, and which run in guides pressed into the cylinder head. The camshaft actuates the valves directly via followers mounted in the cylinder head. Adjustment of the valve clearances is by means of shims located on top of the followers. The cylinder head contains integral oilways which supply and lubricate the followers.

The crankshaft is supported by five main bearings, and endfloat is controlled by a thrust bearing fitted to the upper section of the centre main bearing.

Engine coolant is circulated by a pump, driven by the timing belt. For details of the cooling system, refer to Chapter 3.

Lubricant is circulated under pressure by a pump, driven from the front of the crankshaft.

Oil is drawn from the sump through a strainer, and then forced through an externally-mounted, replaceable screw-on filter. From there, it is distributed to the cylinder head, where it lubricates the camshaft journals and tappets, and also to the crankcase, where it lubricates the main bearings, connecting rod big and small-ends, gudgeon pins and cylinder bores.

Repair operations possible with the engine in the car

The following work can be carried out with the engine in the car:

a) Auxiliary drivebelt - removal and refitting
b) Camshaft - removal and refitting
c) Camshaft oil seals - renewal
d) Camshaft sprocket - removal and refitting
e) Coolant pump - removal and refitting (refer to Chapter 3)
f) Crankshaft oil seals - renewal
g) Crankshaft sprocket - removal and refitting
h) Cylinder head - removal and refitting
i) Engine mountings - inspection and renewal
j) Oil pump and pickup assembly - removal and refitting
k) Sump
l) Timing belt, sprockets and cover - removal, inspection and refitting

*Cylinder head dismantling procedures are detailed in Chapter 2C, with details of camshaft and tappet removal.

Note: It is possible to remove the pistons and connecting rods (after removing the cylinder head and sump) without removing the engine. However, this is not recommended. Work of this nature is more easily and thoroughly completed with the engine on the bench, as described in Chapter 2C.

2 Location of TDC on No 1 cylinder

General information

1 The camshaft is driven by the crankshaft, by means of sprockets and a timing belt. Both sprockets rotate in phase with each other and this provides the correct valve timing as the engine rotates. When the timing belt is removed during servicing or repair, it is possible for the camshaft and crankshaft to rotate independently of each other and the correct valve timing is then lost.

2 The design of the OHC engine covered in this Chapter is such that potentially damaging piston-to-valve contact may occur if the camshaft is rotated when any of the pistons are stationary at, or near, the top of its stroke.

3 For this reason, it is important that the correct phasing between the camshaft and crankshaft is preserved whilst the timing belt is off the engine. This is achieved by setting the engine in a reference condition (known as Top Dead Centre or TDC) before the timing belt is removed and then preventing the camshaft and crankshaft from rotating until the belt is refitted. Similarly, if the engine has been dismantled for overhaul, the engine can be set to TDC during reassembly to ensure that the correct shaft phasing is restored.

4 TDC is the highest position a piston reaches within its respective cylinder - in a four stroke engine, each piston reaches TDC twice per cycle; once on the compression stroke and once on the exhaust stroke. In this case, TDC refers to cylinder No 1 on the compression stroke. (Note that the cylinders are numbered one to four from the timing belt end of the engine).

5 The camshaft sprocket is equipped with a marking which, when aligned with a reference marking on the cylinder head, indicates that camshaft is correctly positioned for cylinder No 1 at TDC on its compression stroke.

6 The crankshaft sprocket is also equipped with a timing mark - when this is aligned with a reference marking on the oil pump cover, the engine is set with cylinders No 1 and 4 at TDC. Note that it is the camshaft positioning that determines whether a cylinder is on its compression or exhaust stroke.

7 The following sub-Sections describe setting the engine to TDC on cylinder No 1.

Location of TDC on cylinder No 1

8 Remove the air cleaner and ducting as described in Chapter 4. Remove the spark plug from No 1 cylinder as described in Chapter 1.

9 Apply the handbrake then jack up the front of the vehicle and support it on axle stands (see "Jacking and vehicle support").

10 Remove the auxiliary drivebelt as described in Chapter 1.

11 Unbolt and remove the crankshaft pulley. To keep the engine stationary during this operation, unbolt the flywheel protection plate from the underside of the transmission belhousing and wedge a stout screwdriver between the flywheel ring gear and the bellhousing casting **(see illustrations)**.

12 Unbolt and remove the upper section of the timing belt cover, as described in Section 5.

2.11a Unbolt the flywheel protection plate from the underside of the transmission belhousing . . .

2.11b . . . and wedge a screwdriver between the flywheel ring gear and the bellhousing casting

2.11c Slacken and withdraw the bolts . . .

13 Turn the engine (by means of a socket and wrench on the crankshaft sprocket) in its normal direction of rotation, until pressure can be felt at cylinder No 1 spark plug hole.

 HAYNES HiNT *Removing all four spark plugs will make the engine easier to turn; refer to Chapter 1 for details.*

14 Continue turning the engine until the camshaft sprocket TDC timing mark is aligned with the mark on the cylinder head and the crankshaft sprocket timing mark is aligned with the mark on the oil pump cover **(see illustrations)**.
15 The engine is now at TDC on No 1 cylinder.

3 Cylinder compression test

1 When engine performance is down, or if misfiring occurs which cannot be attributed to the ignition or fuel systems, a compression test can provide diagnostic clues as to the engine's condition. If the test is performed regularly, it can give warning of trouble before any other symptoms become apparent.

2.11d . . . then remove the crankshaft sprocket

2 The engine must be fully warmed-up to normal operating temperature, the battery must be fully charged, and all the spark plugs must be removed (see Chapter 1). The aid of an assistant will also be required.
3 Disable the ignition system by disconnecting the LT supply to the ignition coils.
4 Fit a compression tester to the No 1 cylinder spark plug hole - the type of tester which screws into the plug thread is to be preferred.
5 Have the assistant hold the throttle wide open, and crank the engine on the starter motor; after one or two revolutions, the compression pressure should build up to a maximum figure, and then stabilise. Record the highest reading obtained.
6 Repeat the test on the remaining cylinders, recording the pressure in each.
7 All cylinders should produce very similar pressures; any excessive difference indicates the existence of a fault. Note that the compression should build up quickly in a healthy engine; low compression on the first stroke, followed by gradually increasing pressure on successive strokes, indicates worn piston rings. A low compression reading on the first stroke, which does not build up during successive strokes, indicates leaking valves or a blown head gasket (a cracked head could also be the cause).

8 If the pressure in any cylinder is very low, carry out the following test to isolate the cause. Introduce a teaspoonful of clean oil into that cylinder through its spark plug hole and repeat the test.
9 If the addition of oil temporarily improves the compression pressure, this indicates that bore or piston wear is responsible for the pressure loss. No improvement suggests that leaking or burnt valves, or a blown head gasket, may be to blame.
10 A low reading from two adjacent cylinders is almost certainly due to the head gasket having blown between them; the presence of coolant in the engine oil will confirm this.
11 If one cylinder is about 20 percent lower than the others and the engine has a slightly rough idle, a worn camshaft lobe could be the cause.
12 On completion of the test, refit the spark plugs and reconnect the ignition HT coil lead.

4 Auxiliary drivebelts - removal and refitting

Refer to the information given in Chapter 1.

5 Timing belt and covers - removal and refitting

Note: *Refer to Chapter 1 for details of the timing belt renewal interval.*

General information
1 The function of the timing belt is to drive the camshaft and water pump. Should the belt slip or break in service, the valve timing will be disturbed and piston-to-valve contact will occur, resulting in serious engine damage.
2 For this reason, it is important that the timing belt is tensioned correctly, and inspected regularly for signs of wear or deterioration.

2.14a Crankshaft sprocket and oil pump cover TDC markings (arrowed) aligned

2.14b Camshaft sprocket and cylinder head TDC markings (arrowed) aligned - (timing belt removed)

5.6a Remove the securing bolts . . .

5.6b . . . and lift off the upper section of the timing belt cover

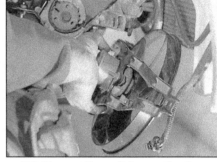

5.7 Remove the radiator cooling fan, together with its support frame

Removal

3 Jack up the front of the vehicle and support on axle stands (see "*Jacking and vehicle support*"). Remove the right-hand front wheel, then undo the screws and remove both sections of the right hand inner wheel arch liner.

4 Remove the air cleaner and air ducting as described in Chapter 4. Unbolt the coolant expansion tank from the inner wing and move it to one side, away from the timing belt cover - there is no need to disconnect the coolant hoses, but ensure that they are not placed under excessive strain.

5 Slacken and remove the auxiliary drivebelt, then remove the spark plugs (refer to Chapter 1).

6 Unbolt and remove the upper section of the timing belt cover **(see illustrations)**. Note the

5.9 Undo the bolts and remove the lower section of the timing belt cover

electrical wiring clipped to the top of the cover.

7 Refer to Chapter 3 and remove the radiator cooling fan, together with its support frame **(see illustration)**.

8 Unbolt and remove the crankshaft pulley. To keep the engine stationary during this operation, unbolt the flywheel protection plate from the underside of the transmission bellhousing and wedge a stout screwdriver between the flywheel ring gear and the bellhousing casting **(see illustrations 2.11a to 2.11d)**.

9 Undo the bolts and remove the lower section of the timing belt cover **(see illustration)**.

10 Set the engine to TDC on cylinder No 1 as described in Section 2.

11 Slacken the nut on the timing belt tensioner and pivot the tensioner pulley away from the belt. Retighten the nut to hold the pulley in the retracted position **(see illustration)**.

12 Slide the timing belt from the sprockets and remove it from the engine compartment **(see illustrations)**.

Refitting

13 When refitting the new belt, make sure that the sprocket timing marks are still in alignment and fit the belt so that the arrows on the belt point in the direction of engine rotation, and the lines of the belt coincide with the sprocket marks.

14 Engage the timing belt with the crankshaft sprocket first, then place it around the coolant

pump sprocket and the camshaft sprocket. Finally, slip the belt around the tensioner pulley.

15 Release the tensioner nut and insert the jaws of a pair of right-angled pliers (or similar) into the two holes on the front face of the tensioner pulley.

16 Rotate the pulley anticlockwise against the belt to set the tension, checking that the sprocket timing marks have not moved out of alignment. Maintain the effort applied to the tensioner pulley, then tighten the securing nut.

17 Turn the crankshaft through two complete turns in the normal direction of rotation to settle the belt and equalise the tension. The belt tension is correct when the centre of the longest run of the belt is gripped between the finger and thumb; it can just be twisted through 90° (quarter of a turn). If the belt appears to be too slack, or too tight, slacken the tensioner nut and repeat steps 13 to 14 until the correct tension is achieved.

Caution: The above procedure serve only as a rough guide to setting the belt tension. The tension must be checked accurately, using specialised test equipment, by a FIAT dealer at the earliest opportunity.

18 Refit all components removed for access then refit and tension the auxiliary drivebelt, with reference to Chapter 1.

19 Refit the wheel arch liner and front wheel(s), lower the vehicle to the ground and tighten the wheel bolts to the specified torque setting.

5.11 Slacken the nut on the timing belt tensioner and pivot the pulley away from the belt

5.12a Slide the timing belt from the crankshaft . . .

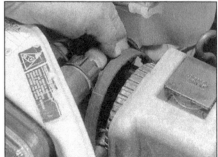

5.12b . . . and camshaft sprockets and remove it from the engine compartment

6 Timing belt sprockets and tensioner - removal and refitting

Timing belt tensioner

Removal

1 Jack up the front of the vehicle and support on axle stands (see "*Jacking and vehicle support*"). Remove the right-hand front wheel.
2 Remove the air cleaner and air ducting as described in Chapter 4.
3 Slacken and remove the auxiliary drivebelt as described in Chapter 1.
4 Remove the timing belt covers as described in Section 5.
5 Set the engine to TDC on cylinder No 1, with reference to Section 2.
6 Loosen the nut on the timing belt tensioner and move the pulley away from the belt.
7 Completely unscrew the nut and slide the tensioner pulley off the mounting stud **(see illustration)**.

Inspection

8 Wipe the tensioner clean but do not use solvents that may contaminate the bearings. Spin the tensioner pulley on its hub by hand. Stiff movement or excessive freeplay is an indication of severe wear; the tensioner is not a serviceable component and should be renewed.

Refitting

9 Slide the tensioner pulley over the mounting stud and fit the securing nut.

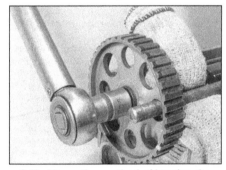

6.15 Alternative method of bracing the camshaft sprocket

6.16a Unscrew the securing bolt and washer . . .

6.7 Timing tensioner securing nut (arrowed)

10 Check and adjust the tension of the belt with reference to Section 5.
11 Refit all components removed for access. On completion, refit and tension the auxiliary drivebelt (refer to Chapter 1).
12 Refit the wheel, lower the vehicle to the ground and tighten the wheel bolts to the specified torque setting.

Camshaft sprocket

Removal

13 Remove the timing belt as described in Section 5.
14 The camshaft sprocket must now be held stationary while the retaining bolt is loosened. To do this, make up a tool as follows and engage it with the holes in the sprocket **(see Tool Tip)**.
15 Alternatively, pass a rod through one of the holes in the camshaft sprocket to prevent it rotating. Position a pad of rag or a piece of wood under the rod to avoid damaging the cylinder head **(see illustration)**.
16 Unscrew the bolt and slide the sprocket from the end of the camshaft. Note the integral location key on the inner face of the sprocket **(see illustrations)**.

Inspection

17 With the sprocket removed, examine the camshaft oil seal for signs of leaking. If necessary, refer to Section 8 and renew it.
18 Check the sprocket teeth for damage.
19 Wipe clean the sprocket and camshaft mating surfaces.

6.16b . . . and slide the sprocket from the end of the camshaft. Integral location key (arrowed)

To make a camshaft sprocket holding tool, obtain two lengths of steel strip about 6 mm thick by 30 mm wide or similar, one 600 mm long, the other 200 mm long (all dimensions approximate). Bolt the two strips together to form a forked end, leaving the bolt slack so that the shorter strip can pivot freely. At the end of each 'prong' of the fork, secure a bolt with a nut and a locknut, to act as the fulcrums; these will engage with the cut-outs in the sprocket, and should protrude by about 30 mm

Refitting

20 Locate the sprocket on the end of the camshaft, then refit the bolt and washer and tighten to the specified torque while holding the camshaft stationary using the method described previously.
21 Refit the timing belt as described in Section 5.

Crankshaft sprocket

Removal

22 Remove the timing belt as described in Section 5.
23 Working beneath the engine unbolt and remove the flywheel lower cover, then hold the flywheel stationary preferably using a tool which engages the flywheel starter ring gear (see Section 2).
24 Unscrew the crankshaft sprocket retaining bolt and slide the sprocket off the end of the crankshaft. The sprocket may have an integral location key on its inner face **(see illustration)**, or a separate key which locates in a groove in the crankshaft nose may be fitted.

6.24 Crankshaft sprocket located by integral key

6.28 Tighten the crankshaft sprocket securing bolt to the specified torque

Inspection

25 With the sprocket removed, examine the crankshaft oil seal for signs of leaking. If necessary, refer to Section 9 and renew it.
26 Check the sprocket teeth for damage.
27 Wipe clean the sprocket and crankshaft mating surfaces.

Refitting

28 Slide the sprocket onto the crankshaft making sure it engages the integral key or separate key. Refit the bolt and washer and tighten the bolt to the specified torque while holding the crankshaft stationary using the method described (Section 2) **(see illustration)**.
29 Refit the timing belt as described in Section 5.

7 Camshaft cover - removal and refitting

Removal

1 Remove the air cleaner assembly and inlet duct as described in Chapter 4.
2 Progressively unscrew the mounting bolts from the top of the camshaft cover and lift off the cover - note the location of any supports on the bolts **(see illustration)**. If it sticks, do not attempt to lever it off - instead free it by working around the cover and tapping it lightly with a soft-faced mallet.
3 Recover the camshaft cover gasket. Inspect the gasket carefully, and renew it if damage or deterioration is evident.

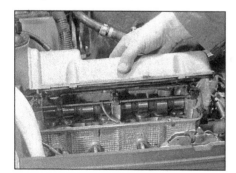

7.2 Progressively unscrew the mounting bolts and lift off the camshaft cover

4 Clean the mating surfaces of the cylinder head and camshaft cover thoroughly, removing all traces of oil and old gasket - take care to avoid damaging the surfaces as you do this.

Refitting

5 Locate a new gasket on the camshaft cover and make sure it is correctly seated **(see illustration)**.
6 Lower the cover onto the cylinder head making sure the gasket is not displaced.
7 Insert the mounting bolts and tighten them progressively to the specified torque.
8 Refit the air cleaner assembly and inlet duct with reference to Chapter 4.

8 Camshaft oil seal - renewal

Right-hand seal

1 Remove the timing belt and camshaft sprocket as described in Sections 5 and 6.
2 Using a suitable hooked instrument, prise the oil seal from the cylinder head taking care not to damage the surface of the camshaft, or the seal housing. Alternatively, drill two small holes opposite each other in the front face of the seal and thread two self-tapping screws into them. Be very careful to avoid drilling into the seal housing or the surface of the camshaft. Grip the screw heads with pliers and use them to draw the seal from its housing.
3 Clean the seal housing in the cylinder head and the end of the camshaft. To prevent damage to the new oil seal as it is being fitted, wrap some adhesive tape around the end of the camshaft and lightly oil it.
4 Dip the new oil seal in oil then locate it over the camshaft making sure that the sealing lips are facing inwards.
5 Using a suitable tubular drift, drive the oil seal squarely into the cylinder head. Ensure that the drift bears only on the hard outer face of the seal, and not the softer inner lip. Remove the adhesive tape from the camshaft.
6 Refit the camshaft sprocket and timing belt with reference to Sections 6 and 5.

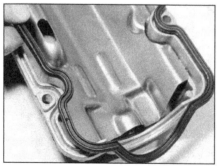

7.5 Locate a new gasket on the camshaft cover and make sure it is correctly seated

Left-hand seal

7 The OHC engine utilises direct ignition and so does not have an HT distributor (see Chapter 5B for details). The mounting bracket for the ignition coils is mounted where the distributor would normally be and has an O-ring oil seal fitted to its inner boss.
8 If the O-ring is leaking, remove the ignition coil mounting bracket from the cylinder head as described in Section 10. Prise out the old seal and thoroughly clean the housing.
9 Fit a new seal to the groove in the housing, then refit the ignition coil mounting bracket.

9 Crankshaft oil seals - renewal

Front (right-hand side) oil seal

1 The front oil seal is located in the oil pump on the front of the crankshaft. Remove the timing belt as described in Section 5 and the crankshaft sprocket as described in Section 6.
2 Using a hooked instrument, prise the oil seal from the oil pump casing taking care not to damage the surface of the crankshaft. Alternatively, drill two small holes opposite each other in the front face of the seal and thread two self-tapping screws into them. Be very careful to avoid drilling into the seal housing or the surface of the crankshaft. Grip the screw heads with pliers and use them to draw the seal from its housing.
3 Clean the seating in the housing and the surface of the crankshaft. To prevent damage to the new oil seal as it is being fitted, wrap some adhesive tape around the end of the crankshaft and lightly oil it.
4 Dip the new oil seal in oil then offer it up to the oil pump casing making sure that the sealing lips are facing inwards.
5 Using a suitable tubular drift, drive the oil seal squarely into the casing. Ensure that the drift bears only on the hard outer face of the seal, and not the softer inner lip. Remove the adhesive tape.
6 Refit the crankshaft sprocket and timing belt with reference to Sections 5 and 6.

Rear (left-hand side) oil seal

Note: *The following paragraphs describe renewal of the rear oil seal leaving the housing in position. Refer to Chapter 2C for details of removing the housing.*
7 Remove the flywheel/driveplate as described in Section 11.
8 Using a suitable hooked instrument, prise the oil seal from the rear oil seal housing taking care not to damage the surface of the crankshaft. Alternatively, drill two small holes opposite each other in the front face of the seal and thread two self-tapping screws into them. Be very careful to avoid drilling into the seal housing or the surface of the crankshaft. Grip the screw heads with pliers and use them to draw the seal from its housing.

9 Clean the seating in the housing and the surface of the crankshaft. Check the crankshaft for burrs which may damage the oil seal lip of the new seal, and if necessary use a fine file to remove them.

10 Dip the new seal in clean engine oil and carefully locate it over the crankshaft rear flange making sure that it is the correct way round.

11 Progressively tap the oil seal into the housing keeping it square to prevent distortion. A block of wood is useful for this purpose. Ensure that the wood bears only on the hard outer face of the seal, and not the softer inner lip.

12 Refit the flywheel/driveplate with reference to Section 11.

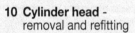

10 Cylinder head - removal and refitting

Removal

1 Disconnect the battery earth lead. Drain the cooling system as described in Chapter 1.

2 Remove the air cleaner and ducting (see Chapter 4).

3 Disconnect the accelerator cable and controls from the throttle housing (see Chapter 4).

4 Slacken the hose clips and disconnect the fuel supply and return hoses from the throttle body (see Chapter 4). Note that hoses have colour coded markings; the fuel supply hose has a red marking. Similarly, loosen the clips and disconnect the coolant hoses from the throttle body.

5 Disconnect the coolant, vacuum and breather hoses from the cylinder head and inlet manifold, making a careful note of their fitted locations to aid refitting later. If the brake servo vacuum hose is difficult to disconnect from the manifold port, prise the non-return valve from the front of the brake servo instead, as described in Chapter 9.

6 With reference to Chapter 4, unplug the electrical wiring connectors from the fuel injector, throttle position sensor, idle speed actuator and inlet air temperature sensor. Label each connector carefully to aid correct refitting later.

7 Remove the ignition coils from their mounting bracket with reference to Chapter 5B. Remove the bolts and withdraw the mounting bracket from the cylinder head. Note that the O-ring seal should be renewed as a matter of course (see Section 8).

8 Unplug the wiring from the coolant temperature sensor on the inlet manifold, and the gauge sender unit on the rear of the cylinder head. Label the connectors to aid correct refitting.

9 Unbolt the HT lead support bracket from the rear of the cylinder head. Disconnect the HT leads from the spark plugs and the ignition coils, then remove them from the engine.

10.14 Loosen the hose clips and disconnect the coolant hose from the thermostat housing

10 Unbolt the harness support bracket from the underside of the inlet manifold and position it to one side.

11 Set No 1 piston to TDC as described in Section 2. Release the timing belt tensioner, and slide the timing belt from the camshaft sprocket as described in Section 5.

12 Remove the throttle body from the inlet manifold, then unbolt the inlet manifold from the cylinder head; refer to Chapter 4 for details.

13 Unbolt the exhaust front pipe from the exhaust manifold as described in Chapter 4, then remove the nuts and free the front pipe from the bracket on the underside of the engine. Unbolt the exhaust manifold from the cylinder head.

14 Loosen the hose clips and disconnect the coolant hose from the thermostat housing at the left hand end of the cylinder head **(see illustration)**.

15 Unscrew the cylinder head bolts half a turn at a time, following the tightening sequence *in reverse* **(see illustration 10.25b)**. When the bolts are free from their threads, withdraw them from the cylinder head together with their washers **(see illustration)**.

16 Lift the cylinder head from the block **(see illustration)**. If it is stuck tight insert wooden dowels into the exhaust or inlet ports, and use them as levers to rock the head off the block. On no account drive levers into the gasket joint, nor attempt to tap the head sideways, as it is located on positioning dowels.

17 Remove and discard the cylinder head gasket and the manifold gaskets.

10.16 Lift the cylinder head from the block

10.15 Unscrew the cylinder head bolts half a turn at a time, following the tightening sequence in reverse

18 If required, the cylinder head can now be dismantled as described in Chapter 2C.

19 If the valves have been ground-in, the valve clearances will require adjusting, as described in Chapter 1. This should be done before the cylinder head is refitted to the engine.

Refitting

20 Before refitting the assembled cylinder head, make sure that the head and block mating surfaces are perfectly clean, and that the bolt holes in the cylinder block have been mopped out to clear any oil.

21 The camshaft sprocket timing mark must be aligned with the mark on the cylinder head (see Section 2).

22 The new gasket should not be removed from its nylon cover until required for use. Fit the gasket dry, and make sure that the mating surfaces on the head and block are perfectly clean.

23 Place the gasket on the cylinder block so that the "ALTO" marking can be read from above **(see illustration)**.

24 Lower the cylinder head onto the block so that it locates on the positioning dowel.

25 The cylinder head bolt threads must be clean. Dip the bolts in clean engine oil, then allow them to drain for thirty minutes, to remove the surplus oil. Screw the bolts in finger-tight, and tighten them in the sequence shown in the accompanying illustration and in the stages given in the *Specifications* **(see illustrations)**.

10.23 Place the gasket on the cylinder block so that the "ALTO" marking can be read from above

10.25a Dip the cylinder head bolts in clean engine oil and allow them to drain for thirty minutes before refitting

26 The remainder of the refitting procedure is a reversal of the removal procedure, noting the following points:

a) *Use new gaskets when refitting the throttle body, inlet and exhaust manifolds.*

b) *After refitting the timing belt, adjust the tension as described in Section 5.*

c) *Ensure that all coolant, fuel and vacuum hoses are refitted according to the notes made during removal.*

d) *Ensure that all electrical wiring is reconnected according to the labels made during removal.*

e) *Reconnect the accelerator cable to the throttle body with reference to Chapter 4.*

f) *Refill and bleed the cooling system as described in Chapter 1.*

11 Flywheel/driveplate -
removal, inspection and refitting

Removal

1 Remove the transmission as described in Chapter 7, then remove the clutch as described in Chapter 6.

2 Mark the position of the flywheel with respect to the crankshaft using a dab of paint. Note that on some models although there is only one location dowel on the flywheel there are two holes in the end of the crankshaft and it is therefore possible to locate the flywheel 180° out. The flywheel must now be held stationary while the bolts are loosened. A

11.2 Home-made flywheel locking tool in place

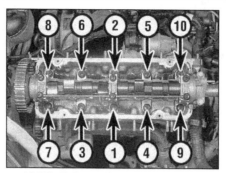

10.25b Cylinder head bolt tightening sequence

home-made locking tool may be fabricated from a piece of scrap metal and used to lock the ring gear. Bolt the tool to one of the transmission bellhousing mounting holes **(see illustration)**.

3 Unscrew and remove the mounting bolts then lift off the flywheel. Recover the spacer plate (where applicable).

Inspection

4 If the flywheel's clutch mating surface is deeply scored, cracked or otherwise damaged, the flywheel must be renewed. However, it may be possible to have it surface-ground; seek the advice of a FIAT dealer or engine reconditioning specialist.

5 If the ring gear is badly worn or has missing teeth, the flywheel must be renewed.

Refitting

6 Clean the mating surfaces of the flywheel and crankshaft. Remove any remaining locking compound from the threads of the crankshaft holes, using the correct-size tap, if available.

 TOOL TiP *If a suitable tap is not available, cut two slots down the threads of one of the old bolts with a hacksaw, and use the bolt to remove the locking compound from the threads.*

7 If the new retaining bolts are not supplied with their threads already pre-coated, apply a suitable thread-locking compound to the threads of each bolt.

11.9 Tighten the flywheel retaining bolts to the specified torque

10.25c Use an angle gauge to tighten the cylinder head bolts to second and third stage torque settings

8 Offer up the flywheel to the crankshaft, using the alignment marks made during removal, and fit the new retaining bolts (together with the spacer plate, where applicable).

9 Lock the flywheel using the method employed during dismantling, and tighten the retaining bolts to the specified torque **(see illustration)**.

10 Refit the clutch as described in Chapter 6.

11 Refit the transmission as described in Chapter 7.

12 Engine mountings -
inspection and renewal

Inspection

1 Jack up the front of the vehicle and support on axle stands (see "*Jacking and vehicle support*").

2 Check the mounting rubbers to see if they are cracked, hardened or separated from the metal at any point; renew the mounting if any such damage or deterioration is evident.

3 Check that all the mountings fasteners are securely tightened; use a torque wrench to check if possible.

4 Using a large screwdriver or a crowbar, check for wear in the mounting by carefully levering against it to check for free play. Where this is not possible enlist the aid of an assistant to move the engine/transmission back and forth, or from side to side, while you watch the mounting. While some free play is to be expected even from new components, excessive wear should be obvious. If excessive free play is found, check first that the fasteners are correctly secured, then renew any worn components as described below.

Renewal

Right-hand mounting

5 Raise the front of the vehicle and support it securely on axle stands (see "*Jacking and vehicle support*").

6 Place a trolley jack beneath the right-hand side of the engine, with a block of wood on the jack head. Raise the jack until it is supporting the weight of the engine.

12.7 Unscrew the through-bolt securing the right-hand engine mounting to the chassis

12.8 Right-hand engine mounting bracket to cylinder block securing nuts/bolts (arrowed)

12.14 Unscrew the two bolts securing the left-hand mounting to the underside of the chassis

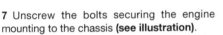

12.15 Unscrew the bolts securing the engine mounting bracket to the transmission casing

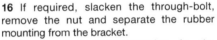

12.22 Unscrew the bolts securing the rear engine mounting to the underbody

12.23 Unbolt the rear mounting assembly from the transmission and withdraw from under the vehicle

7 Unscrew the bolts securing the engine mounting to the chassis **(see illustration)**.

8 Lower the engine slightly then unbolt the mounting from the engine bracket. If required, the engine bracket may be unbolted from the cylinder block, but access is limited with the engine in situ. The illustration shows the right-hand mounting viewed with the engine lowered, during engine/transmission removal **(see illustration)**.

9 Locate the new mounting on the bracket, insert the bolts and tighten to the specified torque.

10 Raise the engine and locate the mounting on the chassis. Refit the bolt and tighten to the specified torque.

11 Remove the trolley jack and lower the vehicle to the ground.

Left-hand mounting

12 Raise the front of the vehicle and support it securely on axle stands (see "*Jacking and vehicle support*").

13 Place a trolley jack beneath the transmission, with a block of wood on the jack head. Raise the jack until it is supporting the weight of the engine/transmission.

14 Unscrew the two bolts securing the left-hand mounting to the underside of the chassis **(see illustration)**.

15 Lower the transmission on the jack slightly, then slacken and unscrew the bolts securing the engine mounting bracket to the transmission casing **(see illustration)**.

16 If required, slacken the through-bolt, remove the nut and separate the rubber mounting from the bracket.

17 Locate the new mounting in the transmission bracket, refit the through-bolt and tighten the nut to the specified torque. Fit the mounting and bracket to the transmission casing, then insert the bolts and tighten them to the specified torque.

18 Raise the engine and transmission on the jack, then refit the mounting-to-chassis bolts. Tighten the bolts to the specified torque.

19 Remove the trolley jack and lower the vehicle to the ground.

Rear mounting

20 Raise the front of the vehicle and support it securely on axle stands (see "*Jacking and vehicle support*").

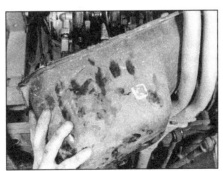

13.4 Removing the sump pan

21 Temporarily support the weight of the engine/transmission using a trolley jack.

22 Working beneath the vehicle, unscrew the bolts securing the rear engine mounting to the underbody **(see illustration)**.

23 Unbolt the rear mounting assembly from the transmission and withdraw from under the vehicle **(see illustration)**.

24 If required, unscrew the bolt and separate the bracket from the mounting.

25 Fitting the new mounting is a reversal of the removal procedure.

13 Sump -
removal and refitting

Removal

1 Jack up the front of the vehicle and support on axle stands (see "*Jacking and vehicle support*"). Drain the engine oil (see Chapter 1).

2 Unbolt and remove the cover plate from the lower part of the flywheel housing.

3 Refer to Chapter 4 and unbolt the exhaust front pipe from the exhaust manifold. Undo the nuts and lower the front pipe from the bracket on the underside of the engine.

4 Unscrew the sump securing nuts and screws and pull the sump downwards to remove it **(see illustration)**. The joint sealant will require cutting with a sharp knife to release the pan. Clean away all old gasket material.

14.8a Removing the oil pump pressure relief valve

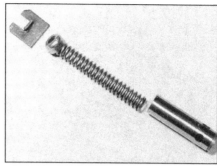

14.8b Components of the oil pump pressure relief valve

14.9 Using an impact screwdriver to remove the oil pump rear cover plate screws

Refitting

5 When refitting, a bead of RTV silicone instant gasket 3 mm in diameter should be applied to the sump flange. Fit the sump, screw in the fixing screws and tighten to the specified torque. Note the flange end fixing nuts.

6 Wait one hour for the gasket compound to harden before filling with engine oil.

7 Refit the flywheel housing cover plate and exhaust systems front pipe.

8 Lower the vehicle to the ground and fill the engine with oil (see Chapter 1). Check the oil level after running the engine for a few minutes, then check around the sump sealing surface for signs of leakage.

14 Oil pump and pick-up tube - removal, inspection and refitting

Removal

1 Drain the engine oil and remove the sump as described in Section 13.

2 Unscrew and remove the oil filter (see Chapter 1).

3 Remove the timing belt as described in Section 5.

4 Lock the crankshaft against rotation either by placing a block of wood between a crankshaft web and the inside of the crankcase, or by jamming the flywheel starter ring gear with a suitable tool (refer to Section 2 for details).

5 Unscrew and remove the crankshaft sprocket bolt and take off the sprocket. If it is tight, use two screwdrivers to lever it off, or use a two or three-legged puller.

6 Unbolt and remove the oil pick-up/filter screen assembly. Note the sealing washer.

7 Extract the oil pump fixing bolts and withdraw the pump. Remove the gasket.

Inspection

8 The oil pump incorporates a pressure relief valve, which can be removed for examination by depressing the spring plunger and pulling out the keeper plate (see illustrations).

9 If pump wear is suspected, check the gears in the following way. Extract the fixing screws and remove the rear cover plate. The screws are very tight, and will probably require the use of an impact screwdriver (see illustration).

10 Check the clearance between the outer gear and the pump housing using feeler blades. Check the gear endfloat by placing a straight edge across the pump body, and checking the gap between the straight edge and gear face (see illustrations). If the clearances are outside the specified tolerance, renew the oil pump complete.

11 If the pump is unworn, refit the rear cover plate and tighten the screws fully.

12 Apply air pressure from a tyre pump to the oil pump oil ducts, to clear any sludge or other material. Prime the pump by pouring clean engine oil into its inlet duct, at the same time turning the oil pump inner gear with the fingers.

13 Lever out the oil seal and drive a new one squarely into the oil pump casing (see illustrations). Lubricate the oil seal lips.

Refitting

14 Bolt the pump into position using a new joint gasket (see illustrations). Note that one bolt is longer than the others.

15 Bolt on the oil pick-up assembly using a new sealing washer.

16 Lock the crankshaft as described in paragraph 4, then fit the crankshaft sprocket and tighten the bolt to the specified torque.

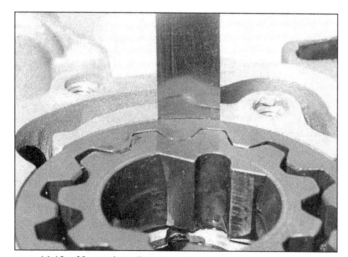

14.10a Measuring oil pump outer gear-to-pump housing clearance

14.10b Measuring oil pump gear endfloat

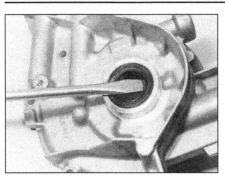

14.13a Removing the oil pump seal

14.13b Using a socket to fit a new oil seal to the oil pump

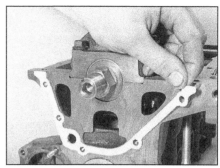

14.14a Using a new gasket . . .

14.14b . . . refit the oil pump

17 Fit and tension the timing belt as described in Section 5.

18 Fit the sump as described in Section 13. Screw on a new oil filter cartridge.

19 Fill the engine with oil (see Chapter 1).

20 Run the engine for a few minutes, then check and top-up the oil level (see *"Weekly Checks"*).

15 Valve clearances - measurement and adjustment

General information

1 The clearance between each camshaft lobe and its respective follower governs valve lift and timing, which in turn affects engine performance and efficiency. Too much clearance will cause noisy operation and poor performance. Too little clearance will also reduce performance and can ultimately lead to burning of the valves and valve seats.

2 The clearance is set by means of a solid shim, fitted to the top of each camshaft follower. Engine wear will alter the valve clearances and for this reason, they must be checked at the specified intervals and adjusted if necessary.

3 Valve clearance measurement must always be carried with the engine cold.

Measurement

4 Disconnect the battery negative cable and position it away from the terminal.

5 Refer to Section 7 and remove the camshaft cover. Remove the spark plugs as described in Chapter 1 (the lack of compression will make it easier to turn the engine over).

6 Raise the front of the vehicle and support it securely on axle stands (see *"Jacking and vehicle support"*). Select fifth gear, to allow you to turn the engine over by rotating one of the front wheels.

7 Each valve clearance must be checked with the high point of the camshaft lobe pointing upwards, directly away from the top of the follower.

8 Check the valves by following the firing order (1, 3, 4, 2 - cylinder No 1 is at the timing

belt end of the engine); this will minimise the number of crankshaft revolutions required.

9 Insert the appropriate feeler blade between the heel of the cam and the cam follower shim of the first valve **(see illustration)**. If necessary alter the thickness of the feeler blade until a stiff, sliding fit is achieved. The blade thickness represents the valve clearance for this particular valve - make a note of the thickness on paper.

10 Turn the engine, until the cam lobe for the second valve is pointing upwards, measure the clearance and record the value in a similar manner.

11 Repeat the operations on all the remaining valves, recording their respective clearances.

12 Remember that the clearances for the inlet and exhaust valves are different - see *Specifications*. Counting from the timing cover end of the engine, the valve sequence is:

> *Inlet: 2-4-5-7*
> *Exhaust: 1-3-6-8*

Adjustment

13 Where clearances are incorrect, the particular shim will have to be changed. To remove the shim, turn the crankshaft until the high point of the cam is pointing directly upward. The cam follower will now have to be depressed so that the shim can be extracted. Special tools are available from your Fiat dealer to do the job, otherwise you will have to make up a forked lever to locate on the rim of the cam follower. This must allow room for the shim to be prised out by means of the cut-outs provided in the cam follower rim **(see illustration)**.

15.9 Checking a valve clearance with a feeler blade

14 Once the shim is extracted, establish its thickness and change it for a thicker or thinner one to bring the previously recorded clearance within specification. For example, if the measured valve clearance was 1.27 mm too great, a shim *thicker* by this amount will be required. Conversely, if the clearance was 1.27 mm too small, a shim *thinner* by this amount will be required.

15 Shims have their thickness (mm) engraved on them; although the engraved side should be fitted so as not to be visible, wear still occurs and often obliterates the number. In this case, measuring their thickness with a metric micrometer is the only method to establish their thickness **(see illustration)**.

16 In practice, if several shims have to be changed, they can often be interchanged, so avoiding the necessity of having to buy more new shims than is necessary.

15.13 Use a modified C-spanner and a screwdriver to remove a shim

15.15 Shim thickness is marked on the lower face (this example is 4.20 mm)

17 If more than two or three valve clearances are found to be incorrect, it will be more convenient to remove the camshaft for easier removal of the shims.

18 Where no clearance can be measured, even with the thinnest available shim in position, the valve will have to be removed and the end of its stem ground off squarely. This will reduce its overall length by the minimum amount to provide a clearance. This job should be entrusted to your dealer, or engine reconditioning specialist, as it is important to keep the end of the valve stem perfectly square.

19 On completion, refit the camshaft cover and gasket, air cleaner and duct, and spark plugs, then lower the vehicle to the ground.

Chapter 2 Part C:
Engine removal and overhaul procedures

Contents

Degrees of difficulty

Easy, suitable for novice with little experience	**Fairly easy,** suitable for beginner with some experience	**Fairly difficult,** suitable for competent DIY mechanic 	**Difficult,** suitable for experienced DIY mechanic	**Very difficult,** suitable for expert DIY or professional

Specifications

OHC engines

Engine codes
See Chapter 2B.

Cylinder head
Camshaft bearing diameters:
  No 1 bearing . . . . 24.045 to 24.070 mm
  No 2 bearing . . . . 23.545 to 23.570 mm
  No 3 bearing . . . . 24.045 to 24.070 mm
Valve seat angle . . . . 45° 30' ± 5'
Valve guide-to-bore in cylinder head:
  Inlet . . . . 0.033 to 0.080 mm (interference fit)
  Exhaust . . . . 0.033 to 0.080 mm (interference fit)
Valve follower (tappet) running clearance in head . . . . 0.005 to 0.050 mm

Valves
Valve stem diameter . . . . 6.982 to 7.000 mm
Valve face angle . . . . 45° 30' ± 5'
Valve face width . . . . 2.0 mm
Valve stem-to-guide clearance . . . . 0.022 to 0.058 mm
Valve follower (tappet) shim sizes . . . . 3.2 to 4.7 mm in increments of 0.05 mm

Camshaft
Camshaft bearing running clearance . . . . 0.03 to 0.07 mm
Camshaft endfloat . . . . 0.07 to 0.25 mm

Cylinder block
Bore diameter . . . . 70.000 to 70.030 mm
Undersizes . . . . Increments of 0.010 mm

Pistons and piston rings

Piston diameter:
    Grade A . . . . 69.96 to 69.97 mm
    Grade B . . . . 69.97 to 69.98 mm
    Grade C . . . . 69.98 to 69.99 mm
Piston to bore clearance . . . . 0.03 to 0.05 mm
Maximum difference in weight between pistons . . . . ± 5.0 g
Gudgeon pin diameter . . . . 17.970 to 17.974 mm
Gudgeon pin to piston clearance . . . . 0.008 to 0.016 mm
Piston ring-to-ring wall clearance:
    Top compression ring . . . . 0.04 to 0.08 mm
    2nd compression ring . . . . 0.02 to 0.055 mm
    Oil control ring . . . . 0.02 to 0.055 mm
Piston ring end gap:
    Top compression ring . . . . 0.25 to 0.45 mm
    2nd compression ring . . . . 0.25 to 0.45 mm
    Oil control ring . . . . 0.2 to 0.45 mm

Connecting rods

Gudgeon pin-to-small end clearance . . . . 0.014 to 0.035 mm (interference fit)

Crankshaft

Main bearing journal diameters:
    Grade 1 . . . . 43.994 to 44.000 mm
    Grade 2 . . . . 43.988 to 43.994 mm
    Grade 3 . . . . 43.982 to 43.988 mm
Crankpin journal diameters . . . . 37.990 to 38.008 mm
Main bearing running clearance . . . . 0.025 to 0.047 mm
Big-end bearing running clearance . . . . 0.024 to 0.060 mm
Crankshaft endfloat . . . . 0.055 to 0.265 mm

OHV engines

Engine codes

See Chapter 2A.

Cylinder head

Valve seat angle . . . . 45° 0' ± 5'
Valve guide-to-bore in cylinder head:
    Inlet . . . . 0.033 to 0.080 mm (interference fit)
    Exhaust . . . . 0.033 to 0.080 mm (interference fit)

Valves

Valve stem diameter . . . . 6.982 to 7.000 mm
Valve face angle . . . . 45° 30' ± 5'
Valve face width . . . . 2.0 mm
Valve stem-to-guide clearance . . . . 0.022 to 0.058 mm

Rocker gear

Rocker shaft diameter . . . . 14.978 mm
Rocker shaft-to-rocker arm clearance . . . . 0.020 to 0.052 mm
Rocker shaft-to-support pedestal clearance . . . . 0.02 to 0.05 mm
Hydraulic tappet diameter . . . . 11.94 to 11.99 mm
Rocker arm-to-hydraulic tappet clearance . . . . 0.010 to 0.083 mm

Camshaft

Camshaft journal diameter:
    No 1 journal . . . . 30.975 to 31.000 mm
    No 2 journal . . . . 43.348 to 43.373 mm
    No 3 journal . . . . 37.975 to 38.000 mm
Camshaft journal-to-bearing clearance:
    No 1 journal . . . . 0.026 to 0.071 mm
    No 2 journal . . . . 0.031 to 0.076 mm
    No 3 journal . . . . 0.025 to 0.075 mm

Cylinder block

Bore diameter . . . . 65.000 to 65.050 mm
Undersizes . . . . Increments of 0.010 mm
Cam follower diameter . . . . 13.982 to 14.000 mm
Cam follower-to-bore clearance . . . . 0.010 to 0.046 mm

Pistons and piston rings

Piston diameter:
Grade A	64.95 to 64.96 mm
Grade C	64.97 to 64.98 mm
Grade E	64.99 to 65 mm

Piston to bore clearance:
Up to engine No 8600000	0.011 to 0.039 mm
From engine No 8600000	0.05 to 0.07 mm
Maximum difference in weight between pistons	± 5.0 g
Gudgeon pin diameter	19.974 to 19.978 mm
Gudgeon pin to piston clearance	0.008 to 0.017 mm

Piston ring-to-ring wall clearance
Top compression ring	0.045 to 0.077 mm
2nd compression ring	0.045 to 0.080 mm
Oil control ring	0.020 to 0.052 mm

Piston ring end gap:
Top compression ring	0.025 to 0.045 mm
2nd compression ring	0.02 to 0.04 mm
Oil control ring	0.020 to 0.045 mm

Connecting rods

Gudgeon pin-to-small end clearance	0.014 to 0.038 mm (interference fit)

Crankshaft

Main bearing journal diameters:
Grade 1	50.795 to 50.805 mm
Grade 2	50.785 to 50.795 mm
Crankpin journal diameters	39.985 to 40.005 mm
Main bearing running clearance	0.026 to 0.061 mm
Big-end bearing running clearance	0.026 to 0.074 mm
Crankshaft endfloat	0.06 to 0.26 mm

Torque wrench settings

	Nm	lbf ft
OHC engines		
Big-end bolts/nuts	41	30
Main bearing cap:		
Stage 1	40	30
Stage 2	Angle-tighten 90°	
OHV engines		
Big-end bolts	41	30
Crankshaft rear oil seal housing bolts	10	7
Main bearing cap bolts	69	51

1 Engine and transmission removal - preparation and precautions

If you have decided the engine must be removed for overhaul or major repair work, several preliminary steps should be taken.

Locating a suitable place to work is extremely important. Adequate work space, along with storage space for the vehicle, will be needed. If a workshop or garage isn't available, at the very least a flat, level, clean work surface is required.

If possible, clear some shelving close to the work area and use it to store the engine components and ancillaries as they are removed and dismantled. In this manner, the components stand a better chance of staying clean and undamaged during the overhaul. Laying out components in groups together with their fixings bolts, screws etc will save time and avoid confusion when the engine is refitted.

Clean the engine compartment and engine/transmission before beginning the removal procedure; this will help visibility and help to keep tools clean.

The help of an assistant should be available; there are certain instances when one person cannot safely perform all of the operations required to remove the engine from the vehicle. Safety is of primary importance, considering the potential hazards involved in this kind of operation. A second person should always be in attendance to offer help in an emergency. If this is the first time you have removed an engine, advice and aid from someone more experienced would also be beneficial.

Plan the operation ahead of time. Before starting work, obtain (or arrange for the hire of) all of the tools and equipment you will need. Access to the following items will allow the task of removing and refitting the engine/transmission to be completed safely and with relative ease; a heavy-duty trolley jack - rated in excess of the combined weight of the engine and transmission, complete sets of spanners and sockets as described in the front of this manual, wooden blocks, and plenty of rags and cleaning solvent for mopping up spilled oil, coolant and fuel. A selection of different sized plastic storage bins will also prove useful for keeping dismantled components grouped together. If any of the equipment must be hired, make sure that you arrange for it in advance, and perform all of the operations possible without it beforehand; this may save you time and money.

Plan on the vehicle being out of use for quite a while, especially if you intend to carry out an engine overhaul. Read through the whole of this section and work out a strategy based on your own experience and the tools, time and workspace available to you. Some of the overhaul processes may have to be carried out by a FIAT dealer or an engineering works - these establishments often have busy schedules, so it would be prudent to consult them before removing or dismantling the engine, to get an idea of the amount of time required to carry out the work.

When removing the engine from the vehicle, be methodical about the disconnection of external components. Labelling cables and hoses as they are removed will greatly assist the refitting process.

Always be extremely careful when lifting the engine/transmission assembly from the engine bay. Serious injury can result from careless actions. If help is required, it is better to wait until it is available rather than risk personal injury and/or damage to components by continuing alone. By planning ahead and taking your time, a job of this nature, although major, can be accomplished successfully and without incident.

On all models described in this manual, the engine and transmission are removed as a complete assembly, or as separate units, via the underside of the engine compartment.

2 Engine and transmission - removal, separation, connection and refitting

Note: *This procedure describes the removal of the engine and transmission as a complete assembly and their separation on the bench. Removal of the transmission alone is described in Chapter 7.*

Removal

1 Select a solid, level surface to park the vehicle upon. Give yourself enough space to move around it easily. Disconnect the battery negative cable and position it away from the terminal (see *"Disconnecting the battery"*).
2 Remove the bonnet and disconnect the washer tubing as described in Chapter 11. Although the engine can be removed with the bonnet in situ, its removal will allow greater freedom when positioning the engine lifting equipment.
3 Apply the handbrake firmly and chock both rear wheels. Jack up the front of the vehicle and support securely on axle stands (see *"Jacking and vehicle support"*). In order to remove the engine/transmission assembly in an upright position from under the vehicle, there must be a minimum of approximately 620 mm between the floor and the lower edge of the engine compartment front cross-

2.28 Removing the engine and transmission as an assembly, via the underside of the engine compartment

member, with the front bumper removed (see Chapter 11). Remember that additional clearance will be necessary if the assembly is to be lowered onto a trolley.
4 Remove the screws and detach the engine compartment lower cover(s).
5 Remove both front wheels, then undo the screws and remove the two-piece plastic liners from both front wheel arches.
6 Drain the coolant from the engine with reference to Chapter 1.
7 Refer to Chapter 10 and separate both front suspension lower arms from their respective hub carriers. Remove the gaiter clips and disconnect the inner CV joints from the transmission plunge cups, with reference to Chapter 8. Secure the driveshafts away from the engine, to prevent them from obstructing the removal of the engine.
8 Unbolt the exhaust system front pipe from the exhaust manifold and the support bracket on the underside of the engine, with reference to Chapter 4. Remove the front pipe from the engine compartment.
9 Refer to Chapter 5A and remove the starter motor.
10 Remove the bolts and lower the flywheel protection plate away from the bottom of the bellhousing.
11 Remove the charcoal canister, together with its support bracket, from the front of the transmission casing with reference to Chapter 4. Secure the vacuum/vapour hoses away from the engine.
12 Remove the air cleaner and ducting as described in Chapter 4.
13 Disconnect the clutch cable from the transmission (refer to Chapter 6).
14 Refer to Chapter 7 and detach the gear change and selector cables from the transmission.
15 Unscrew the ferrule and disconnect the speedometer cable from the rear of the differential casing.
16 With reference to Chapter 7, disconnect the reverse gear inhibitor cable (where applicable) from the transmission casing, then unplug the wiring from the reversing lamp switch at the connector.
17 Unscrew the bolt and disconnect the earth lead from the transmission.
18 Release the plastic clips and free the main engine wiring harness from the top of the transmission casing.
19 Refer to Chapter 1 and remove the auxiliary drivebelt. Pivot the alternator as far as possible towards the engine, then tighten the upper mounting bolt to secure it in position. Refer to Chapter 5A and disconnect the electrical wiring from the alternator.
20 Refer to Chapter 3 and disconnect the radiator top and bottom hoses from the engine. Similarly, disconnect the coolant hose from the thermostat housing at the left-hand end of the cylinder head.
21 Remove the throttle body from the inlet manifold/mounting flange (as applicable), as described in Chapter 4.

22 Disconnect the coolant, vacuum and breather hoses from the cylinder head and inlet manifold (where applicable), making a careful note of their fitted locations to aid refitting later. If the brake servo vacuum hose is difficult to disconnect from the manifold port, prise the non-return valve from the front of the brake servo instead, as described in Chapter 9.
23 Unplug the wiring from the coolant temperature sensor on the inlet manifold, and the gauge sender unit on the rear of the cylinder head (or the top of the cylinder head on OHV engines). Label the connectors to aid correct refitting.
24 Release the clips and free the engine harness from the support brackets at the underside of the inlet manifold (OHC engines) and the left-hand end of the cylinder head.
25 Work around the engine compartment and check that nothing remains connected to the engine or transmission that might prevent removal. Ensure that all disconnected hoses, pipes and electrical cables are secured away from the engine.
26 Attach a suitable hoist to the engine and transmission lifting eyes. The left-hand eye is located on the transmission bellhousing and the other on the right-hand side of the engine. Take the weight of the engine/transmission.
27 Working beneath the vehicle, unscrew the bolts securing the rear, left hand and right hand engine mountings to the underbody (in that order); refer to Chapter 2A or B as applicable.
28 With the help of an assistant lower the engine/transmission from the engine compartment taking care not to damage the surrounding components **(see illustration)**.
Note: *Extra clearance can be gained by removing the front bumper (see Chapter 11), radiator and cooling fan (see Chapter 3).*
29 Ideally, the unit should be lowered onto a low level trolley so that it may be easily withdrawn from under the vehicle. Disconnect the hoist from the assembly.

Separation

30 Rest the engine and transmission assembly on a firm, flat surface and use wooden blocks as wedges to keep the unit steady as required.
31 Support the transmission with blocks of wood, then with reference to Chapter 7, unscrew the transmission-to-engine bolts.
32 Lift the transmission directly from the side of the engine, taking care to keep it level so that the transmission input shaft does not hang on the clutch.

Connection

33 If the engine and transmission have not been separated, proceed from paragraph 35.
34 Smear a little high-melting-point grease on the splines of the transmission input shaft. **Do not** use an excessive amount as there is the risk of contaminating the clutch friction plate.

35 Carefully offer up the transmission to the engine cylinder block, guiding the input shaft through the clutch friction plate.

36 With reference to Chapter 7, refit the transmission-to-engine bolts and the single nut, hand tightening them to secure the transmission in position. **Note:** *Do not tighten them to force the engine and transmission together.* Ensure that the bellhousing and cylinder block mating faces will butt together evenly without obstruction, before tightening the bolts and nut to their specified torque.

Refitting

37 Locate the engine/transmission assembly beneath the engine compartment and attach the hoist to the lifting eyes.

38 Carefully lift the assembly up into the engine compartment taking care not to damage the surrounding components.

39 Guide the rear engine mounting into place on the underbody - insert the securing bolts but only partially tighten them at this stage.

40 Raise the engine and transmission and guide the left and right hand engine mountings into position. Insert the securing bolts, then tighten them (together with those at the rear engine mounting) to the specified torque as described in Chapter 2A or B as applicable.

41 The remainder of the refitting procedure is the direct reverse of the removal procedure, noting the following points:

a) Ensure that all sections of the wiring harness follow their original routing, to keep them away from sources of heat and abrasion.

b) Ensure that all hoses are correctly routed and are secured with the correct hose clips, where applicable. If the existing hose clips are of the crimp-type, they cannot be used again; proprietary worm drive clips should be fitted in their place.

c) Refill the cooling system as described in Chapter 1.

d) Reconnect the clutch cable and adjust the pedal travel as described in Chapter 6.

e) Ensure that the brake servo vacuum hose is securely reconnected with reference to Chapter 9.

f) Refit and adjust the auxiliary drivebelt with reference to Chapter 1.

g) Reconnect and if necessary adjust the accelerator cable with reference to Chapter 4.

h) When the engine is started for the first time, check for air, coolant, lubricant and fuel leaks from manifolds, hoses etc. If the engine has been overhauled, read the notes in Section 12 before attempting to start it.

3 Engine overhaul - preliminary information

It is much easier to dismantle and work on the engine if it is mounted on a portable engine stand. These stands can often be hired from a tool hire shop. Before the engine is mounted on a stand, the flywheel should be removed, so that the stand bolts can be tightened into the end of the cylinder block/crankcase.

If a stand is not available, it is possible to dismantle the engine with it blocked up on a sturdy workbench, or on the floor.

⚠ **Warning: Be very careful not to tip or drop the engine when working without a stand.**

If you intend to obtain a reconditioned engine, all ancillaries must be removed first, to be transferred to the replacement engine (just as they will if you are doing a complete engine overhaul yourself).

Note: *When removing the external components from the engine, pay close attention to details that may be helpful or important during refitting. Note the fitted position of gaskets, seals, spacers, pins, washers, bolts, and other small components.*

If you are obtaining a "short" engine (the engine cylinder block/crankcase, crankshaft, pistons and connecting rods, all fully assembled), then the cylinder head, sump, oil pump, timing belt/chain and sprockets, auxiliary belt, coolant pump, thermostat housing, coolant outlet elbows, oil filter housing and where applicable oil cooler will also have to be removed.

If you are planning a full overhaul, the engine can be dismantled in the order given below:

a) Timing belt, sprockets, and tensioner (OHC engine).
b) Timing chain, sprockets and tensioner (OHV engine).
c) Camshaft and followers (OHV engine).
d) Flywheel.
e) Inlet and exhaust manifolds.
f) Cylinder head.
g) Sump.
h) Oil pump.
i) Pistons and crankshaft.

4 Cylinder head - dismantling, cleaning, inspection and reassembly

Note: *New and reconditioned cylinder heads are available from the manufacturer or engine overhaul specialists. Be aware that some specialist tools are required for the dismantling and inspection procedures, and new components may not be readily available. It may therefore be more practical and economical for the home mechanic to purchase a reconditioned head, rather than dismantle, inspect and recondition the original head.*

Dismantling

1 Remove the cylinder head as described in Part A or B of this Chapter (as applicable). On OHV engines, this entails removing the rocker gear from the cylinder head first.

2 If not already done, remove the inlet and exhaust manifolds with reference to Chapter 4, and the spark plugs as described in Chapter 1.

3 On OHC engines, remove the camshaft sprocket with reference to Chapter 2B.

OHC engines

4 Mark the positions of the camshaft bearing caps, numbering them from the timing end.

5 Unbolt and remove the lubrication pipe (prise the oil feed stub out with a screwdriver). Unscrew the remaining bolts and take off the bearing caps **(see illustrations)**.

6 Lift the camshaft carefully from the cylinder head, checking that the valve clearance shims and cam followers are not withdrawn by the adhesion of the oil **(see illustration)**.

4.5a Removing the camshaft oil feed pipe (OHC engine)

4.5b Unscrewing the camshaft bearing/banjo union bolt (OHC engine)

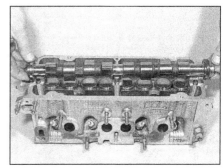

4.6 Removing the camshaft from the cylinder head (OHC engine)

4.7 Removing a follower (OHC engine)

7 Remove the shims and cam followers, but keep them in their originally fitted order **(see illustration)**.

All engines

8 Stand the cylinder head on its end. Using a valve spring compressor, compress each valve spring in turn, extracting the split collets when the upper valve spring seat has been pushed far enough down the valve stem to free them. If the spring seat sticks, lightly tap the upper jaw of the spring compressor with a hammer to free it.

9 Release the valve spring compressor and remove the upper spring seat, valve spring and lower spring seat.

10 Withdraw the valve from the head gasket side of the cylinder head, then use a pair of pliers to extract the valve stem oil seal from the top of the guide **(see illustrations)**. If the valve sticks in the guide, carefully deburr the end face with fine abrasive paper. Repeat this process for the remaining valves.

11 It is essential that each valve is stored together with its collets, spring, and spring seats. The valves should also be kept in their correct sequence, unless they are so badly worn that they are to be renewed. If they are going to be kept and used again, place each valve assembly in a labelled polythene bag or similar small container. Note that No 1 valve is at the timing belt/chain end of the engine.

Cleaning

12 Using a suitable degreasing agent, remove all traces of oil deposits from the cylinder head, paying particular attention to the journal bearings, valve follower bores, valve guides and oilways. Scrape off any traces of old gasket from the mating surfaces, taking care not to score or gouge them. If using emery paper, do not use a grade of less than 100. Turn the head over and using a blunt blade, scrape any carbon deposits from the combustion chambers and ports.
Caution: Do not erode the sealing surface of the valve seat.

13 Finally, wash the entire head casting with a suitable solvent to remove the remaining debris.

14 Clean the valve heads and stems using a fine wire brush. If the valve is heavily coked, scrape off the majority of the deposits with a blunt blade first, then use the wire brush.
Caution: Do not erode the sealing surface of the valve face.

15 Thoroughly clean the remainder of the components using solvent and allow them to dry completely. Discard the oil seals, as new items must be fitted when the cylinder head is reassembled.

Inspection

Cylinder head

16 Inspect the head very carefully for cracks, evidence of coolant leakage, and other damage. If cracks are found, a new cylinder head should be obtained.

17 Use a straight-edge and feeler blade to check that the cylinder head gasket surface is not distorted. If it is, it may be possible to have it machined, provided that the cylinder head is not reduced to less than the specified height. Seek the advice of an engine overhaul specialist.

18 Examine the valve seats in each of the combustion chambers. If they are severely pitted, cracked, or burned, they will need to be renewed or re-cut by an engine overhaul specialist. If they are only slightly pitted, this can be removed by grinding-in the valve heads and seats with fine valve-grinding compound, as described below.

19 Check the valve guides for wear by inserting the relevant valve, and checking for side-to-side motion of the valve. A very small amount of movement is acceptable. If the movement seems excessive, remove the valve. Measure the valve stem diameter at several points, and renew the valve if it is worn. If the valve stem is not worn, the wear must be in the valve guide, and the guide must be renewed. The renewal of valve guides is best carried out by an engine overhaul specialist, who will have the necessary tools available.

20 If renewing the valve guides, the valve seats should be re-cut or re-ground only *after* the guides have been fitted.

Camshaft (OHC engines)

21 Inspect the camshaft for wear on the surfaces of the lobes and journals. Normally their surfaces should be smooth and have a dull shine; look for scoring and pitting. Accelerated wear will occur once the hardened exterior of the camshaft has been damaged.

22 Examine the bearing cap and journal surfaces for signs of wear.

23 To measure the camshaft endfloat, temporarily refit the camshaft then push the camshaft to one end of the cylinder head as far as it will travel. Attach a dial test indicator to the cylinder head and zero it, then push the camshaft as far as it will go to the other end of the cylinder head and record the gauge reading. Verify the reading by pushing the camshaft back to its original position and checking that the gauge indicates zero again.

24 The camshaft bearing running clearance may be checked using Plastigauge, using the method described later in this Chapter for checking the crankshaft running clearances.

25 Where the camshaft and bearings are worn excessively consider renewing the complete cylinder head together with camshaft and cam followers. A reconditioned head may be available from engine repairers. Wear of cam followers may be checked using a micrometer.

Valves and associated components

26 Examine the head of each valve for pitting, burning, cracks, and general wear. Check the valve stem for scoring and wear ridges. Rotate the valve, and check for any obvious indication that it is bent. Look for pits or excessive wear on the tip of each valve stem. Renew any valve that shows any such signs of wear or damage.

27 If the valve appears satisfactory at this stage, measure the valve stem diameter at several points using a micrometer. Any significant difference in the readings obtained indicates wear of the valve stem. Should any of these conditions be apparent, the valve(s) must be renewed.

28 If the valves are in satisfactory condition, they should be ground (lapped) into their respective seats, to ensure a smooth, gas-tight seal. If the seat is only lightly pitted, or if it has been re-cut, fine grinding compound *only* should be used to produce the required finish. Coarse valve-grinding compound should *not* be used, unless a seat is badly burned or deeply pitted. If this is the case, the cylinder head and valves should be inspected by an expert, to decide whether seat re-cutting, or even the renewal of the valve or seat insert (where possible) is required.

4.10a Withdraw the valves from the head gasket side of the cylinder head

4.10b Use a pair of pliers to extract the valve stem oil seal from the top of the guide

4.39 Compress the valve spring and locate the split collets (arrowed) in the recess in the valve stem

4.43 The locating dowels have different lengths, to ensure correct cap orientation (OHC engine)

29 Valve grinding is carried out as follows. Place the cylinder head upside-down on a bench.

30 Smear a trace of (the appropriate grade of) valve-grinding compound on the seat face, and press a suction grinding tool onto the valve head. With a semi-rotary action, grind the valve head to its seat, lifting the valve occasionally to redistribute the grinding compound. A light spring placed under the valve head will greatly ease this operation.

31 If coarse grinding compound is being used, work only until a dull, matt even surface is produced on both the valve seat and the valve, then wipe off the used compound, and repeat the process with fine compound. When a smooth unbroken ring of light grey matt finish is produced on both the valve and seat, the grinding operation is complete. *Do not grind-in the valves any further than absolutely necessary, or the seat will be prematurely sunk into the cylinder head.*

32 When all the valves have been ground-in, carefully wash off *all* traces of grinding compound using paraffin or a suitable solvent, before reassembling the cylinder head.

33 Examine the valve springs for signs of damage and discoloration. If possible compare the length of the springs with new ones and renew them if necessary.

34 Stand each spring on a flat surface, and check it for squareness. If any of the springs are damaged, distorted or have lost their tension, obtain a complete new set of springs. It is normal to renew the valve springs as a matter of course if a major overhaul is being carried out.

35 Renew the valve stem oil seals regardless of their apparent condition.

Rocker gear (OHV engines)

Refer to the information given in Chapter 2A.

Reassembly

36 Lubricate the stems of the valves, and insert the valves into their original locations. If new valves are being fitted, insert them into the locations to which they have been ground.

37 Refit the spring seat then, working on the first valve, dip the new valve stem seal in fresh engine oil. Carefully locate it over the valve and onto the guide. Take care not to damage the seal as it is passed over the valve stem.

Use a suitable socket or metal tube to press the seal firmly onto the guide.

38 Locate the valve spring on top of its seat, then refit the spring retainer.

39 Compress the valve spring and locate the split collets in the recess in the valve stem. Release the compressor, then repeat the procedure on the remaining valves **(see illustration)**.

> **HAYNES HiNT**
> *Use a dab of grease to hold the collets in position on the valve stem while the spring compressor is released.*

40 With all the valves installed, place the cylinder head flat on the bench and, using a hammer and interposed block of wood, tap the end of each valve stem to settle the components.

OHC engines

41 Oil the valve followers and locate them in their correct positions in the cylinder head. Locate the shims in the valve followers making sure they are in their original positions.

42 Oil the journals then locate the camshaft in the cylinder head with the cam lobes of No 1 cylinder facing upwards (ie No 1 cylinder at TDC).

43 Refit the bearing caps in their correct positions and progressively tighten the nuts/bolts to the specified torque. Note that the locating dowels have different lengths to provide bearing cap orientation **(see**

illustration). Locate the lubrication pipe on the head and press in the oil feed stub before refitting the bolts.

44 Refit the camshaft sprocket with reference to Chapter 2A or 2B.

All engines

45 Refit the spark plugs as described in Chapter 1. On OHV engines, refit the rocker gear and then adjust the hydraulic tappet pre-load at each rocker arm, with reference to Chapter 2A.

46 If required, refit the inlet and exhaust manifolds at this point. On OHC engines, the valve clearances can also be checked now. The cylinder head is now ready for refitting as described in Part A or B of this Chapter (as applicable).

5 Camshaft and followers (OHV engine) - removal, inspection and refitting

Removal

1 Refer to the relevant Sections in Chapter 2A and remove the cylinder head, timing chain and camshaft sprocket, sump and oil pump.

2 Invert the engine so that it is supported on its cylinder head face (on a clean work area). This is necessary to make all of the followers slide to the top of their stroke, thus allowing the camshaft to be withdrawn. Rotate the camshaft through a full turn, to ensure that all of the followers slide up their bores, clear of the camshaft.

3 Before removing the camshaft, check its endfloat using a dial gauge mounted on the front face of the engine. Pull the camshaft longitudinally in one direction, zero the DTI gauge probe on the end of the camshaft, then push the camshaft to the end of its travel in the other direction. The camshaft endfloat must be as specified by your FIAT dealer.

4 Undo the lockscrew, and remove the camshaft front bearing **(see illustrations)**.

5 Carefully withdraw the camshaft from the front end of the engine, ensuring that the camshaft lobes do not scratch the remaining bearings as the shaft is removed. **(see illustration)**.

5.4a Undo the lockscrew . . .

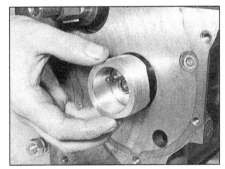

5.4b . . . and remove the camshaft front bearing

5.5 Withdrawing the camshaft from the engine

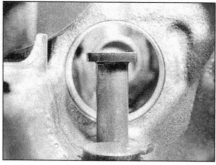

5.6 Camshaft followers (viewed with cylinder block inverted)

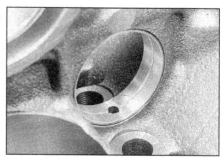

5.8 Examine the camshaft centre and rear bearings for signs of damage or excessive wear

6 Extract each follower in turn. Keep them in order of fitting by inserting them in a card with eight holes in it, numbered 1 to 8 (from the timing chain end of the engine). A valve grinding suction tool will be found to be useful for the removal of followers **(see illustration)**.

Inspection

7 Examine the camshaft bearing journals and lobes for damage or excessive wear. If evident, the camshaft must be renewed.
8 Examine the camshaft bearing internal surfaces for signs of damage or excessive wear **(see illustration)**. If evident, the bearings must be renewed. Renewal of the centre and rear bearings should be entrusted to a Fiat dealer or engine reconditioning workshop, as access to specialist equipment is required.
9 If not carried out on removal, check the camshaft endfloat as described in paragraph 3. If the endfloat exceeds the specified tolerance, renew the front bearing.
10 It is seldom that the followers wear excessively in their bores, but it is likely that after a high mileage, the cam lobe contact surfaces will show signs of depression or grooving.
11 Where this condition is evident, renew the followers. Grinding out the grooves and wear marks will reduce the thickness of the surface hardening, and will accelerate further wear.

Refitting

12 To refit the followers and the camshaft, it is essential that the crankcase is inverted (cylinder head mating surface facing downwards).

6.6 Removing a big-end bearing cap (OHC engine shown)

13 Lubricate the followers and their bores. Insert each follower fully into its original bore in the cylinder block.
14 Lubricate the camshaft bearings, camshaft and thrust plate, then insert the camshaft into the crankcase from the timing case end.
15 Fit the front bearing and tighten the lockscrew securely. Check that the camshaft is able to rotate freely, and that the endfloat is as specified (see Specifications).
16 Refit the oil pump, sump, camshaft sprocket, timing chain and cylinder head as described in Chapter 2A. On completion, adjust the hydraulic tappet pre-load (also described in Chapter 2A).

6 Pistons and connecting rods - removal, inspection, refitting and clearance check

Removal

1 Remove the sump and gasket with reference to Chapter 2A or 2B.
2 Unbolt and remove the oil pump pick-up/filter screen assembly.
3 The big-end bearing shells can be renewed without having to remove the cylinder head, if the caps are unbolted and the piston/connecting rod pushed gently about one inch up the bore (the crankpin being at its lowest point). If these shells are worn, however, the main bearing shells will almost certainly be worn as well. In this case, the crankshaft should be removed for inspection.
4 To remove the pistons and connecting rods, remove the cylinder head first with reference to Chapter 2A or 2B.
5 The big-end caps and the connecting rods are numbered 1, 2, 3 and 4 from the timing belt/chain end of the engine. The numbers are located on the engine oil dipstick tube side (OHC engines) or on the side furthest away from the camshaft (OHV engines). These markings indicate which way round, and to which connecting rod, each cap should be fitted. If the manufacturers markings are not visible, make your own using a centre punch and small mallet, or a sharp file.

6 Turn the crankshaft as necessary to bring the first crankpin to its lowest point, then unscrew the bolts/nuts (as applicable) and remove the big-end cap and shell bearing **(see illustration)**.
7 Push the piston/rod assembly up the bore and out of the cylinder block. If a wear ridge has developed at the top of the bores, remove this by careful scraping before trying to extract the piston/rod assemblies. The ridge will otherwise prevent removal, or will break the piston rings during the attempt. On OHC engines, note the arrow markings on the top of the piston crown; these point towards the timing belt/chain end of the engine.
8 Remove the remaining pistons/rods in a similar way. If the bearing shells are to be used again, tape them to their respective caps or rods, to keep them in the correct order.

Inspection

9 Before the inspection process can begin, the piston/connecting rod assemblies must be cleaned, and the original piston rings removed from the pistons.
10 Carefully expand the old rings over the top of the pistons. The use of two or three old feeler blades will be helpful in preventing the rings dropping into empty grooves. Always remove the rings from the top of the piston. Keep each set of rings with its piston if the old rings are to be re-used.
Caution: Be careful not to scratch the piston with the ends of the ring. The rings are brittle, and will snap if they are spread too far. They are also very sharp - protect your hands and fingers.
11 Scrape away all traces of carbon from the top of the piston. A hand-held wire brush (or a piece of fine emery cloth) can be used, once the majority of the deposits have been scraped away.
12 Remove the carbon from the ring grooves in the piston, using an old ring. Break the ring in half to do this (be careful not to cut your fingers - piston rings are sharp).
Caution: Be careful to remove only the carbon deposits - do not remove any metal, and do not nick or scratch the sides of the ring grooves.
13 Once the deposits have been removed, clean the piston/connecting rod assembly

with paraffin or a suitable solvent, and dry thoroughly. Make sure that the oil return holes in the ring grooves are clear.

14 If the pistons and cylinder bores are not damaged or worn excessively, and if the cylinder block does not need to be rebored, the original pistons can be refitted. Normal piston wear shows up as even vertical wear on the piston thrust surfaces, and slight looseness of the top ring in its groove. New piston rings should always be used when the engine is reassembled.

15 Carefully inspect each piston for cracks around the skirt, around the gudgeon pin holes, and at the piston ring "lands" (between the ring grooves).

16 Look for scoring and scuffing on the piston skirt, holes in the piston crown, and burned areas at the edge of the crown. If the skirt is scored or scuffed, the engine may have been suffering from overheating, and/or abnormal combustion which caused excessively high operating temperatures. The cooling and lubrication systems should be checked thoroughly. Scorch marks on the sides of the pistons show that blow-by has occurred. A hole in the piston crown, or burned areas at the edge of the piston crown, indicates that abnormal combustion has been occurring. If any of the above problems exist, the causes must be investigated and corrected, or the damage will occur again. The causes may include incorrect ignition timing, or a faulty injector (as applicable).

17 Corrosion of the piston, in the form of pitting, indicates that coolant has been leaking into the combustion chamber and/or the crankcase. Again, the cause must be corrected, or the problem may persist in the rebuilt engine.

18 Examine each connecting rod carefully for signs of damage, such as cracks around the big-end and small-end bearings. Check that the rod is not bent or distorted. Damage is highly unlikely, unless the engine has been seized or badly overheated. Detailed checking of the connecting rod assembly can only be carried out by an engine repair specialist with the necessary equipment.

19 Although not essential, it is highly recommended that the big-end cap bolts/nuts (as applicable) are renewed as a complete set prior to refitting.

20 Check the fit of the gudgeon pin by twisting the piston and connecting rod in opposite directions. Any noticeable play indicates excessive wear, which must be corrected. On both the OHV and OHC engines, connecting rod/gudgeon pin renewal should be entrusted to an engine repair specialist, as the gudgeon pins are an interference fit in the connecting rod small ends.

21 Check the piston-to-bore clearance by measuring the cylinder bore (see Section 8) and the piston diameter. Measure the piston across the skirt, at a 90° angle to the gudgeon pin, approximately half way down the skirt. Subtract the piston diameter from the bore

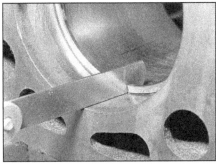

6.23 Checking the end gap of piston ring

diameter to obtain the clearance. If this is greater than the figures given in the Specifications, the block will have to be rebored and new pistons and rings fitted.

22 If new rings are being fitted to the old pistons, measure the piston ring-to-groove clearance by placing a new piston ring in each ring groove and measuring the clearance with a feeler blade. Check the clearance at three or four places around each groove. If the measured clearance exceeds the limit listed in the Specifications, new pistons will be required. If the new ring is excessively tight, the most likely cause is dirt remaining in the groove.

23 Before refitting the rings to the pistons, check their end gaps by inserting each of them in their cylinder bores. Use the piston to make sure that they are square. Using feeler blades, check that the gaps are within the tolerances given in the Specifications **(see illustration)**. Genuine rings are supplied pre-gapped; no attempt should be made to adjust the gaps by filing.

Reassembly

24 Install the new rings by fitting them over the top of the piston, starting with the oil control ring. Use feeler blades in the same way as when removing the old rings. New rings generally have their top surfaces identified 'TOP', and must be fitted the correct way round. Note that the first and second compression rings have different cross-sections; the upper ring is thinner and the second ring has a stepped base. Be careful when handling the compression rings; they will break if they are handled roughly or

6.24b Piston ring markings

6.24a Using feeler blades to fit piston rings

expanded too far. With all the rings in position, space the ring gaps at 120° to each other and use a feeler blade to check the ring-to-groove clearance **(see illustrations)**.

Refitting and big-end bearing running clearance check

25 Prior to refitting the piston/connecting rod assemblies, it is recommended that the big-end bearing running clearance is checked as follows.

Big-end bearing running clearance check

26 Clean the backs of the bearing shells, and the bearing locations in both the connecting rod and bearing cap.

27 Press the bearing shells into their locations, ensuring that the tab on each shell engages in the notch in the connecting rod and cap. Take care not to touch any shell's bearing surface with your fingers. If the original bearing shells are being used for the check, ensure that they are refitted in their original locations. The clearance can be checked in either of two ways.

28 One method is to refit the big-end bearing cap to the connecting rod, ensuring that they are fitted the correct way around, with the bearing shells in place. With the cap retaining bolts/nuts correctly tightened, use an internal micrometer or vernier caliper to measure the internal diameter of each assembled pair of bearing shells. If the diameter of each corresponding crankshaft journal is measured and then subtracted from the bearing internal diameter, the result will be the big-end bearing running clearance.

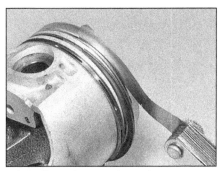

6.24c Measuring the piston ring-to-groove clearance

6.38a Fitting a piston/connecting rod assembly

6.38b Piston orientation arrow

6.40a Orientation/identification marks on the connecting rod and bearing cap must match and face each other

29 The second, and more accurate method is to use a product called Plastigauge. Ensure that the bearing shells are correctly fitted then place a strand of Plastigauge on each (cleaned) crankpin journal.
30 Refit the (clean) piston/connecting rod

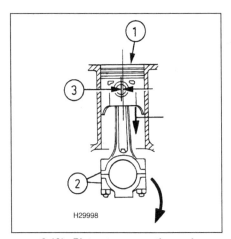

6.40b Piston to connecting rod relationship (OHC engine) - arrow indicates crankshaft direction of rotation

1 Piston orientation arrow
2 Rod/cap orientation/identification markings
3 Gudgeon pin offset in piston

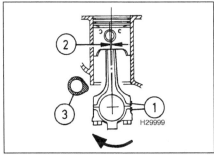

6.40c Piston to connecting rod relationship (OHV engine) - arrow indicates crankshaft direction of rotation

1 Rod/cap orientation/ident-ification markings
2 Gudgeon pin offset in piston
3 Camshaft

assemblies to the crankshaft, and refit the big-end bearing caps, using the marks made or noted on removal to ensure that they are fitted the correct way around.
31 Tighten the bearing cap bolts/nuts taking care not to disturb the Plastigauge or rotate the connecting rod during the tightening sequence.
32 Dismantle the assemblies without rotating the connecting rods or crankshaft. Use the scale printed on the Plastigauge envelope to obtain the big-end bearing running clearance.
33 If the clearance is significantly different from that expected, the bearing shells may be the wrong size (or excessively worn, if the original shells are being re-used). Make sure that no dirt or oil was trapped between the bearing shells and the caps or block when the clearance was measured. If the Plastigauge was wider at one end than at the other, the crankshaft journal may be tapered.
34 On completion, carefully scrape away all traces of the Plastigauge material from the crankshaft and bearing shells. Use your fingernail, or some other object which is unlikely to score the bearing surfaces.

Final piston/connecting rod refitting

35 Ensure that the bearing shells are correctly fitted. If new shells are being fitted, ensure that all traces of the protective grease are cleaned off using paraffin. Wipe dry the shells and connecting rods with a lint-free cloth.
36 Lubricate the cylinder bores, the pistons and piston rings, then lay out each piston /connecting rod assembly in its respective position.

6.41a Refitting a big-end bearing cap

37 Start with assembly No 1. Ensure that the piston ring gaps are still 120° apart, then clamp them in position with a piston ring compressor.
38 Insert the piston/connecting rod assembly into the top of cylinder making sure it is the correct way round. On OHC engines, ensure that the arrow on the piston crown is pointing towards the timing belt/chain end of the engine. On OHV engines, ensure that the connecting rod/bearing cap markings face **away** from the camshaft side of the engine. Using a block of wood or hammer handle against the piston crown, tap the assembly into the cylinder until the piston crown is flush with the top of the cylinder (see illustrations).
39 Ensure that the bearing shell is still correctly installed. Liberally lubricate the crankpin and both bearing shells. Taking care not to mark the cylinder bores, pull the piston/connecting rod assembly down the bore and onto the crankpin.
40 Refit the big-end bearing cap, tightening its retaining bolts/nuts finger-tight at first. Note that the surfaces with the identification marks must match and face each other (see illustrations).
41 Tighten the bearing cap retaining bolts/nuts evenly and progressively to the specified torque setting (see illustrations).
42 Once the bearing cap retaining bolts have been correctly tightened, rotate the crankshaft. Check that it turns freely; some stiffness is to be expected if new components have been fitted, but there should be no signs of binding or tight spots.

6.41b Tighten the big end bolts to the specified torque

7.4 Checking crankshaft endfloat using a DTI gauge

43 Refit the remaining three piston/connecting rod assemblies in the same way.
44 Refit the cylinder head, oil pump pick-up/filter screen assembly and sump with reference to Chapter 2A or 2B.

7 Crankshaft - removal and inspection

Removal

1 Remove the sump, oil pump and pick-up tube, and flywheel with reference to the relevant Sections of Parts A or B.
2 Remove the pistons and connecting rods, as described in Section 6. However, if no work is to be done on the pistons and connecting rods there is no need to remove the cylinder head, or to push the pistons out of the

7.7 Removing a main bearing cap (OHC engine shown)

7.8a Removing the crankshaft from the crankcase (OHC engine shown)

7.5 Checking crankshaft endfloat using a feeler blade

cylinder bores. The pistons should just be pushed far enough up the bores so that they are positioned clear of the crankshaft journals.
3 Unbolt the crankshaft rear oil seal housing from the cylinder block and recover the gasket where fitted.
4 Before removing the crankshaft, check the endfloat using a DTI gauge. Push the crankshaft fully one way, and then zero the gauge. Push the crankshaft fully the other way, and check the endfloat (see illustration). The result can be compared with the specified amount, and will give an indication as to whether new thrustwashers are required.
5 If a dial gauge is not available, feeler blades can be used. First push the crankshaft fully towards the flywheel end of the engine, then use feeler blades to measure the gap between the centre main bearing thrustwasher and the crankshaft web (see illustration).
6 On OHC engines, note the markings on the main bearing caps. There is one line ('I') on the cap nearest the timing end, 'II' on the second cap, C on the centre cap, then 'III' and 'IIII' on the remaining caps (see illustration). On OHV engines, the bearing cap arrangement is self-evident as there are only three main bearings and each cap is shaped differently.
7 Loosen and remove the main bearing cap retaining bolts, and lift off each bearing cap. Recover the lower bearing shells, and tape them to their respective caps for safe-keeping (see illustration).
8 Lift the crankshaft from the crankcase and remove the upper bearing shells from the crankcase. If the shells are to be used again,

7.8b Remove the thrustwashers (arrowed) from their position either side of the centre main bearing (OHV engine)

7.6 Main bearing cap markings (OHC engine)

keep them identified for position. Also remove the thrustwashers from their position either side of the centre main bearing (see illustrations).

Inspection

9 Wash the crankshaft in a suitable solvent and allow it to dry. Flush the oil holes thoroughly, to ensure that they are not blocked - use a pipe cleaner or a needle brush if necessary. Remove any sharp edges from the edge of the holes which may damage the new bearings when they are installed.
10 Inspect the main bearing and crankpin journals carefully; if uneven wear, cracking, scoring or pitting are evident then the crankshaft should be reground by an engineering workshop, and refitted with engine with undersize bearings.
11 Use a micrometer to measure the diameter of each main and crankpin bearing journal (see illustration). Taking a number of measurements on the surface of each journal will reveal if it is worn unevenly. Differences in diameter measured at 90° intervals indicate that the journal is out of round. Differences in diameter measured along the length of the journal, indicate that the journal is tapered. Again, if wear is detected, the crankshaft can be reground by an engineering workshop and refitted with undersize bearings.
12 Check the oil seal journals at either end of the crankshaft. If they appear excessively scored or damaged, they may cause the new seals to leak when the engine is reassembled. It may be possible to repair the journal; seek the advice of an engineering workshop.

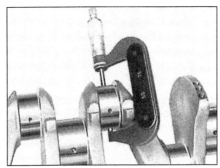

7.11 Measuring the diameter of a crankpin journal

13 Measure the crankshaft runout by setting up a DTI gauge on the centre main bearing journal and rotating the shaft in V-blocks. The maximum deflection of the gauge will indicate the runout. Take precautions to protect the bearing journals and oil seal mating surfaces from damage during this procedure. A maximum runout figure is not quoted by the manufacturer, but use the figure of 0.05 mm as a rough guide. If the runout exceeds this figure, crankshaft renewal should be considered - consult your FIAT dealer or an engine rebuilding specialist for advice.

14 Refer to Section 9 for details of main and big-end bearing inspection.

8 Cylinder block/crankcase - cleaning and inspection

Cleaning

1 Remove all external components and brackets from the block including the rear engine plate, injection pump/oil filter bracket and gasket, intermediate shaft bracket, oil vapour breather casing, and water pump. Also unbolt and remove the oil return tube from the crankcase. For complete cleaning, the core plugs should ideally be removed. Drill a small hole in the plugs, then insert a self-tapping screw into the hole. Pull out the plugs by pulling on the screw with a pair of grips, or by using a slide hammer.

2 Scrape all traces of gasket from the cylinder block/crankcase, taking care not to damage the gasket/sealing surfaces.

3 Remove all oil gallery plugs (where fitted). The plugs are usually very tight - they may have to be drilled out, and the holes re-tapped. Use new plugs when the engine is reassembled.

4 If the block is very dirty have it steam-cleaned, otherwise use paraffin to clean it.

5 Clean all oil holes and oil galleries again and dry thoroughly, then apply a light film of oil to all mating surfaces, to prevent rusting. Smear the cylinder bores with a light coating of oil.

6 All threaded holes must be clean, to ensure accurate torque readings during reassembly. To clean the threads, run the correct-size tap into each of the holes to remove rust, corrosion, thread sealant or sludge, and to restore damaged threads. If possible, use compressed air to clear the holes of debris produced by this operation.

7 Apply suitable sealant to the new oil gallery plugs, and insert them into the holes in the block. Tighten them securely.

8 Fit the new core plugs with sealant applied to their perimeters before using a suitable metal tube to drive them into position.

9 Refit the oil return tube to the crankcase and tighten the mounting bolts.

10 Refit the injection pump/oil filter bracket together with a new gasket and tighten the bolts.

11 Refit the rear engine plate and tighten the bolts. Also refit any other removed brackets etc.

Inspection

12 Visually check the cylinder block for cracks and corrosion. Look for stripped threads in the threaded holes. If there has been any history of internal water leakage, it may be worthwhile having an engine overhaul specialist check it with special equipment.

13 Check each cylinder bore for scuffing and scoring. Check for signs of a wear ridge at the top of the cylinder, indicating that the bore is excessively worn.

14 If the necessary measuring equipment is available, measure the bore diameters at the top (just under the wear ridge), centre and bottom, parallel to the crankshaft axis.

15 Next, measure the bore diameters at the same three locations, at right-angles to the crankshaft axis. If there is any doubt about the condition of the cylinder bores seek the advice of a FIAT dealer or suitable engine reconditioning specialist.

16 If the engine is not going to be reassembled right away, cover it with a large plastic bag to keep it clean and prevent rusting. If the engine is ready for reassembly, refit all the components and brackets removed.

9 Main and big-end bearings - inspection and selection

Inspection

1 Even though the main and big-end bearings should be renewed during the engine overhaul, the old bearings should be retained for close examination, as they may reveal valuable information about the condition of the engine. The bearing shells are available in different thicknesses to match the diameter of the journal.

2 Bearing failure can occur due to lack of lubrication, the presence of dirt or other foreign particles, overloading the engine, or corrosion. Regardless of the cause of bearing failure, the cause must be corrected (where applicable) before the engine is reassembled, to prevent it from happening again.

3 When examining the bearing shells, remove them from the cylinder block/crankcase, the main bearing caps, the connecting rods and the connecting rod big-end bearing caps. Lay them out on a clean surface in the same general position as their location in the engine. This will enable you to match any bearing problems with the corresponding crankshaft journal.

Caution: Do not touch any shell's bearing surface with your fingers while checking it.

4 Dirt and other foreign matter gets into the engine in a variety of ways. It may be left in the engine during assembly, or it may pass

through filters or the crankcase ventilation system. It may get into the oil, and from there into the bearings. Metal chips from machining operations and normal engine wear are often present. Abrasives are sometimes left in engine components after reconditioning, especially when parts are not thoroughly cleaned using the proper cleaning methods. Whatever the source, these foreign objects often end up embedded in the soft bearing material, and are easily recognised. Large particles will not embed in the bearing, and will score or gouge the bearing and journal. The best prevention for this cause of bearing failure is to clean all parts thoroughly, and keep everything spotlessly-clean during engine assembly. Frequent and regular engine oil and filter changes are also recommended.

5 Lack of lubrication (or lubrication breakdown) has a number of interrelated causes. Excessive heat (which thins the oil), overloading (which squeezes the oil from the bearing face) and oil leakage (from excessive bearing clearances, worn oil pump or high engine speeds) all contribute to lubrication breakdown. Blocked oil passages, which can be the result of misaligned oil holes in a bearing shell, will also oil-starve a bearing, and destroy it. When lack of lubrication is the cause of bearing failure, the bearing material is wiped or extruded from the steel backing of the bearing. Temperatures may increase to the point where the steel backing turns blue, or multi-coloured, from overheating.

6 Driving habits can have a definite effect on bearing life. Full-throttle, low-speed operation (labouring the engine) puts very high loads on bearings, tending to squeeze out the oil film. These loads cause the bearings to flex, which produces fine cracks in the bearing face (fatigue failure). Eventually, the bearing material will loosen in pieces, and tear away from the steel backing.

7 Short-distance driving leads to corrosion of bearings, because insufficient engine heat is produced to drive off the condensed water and corrosive gases. These products collect in the engine oil, forming acid and sludge. As the oil is carried to the engine bearings, the acid attacks and corrodes the bearing material.

8 Incorrect bearing installation during engine assembly will lead to bearing failure as well. Tight-fitting bearings leave insufficient bearing running clearance, and will result in oil starvation. Dirt or foreign particles trapped behind a bearing shell result in high spots on the bearing, which lead to failure.

Caution: Do not touch any shell's bearing surface with your fingers during reassembly; there is a risk of scratching the delicate surface, or of depositing particles of dirt on it.

9 As mentioned at the beginning of this Section, the bearing shells should be renewed as a matter of course during engine overhaul; to do otherwise is false economy.

Selection

10 Main and big-end bearings are available in standard sizes and a range of undersizes to suit reground crankshafts - refer to *Specifications* for details. The engine reconditioner will select the correct bearing shells for machined crankshaft.

11 The running clearances can be checked when the crankshaft is refitted with its new bearings.

10 Engine overhaul -
reassembly sequence

1 Before reassembly begins, ensure that all new parts have been obtained, and that all necessary tools are available. Read through the entire procedure to familiarise yourself with the work involved, and to ensure that all items necessary for reassembly of the engine are at hand. In addition to all normal tools and materials, thread-locking compound will be needed. A tube of sealant will also be required for the joint faces that are fitted without gaskets.

2 In order to save time and avoid problems, engine reassembly can be carried out in the following order:
  a) *Crankshaft (Section 11).*
  b) *Piston/connecting rod assemblies (Section 6).*
  c) *Oil pump (see Part A or B - as applicable).*
  d) *Sump (see Part A or B - as applicable).*
  e) *Flywheel (see Part A or B - as applicable).*
  f) *Cylinder head (see Part A or B - as applicable).*
  g) *Water pump (see Chapter 3)*
  h) *Timing belt/chain and associated components (see Chapter A or B as applicable)*
  i) *Engine external components.*

3 At this stage, all engine components should be absolutely clean and dry, with all faults repaired. The components should be laid out on a completely clean work surface.

11 Crankshaft -
refitting and main bearing running clearance check

Crankshaft - initial refitting

1 Crankshaft refitting is the first stage of engine reassembly following overhaul. At this point, it is assumed that the crankshaft, cylinder block/crankcase and bearings have been cleaned, inspected and reconditioned or renewed.

2 Place the cylinder block on a clean, level work surface, with the crankcase facing upwards. Where necessary, unbolt the bearing caps and lay them out in order to ensure correct reassembly. If they are still in place, remove the bearing shells from the caps and the crankcase and wipe out the

11.3 Ensure that the orientation lugs engage with the recesses in the saddles and that the oil holes are correctly aligned

inner surfaces with a clean rag - they must be kept spotlessly clean.

3 Clean the rear surface of the new bearing shells with a rag and fit them on the bearing saddles. Ensure that the orientation lugs on the shells engage with the recesses in the saddles and that the oil holes are correctly aligned **(see illustration)**. Do not hammer or otherwise force the bearing shells into place. It is critically important that the surfaces of the bearings are kept free from damage and contamination.

4 Give the newly fitted bearing shells and the crankshaft journals a final clean with a rag. Check that the oil holes in the crankshaft are free from dirt, as any left here will become embedded in the new bearings when the engine is first started.

5 Carefully lay the crankshaft in the crankcase, taking care not to dislodge the bearing shells **(see illustration)**.

Main bearing running clearance check

6 When the crankshaft and bearings are refitted, a clearance must exist between them to allow lubricant to circulate. This clearance is impossible to check using feeler blades, however Plastigauge can be used. This consists of a thin strip of soft plastic that is crushed between the bearing shells and journals when the bearing caps are tightened up. Its width then indicates the size of the clearance gap.

7 Cut off five pieces of Plastigauge, just shorter than the length of the crankshaft journal. Lay a piece on each journal, in line with its axis.

8 Wipe off the rear surfaces of the new lower half main bearing shells and fit them to the main bearing caps, again ensuring that the locating lugs engage correctly.

9 Fit the caps in their correct locations on the bearing saddles, using the manufacturers markings as a guide. Ensure that they are correctly orientated - the caps should be fitted such that the recesses for the bearing shell locating lugs are on the same side as those in the bearing saddle.

10 Insert and tighten the bolts until they are all correctly torqued. **Do not** allow the

11.5 Refitting the crankshaft (OHV engine shown)

crankshaft to rotate at all whilst the Plastigauge is in place. Progressively unbolt the bearing caps and remove them, taking care not to dislodge the Plastigauge.

11 The width of the crushed Plastigauge can now be measured, using the scale provided. Use the correct scale, as both imperial and metric are printed. This measurement indicates the running clearance - compare it with that listed in *Specifications*. If the clearance is outside the tolerance, it may be due to dirt or debris trapped under the bearing surface; try cleaning them again and repeat the clearance check. If the results are still unacceptable, re-check the journal diameters and the bearing sizes. Note that if the Plastigauge is thicker at one end, the journals may be tapered and as such, will require regrinding.

12 When you are satisfied that the clearances are correct, carefully remove the remains of the Plastigauge from the journals and bearings faces. Use a soft, plastic or wooden scraper as anything metallic is likely to damage the surfaces.

Crankshaft - final refitting

13 Lift the crankshaft out of the crankcase. Wipe off the surfaces of the bearings in the crankcase and the bearing caps. Fit the thrust bearings using grease to hold them in position. Ensure that they are seated correctly in the machined recesses, with the oil grooves facing outwards **(see illustration)**.

11.13 Ensure the thrustwashers are seated correctly in the crankcase machined recesses, with the oil grooves facing outwards

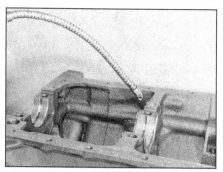

11.14 Liberally coat the bearing shells in the crankcase with clean engine oil

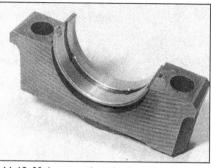

11.16 Make sure that the locating lugs on the shells are engaged with the corresponding recesses in the caps

11.18 Tightening a main bearing cap bolt to its stage one torque setting (OHC engine shown)

14 Liberally coat the bearing shells in the crankcase with clean engine oil **(see illustration)**.

15 Lower the crankshaft into position in the crankcase.

16 Lubricate the lower bearing shells in the main bearing caps with clean engine oil. Make sure that the locating lugs on the shells are still engaged with the corresponding recesses in the caps **(see illustration)**.

17 Fit the main bearing caps in the correct order and orientation. Insert the bearing cap bolts and hand tighten them only.

18 Working from the centre bearing cap outwards, tighten the retaining bolts to their specified torque. On OHC engines, after tightening the bolts to the first stage torque setting, angle tighten the bolts to their stage two setting **(see illustration)**.

19 Fit a new oil seal to the crankshaft rear oil seal housing. Apply grease to the seal lips. On OHC engines a conventional gasket is not used at the oil seal retainer joint face, but a 3 mm diameter bead of RTV (instant) silicone gasket must be applied as shown - allow at least one hour for the gasket to cure before oil contacts it. On all other engines a gasket is fitted. Tighten the housing bolts to the specified torque **(see illustrations)**.

20 Check that the crankshaft rotates freely by turning it by manually. If resistance is felt, re-check the running clearances.

21 Carry out a check of the crankshaft endfloat as described at the beginning of Section 7. If the thrust surfaces of the crankshaft have been checked and new thrust bearings have been fitted, then the endfloat should be within specification.

22 Refit the pistons and connecting rods as described in Section 6.

23 Refit the flywheel/driveplate, oil pump and pick-up tube, and sump with reference to the relevant Sections of Parts A or B **(see illustration)**.

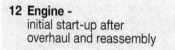
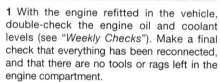

12 Engine - initial start-up after overhaul and reassembly

1 With the engine refitted in the vehicle, double-check the engine oil and coolant levels (see "Weekly Checks"). Make a final check that everything has been reconnected, and that there are no tools or rags left in the engine compartment.

2 Remove the spark plugs, then disconnect the fuel injection ECU (refer to Chapter 4 if necessary).

3 Turn the engine on the starter until the oil pressure warning light goes out. Refit the spark plugs, and reconnect the ECU.

4 Start the engine, noting that this may take a little longer than usual, due to the fuel system components having been disturbed.

5 While the engine is idling, check for fuel, water and oil leaks. Don't be alarmed if there are some odd smells and smoke from parts getting hot and burning off oil deposits.

6 Assuming all is well, keep the engine idling until hot water is felt circulating through the top hose, then switch off the engine.

7 Recheck the oil and coolant levels as described in "Weekly Checks", and top-up as necessary.

8 There is no need to re-tighten the cylinder head bolts once the engine has first run after reassembly.

9 If new pistons, rings or crankshaft bearings have been fitted, the engine must be treated as new, and run-in for the first 500 miles (800 km). *Do not* operate the engine at full-throttle, or allow it to labour at low engine speeds in any gear. It is recommended that the oil and filter be changed at the end of this period.

10 Note that the engine management system has a 'learning' capability which allows the electronic control unit (ECU) to store details of the engine's running characteristics in its memory. This memory will be erased by the disconnection of the battery cables, with the result that the engine may idle roughly, or lack performance for a while, until the engine's characteristics are 're-learnt'; see Chapter 4 for further details.

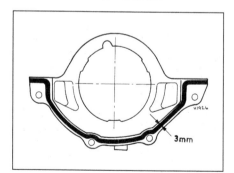

11.19a Application area for silicone gasket on crankshaft rear oil seal retainer

11.19b Fitting the crankshaft rear oil seal retainer

11.23 Refitting the oil pump (OHC engine)

Chapter 3
Cooling, heating and air conditioning systems

Contents

Degrees of difficulty

Easy, suitable for novice with little experience	Fairly easy, suitable for beginner with some experience	Fairly difficult, suitable for competent DIY mechanic	Difficult, suitable for experienced DIY mechanic	Very difficult, suitable for expert DIY or professional

Specifications

General

Expansion tank pressure relief cap opening pressure	0.98 bar

Thermostat

Opening temperature:	
Starts to open	85 to 89°C
Fully open	96 to 100°C

Electric cooling fan

Cut-in temperature	90 to 94°C
Cut-out temperature	85 to 89°C

Torque wrench settings

	Nm	lbf ft
Coolant pump:		
Securing bolts (OHC engine)	8	6
Securing nuts (OHC engine)	10	7
Rear cover bolts (OHV engine)	7	5

1 General information and precautions

General information

The cooling system is of pressurised type, comprising a pump driven by the auxiliary drivebelt (OHV engines) or the timing belt (OHC engines), an aluminium crossflow radiator, electric cooling fan and a thermostat. The system functions as follows. Cold coolant from the radiator passes through the hose to the coolant pump, where it is pumped around the cylinder block and head passages. After cooling the cylinder bores, combustion surfaces and valve seats, the coolant reaches the underside of the thermostat, which is initially closed. The coolant passes through the heater, and is returned via the cylinder block to the coolant pump.

When the engine is cold, the coolant circulates only through the cylinder block, cylinder head and heater. When the coolant reaches a predetermined temperature, the thermostat opens and the coolant passes through to the radiator. As the coolant circulates through the radiator, it is cooled by the inrush of air when the car is in forward motion. Airflow is supplemented by the action of the electric cooling fan when necessary. Once the coolant has passed through the radiator, and has cooled, the cycle is repeated.

The electric cooling fan, mounted on the rear of the radiator, is controlled by a thermostatic switch. At a predetermined coolant temperature, the switch actuates the fan.

An expansion tank is fitted to allow for the expansion of the coolant when hot. The expansion tank is connected to the top of the radiator.

Refer to Section 10 for information on the air conditioning system.

Precautions

Warning: *Do not attempt to remove the radiator filler cap, or disturb any part of the cooling system, while the engine is hot; there is a high risk of scalding. If the radiator filler cap must be removed before the engine and radiator have fully cooled (even though this is not recommended) the pressure in the cooling system must first be relieved. Cover the cap with a thick layer of cloth, to avoid scalding, and slowly unscrew the filler cap until a hissing sound can be heard. When the hissing has stopped, indicating that the pressure has reduced, slowly unscrew the filler cap until it can be removed; if more hissing sounds are heard, wait until they have stopped before unscrewing the cap completely. At all times, keep well away from the filler cap opening.*

Warning: *Do not allow antifreeze to come into contact with skin, or with the painted surfaces of the vehicle. Rinse off spills immediately, with plenty of water. Never leave antifreeze lying around in an open container, or in a puddle on the driveway or garage floor. Children and pets are attracted by its sweet smell, but antifreeze can be fatal if ingested.*

Warning: *If the engine is hot, the electric cooling fan may start rotating even if the engine is not running; be careful to keep hands, hair and loose clothing well clear when working in the engine compartment.*

Warning: *Refer to Section 10 for precautions to be observed when working on models equipped with air conditioning.*

2 Cooling system hoses – disconnection and renewal

Note: *Refer to the warnings given in Section 1 of this Chapter before proceeding. Do not attempt to disconnect any hose while the system is still hot.*

1 If the checks described in Chapter 1 reveal a faulty hose, it must be renewed as follows.

2.3 Slackening the radiator bottom hose clip

2 First drain the cooling system (see Chapter 1). If the coolant is not due for renewal, it may be re-used if it is collected in a clean container.

3 Before disconnecting a hose, first note its routing in the engine compartment, and whether it is secured by any clips or ties. Use a screwdriver to slacken the clips, then move the clips along the hose, clear of the relevant inlet/outlet union. Carefully work the hose free **(see illustration)**.

4 Note that the radiator inlet and outlet unions are fragile; do not use excessive force when attempting to remove the hoses. If a hose proves to be difficult to remove, try to release it by rotating the hose ends before attempting to free it.

 HAYNES HiNT *If all else fails, cut the coolant hose with a sharp knife, then slit it so that it can be peeled off in two pieces. Although this may prove expensive if the hose is otherwise undamaged, it is preferable to buying a new radiator.*

5 When fitting a hose, first slide the clips onto the hose, then work the hose into position. If clamp-type clips were originally fitted, it is a good idea to replace them with screw-type clips when refitting the hose. If the hose is stiff, use a little soapy water (washing-up liquid is ideal) as a lubricant, or soften the hose by soaking it in hot water.

6 Work the hose into position, checking that it is correctly routed and secured. Slide each clip along the hose until it passes over the

2.6 The cut-out (arrowed) in the end of the bottom hose must engage with the lug on the radiator union

flared end of the relevant inlet/outlet union, before tightening the clips securely. Note that some of the hoses have a cut-out in the end, which should engage with a lug on the relevant inlet/outlet union **(see illustration)**.

7 Refill the cooling system with reference to Chapter 1.

8 Check thoroughly for leaks as soon as possible after disturbing any part of the cooling system.

3 Radiator – removal, inspection and refitting

Removal

1 Disconnect the battery negative lead.

2 Apply the handbrake, then jack up the front of the vehicle and support securely on axle stands (see *"Jacking and Vehicle Support"*).

3 Where applicable, remove the securing screws and withdraw the radiator splash shield from under the vehicle.

4 Drain the cooling system as described in Chapter 1.

5 Working under the vehicle, slacken the hose clip, and disconnect the top hose from the radiator **(see illustration)**.

6 Disconnect the wiring plug from the cooling fan switch, located in the side of the radiator, and disconnect the wiring plug from the cooling fan **(see illustration)**.

7 Release the cooling fan wiring harness and the coolant pipe from the clips on the cooling fan shroud **(see illustrations)**.

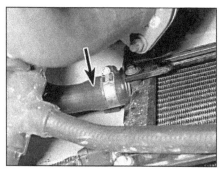

3.5 Disconnect the top hose (arrowed) from the radiator

3.6 Disconnecting the cooling fan wiring plug

3.7a Release the cooling fan wiring harness . . .

3.7b ... and the coolant pipe from the clips on the cooling fan shroud

3.8 Unscrewing the plug from the end of the radiator bleed hose

3.9 Radiator support bracket-to-body bolts (arrowed)

8 Working in the engine compartment, release the cable-tie securing the radiator bleed hose in the engine compartment. Unscrew the plug from the end of the bleed hose **(see illustration)**.

9 Working at the top left-hand corner of the radiator, unscrew the two bolts securing the radiator support bracket to the body, then lower the radiator and release the lugs on the radiator from the support rubbers in the right-hand body panel **(see illustration)**. Feed the radiator bleed hose from the engine compartment down through the body panel as the radiator/cooling fan assembly is withdrawn.

Inspection

10 If the radiator has been removed due to suspected blockage, reverse-flush it as described in Chapter 1. Clean dirt and debris from the radiator fins, using an air line (in which case, wear eye protection) or a soft brush.
Caution: Be careful, as the fins are easily damaged, and are sharp.
11 If necessary, a radiator specialist can perform a "flow test" on the radiator, to establish whether an internal blockage exists.
12 A leaking radiator must be referred to a specialist for permanent repair.
Caution: Do not attempt to weld or solder a leaking radiator, as damage may result.
13 In an emergency, minor leaks from the radiator can be cured by using a suitable radiator sealant (in accordance with its manufacturer's instructions) with the radiator *in situ*.

14 Inspect the radiator mounting rubbers, and renew them if necessary.

Refitting

15 Refitting is a reversal of removal, bearing in mind the following points:
a) *Feed the radiator bleed hose up through the body panel into the engine compartment as the radiator is refitted, and secure the hose in position using a new cable-tie.*
b) *On completion, refill the cooling system as described in Chapter 1.*

---

4 Thermostat –
removal, testing and refitting

OHV engines

Note: *A new thermostat housing gasket will be required on refitting.*

Removal

1 The thermostat is located at the left-hand front corner of the cylinder head. The thermostat is integral with the thermostat housing and the thermostat/housing can only be renewed as an assembly **(see illustration)**.
2 Disconnect the battery negative lead.
3 Drain the cooling system as described in Chapter 1.
4 Disconnect the wiring plug from the coolant temperature sensor, mounted in the top of the thermostat housing.

5 Where applicable, release the wiring harness from its retaining clips, and move it clear of the thermostat housing.
6 Slacken the hose clips and disconnect the coolant hoses from the thermostat housing.
7 Unscrew the securing nuts, then lift the thermostat/housing assembly from the studs on the cylinder head. Note the locations of any wiring and/or brackets secured by the nuts **(see illustration)**. If the assembly sticks, tap gently to free it – do not lever between the housing and cylinder head mating faces. Recover the gasket.

Testing

8 A rough test of the thermostat's operation may be made by suspending it with a piece of string in a container full of water. Heat the water to bring it to the boil - the thermostat must open by the time the water boils. If not, renew it.
9 The opening temperature is usually marked on the thermostat. If a thermometer is available, the precise opening temperature of the thermostat may be determined, and compared with the values given in the Specifications **(see illustration)**.
10 A thermostat which fails to close as the water cools must also be renewed.

Refitting

11 Thoroughly clean the mating faces of the thermostat housing and the cylinder head, then lay a new gasket in position over the studs on the cylinder head.
12 Lower the thermostat/housing assembly over the studs, then refit the securing nuts,

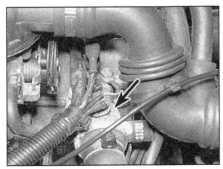

4.1 Thermostat housing location (arrowed) – OHV engine

4.7 Note the location of the wire (arrowed) secured by the thermostat housing securing nut

4.9 Testing the thermostat opening temperature

4.20 Removing the thermostat/cover assembly – OHC engine

ensuring that the wiring/hose bracket is in place, and tighten the nuts securely.

Caution: Take care not to overtighten the nuts, as the alloy thermostat housing is easily damaged.

13 If a new thermostat/housing assembly has been fitted, transfer the coolant temperature sensor to the new assembly.

14 Further refitting is a reversal of the removal procedure, but refill the cooling system as described in Chapter 1.

OHC engines

Note: *A new thermostat cover gasket will be required on refitting.*

Removal

15 The thermostat is located at the left-hand end of the cylinder head. The thermostat is integral with the thermostat cover and the thermostat/cover can only be renewed as an assembly.

16 Disconnect the battery negative lead.

17 Drain the cooling system as described in Chapter 1.

18 To improve access, remove the exhaust manifold hot air hose. If desired, the ignition coil can also be removed (see Chapter 5B), but it should be possible to reach the thermostat cover bolts with the coil in place.

19 Slacken the hose clip and disconnect the coolant hose from the thermostat cover.

20 Unscrew the securing bolts and withdraw the thermostat/cover assembly from the cylinder head **(see illustration)**. Recover the gasket.

Testing

21 Proceed as described in paragraphs 8 to 10 inclusive.

Refitting

22 Thoroughly clean the mating faces of the thermostat cover and the cylinder head.

23 Refit the thermostat/cover assembly using a new gasket, and tighten the securing bolts securely.

24 Reconnect the coolant hose to the thermostat cover and tighten the hose clip securely.

25 Refill the cooling system as described in Chapter 1, then reconnect the battery negative lead.

---

5 Electric cooling fan – testing, removal and refitting

Testing

1 Disconnect the battery negative lead.

2 Disconnect the cooling fan wiring connector.

3 Connect a 12-volt power supply across the fan wiring plug terminals, and check that the fan operates smoothly, without sticking.

4 To test the cooling fan switch, reconnect the battery negative lead, then run the engine until it reaches normal operating temperature, and continue to run the engine at idle speed. If the cooling fan does not cut in within a few minutes, switch off the ignition and disconnect the wiring from the switch in the radiator **(see illustration)**. Bridge the two wires (or the two pins in the wiring plug, as applicable) using a length of wire, and switch on the ignition. If the fan now operates, the switch is probably faulty and should be renewed.

Removal

5 Disconnect the battery negative lead.

6 Apply the handbrake, then jack up the front of the vehicle and support securely on axle stands (see *"Jacking and Vehicle Support"*).

7 Where applicable, remove the securing screws and withdraw the radiator splash shield from under the vehicle.

8 Disconnect the cooling fan wiring plug, and release the wiring harness from the clip on the cooling fan shroud.

9 Release the clips securing the coolant pipe to the cooling fan shroud.

10 Unscrew the three screws securing the fan shroud assembly to the radiator, then lower the cooling fan assembly from under the front of the vehicle **(see illustrations)**.

11 If desired, the cooling fan motor can be removed from the shroud by unscrewing the three securing nuts, and the fan blades can be removed from the motor shaft after releasing the metal securing clip.

Refitting

12 Refitting is a reversal of removal.

---

6 Cooling system electrical switches and sensors – testing, removal and refitting

Coolant temperature sensor

1 Refer to Chapter 4.

Cooling fan switch

Testing

2 The switch is located in the left or right-hand side of the radiator, depending on model. Refer to the cooling fan test procedure in Section 5 for details of testing the switch.

Removal

3 Disconnect the battery negative lead.

4 Apply the handbrake, then jack up the front of the vehicle and support securely on axle stands (see *"Jacking and Vehicle Support"*).

5 Either drain the cooling system to below the level of the switch (see Chapter 1), or have ready a suitable plug which can be used to plug the switch aperture in the radiator whilst the switch is removed. If a plug is used, take great care not to damage the radiator, and do not use anything which will allow foreign matter to enter the radiator.

6 Disconnect the wiring plug from the switch.

7 Carefully unscrew the switch from the radiator and recover the sealing ring.

5.4 Disconnecting the cooling fan switch wiring connector

5.10a Cooling fan assembly left-hand . . .

5.10b . . . and right-hand securing screws (arrowed)

6.9a Coolant temperature gauge sender location (arrowed) –
OHV engine

6.9b Coolant temperature gauge sender location (arrowed) –
OHC engine

Refitting

8 Refitting is a reversal of removal, but examine the condition of the sealing ring, and fit a new one if necessary. Top up or refill the cooling system, as described in *"Weekly checks"* and Chapter 1 respectively.

Coolant temperature gauge sender

Testing

9 On OHV engines, the sender is located at the front right-hand corner of the cylinder head, and on OHC engines, the sender is located at the rear right-hand corner of the cylinder head **(see illustrations)**.
10 The coolant temperature gauge is fed with a stabilised voltage supply from the instrument panel feed (via the ignition switch and a fuse), and its earth is controlled by the sender.
11 The sender contains a thermistor (thermal resistor), an electronic component whose electrical resistance decreases at a predetermined rate as its temperature rises. When the coolant is cold, the sender resistance is high, current flow through the gauge is reduced, and the gauge needle points towards the "cold" end of the scale. If the sender is faulty, it must be renewed.
12 If the gauge develops a fault, first check the other instruments; if they do not work at all, check the instrument panel electrical feed. If the readings are erratic, there may be a fault in the voltage stabiliser, which will necessitate renewal of the stabiliser (see Chapter 12). If the fault lies in the temperature gauge alone, check it as follows.
13 If the gauge needle remains at the "cold" end of the scale, disconnect the sender wire, and earth it to the cylinder head. If the needle then deflects when the ignition is switched on, the sender unit is proved faulty, and should be renewed. If the needle still does not move, remove the instrument panel (Chapter 12) and

check the continuity of the wiring between the sender unit and the gauge, and the feed to the gauge unit. If continuity is shown, and the fault still exists, then the gauge is faulty and should be renewed.
14 If the gauge needle remains at the "hot" end of the scale, disconnect the sender wire. If the needle then returns to the "cold" end of the scale when the ignition is switched on, the sender unit is proved faulty and should be renewed. If the needle still does not move, check the remainder of the circuit as described previously.

Removal

Note: *Suitable sealant will be required to coat the threads of the sender on refitting.*
15 Either partially drain the cooling system to just below the level of the sender (as described in Chapter 1), or have ready a suitable plug which can be used to block the sender aperture whilst it is removed. If a plug is used, take great care not to damage the internal threads, and do not use anything which will allow foreign matter to enter the cooling system.
16 Disconnect the battery negative lead.
17 Disconnect the wiring from the sender, then unscrew the unit from its location.

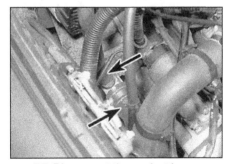

7.7 Disconnect the coolant hoses
(arrowed) from the coolant pump –
OHV engine

Refitting

18 Ensure the sender threads are clean, and apply a smear of suitable sealant to them.
19 Refit the sender, tightening it securely, and reconnect the wiring.
20 Top-up/refill the cooling system as described in *"Weekly checks"* and Chapter 1.
21 On completion, start the engine and check the operation of the temperature gauge. Also check for coolant leaks.

7 Coolant pump –
removal, inspection
and refitting

OHV engines

Note: *A new coolant pump gasket will be required on refitting.*

Removal

1 The coolant pump is located at the front right-hand corner of the cylinder block, and is driven by an auxiliary drivebelt. Disconnect the battery negative lead.
2 Apply the handbrake, then jack up the front of the vehicle and support securely on axle stands (see *"Jacking and Vehicle Support"*). Remove the front right-hand roadwheel.
3 Drain the cooling system as described in Chapter 1.
4 Remove the securing screws and withdraw the radiator shield from under the vehicle.
5 Remove the securing screws and withdraw the front right-hand wheel arch liner.
6 Remove the alternator/coolant pump drivebelt, as described in Chapter 1.
7 Working under the vehicle, slacken the hose clips and disconnect the two coolant hoses from the pump **(see illustration)**.
8 Unscrew the three bolts securing the coolant pump to the cylinder block, then withdraw the coolant pump **(see illustration)**. Recover the gasket.

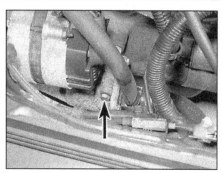

7.8 Coolant pump securing bolt (arrowed) – OHV engine

7.16 Coolant pump securing bolts and nut (arrowed) – OHC engine

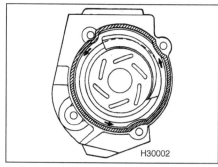

7.19 Apply a bead of sealant (heavy line) to the impeller housing on the pump – OHC engine

Inspection

9 Check the pump body and impeller for signs of excessive corrosion. Turn the impeller, and check for stiffness due to corrosion, or roughness due to excessive endplay.

10 Note that the pump rear cover can be unbolted for access to the impeller – thoroughly clean the mating faces of the pump and cover, and use a new gasket on refitting.

Refitting

11 Commence refitting by thoroughly cleaning the mating faces of the coolant pump and cylinder block.

12 Refit the coolant pump, using a new gasket, and tighten the securing bolts.

13 Further refitting is a reversal of the removal procedure, tightening the pump rear cover bolts to the specified torque if applicable. Refit and adjust the alternator/coolant pump drivebelt, and refill the cooling system, as described in Chapter 1.

OHC engines

Note: *Suitable waterproof silicone grease will be required to seal the coolant pump on refitting.*

Removal

14 The pump is located at the right-hand end of the engine, and is driven by the timing belt. Disconnect the battery negative lead.

15 Remove the timing belt as described in Chapter 2A.

16 Unscrew the securing bolts and nuts, and withdraw the coolant pump from the cylinder block **(see illustration)**. If the pump is stuck, tap it gently using a soft-faced mallet – do not lever between the pump and cylinder block mating faces.

Inspection

17 Proceed as described in paragraph 9.

Refitting

18 Thoroughly clean the mating faces of the pump and the cylinder block. Remove all traces of sealant.

19 Apply a continuous bead of silicone sealant around the edge of the impeller housing on the pump **(see illustration)**. Take care not to apply excessive sealant, which could find its way into the pump and the engine coolant passages.

20 Offer the pump into position in the cylinder block, then refit and tighten the securing bolts and nuts to the specified torque.

21 Refit the timing belt as described in Chapter 2A, then reconnect the battery negative lead.

8 Heating and ventilation system – general information

The heater/ventilation system consists of a three-speed blower motor (housed in the engine compartment), face-level vents in the centre and at each end of the facia, and air ducts to the front footwells.

The control panel is located in the facia, and the controls operate flap valves to deflect and mix the air flowing through the various parts of the heater/ventilation system. The flap valves are contained in the air distribution housing, which acts as a central distribution unit, passing air to the various ducts and vents.

Cold air enters the system through the grille at the rear of the engine compartment.

The air (boosted by the blower fan if required) then flows through the various ducts, according to the settings of the controls. Stale air is expelled through ducts at the rear of the vehicle. If warm air is required, the cold air is passed through the heater matrix, which is heated by the engine coolant.

9 Heater/ventilation system components – removal and refitting

Note: *The following procedures are for models without air conditioning. Refer to Section 11 for models with air conditioning.*

Heater/ventilation control panel

1 The control panel can only be removed with the complete heater assembly, as described later in this Section.

Heater/ventilation control cables

Removal

2 Remove the complete heater assembly as described later in this Section.

3 With the heater assembly removed, release the relevant cable securing clips and/or screws, and disconnect the ends of the relevant cable from the heater control panel and the levers on the heater casing **(see illustrations)**. Note the routing of the cable to aid refitting.

Refitting

4 Refitting is a reversal of removal, but make sure that the cable is routed as noted before removal, and ensure that the cable is free from kinks and clear of surrounding components. Refit the heater assembly as described later in this Section.

9.3a Remove the securing screw (1) and unhook the control cable from the lever (2)

9.3b Remove the securing screw (1) and prise off the securing clip (2) to disconnect the control cable

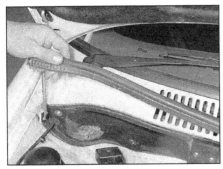

9.7 Pull the weatherstrip from the scuttle panel

9.8a Unscrew the six screws . . .

9.8b . . . securing the heater coolant pipe support plate to the bulkhead

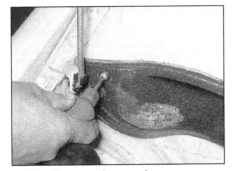

9.9a Unscrew the securing screw . . .

9.9b . . . and remove the insulating panel from the bulkhead

9.10 Disconnect the two coolant hoses from the heater matrix

Heater matrix

Removal

5 Drain the cooling system as described in Chapter 1.

6 Remove the battery, as described in Chapter 5A.

7 Working in the engine compartment, carefully pull the weatherstrip from the front edge of the scuttle panel (see illustration).

8 Unscrew the six screws securing the heater coolant pipe support plate to the engine compartment bulkhead (see illustrations).

9 Unscrew the securing screw, and remove the insulating panel from the right-hand side of the bulkhead (see illustrations).

10 Release the hose clips, and disconnect the two coolant hoses from the top of the heater matrix (see illustration).

11 Unscrew the three securing screws, then carefully withdraw the heater matrix from its housing (see illustrations).

Refitting

12 Refitting is a reversal of removal but, on completion, refill the cooling system as described in Chapter 1.

Complete heater assembly

Removal

13 Disconnect the battery negative lead.

14 Working inside the vehicle, unscrew the three lower instrument panel surround securing screws (see illustration).

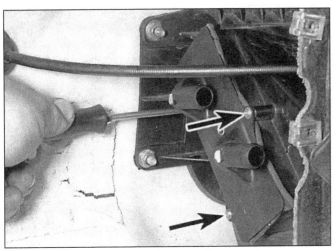

9.11a Unscrew the three securing screws . . .

9.11b . . . and withdraw the heater matrix

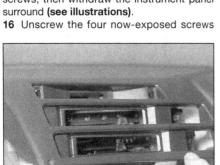

9.14 Unscrewing a lower instrument panel surround securing screw

9.15a Prise out the covers . . .

9.15b . . . and unscrew the upper instrument panel surround securing screws

15 Prise out the covers and unscrew the two upper instrument panel surround securing screws, then withdraw the instrument panel surround (see illustrations).

16 Unscrew the four now-exposed screws

securing the heater control panel to the facia (see illustration).

17 Proceed as described in paragraphs 6 to 10 of this Section.

18 Remove the windscreen wiper motor/

linkage assembly as described in Chapter 12.

19 Unclip the speedometer cable from the heater hose, and move the cable to one side, clear of the heater assembly.

20 Remove the air cleaner assembly as described in Chapter 4.

21 Where applicable, unscrew the two studs from the top of the throttle body, then cover the throttle body with a wad of cloth to prevent dirt entry (see illustration).

22 Working in the scuttle at the rear of the engine compartment, unscrew the four nuts securing the heater assembly to the bulkhead (see illustrations).

23 Carefully pull the heater assembly forwards from the bulkhead then, working at the rear of the assembly, pull the heater blower motor wiring loom through the hole in the bulkhead into the engine compartment, and separate the two halves of the wiring connector (see illustrations).

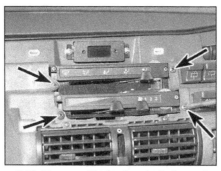

9.15c Withdrawing the instrument panel surround

9.16 Unscrew the heater control panel securing screws (arrowed)

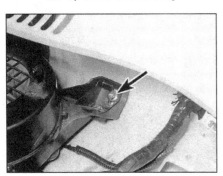

9.21 Unscrew the studs (arrowed) from the top of the throttle body

9.22a Unscrew the right-hand . . .

9.22b . . . the upper left-hand . . .

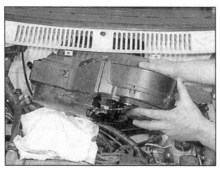

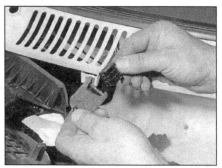

9.22c . . . and the lower left-hand heater assembly securing nuts

9.23a Pull the heater assembly from the bulkhead . . .

9.23b . . . and separate the two halves of the heater blower motor wiring connector

9.24 Removing the heater assembly

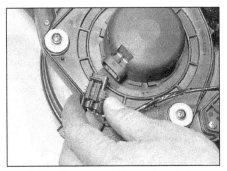

9.27a Disconnect the motor wiring plug . . .

9.27b . . . then unscrew the three securing screws . . .

24 Have an assistant working inside the vehicle feed the heater control panel through the hole in the bulkhead as the heater assembly is withdrawn from the engine compartment **(see illustration)**.

Refitting

25 Refitting is a reversal of removal, bearing in mind the following points:
  a) *Have an assistant guide the heater control panel through the hole in the bulkhead into the passenger compartment, taking care not to bend the heater control levers.*
  b) *Remember to reconnect the heater blower motor wiring connector before refitting the heater assembly into position on the bulkhead.*
  c) *Refit the windscreen wiper motor/linkage assembly as described in Chapter 12.*
  d) *On completion, refill the cooling system as described in Chapter 1.*

Heater blower motor

Removal

26 Remove the complete heater assembly as described previously in this Section.
27 Disconnect the blower motor wiring plug, then unscrew the three securing screws, and withdraw the heater blower motor assembly

9.27c . . . and withdraw the blower motor

from the heater housing **(see illustrations)**. Note that the motor, support plate and fan blades are only available as an assembly, and the parts cannot be renewed independently.

Refitting

28 Refitting is a reversal of removal, but refit the heater assembly with reference to paragraph 25.

Heater blower motor resistor

Removal

29 The resistor is located in the bottom of the heater assembly, next to the blower motor.

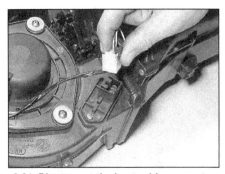

9.31 Disconnect the heater blower motor resistor wiring plug . . .

30 Remove the complete heater assembly as described previously in this Section.
31 Disconnect the wiring plug from the resistor **(see illustration)**.
32 Remove the two securing screws, and withdraw the resistor from the housing **(see illustrations)**.

Refitting

33 Refitting is a reversal of removal, but refit the heater assembly with reference to paragraph 25.

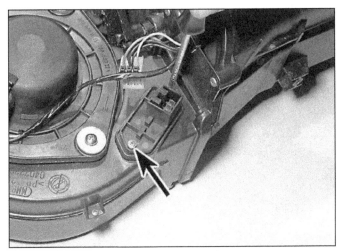

9.32a . . . then remove the securing screws . . .

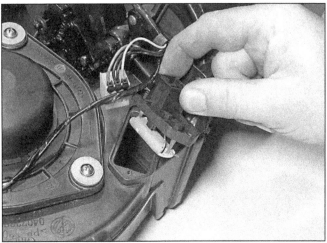

9.32b . . . and withdraw the resistor

10 Air conditioning system –
general information and precautions

General information

Air conditioning is available on certain models. It enables the temperature of incoming air to be lowered, and also dehumidifies the air, which makes for rapid demisting and increased comfort.

The cooling side of the system works in the same way as a domestic refrigerator. Refrigerant gas is drawn into a belt-driven compressor, and passes into a condenser mounted behind the front bumper, where it loses heat and becomes liquid. The liquid passes through an expansion valve to an evaporator, where it changes from liquid under high pressure to gas under low pressure. This change is accompanied by a drop in temperature, which cools the evaporator. The refrigerant returns to the compressor, and the cycle begins again.

Air blown through the evaporator passes to the heater assembly, where it is mixed with hot air blown through the heater matrix, to achieve the desired temperature in the passenger compartment.

The heating side of the system works in the same way as on models without air conditioning (see Section 8).

The operation of the system is controlled by an on/off switch and a recirculation switch on the facia, in addition to the conventional heater/ventilation controls. Any problems with the system should be referred to a Fiat dealer or an air conditioning specialist.

Precautions

It is necessary to observe special precautions whenever dealing with any part of the system, its associated components and any items which necessitate disconnection of the system.

 Warning: The refrigeration circuit contains a liquid refrigerant (Freon). This refrigerant is potentially dangerous, and should only be handled by qualified persons. If it is splashed onto the skin, it can cause frostbite. It is not itself poisonous, but in the presence of a naked flame it forms a poisonous gas; inhalation of the vapour through a lighted cigarette could prove fatal. Uncontrolled discharging of the refrigerant is dangerous, and potentially damaging to the environment. It is therefore dangerous to disconnect any part of the system without specialised knowledge and equipment. If for any reason the system must be disconnected, entrust this task to an authorised Fiat dealer or an air conditioning specialist. Caution: Do not operate the air conditioning system if it is known to be short of refrigerant, as this may damage the compressor.

11 Air conditioning system components –
removal and refitting

 Warning: Do not attempt to open the refrigerant circuit. Refer to the precautions in Section 10.

The only operation which can be carried out easily without discharging the refrigerant is the renewal of the compressor drivebelt (see Chapter 1). All other operations must be referred to a Fiat dealer or air conditioning specialist.

If necessary, the compressor can be unbolted and moved to one side, without disconnecting the flexible hoses, after removing the drivebelt.

Chapter 4
Fuel, exhaust and emission control systems

Contents

Degrees of difficulty

Easy, suitable for novice with little experience		Fairly easy, suitable for beginner with some experience		Fairly difficult, suitable for competent DIY mechanic		Difficult, suitable for experienced DIY mechanic		Very difficult, suitable for expert DIY or professional	

Specifications

System type
OHV and OHC engines . . . . Weber-Marelli integrated single-point fuel injection/ignition system

Fuel system data
Fuel pump type . . . . Electric, immersed in fuel tank
Fuel pump delivery rate . . . . 110 litres/hour minimum
Regulated fuel pressure:
   OHV engine . . . . 1.1 ± 0.2 bar
   OHC engine . . . . 1.0 ± 0.2 bar
Pressure relief valve opens at . . . . 2.6 bar
Coolant temperature resistance (approx.):
   At 0°C . . . . 10 kΩ
   At 20°C . . . . 5 kΩ
   At 60°C . . . . 10 Ω
Crankshaft TDC sensor resistance at 20°C . . . . 575 to 720 Ω
TDC sensor-to-reluctor wheel clearance . . . . 0.5 to 1.5 mm
Injector duration (at idle) . . . . 1.5 ms
Lambda sensor heater resistance at 20°C . . . . 2.5 to 4.5 Ω
Engine idle speed . . . . See Chapter 1
CO% . . . . See Chapter 1

Recommended fuel
Minimum octane rating . . . . 95 RON unleaded

Torque wrench settings

	Nm	lbf ft
Coolant temperature sensor	2.5	1.8
Exhaust downpipe bracket (OHC engine)	24	18
Exhaust downpipe to manifold	18	13
Exhaust manifold	18	13
Exhaust system clamp bolts/nuts	24	18
Fuel filter collar nut	5	4
Fuel tank	28	21
Idle control stepper motor	4	3
Inlet manifold (OHC engine)	27	20
Lambda sensor	50	37
Throttle body to manifold	7	5
Throttle potentiometer	2.5	1.8

1 General information and precautions

General information

The IAW Weber-Marelli single point injection (SPI) system is a self-contained engine management system, which controls both the fuel injection and ignition. This Chapter deals with the fuel injection system components only - refer to Chapter 5B for details of the ignition system components.

The fuel injection system comprises a fuel tank, an electric fuel pump, a fuel filter, fuel supply and return lines, a throttle body with an integral electronic fuel injector, and an Electronic Control Unit (ECU) together with its associated sensors, actuators and wiring.

The fuel pump delivers a constant supply of fuel through a cartridge filter to the throttle body, and the fuel pressure regulator (integral with the throttle body) maintains a constant fuel pressure at the fuel injector and returns excess fuel to the tank via the return line. This constant flow system also helps to reduce fuel temperature and prevents vaporisation.

The fuel injector is opened and closed by an Electronic Control Unit (ECU), which calculates the injection timing and duration according to engine speed, throttle position and rate of opening, inlet air temperature, coolant temperature and exhaust gas oxygen content information, received from sensors mounted on the engine.

Inlet air is drawn into the engine through the air cleaner, which contains a renewable paper filter element. The inlet air temperature is regulated by a vacuum operated valve mounted in the air ducting, which blends air at ambient temperature with hot air, drawn from over the exhaust manifold.

Idle speed is controlled by a stepper motor located on the side of the throttle body. Cold starting enrichment is controlled by the ECU using the coolant temperature and inlet air temperature parameters to increase the injector opening duration.

The exhaust gas oxygen content is constantly monitored by the ECU via the Lambda sensor, which is mounted in the exhaust downpipe. The ECU then uses this information to modify the injection timing and duration to maintain the optimum air/fuel ratio. An exhaust catalyst is fitted to all SPI models. The ECU also controls the operation of the activated charcoal filter evaporative loss system.

It should be noted that fault diagnosis of the IAW Weber-Marelli system is only possible with dedicated electronic test equipment. Problems with the system should therefore be referred to a FIAT dealer for assessment. Once the fault has been identified, the removal/refitting procedures detailed in the following Sections can then be followed.

Emission control systems

All models use unleaded petrol and are controlled by engine management systems that are "tuned" to give the best compromise between driveability, fuel consumption and exhaust emission production. In addition, a number of systems are fitted that help to minimise other harmful emissions; a crankcase emission-control system that reduces the release of pollutants from the crankcase, an evaporative loss emission control system to reduce the release of hydrocarbons from the fuel system, and a catalytic converter to reduce exhaust gas pollutants.

Crankcase emission control

To reduce the emission of unburned hydrocarbons from the crankcase into the atmosphere, the engine is sealed and the combustion blow-by gases and oil vapour are drawn from inside the crankcase, through a flame trap, into the inlet tract to be burned by the engine during normal combustion.

Under conditions of high manifold depression (idling, deceleration) the gases will by sucked positively out of the crankcase. Under conditions of low manifold depression (acceleration, or wide open throttle) the gases are forced out of the crankcase by the (relatively) higher crankcase pressure; if the engine is worn, the raised crankcase pressure (due to increased blow-by) will cause some of the flow to return under all manifold conditions.

Exhaust emission control

To minimise the amount of combustion pollutants released into the atmosphere, a catalytic converter is fitted to the exhaust system. The fuel system is of the closed-loop type; a Lambda sensor mounted in the exhaust pipe measures the oxygen content of the exhaust gas and provides the engine management system ECU with constant feedback. This enables the ECU to adjust the air/fuel mixture to optimise combustion.

The Lambda sensor has a heating element built-in that is controlled by the ECU through the Lambda sensor relay to quickly bring the sensor's tip to its optimum operating temperature. The sensor's tip is sensitive to oxygen and relays a voltage signal to the ECU that varies according to the amount of oxygen in the exhaust gas. If the inlet air/fuel mixture is too rich, the exhaust gases are low in oxygen so the sensor sends a low-voltage signal, the voltage rising as the mixture weakens and the amount of oxygen rises in the exhaust gases. Peak conversion efficiency of all major pollutants occurs if the inlet air/fuel mixture is maintained at the chemically-correct ratio for the complete combustion of petrol of 14.7 parts (by weight) of air to 1 part of fuel (the 'stoichiometric' ratio). The sensor output voltage alters in a large step at this point, the ECU using the signal change as a reference point and correcting the inlet air/fuel mixture accordingly by altering the fuel injector pulse width.

Evaporative loss control system

To minimise the escape of unburned hydrocarbons into the atmosphere, an evaporative loss emission control system is fitted to all models. The fuel tank filler cap is sealed and a charcoal-filled canister, mounted in the engine compartment collects the petrol vapours released from the fuel contained in the fuel tank. It stores them until they can be drawn from the canister (under the control of the fuel injection/ignition system ECU) via the purge valve into the inlet air tract, where they are then burned by the engine during normal combustion.

To ensure that the engine runs correctly when it is cold and/or idling and to protect the catalytic converter from the effects of an over-rich mixture, the purge control valve is not opened by the ECU until the engine has warmed up, and the engine is under load; the purge valve is then modulated on and off to allow the stored vapour to pass into the inlet tract.

A multi-function valve mounted on the top of the fuel tank controls the flow of fuel vapour from the tank and prevents liquid fuel from flowing through the system when the fuel tank is full, or if the vehicle overturns during an accident.

Exhaust systems

The exhaust system comprises the exhaust manifold, an exhaust downpipe incorporating a catalytic converter, an intermediate pipe with silencer and a flexible joint, and a tailpipe with a second silencer.

Precautions

Warning: Many procedures in this Chapter require the removal of fuel lines and connections, which may result in fuel spillage. Before carrying out any operation on the fuel system, refer to the precautions given in "Safety first!" at the beginning of this manual, and follow them implicitly. Petrol is a highly dangerous and volatile liquid, and the precautions necessary when handling it cannot be overstressed. Note that residual pressure will remain in the fuel lines long after the vehicle was last used. When disconnecting any fuel line, first depressurise the fuel system, as described in Section 8.

2 Air cleaner and inlet system - removal and refitting

Removal

OHC engines

1 Remove the air cleaner element as described in Chapter 1.

2 Release the clips and disconnect the breather hoses from the air cleaner **(see illustration)**.

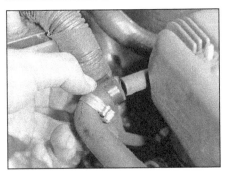

2.2 Disconnect the breather hoses from the air cleaner

2.3a Prise off the plastic caps . . .

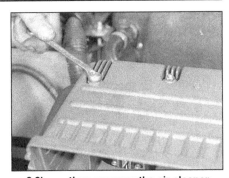

2.3b . . . then unscrew the air cleaner retaining nuts

3 Prise off the plastic caps, then unscrew the air cleaner retaining nuts **(see illustrations)**.
4 Lift the air cleaner away from the throttle body slightly, then disconnect the hoses from the thermostatic vacuum switch, on the underside of the air cleaner **(see illustration)**.
5 Remove the air cleaner from the engine compartment **(see illustration)**.
6 Remove the two screws and detach the cold air intake ducting from the wiring harness bracket. Disconnect the flexible air cleaner ducting, then release the clip and disconnect the hot air intake hose from the exhaust manifold collector box. Remove the intake ducting components from the engine compartment **(see illustrations)**.

OHV engines

7 Remove the air cleaner element as described in Chapter 1.

8 Release the hose clip and disconnect the hot air hose from the rear of the air cleaner.
9 Slacken and withdraw the two bolts securing the air box to the top of the throttle body.
10 Disconnect the breather hose from the side of the inlet trunking.
11 Lift the top of the air cleaner, the inlet trunking and air box away from the engine.
12 Remove the securing nuts and lift the lower section of the air cleaner away from the engine compartment.
13 Wipe clean the inner surfaces of the upper and lower sections of the air cleaner. Renew the throttle body rubber seal if it shows signs of deterioration.

Refitting

14 Refitting is a reversal of removal but renew the throttle body rubber seal if it shows signs of deterioration.

3 Inlet air temperature regulation system components - removal and refitting

General information

1 On OHC engines, the thermostatic vacuum switch is located inside the rear section of the air cleaner casing. The flap valve is mounted in the inlet trunking, between the intake duct and the air cleaner casing. On OHV engines, the flap valve is located inside the lower section of the air cleaner casing and is controlled by a waxstat capsule mounted next to it **(see illustrations)**.

OHC engines

2 To check the operation system, disconnect the air inlet duct with the engine cold and use

2.4 Disconnect the hoses from the thermostatic vacuum switch, on the underside of the air cleaner

2.5 Remove the air cleaner from the engine compartment

2.6a Disconnect the flexible air cleaner ducting . . .

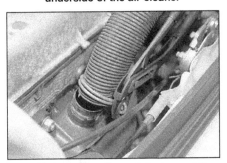

2.6b Release the clip and disconnect the hot air intake hose from the exhaust manifold collector box

2.6c Remove the intake ducting components from the engine compartment

3.1a Thermostatic vacuum switch location on OHC engines

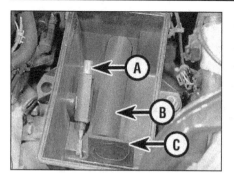

3.1b Inlet air temperature regulation system components - OHV engine

A *Waxstat capsule*   C *Flap valve*
B *Hot air intake*

a mirror to check that the flap is positioned to admit only hot air from the shroud on the exhaust manifold. Next, warm up the engine and check that the flap pivots, closing off the hot air inlet and admitting only cold air from the inlet duct.

3 If the system does operate as described, disconnect the vacuum pipe from the top of the flap valve unit and check that vacuum is present at the end of the pipe only when the engine is cold. Apply vacuum directly to the flap valve unit, by means of a hand-operated pump, to check its operation.

OHV engines

4 Switch off the engine and allow it to cool completely. Refer to Chapter 1 and remove the air filter element.

5 The flap valve should be in the open position - the port leading to the hot air inlet hose at the rear of the air cleaner casing is uncovered.

6 Gently heat the waxstat capsule with a hairdryer, or a heat gun on its lowest setting. The flap should pivot towards the rear of the air cleaner casing, closing off the hot air inlet port.

Removal

OHC engines

7 Remove the air cleaner element as described in Chapter 1, then remove the rear section of the air cleaner casing as described in Section 2.

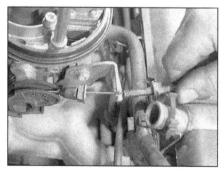

4.3a Release the outer cable from its mounting bracket

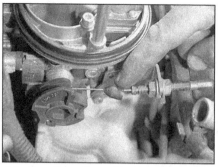

4.2a To release the cable from the throttle body, slide off the plastic ferrule ...

8 Carefully prise off the metal spring clip and withdraw the vacuum switch from the air cleaner housing.

9 The flap valve unit is an integral part of the inlet trunking but can be renewed after disconnecting the associated flexible hoses.

OHV engines

10 The inlet air temperature regulation system components are integral with the lower section of the air cleaner and cannot be renewed separately.

Refitting

11 Refitting is a reversal of removal.

4 Accelerator cable - removal, refitting and adjustment

Removal

1 Remove the air cleaner and air inlet ducting as described in Section 2.

2 To release the cable from the throttle body, slide off the plastic ferrule and unscrew the outer cable locknuts (see illustrations).

3 Hold the throttle open by hand, then release the outer cable from its mounting bracket and disengage the inner cable from the throttle cam (see illustrations).

4 Working under the facia inside the vehicle, unhook the cable from the fork at the top of the pedal arm.

5 Release the bulkhead grommet and withdraw the accelerator cable from inside the engine compartment.

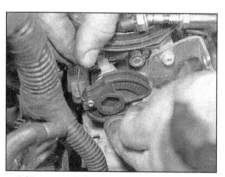

4.3b ... and disengage the inner cable from the throttle cam

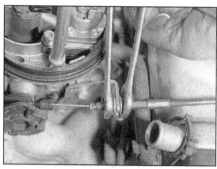

4.2b ... and unscrew the outer cable locknuts

Refitting and adjustment

6 Refitting is a reverse of the removal process, but adjust the cable (by means of the outer cable locknuts) so that all free play is removed from the throttle body end of the inner cable. Have an assistant depress the accelerator pedal, and check that the throttle cam opens fully and returns to the at-rest position, then securely tighten the cable locknuts.

5 Engine management system components - removal and refitting

Note: *Refer to the warning given in Section 1 before proceeding.*

Throttle body assembly

Removal

1 Remove the air cleaner and air duct as described in Section 2.

2 Disconnect the wiring connectors from the throttle potentiometer, idle control stepper motor, inlet air temperature sensor and the injector wiring loom connector situated on the front of the throttle body (refer to the relevant sub-Sections).

3 Depressurise the fuel system with reference to Section 8, then release the retaining clips and disconnect the fuel feed and return hoses from the throttle body assembly (see illustrations). If the original FIAT retaining

5.3a Release the retaining clips and disconnect the fuel feed ...

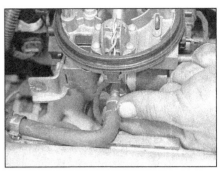

5.3b . . . and return hoses from the throttle body assembly

5.6a Disconnect the coolant supply . . .

5.6b . . . and return hoses from the throttle body assembly

clips are still fitted, cut the clips and discard them; replace them with standard fuel hose clips on refitting.

4 Slacken the accelerator cable locknuts, then disengage the inner cable from the throttle cam and free the outer cable from its retaining bracket (see Section 4). Position the cable clear of the throttle body.

5 Disconnect the EVAP purge valve vacuum hose, the MAP sensor vacuum hose, and the engine breather hose from the ports at the rear of the throttle body.

6 Release the retaining clips and disconnect the coolant hoses from the front and rear of the throttle body assembly **(see illustrations)**.

7 Slacken and remove the bolts securing the throttle body assembly to the inlet manifold, then remove the assembly along with its insulating spacer and gasket **(see illustrations)**.

Refitting

8 Refitting is a reversal of the removal procedure, bearing in mind the following points:

a) Examine the insulating spacer for signs of damage, and renew if necessary. Use a new gasket on refitting.

b) Ensure that the throttle body, inlet manifold and insulating spacer mating surfaces are clean and dry, then fit the throttle body and spacer, and securely tighten the retaining bolts.

c) Ensure that all hoses are correctly reconnected and their retaining clips are securely tightened.

d) Adjust the accelerator cable as described in Section 4.

Fuel injector

Note: If a faulty injector is suspected, it is worth trying the effect of one of the proprietary injector cleaning treatments, before considering its renewal.

Removal

9 Depressurise the fuel system as described in Section 8.

10 Remove the air cleaner and air duct as described in Section 2.

11 Disconnect the injector wiring at the connector **(see illustration)**.

12 Unscrew the mounting screw and lift off the clamp plate. Carefully withdraw the injector from the throttle body **(see illustrations)**. Be prepared for some fuel spillage - pad the surrounding area with absorbent rags.

13 Check the condition of the O-ring seals; renew them if they show signs of deterioration. Examine the gauze filter at the base of the injector for signs of damage or corrosion.

5.7a Slacken and remove the bolts . . .

5.7b . . . then remove the throttle body assembly from the inlet manifold . . .

5.7c . . . together with its insulating spacer and gasket

5.11 Disconnect the injector wiring

5.12a Unscrew the mounting screw . . .

5.12b . . . and lift off the clamp plate

5.12c Carefully withdraw the injector from the throttle body

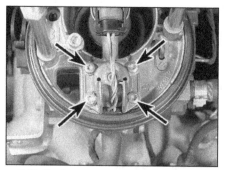

5.16 Fuel pressure regulator retaining screws (arrowed)

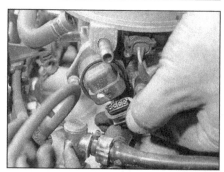

5.21a Unplug the wiring from the stepper motor at the connector

Refitting

14 Refitting is a reversal of removal. Ensure that the O-ring seals seat securely in the injector housing.

Fuel pressure regulator

Removal

15 Remove the air cleaner and air duct as described in Section 2. Cover the throttle opening to prevent components from being accidentally dropped into the throttle body.

16 Using a marker pen, make alignment marks between the regulator cover and the throttle body, then undo the four retaining screws (see illustration). As the screws are loosened, place a rag over the cover to catch any fuel spray which may be released.

17 Carefully lift off the cover, then remove the spring and withdraw the diaphragm, noting its correct fitted orientation. Remove all traces of dirt, and examine the diaphragm for signs of splitting.

Refitting

18 Refitting is a reversal of removal ensuring that the diaphragm and cover are fitted the correct way round, and that the retaining screws are securely tightened.

Idle control stepper motor

Removal

19 Disconnect the battery negative cable and position it away from the terminal.

20 Remove the air cleaner and air duct as described in Section 2.

21 Unplug the wiring from the stepper motor at the connector, then unscrew the mounting screws and remove the stepper motor from the throttle body (see illustrations). Recover the gasket.

Note: The mounting screws are covered with a locking agent and must be renewed every time they are removed.

22 Clean the throttle body motor housing and check for damage and wear.

Refitting

23 Fit a new gasket to the throttle body, then place the motor in position. Insert the mounting screws and tighten them to the specified torque.

Caution: Do not try to alter the position of the motor plunger by hand during refitting.

24 Leave the battery negative cable disconnected for about 20 minutes, then reconnect the cable and switch on the ignition. The engine management system ECU will set the position of the idle control stepper motor as the ignition is switched on.

Throttle potentiometer

Removal

25 Remove the air cleaner and air duct as described in Section 2.

26 Disconnect the wiring from the throttle potentiometer (see illustration).

27 Unscrew the mounting screws and withdraw the unit from the throttle body (see illustration).

Note: The mounting screws are covered with a locking agent and must be renewed every time they are removed.

Refitting

28 When refitting the unit make sure that the pin is correctly engaged with the throttle disc shaft and tighten the mounting screws to the specified torque.

29 If a Fiat test instrument is available, the operation of the throttle potentiometer can be checked at this stage. Before reconnecting the potentiometer wiring first turn the ignition key to position "MAR" and wait a few seconds, then return the key to the "STOP" position. Reconnect the potentiometer wiring and connect the test instrument. Turn the ignition key to the "MAR" position and cancel the error that will appear. The throttle position indicated should be between 0° and 14°. If greater than this, check that the accelerator cable is correctly adjusted, however if the correct reading cannot be obtained renew the unit.

30 If a FIAT tester is not available, the alignment of the throttle potentiometer must be set by a FIAT dealer or a fuel injection systems specialist.

Inlet air temperature sensor

Removal

31 Remove the throttle body assembly as described earlier in this Section.

32 Extract the plastic pins and remove the press-fit cover from the top of the throttle body.

33 Invert the cover then unscrew the mounting screws and remove the inlet air temperature sensor from the cover (see illustrations).

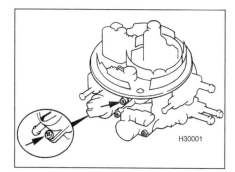

5.21b Removing the idle control stepper motor screws

5.26 Disconnect the wiring from the throttle potentiometer

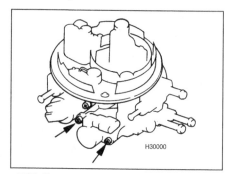

5.27 Unscrew the throttle potentiometer mounting screws (arrowed)

5.33a Inlet air temperature sensor (arrowed)

5.33b Disconnecting the wiring from the inlet air temperature sensor

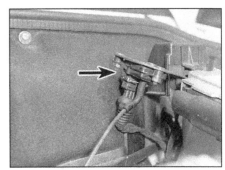

5.35 Manifold/absolute pressure sensor location (OHC model shown)

Refitting

34 Refitting is a reversal of removal.

Manifold/absolute pressure (MAP) sensor

Removal

35 The sensor is located on a bracket at the left-hand side of the bulkhead (see illustration).
36 Unscrew the mounting screws and remove the sensor from the bulkhead. Disconnect the wiring and vacuum pipe.

Refitting

37 Refitting is a reversal of removal, but check the condition of the vacuum pipe and renew it if necessary.

Coolant temperature sensor

Removal

38 The sensor is located on the left-hand side of the inlet manifold on OHC engines, and at

the top of the thermostat housing on OHV engines. Allow the engine to cool completely, then partially drain the cooling system with reference to Chapter 1, before removing it.
39 Disconnect the wiring from the sensor at the connector.
40 Unscrew the sensor and remove it from the inlet manifold. Use the correct size of spanner to remove the sensor, rather than a socket and take care not to damage the wiring connector on the sensor.

Refitting

41 Refitting is a reversal of removal but tighten the sensor to the specified torque.
Caution: Do not exceed the specified torque otherwise the unit may be damaged.

Crankshaft TDC sensor

Removal

42 The crankshaft TDC sensor is located on the front side of the crankshaft pulley. Apply the handbrake then jack up the front of the vehicle and support on axle stands (see "*Jacking and vehicle support*"). Remove the right-hand front wheel and plastic cover.
43 Disconnect the sensor wiring plug on the front of the engine.
44 On OHC engines, slacken the locking screw, then withdraw the sensor from its mounting bracket. On OHV engines, slacken and remove the two sensor-to-bracket screws and withdraw the sensor (see illustrations).
Caution: DO NOT slacken or remove the bracket-to-timing case bolts, as the sensor alignment will be disturbed.

Refitting

45 After refitting the sensor, use a feeler blade to check that the gap between the sensor and the serrated part of the toothed reluctor wheel is as listed in the Specifications. No adjustment is possible and if the gap is incorrect the sensor and pulley should be checked for possible damage.

Electronic control unit (ECU)

Note: *The engine management system has a 'learning' capability which allows the ECU to store details of the engine's running characteristics in its memory. This memory will be erased by the disconnection of the battery cables, with the result that the engine may idle roughly, or lack performance for a while, until the engine's characteristics are 're-learnt'.*

Removal

46 The ECU (electronic control unit) is located on the left-hand inner wing (see illustration). The 3-pin socket by the ECU is for use of a FIAT code reader.
47 Prior to removal, disconnect the battery negative cable and position it away from the terminal.
48 Disconnect the ECU wiring connector, then undo the retaining nuts and remove the unit from the bracket in the engine compartment.

Refitting

49 Refitting is a reversal of removal making sure that the wiring connector is securely reconnected. Reconnect the battery, and carry out the following procedure to speed up the self-learning procedure of the ECU memory.

5.44a On OHC engines, slacken the locking screw . . .

5.44b . . . then withdraw the TDC sensor from its mounting bracket

5.44c On OHV engines, remove the two sensor-to-bracket screws (arrowed) and withdraw the sensor

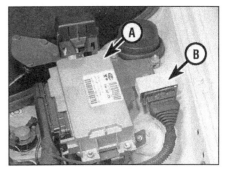

5.46 Engine management system ECU (A) and relays (B) - OHC engines

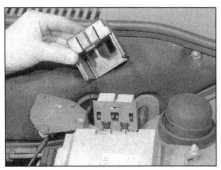

5.56 Engine management system relays - OHV engine

50 Start the engine and run it until it has reached normal operating temperature. Keep the engine running until the cooling fan switches on, then off, then on again for a second time. If at any time during this warm-up procedure the engine stalls, restart it immediately.

51 Once the cooling fan switches on for the second time, switch the engine off and immediately disconnect the battery negative terminal. Leave the battery disconnected for approximately 45 seconds, then reconnect the negative terminal; this will reset the ECU memory.

52 Once the battery is reconnected, immediately start the engine and allow it to idle for approximately 2 minutes. If the engine stalls during these initial 2 minutes, disconnect the battery negative terminal again for a further 45 seconds, then restart the engine and allow it to idle for a further 2 minutes. Repeat this procedure as required until the engine has run for at least 2 minutes without stalling; the ECU is then reprogrammed sufficiently to allow the engine to run and idle smoothly. Note, however, that it will still take a few miles for the ECU to learn the optimum settings for all operating conditions.

Inertia safety switch

Removal

53 The switch is located under the centre of the facia, behind a plastic cover panel. The switch can be reset without removing the plastic cover, by pressing the rubber cap at the top of the switch body.

54 To remove the switch, undo the screws and lift off the cover panel. Disconnect the wiring at the connector, then unbolt the switch from the bodywork.

Refitting

55 Refitting is a reversal of removal.

Fuel injection system relays

Removal

56 The fuel injection system relay is mounted on a bracket at the rear left-hand corner of the engine compartment, next to the ECU **(see illustration)**.

57 On OHC engines, two separate relays are incorporated in the single housing **(see illustration 5.46)**. The main purpose of the relays is to supply current to the fuel pump, ignition coils, oxygen sensor, injectors and EVAP solenoid. The main relay is controlled by the ignition switch.

58 Depress the locking bar and unplug the wiring connector from the base of the relay.

59 Remove the securing screw and detach the relay from its mounting bracket.

Refitting

60 Refitting is a reversal of removal.

6 Fuel pump/fuel gauge sender unit - removal and refitting

Removal

Note: *Refer to the warning given in Section 1 before proceeding.*

1 Disconnect the battery negative cable and position it away from terminal.

2 Remove the rear seat as described in Chapter 11. Briefly release the petrol filler cap, to expel any fuel vapour that may be pressurising the fuel tank.

3 Unscrew the nuts and remove the fuel pump access panel from the floorpan **(see illustrations)**.

4 Slacken and remove the securing nut and washer, lift the locking plate and then withdraw the fuel supply and return pipe unions from the top of the pump unit **(see illustrations)**. Be prepared for some fuel loss - pad the surrounding area with absorbent rags. Ensure that the O-ring seals remain in the grooves at the ends of the fuel pipe unions.

5 Unplug the wiring from the top of the fuel gauge sender unit **(see illustration)**.

6 Insert two stout flat bladed screwdrivers into the slots at the top of the sender unit, then use a third to twist the sender unit anticlockwise, to release it from the fuel pump unit **(see illustration)**.

7 Lift the sender unit carefully from the pump unit, allowing time for the fuel to drain back into the tank **(see illustration)**. Ensure that the O-ring seal remains in place at the top of the sender unit.

8 Unplug the wiring connector from the top of the pump unit **(see illustration)**.

6.3a Unscrew the nuts . . .

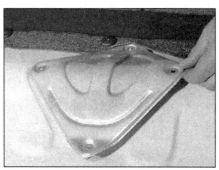

6.3b . . . and remove the fuel pump access panel from the floorpan

6.4a Slacken and remove the securing nut and washer . . .

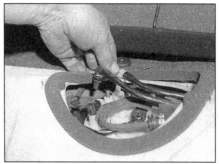

6.4b . . . lift the locking plate then withdraw the fuel supply and return pipe unions

6.5 Unplug the wiring from the top of the fuel gauge sender unit

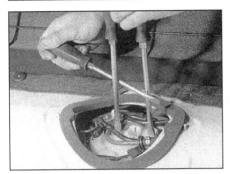

6.6 Using screwdrivers as levers, to release the fuel gauge sender unit from the fuel pump

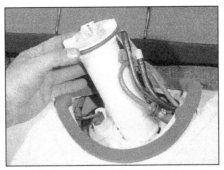

6.7 Lift the sender unit carefully from the pump unit

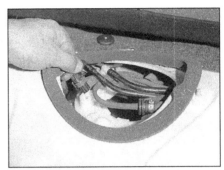

6.8 Unplug the wiring connector from the top of the fuel pump unit

9 Work around the outside of the pump unit locking collar and progressively slacken each of the securing nuts **(see illustration)**.

10 Remove the locking collar and carefully withdraw the pump unit from the fuel tank **(see illustrations)**. Allow plenty of time for the excess fuel to drain from the base of the pump. Note the pump locating tab, protruding from the bottom of the fuel tank.

11 Inspect the gauze filter surrounding the fuel pump for signs of damage or clogging. Dislodge any debris with clean fuel, if required.

Refitting

12 Refitting is a reversal of the removal procedure. Ensure that the base of the fuel pump passes behind the locating tab at the bottom of the fuel tank. This can be a tricky

operation, as the pump is suspended on spring strips, which must be compressed with twisting action as the pump is inserted.

13 Prior to refitting the access cover, reconnect the battery negative cable, then start the engine and check the feed and return unions for signs of leakage. On completion refit the access panel, tighten the nuts securely and refit the rear seat (see Chapter 11).

7 Fuel tank - removal and refitting

Note: *Refer to the warning given in Section 1 before proceeding.*

Removal

1 Before removing the fuel tank, all fuel must be drained from the tank. Since a fuel tank drain plug is not provided, it is therefore preferable to carry out the removal operation when the tank is almost empty. Before proceeding, disconnect the battery negative lead and syphon or hand-pump the remaining fuel from the tank.

2 Remove the fuel pump/fuel gauge sender unit as described in Section 6.

3 Chock the front wheels, then jack up the rear of the vehicle and support on axle stands (see "*Jacking and vehicle support*").

4 Loosen the clip and disconnect the filler pipe from the right-hand side of the fuel tank.

5 Undo the tank mounting bolts **(see illustration)**, then lower the tank out of

position until it is possible to access the hose connections on top of the tank.

6 Loosen the clips and disconnect the EVAP purge hose and breather hose from the fuel tank. If necessary, the filler neck can be detached from the body.

7 Check that all hoses and wiring is disconnected, then remove the tank from underneath the vehicle.

Refitting

8 Refitting is a reversal of the removal procedure, ensuring all hoses are correctly routed and securely reconnected. Tighten the tank mounting bolts to the specified torque setting.

8 Fuel injection system - depressurisation

Note: *Refer to the warning given in Section 1 before proceeding.*

1 The fuel system referred to in this Section is defined as the tank-mounted fuel pump, the fuel filter, the throttle body and pressure regulator components, and the metal pipes and flexible hoses of the fuel lines between these components. All these contain fuel which will be under pressure while the engine is running and/or while the ignition is switched on. The pressure will remain for a considerable time after the ignition has been switched off, due to the presence of a non-return valve in the fuel supply line. This residual pressure

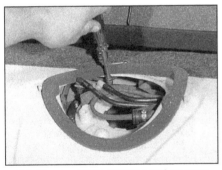

6.9 Progressively slacken and remove each of the securing nuts

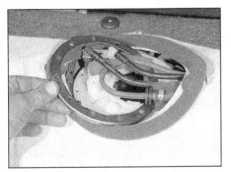

6.10a Remove the locking collar . . .

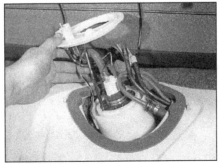

6.10b . . . and carefully withdraw the pump unit from the fuel tank

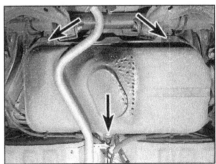

7.5 Fuel tank mounting bolts (arrowed)

must be relieved before any of these components are disturbed for servicing work.

2 Disconnect the battery negative cable and position it away from the terminal (see "*Disconnecting the battery*").

3 Place a container beneath the relevant connection/union to be disconnected, and have a wad of absorbent rags ready to soak up any escaping fuel not being caught by the container.

4 Slowly loosen the connection or union nut (as applicable) to avoid a sudden release of pressure, and wrap the rag around the connection to catch any fuel spray which may be expelled. Once the pressure is released, disconnect the fuel line, and insert plugs to minimise fuel loss and prevent the entry of dirt into the fuel system.

5 It is possible to depressurise the fuel system by disconnecting the fuel pump relay and then cranking and running the engine until the engine cuts out. This method is **NOT** recommended as it introduces the risk of unburned fuel being delivered to the catalytic converter, which can cause irreparable damage.

9 Inlet manifold - removal and refitting

Note: *Refer to the warning given in Section 1 before proceeding.*

Removal

OHV engines

1 The OHV engine has a ported cylinder head and does not have a 'conventional' inlet manifold. The throttle body is bolted to a short mounting flange which is in turn bolted directly to the upper surface of the cylinder head. The mounting flange houses the tapping point for the brake servo vacuum hose.

OHC engines

2 Remove the throttle body assembly as described in Section 5.
3 Drain the cooling system as described in Chapter 1.
4 Disconnect the wiring connector from the

9.9a Undo the manifold retaining nuts and bolts . .

coolant temperature sensor (situated on the left-hand side of the manifold).

5 Undo the bolt securing the accelerator cable mounting bracket to the manifold, and position it clear of the manifold.

6 Where applicable, unbolt and remove the harness support from the underside of the manifold.

7 Slacken the retaining clip and disconnect the coolant hose from the rear of the manifold.

8 Release the clip and disconnect the brake servo vacuum hose. Alternatively, remove the vacuum hose non-return valve from the servo (see Chapter 9), leaving the hose attached to the inlet manifold port.

9 Undo the manifold retaining nuts and bolts, and remove the manifold from the engine **(see illustrations)**. Remove the gasket and discard it; a new one should be used on refitting.

Refitting

10 Refitting is a reverse of the removal procedure, noting the following points:

a) *Ensure that the manifold and cylinder head mating surfaces are clean and dry, and fit a new manifold gasket. Refit the manifold and tighten its retaining nuts securely or to the specified torque setting (where applicable).*

b) *Ensure that all relevant hoses are reconnected to their original positions and are securely held (where necessary) by the retaining clips.*

c) *Refit the throttle body assembly with reference to Section 5.*

d) *On completion, refill the cooling system as described in Chapter 1.*

10 Fuel injection system - testing and adjustment

Testing

1 If a fault appears in the fuel injection system, first ensure that all the system wiring connectors are securely connected and free of corrosion. Then ensure that the fault is not due to poor maintenance; ie, check that the air cleaner filter element is clean, the spark plugs are in good condition and correctly

9.9b . . . and remove the manifold from the engine

gapped, that the valve clearances are correctly adjusted, and that the engine breather hoses are clear and undamaged.

2 If these checks fail to reveal the cause of the problem, the vehicle should be taken to a suitably-equipped FIAT dealer for testing. A wiring block connector is incorporated in the engine management system wiring harness, into which a special electronic diagnostic tester can be plugged. The connector is situated to the right-hand side of the ECU. The tester will locate the fault quickly and simply, alleviating the need to test all the system components individually, which is a time-consuming operation that carries a high risk of damaging the ECU.

Adjustment

3 As mentioned above, the idle speed and mixture adjustment are all monitored and controlled by the ECU, and are not adjustable. Experienced home mechanics with a considerable amount of skill and equipment (including a good-quality tachometer and a good-quality, carefully calibrated exhaust gas analyser) may be able to check the exhaust CO level and the idle speed (see Chapter 1 for details). However, if these are found to be in need of adjustment, the car **must** be taken to a suitably-equipped FIAT dealer for testing using the special test equipment which is plugged into the diagnostic connector.

11 Unleaded petrol - general information and usage

Note: *The information given in this Chapter is correct at the time of writing. If updated information is thought to be required, check with a FIAT dealer. If travelling abroad, consult one of the motoring organisations (or a similar authority) for advice on the fuel available.*

The fuel recommended by FIAT is given in the *Specifications* of this Chapter, followed by the equivalent petrol currently on sale in the UK.

All models are fitted with a catalytic converter and must be run on unleaded fuel *only*. Under no circumstances should leaded fuel (UK "4-star") be used, as this may damage the converter.

Super unleaded petrol (98 octane) can also be used in all models if wished, though there is no advantage in doing so.

12 Exhaust manifold - removal and refitting

Removal

1 Jack up the front of the vehicle and support on axle stands (see "*Jacking and vehicle support*"). The exhaust manifold is located on the front on OHC engines, and at the rear on OHV engines.

2 Where applicable, release the Lambda sensor wiring from its cable clip, then unscrew the nuts and disconnect the exhaust downpipe from the exhaust manifold flange. Rest the downpipe on a raised trolley jack or block of wood. Recover the gasket.

3 Unscrew the mounting nuts, remove the washers, then withdraw the manifold from the studs on the cylinder head **(see illustrations)**.

4 Recover the gaskets from the studs.

Refitting

5 Refitting is a reversal of the removal procedure but fit new gaskets throughout. Tighten the nuts to the specified torque.

13 Exhaust system - general information and component renewal

General information

1 A three section exhaust system is fitted consisting of a front downpipe incorporating a catalytic converter, an intermediate pipe incorporating a flexible joint and a silencer, and a tailpipe incorporating a second silencer. The downpipe-to-manifold joint is of the flange and gasket type, whereas the remaining joints are of the sleeve type secured with clamp rings.

2 The system is suspended throughout its length by rubber mountings. On OHC engined models, the downpipe is bolted to a bracket on the underside of the engine.

Removal

3 Each exhaust section can be removed individually or, alternatively, the complete system can be removed as a unit. Where separation of the rear sleeve joint is necessary, it may be more practical to remove the entire system rather than try and separate the joint in position.

4 To remove the system or part of the system, first jack up the front of the vehicle and support on axle stands (see *"Jacking and vehicle support"*). Alternatively, position the vehicle over an inspection pit or on car ramps.

Downpipe/catalytic converter

5 Support the forward end of the intermediate pipe using an axle stand or blocks of wood. Where applicable, refer to Section 15 and remove the Lambda sensor from the exhaust downpipe. On OHC engined models, remove the nuts and free the downpipe from the support bracket on the underside of the engine.

6 Slacken the nuts and release the clamp ring from the sleeve joint securing the downpipe to the intermediate pipe. Separate the joint, using a twisting action to free the downpipe. If the joint sticks, apply a small quantity of penetrating lubricant and allow it to soak into the joint for several minutes before trying again.

7 Unscrew the nuts securing the downpipe to the exhaust manifold and lower the downpipe. Recover the gasket.

12.3a Unscrew the mounting nuts . . .

Intermediate pipe

8 Support the tailpipe section of the exhaust using an axle stand or blocks of wood.

9 Separate the downpipe from the intermediate pipe as described in the previous sub-Section.

10 Unscrew the clamp bolt and separate the intermediate pipe from the tailpipe section.

11 Release the mounting rubber and remove the intermediate pipe from under the vehicle.

Tailpipe and silencers

12 Support the rearward end of the intermediate pipe using an axle stand or blocks of wood.

13 Unscrew the clamp bolt and separate the intermediate pipe from the tailpipe section.

14 Release the tailpipe section from its mounting rubbers and remove from under the vehicle.

Complete system

15 Disconnect the downpipe from the exhaust manifold as described in paragraph 7.

16 With the aid of an assistant, free the system from all its mounting rubbers and manoeuvre it out from underneath the vehicle.

Heatshields

17 The heatshields are secured to the underbody by a number of bolts and are easily removed once the exhaust system has been lowered out of position.

Refitting

18 Each section is refitted by a reverse of the removal sequence, noting the following points:

a) *Ensure that all traces of corrosion have been removed from the flanges and renew all necessary gaskets.*

b) *Inspect the rubber mountings for signs of damage or deterioration and renew as necessary.*

c) *Before refitting the tailpipe joint, smear some exhaust system jointing paste to the joint mating surfaces to ensure an air-tight seal. Tighten the clamp bolt to the specified torque setting.*

d) *Prior to fully tightening the rear joint clamp, ensure that all rubber mountings are correctly located and that there is adequate clearance between the exhaust system and vehicle underbody.*

12.3b . . . then withdraw the manifold from the studs on the cylinder head

e) *On completion, rock the exhaust system from side to side to ensure that contact with the floorpan or surrounding components does not occur.*

14 Catalytic converter - general information and precautions

The catalytic converter is a reliable and simple device which needs no maintenance in itself, but there are some facts of which an owner should be aware if the converter is to function properly for its full service life.

a) *DO NOT use leaded petrol in a car equipped with a catalytic converter - the lead will coat the precious metals, reducing their converting efficiency and will eventually destroy the converter.*

b) *Always keep the ignition and fuel systems well-maintained in accordance with the manufacturer's schedule.*

c) *If the engine develops a misfire, do not drive the car at all (or at least as little as possible) until the fault is cured.*

d) *DO NOT push- or tow-start the car - this will soak the catalytic converter in unburned fuel, causing it to overheat when the engine does start.*

e) *DO NOT switch off the ignition at high engine speeds.*

f) *DO NOT use fuel or engine oil additives - these may contain substances harmful to the catalytic converter.*

g) *DO NOT continue to use the car if the engine burns oil to the extent of leaving a visible trail of blue smoke.*

h) *Remember that the catalytic converter operates at very high temperatures. DO NOT, therefore, park the car in dry undergrowth, over long grass or piles of dead leaves after a long run.*

i) *Remember that the catalytic converter is FRAGILE - do not strike it with tools during servicing work.*

j) *In some cases a sulphurous smell (like that of rotten eggs) may be noticed from the exhaust, particularly when starting from cold or accelerating. This is common to many catalytic converter-equipped cars and is caused by sulphur in the fuel.*

15.1 Lambda sensor location (OHV model shown)

k) The catalytic converter, used on a well-maintained and well-driven car, should last for between 50 000 and 100 000 miles - if the converter is no longer effective it must be renewed.

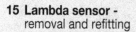

15 Lambda sensor - removal and refitting

Note: The Lambda sensor is delicate and will not work if it is dropped or knocked, if its power supply is disrupted, or if any cleaning materials are used on it.

Removal

1 The sensor is threaded into the exhaust front downpipe **(see illustration)**. Access if best gained from underneath the vehicle. Apply the handbrake then jack up the front of the vehicle and support on axle stands (see "Jacking and vehicle support").
2 Disconnect the sensor wiring connector located on the front of the engine.
3 Working beneath the vehicle, unscrew the sensor, taking care to avoid damaging the sensor probe as it is removed. **Note:** As a flying lead remains connected to the sensor after it has been disconnected, if the correct spanner is not available, a slotted socket will be required to remove the sensor.

16.4 Disconnect the wiring from the purge valve solenoid

Refitting

4 Apply a little anti-seize grease to the sensor threads - avoid contaminating the probe tip.
5 Refit the sensor to the downpipe, tightening it to the correct torque. Reconnect the wiring.
6 Lower the vehicle to the ground.

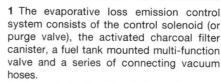

16 Evaporative loss emission control system - component renewal

1 The evaporative loss emission control system consists of the control solenoid (or purge valve), the activated charcoal filter canister, a fuel tank mounted multi-function valve and a series of connecting vacuum hoses.
2 The control solenoid and charcoal canister are both mounted on a bracket, in front of the transmission casing at the left-hand side of the engine compartment.

Component renewal

Purge valve

3 With the bonnet open, disconnect the hoses from the control solenoid on the top of the charcoal canister.
4 Disconnect the wiring and remove the solenoid **(see illustration)**.
5 Refitting is a reversal of removal.

16.6 Disconnect the vapour supply and return hoses from the canister

Charcoal canister

6 Disconnect the vapour supply and return hoses from the canister **(see illustration)**.
7 Slacken and withdraw the securing nuts/screws and remove the canister, together with the purge valve and mounting bracket **(see illustrations)**.
8 Refitting is a reversal of removal.

Multifunction valve

9 The multifunction valve is mounted on top of the fuel tank - refer to Section 7 and lower the fuel tank away from the underside of the vehicle.
10 Remove the securing screws and withdraw the valve from the top of the fuel tank.
11 Refitting is a reversal of removal.

17 Crankcase emission system - general information

The crankcase emission control system consists of a hose from the camshaft cover to the air cleaner with a branch to the throttle housing. The main hose incorporates a flame trap and the inlet to the throttle body incorporates a calibrated hole.

The system requires no attention other than to check at regular intervals that the hoses are free of blockages and undamaged.

16.7a Slacken and withdraw the securing nuts/screws . . .

16.7b . . . and remove the canister

Chapter 5 Part A:
Starting and charging systems

Contents

Degrees of difficulty

| Easy, suitable for novice with little experience | | Fairly easy, suitable for beginner with some experience | | Fairly difficult, suitable for competent DIY mechanic | | Difficult, suitable for experienced DIY mechanic | | Very difficult, suitable for expert DIY or professional | |

Specifications

General
System type . . . . 12-volt, negative earth

Starter motor
Type . . . . Magneti-Marelli, pre-engaged
Output . . . . 0.8 kW
Solenoid pull-in coil resistance . . . . 0.3 Ω
Solenoid hold-in coil resistance . . . . 1.2 to 1.3 Ω

Battery
Capacity . . . . 40 A-hr
Charge condition:
  Poor . . . . 12.5 volts
  Normal . . . . 12.6 volts
  Good . . . . 12.7 volts
Maximum current:
  OHC engine . . . . 200 A
  OHV engine . . . . 150 A

Alternator
Type . . . . Magneti-Marelli
Maximum current:
  OHC engine 65A
  OHV engine 55A
Cut-in speed:
  OHC engine . . . . 1050 to 1150 rpm
  OHV engine . . . . 950 to 1050 rpm
Field winding resistance:
  OHC engine . . . . 2.6 to 2.8 Ω
  OHV engine . . . . 3.0 to 3.2 Ω

Torque wrench settings

	Nm	lbf ft
Alternator mounting bolts	49	36
Battery terminal clamp bolts	4	3
Roadwheel bolts	86	63
Starter motor mounting bolts	45	33

1 General information and precautions

General information

The engine electrical system consists mainly of the charging and starting systems. Because of their engine-related functions, these components are covered separately from the body electrical devices such as the lights, instruments, etc (which are covered in Chapter 12). For details of the ignition system components, refer to Chapter 5B. For details of the fuel injection system electrical components refer to Chapter 4.

The electrical system is of 12-volt negative earth type.

The battery fitted as original equipment is of "maintenance-free" (sealed for life) type and is charged by the alternator, which is belt-driven from the crankshaft pulley. If a non-original battery is fitted it may be of standard or low maintenance type.

The starter motor is of the pre-engaged type incorporating an integral solenoid. On starting, the solenoid moves the drive pinion into engagement with the flywheel ring gear before the starter motor is energised. Once the engine has started, a one-way clutch prevents the motor armature being driven by the engine until the pinion disengages from the flywheel.

Precautions

Further details of the various systems are given in the relevant Sections of this Chapter. While some repair procedures are given, the usual course of action is to renew the component concerned. The owner whose interest extends beyond mere component renewal should obtain a copy of the "Automobile Electrical & Electronic Systems Manual", available from the publishers of this manual.

It is necessary to take extra care when working on the electrical system to avoid damage to semi-conductor devices (diodes and transistors), and to avoid the risk of personal injury. In addition to the precautions given in "Safety first!" at the beginning of this manual, observe the following when working on the system:

Always remove rings, watches, etc before working on the electrical system. Even with the battery disconnected, capacitive discharge could occur if a component's live terminal is earthed through a metal object. This could cause a shock or nasty burn.

Do not reverse the battery connections. Components such as the alternator, electronic control units, or any other components having semi-conductor circuitry could be irreparably damaged.

If the engine is being started using jump leads and a slave battery, connect the batteries *positive-to-positive* and *negative-to-*negative (see *"Booster battery (jump) starting"*). This also applies when connecting a battery charger but in this case both of the battery terminals should first be disconnected.

Never disconnect the battery terminals, the alternator, any electrical wiring or any test instruments when the engine is running.

Do not allow the engine to turn the alternator when the alternator is not connected.

Never "test" for alternator output by "flashing" the output lead to earth.

Never use an ohmmeter of the type incorporating a hand-cranked generator for circuit or continuity testing.

Always ensure that the battery negative lead is disconnected when working on the electrical system.

Before using electric-arc welding equipment on the car, disconnect the battery, alternator and components such as the fuel injection/ignition electronic control unit to protect them from the risk of damage.

The radio/cassette unit fitted as standard equipment by FIAT is equipped with a built-in security code to deter thieves. If the power source to the unit is cut, the anti-theft system will activate. Even if the power source is immediately reconnected, the radio/cassette unit will not function until the correct security code has been entered. Therefore, if you do not know the correct security code for the radio/cassette unit **do not** disconnect the battery negative terminal of the battery or remove the radio/cassette unit from the vehicle. Refer to your FIAT dealer for further information on whether the unit fitted to your car has a security code.

2 Battery - testing and charging

Standard and low maintenance battery - testing

1 If the vehicle covers a small annual mileage, it is worthwhile checking the specific gravity of the electrolyte every three months to determine the state of charge of the battery. Use a hydrometer to make the check and compare the results with the following table. Note that the specific gravity readings assume an electrolyte temperature of 25°C (77°F); for every 10°C (48°F) below 15°C (60°F) subtract 0.007. For every 10°C (48°F) above 15°C (60°F) add 0.007.

	Ambient temperature 25°C (77°F)	
	Above 25°C	Below 25°C
Charged	1.210 to 1.230	1.270 to 1.290
70% charged	1.170 to 1.190	1.230 to 1.250
Discharged	1.050 to 1.070	1.110 to 1.130

2 If the battery condition is suspect, first check the specific gravity of electrolyte in each cell. A variation of 0.040 or more between any cells indicates loss of electrolyte or deterioration of the internal plates.

3 If the specific gravity variation is 0.040 or more, the battery should be renewed. If the cell variation is satisfactory but the battery is discharged, it should be charged as described later in this Section.

Maintenance-free battery - testing

4 In cases where a "sealed for life" maintenance-free battery is fitted, topping-up and testing of the electrolyte in each cell is not possible. The condition of the battery can therefore only be tested using a battery condition indicator or a voltmeter.

5 Certain models may be fitted with a maintenance-free battery with a built-in charge condition indicator. The indicator is located in the top of the battery casing, and indicates the condition of the battery from its colour. If the indicator shows green, then the battery is in a good state of charge. If the indicator turns darker, eventually to black, then the battery requires charging, as described later in this Section. If the indicator shows clear/yellow, then the electrolyte level in the battery is too low to allow further use, and the battery should be renewed.

Caution: Do not attempt to charge, load or jump start a battery when the indicator shows clear/yellow.

6 If testing the battery using a voltmeter, connect the voltmeter across the battery and compare the result with those given in the *Specifications* under "charge condition". The test is only accurate if the battery has not been subjected to any kind of charge for the previous six hours. If this is not the case, switch on the headlights for 30 seconds, then wait four to five minutes before testing the battery after switching off the headlights. All other electrical circuits must be switched off, so check that the doors and tailgate are fully shut when making the test.

7 If the voltage reading is less than 12.2 volts, then the battery is discharged, whilst a reading of 12.2 to 12.4 volts indicates a partially discharged condition.

8 If the battery is to be charged, remove it from the vehicle (see Section 3) and charge it as described later in this Section.

Standard and low maintenance battery - charging

Note: *The following is intended as a guide only. Always refer to the manufacturer's recommendations (often printed on a label attached to the battery) before charging a battery.*

9 Charge the battery at a rate of 3.5 to 4 amps and continue to charge the battery at this rate until no further rise in specific gravity is noted over a four hour period.

10 Alternatively, a trickle charger charging at the rate of 1.5 amps can safely be used overnight.

11 Specially rapid "boost" charges which are claimed to restore the power of the battery in 1 to 2 hours are not recommended, as they can cause serious damage to the battery plates through overheating.

12 While charging the battery, note that the temperature of the electrolyte should never exceed 37.8°C (100°F).

Maintenance-free battery - charging

Note: *The following is intended as a guide only. Always refer to the manufacturer's recommendations (often printed on a label attached to the battery) before charging a battery.*

13 This battery type takes considerably longer to fully recharge than the standard type, the time taken being dependent on the extent of discharge, but it can take anything up to three days.

14 A constant voltage type charger is required, to be set, when connected, to 13.9 to 14.9 volts with a charger current below 25 amps. Using this method, the battery should be usable within three hours, giving a voltage reading of 12.5 volts, but this is for a partially discharged battery and, as mentioned, full charging can take considerably longer.

15 If the battery is to be charged from a fully discharged state (condition reading less than 12.2 volts), have it recharged by your FIAT dealer or local automotive electrician, as the charge rate is higher and constant supervision during charging is necessary.

3 Battery - removal and refitting

Note 1: *If the vehicle has a security coded radio, check that you have a copy of the code number before disconnecting the battery cable; refer to Chapter 12 for details.*

Note 2: *On all models, the engine management system has a 'learning' capability which allows the electronic control unit (ECU) to store details of the engine's running characteristics in its memory. This memory will be erased by the disconnection of the battery cables, with the result that the engine may idle roughly, or lack performance for a while, until the engine's characteristics are 're-learnt'; see Chapter 4 for further details.*

3.2a Slacken both nuts from the battery clamp plate bolts . . .

Removal

1 Loosen the clamp bolt and disconnect the battery negative cable from the terminal (see *"Disconnecting the battery"*).

2 At the top of the battery, slacken both nuts from the battery clamp plate bolts. Unhook the bolts from the battery tray and remove the clamp plate **(see illustrations)**.

3 Loosen the clamp bolt and disconnect the battery positive cable from the terminal. On OHC engines, detach the fusible link housing from the top of the battery **(see illustrations)**.

4 Lift the battery from the engine compartment **(see illustration)**.

Refitting

5 Refitting is a reversal of removal but make sure that the positive terminal is connected first, followed by the negative terminal. Tighten the battery terminal clamp bolts to the specified torque setting.

4 Alternator/charging system - testing in vehicle

Note: *Refer to the warnings given in "Safety first!" and in Section 1 of this Chapter before starting work.*

1 If the ignition warning light fails to illuminate when the ignition is switched on, first check the alternator wiring connections for security. If satisfactory, check that the warning light bulb has not blown, and that the bulbholder is

3.2b . . . then unhook the bolts from the battery tray and remove the clamp plate

secure in its location in the instrument panel. If the light still fails to illuminate, check the continuity of the warning light feed wire from the alternator to the bulbholder. If all is satisfactory, the alternator is at fault and should be renewed or taken to an auto-electrician for testing and repair.

2 If the ignition warning light illuminates when the engine is running, stop the engine and check that the drivebelt is correctly tensioned (see Chapter 1) and that the alternator connections are secure. If all is so far satisfactory, have the alternator checked by an auto-electrician.

3 If the alternator output is suspect even though the warning light functions correctly, the regulated voltage may be checked as follows.

4 Connect a voltmeter across the battery terminals and start the engine.

5 Increase the engine speed until the voltmeter reading remains steady; the reading should be approximately 12 to 13 volts, and no more than 14 volts.

6 Switch on as many electrical accessories (eg, the headlights, heated rear window and heater blower) as possible, and check that the alternator maintains the regulated voltage at around 13 to 14 volts.

7 If the regulated voltage is not as stated, the fault may be due to worn brushes, weak brush springs, a faulty voltage regulator, a faulty diode, a severed phase winding or worn or damaged slip rings. The alternator should be renewed or taken to an auto-electrician for testing and repair.

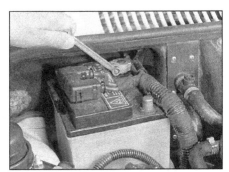

3.3a Loosen the clamp bolt and disconnect the battery positive cable from the terminal

3.3b On OHC engines, detach the fusible link housing from the top of the battery

3.4 Lift the battery from the engine compartment

5.4 Remove the nuts and washers and disconnect the wiring from the stud terminals at the rear of the alternator

5.5 Alternator pivot and adjustment bolts (arrowed); OHV engine shown

5.6a Support the right-hand end of the engine, then unbolt the right-hand engine mounting from the bodywork

5.6b Remove the alternator upper adjustment bolt; engine mounting bracket securing nut arrowed

5.7a Unscrew and withdraw the alternator lower pivot bolt . . .

5.7b . . . then remove the alternator from the engine

5 Alternator -
removal and refitting

Removal

1 Disconnect the battery negative cable and position it away from the terminal.
2 Jack up the front of the vehicle and support on axle stands (see *"Jacking and Vehicle Support"*). Remove the right-hand roadwheel.
3 Undo the securing screws and remove the plastic liner from the right-hand wheelarch, for access to the right-hand side of the engine.
4 Remove the nuts and washers and disconnect the wiring from the stud terminals

at the rear of the alternator. Unplug the remaining wiring at the spade connector **(see illustration)**.
5 Loosen the pivot and adjustment bolts then swivel the alternator towards the engine and slip off the auxiliary drivebelt. Note that the position of the rpm sensor will prevent complete removal of the drivebelt from the crankshaft pulley. If required, remove the securing screw and withdraw the TDC sensor from its mounting bracket **(see illustration)**.
6 On OHC engines only, support the right-hand end of the engine using a lifting beam or hoist, then refer to Chapter 2B and unbolt the right-hand engine mounting from the bodywork. The nuts securing the right-hand engine mounting bracket to the engine block

must now be slackened, to provide enough clearance to allow the alternator upper adjustment bolt to be fully unscrewed and withdrawn **(see illustrations)**.
7 Unscrew and withdraw the alternator lower pivot bolt, then remove the alternator from the engine **(see illustrations)**.

Refitting

8 Refitting is a reversal of removal. Refer to Chapter 1 for details of tensioning the auxiliary drivebelt. On completion tighten the pivot and adjustment bolts/nut and the roadwheel bolts to the specified torque.

6 Alternator -
brush holder/regulator module renewal

1 Remove the alternator as described in Section 5.
2 Extract the two small bolts, remove the plastic grille and withdraw the brush box **(see illustrations)**.
3 Using a steel rule check the length of the brushes. If less than 5.0 mm the complete brush holder assembly should be renewed.
4 Clean the slip rings thoroughly and then check them for signs of excessive wear.
5 Fit the new holder using a reversal of the removal procedure.

6.2a Extract the two small bolts . . .

6.2b . . . and withdraw the brush box

7 Starting system - testing

Note: Refer to the precautions given in "Safety first!" and in Section 1 of this Chapter before starting work.

1 If the starter motor fails to operate when the ignition key is turned to the appropriate position, the following possible causes may be to blame.

a) *The battery is faulty.*
b) *The electrical connections between the switch, solenoid, battery and starter motor are somewhere failing to pass the necessary current from the battery through the starter to earth.*
c) *The solenoid is faulty.*
d) *The starter motor is mechanically or electrically defective.*

2 To check the battery, switch on the headlights. If they dim after a few seconds, this indicates that the battery is discharged - recharge (see Section 2) or renew the battery. If the headlights glow brightly, operate the ignition switch and observe the lights. If they dim, then this indicates that current is reaching the starter motor, therefore the fault must lie in the starter motor. If the lights continue to glow brightly (and no clicking sound can be heard from the starter motor solenoid), this indicates that there is a fault in the circuit or solenoid - see following paragraphs. If the starter motor turns slowly when operated, but the battery is in good condition, then this indicates that either the starter motor is faulty, or there is considerable resistance somewhere in the circuit.

3 If a fault in the circuit is suspected, disconnect the battery leads (including the earth connection to the body), the starter /solenoid wiring and the engine/transmission earth strap. Thoroughly clean the connections, and reconnect the leads and wiring, then use a voltmeter or test lamp to check that full battery voltage is available at the battery positive lead connection to the solenoid, and that the earth is sound. Smear petroleum jelly around the battery terminals to prevent corrosion - a corroded battery connection is one of the most frequent causes of electrical system faults.

8.3 Withdraw the uppermost starter motor securing bolt from the transmission bellhousing - OHC engine

4 If the battery and all connections are in good condition, check the circuit by disconnecting the wire from the solenoid blade terminal. Connect a voltmeter or test lamp between the wire end and a good earth (such as the battery negative terminal), and check that the wire is live when the ignition switch is turned to the "start" position. If it is, then the circuit is sound - if not, the circuit wiring can be checked as described in Chapter 12.

5 The solenoid contacts can be checked by connecting a voltmeter or test lamp across the solenoid. When the ignition switch is turned to the "start" position, there should be a reading or lighted bulb, as applicable. If there is no reading or lighted bulb, the solenoid is faulty and should be renewed.

6 If the circuit and solenoid are proved sound, the fault must lie in the starter motor. In this event, it may be possible to have the starter motor overhauled by a specialist, but check on the cost of spares before proceeding, as it may prove more economical to obtain a new or exchange motor.

8 Starter motor - removal and refitting

General information

On OHV engines, the starter motor is located on the front face of the engine and access is relatively straightforward. On OHC

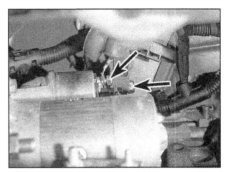

8.6 Remove the nuts and disconnect the wiring from the stud terminals at the rear of the starter motor

engines, the starter motor is mounted on the rear of the engine and access is limited.

Removal

OHC engines

1 Disconnect the battery negative cable and position it away from the terminal.
2 Refer to Chapter 4 and remove the air cleaner and its associated ducting.
3 Slacken and withdraw the uppermost starter motor securing bolt from the transmission bellhousing **(see illustration)**.
4 Apply the handbrake then jack up the front of the vehicle and support on axle stands (see *"Jacking and Vehicle Support"*).
5 With reference to Chapter 4, unbolt the exhaust system downpipe and remove it from the engine.
6 Remove the plastic cap, then slacken and remove the nuts and disconnect the wiring from the stud terminals at the rear of the starter motor **(see illustration)**.
7 Undo the two remaining starter motor securing bolts, then withdraw the motor from the bellhousing **(see illustrations)**.

OHV engines

8 Disconnect the battery negative cable and position it away from the terminal.
9 Slacken and remove the nuts and disconnect the wiring from the stud terminals at the rear of the starter motor.
10 Slacken and withdraw the starter motor securing bolts, then remove the motor from the transmission bellhousing **(see illustration)**.

8.7a Undo the two remaining starter motor securing bolts . . .

8.7b . . . then withdraw the motor from the bellhousing

8.10 Starter motor securing bolts (arrowed) - OHV engine

Refitting

11 Refit the starter motor by following the removal procedure in reverse. Tighten the mounting bolts to the specified torque.

9 Starter motor -
testing and overhaul

If the starter motor is thought to be suspect, it should be removed from the vehicle and taken to an auto-electrician for testing. Most auto-electricians will be able to supply and fit brushes at a reasonable cost. However, check on the cost of repairs before proceeding as it may prove more economical to obtain a new or exchange motor.

Chapter 5 Part B:
Ignition system

Contents

Degrees of difficulty

Easy, suitable for novice with little experience	**Fairly easy,** suitable for beginner with some experience	**Fairly difficult,** suitable for competent DIY mechanic	**Difficult,** suitable for experienced DIY mechanic	**Very difficult,** suitable for expert DIY or professional 

Specifications

General

System type . . . . Weber-Marelli Static (distributorless), "wasted" spark ignition system controlled by engine management ECU

Firing order . . . . 1-3-4-2 (No 1 cylinder at timing end of engine)

Ignition timing:

OHC engine . . . . $8° \pm 3°$ at 900 rpm

OHV engine . . . . $11° \pm 3°$ at 850 rpm

Ignition coil winding resistance (at 20°C):

Primary . . . . 0.5 to 0.6 Ω

Secondary . . . . 6.6 to 8.1 kΩ

Torque wrench settings

	Nm	lbf ft
Roadwheel bolts	86	63
Spark plugs	27	20

1 General information

The ignition system is integrated with the fuel injection system to form a combined engine management system under the control of one ECU (see Chapter 4 for further information).

The ignition side of the system is of the static (distributorless) type, consisting only of two twin-output ignition coils located on the left-hand side of the cylinder head. Each ignition coil supplies two cylinders (one coil supplies cylinders 1 and 4, and the other cylinders 2 and 3). Under the control of the ECU, the ignition coils operate on the "wasted spark" principle, ie. each spark plug sparks twice for every cycle of the engine, once on the compression stroke and once on the exhaust stroke. The spark voltage is greatest in the cylinder which is under compression, the other cylinder having a very weak spark which has no effect on the exhaust gases. The ECU uses its inputs from the various sensors to calculate the required ignition advance setting and coil charging time.

2 Ignition system - testing

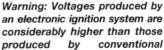 **Warning: Voltages produced by an electronic ignition system are considerably higher than those produced by conventional ignition systems. Extreme care must be taken when working on the system with the ignition switched on. Persons with surgically-implanted cardiac pacemaker devices should keep well clear of the ignition circuits, components and test equipment.**

1 If a fault appears in the engine management (fuel injection/ignition) system first ensure that the fault is not due to a poor electrical connection or poor maintenance; ie, check that the air cleaner filter element is clean, the spark plugs are in good condition and correctly gapped, that the engine breather hoses are clear and undamaged, referring to Chapter 1 for further information. Also check that the accelerator cable is correctly adjusted as described in Chapter 4. If the engine is running very roughly, check the compression pressures and the valve clearances as described in Chapter 1.

2 If these checks fail to reveal the cause of the problem, the vehicle should be taken to a suitably equipped FIAT dealer for testing. A wiring block connector is incorporated in the engine management circuit into which a special electronic diagnostic tester can be plugged. The tester will locate the fault quickly and simply alleviating the need to test all the system components individually which is a time consuming operation that carries a high risk of damaging the ECU.

3 The only ignition system checks which can be carried out by the home mechanic are those described in Chapter 1, relating to the spark plugs, and the ignition coil test described in this Chapter. If necessary, the system wiring and wiring connectors can be checked as described in Chapter 12 ensuring that the ECU wiring connector(s) have first been disconnected.

3.1a Unscrew the bolt . . .

3.1b . . . and remove the plastic cover from the left-hand end of the cylinder head

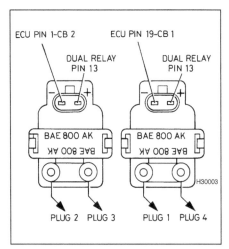

3.2 Ignition coil HT and LT wiring connections

3 Ignition HT coil -
removal, testing and refitting

Removal

1 Refer to Chapter 4 and remove the air cleaner housing and its associated intake ducting. Where applicable, unscrew the bolt and remove the plastic cover from the left-hand end of the cylinder head (see illustrations).
2 Identify the two HT leads for position then disconnect them from the relevant coil HT terminals (see illustration).
3 Disconnect the LT wiring plugs (see illustration).
4 Unscrew the mounting bolts and remove the ignition coil from the end of the cylinder head (see illustration).
5 If required, both ignition coils can be

removed as an assembly, by unbolting their mounting bracket from the cylinder head cover (see illustrations).

Testing

6 Testing of the coil consists of using a multimeter set to its resistance function, to check the primary and secondary windings for continuity and resistance. Compare the results obtained to those given in the Specifications at the start of this Chapter. Note the resistance of the coil windings varies slightly according to the coil temperature; the results in the Specifications are approximate values for the coil at 20°C.
7 Check that there is no continuity between the HT lead terminals and the coil body/mounting bracket.
8 Note that with the ignition switched on and the engine stationary, voltage will only be supplied to the ignition coils for approximately 2

3.3 Disconnect the LT wiring plugs

3.4 Unscrew the mounting bolts and remove the ignition coil from the end of the cylinder head

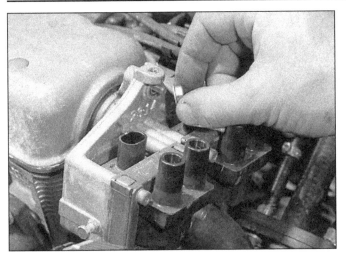

3.5a If required, unscrew the securing nuts . . .

3.5b . . . and remove the ignition coil and mounting bracket assembly from the end of the cylinder head

seconds. However, when the engine is being cranked or running, voltage will be continually supplied. If faulty, the coil should be renewed.

Refitting

9 Refitting is a reversal of the removal procedure ensuring that the wiring and HT leads are correctly reconnected.

4 Ignition timing - checking and adjustment

1 When the engine is running, the ignition timing is constantly being monitored and adjusted by the engine management system. When the engine is idling, small changes are made to the ignition timing, to help maintain a constant idle speed. Although it is possible to check the base ignition timing using a standard timing light, it is not possible to

adjust it. The reading obtained will only be approximate, due to the constantly changing ignition timing.

2 For those wishing to check the ignition timing a stroboscopic timing light will be required, and it will need to be the type which can determine the amount of advance from the TDC markings on the crankshaft pulley or flywheel. It is recommended that the timing mark is highlighted as follows.

3 On OHC engines, remove the plug from the top of the transmission then turn the engine slowly (raise the front right-hand wheel and engage 4th gear) until the timing mark scribed on the edge of the flywheel appears in the aperture. Highlight the line with quick-drying white paint - typist's correction fluid is ideal. On OHV engines, the timing marks are located on the crankshaft pulley and timing gear casing; it will be necessary to remove the right-hand roadwheel and wheel arch liner to gain access.

4 Start the engine and run it to normal operating temperature, then stop it.

5 Connect the timing light to No 1 cylinder spark plug lead (No 1 cylinder is at the timing end of the engine) as described in the timing light manufacturer's instructions.

6 Start the engine, allowing it to idle at the specified speed, and point the timing light at the transmission housing aperture/crankshaft pulley. Adjust the timing light until the TDC marks are aligned with each other and read off the amount of advance.

7 If the ignition timing is incorrect, the car should be taken to a FIAT dealer who will be able to check the system quickly using special diagnostic equipment.

8 After making the check stop the engine, disconnect the timing light, and on OHC engines, refit the plug to the top of the transmission casing. On OHV engines, refit the wheel arch liner and roadwheel and tighten the roadwheel bolts to the specified torque setting.

Notes

Chapter 6
Clutch

Contents

Degrees of difficulty

Easy, suitable for novice with little experience		Fairly easy, suitable for beginner with some experience		Fairly difficult, suitable for competent DIY mechanic		Difficult, suitable for experienced DIY mechanic		Very difficult, suitable for expert DIY or professional	

Specifications

General

Type	Single dry plate with diaphragm spring, cable-operated

Clutch pedal travel:
OHC engine	120 ± 5 mm
OHV engine	110 ± 5 mm

Friction plate diameter:
OHV engine	170.0 mm
OHC engine	181.5 mm

Torque wrench settings

	Nm	lbf ft
Pressure plate retaining bolts	10	7
Release fork securing bolt	25	18

2.2a At the transmission end of the clutch cable, unscrew the locknut . . .

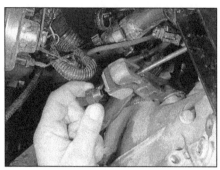

2.2b . . . and adjuster nut . . .

2.2c Note the position of the damper block

2.2d Release the outer cable from the bracket on the transmission housing

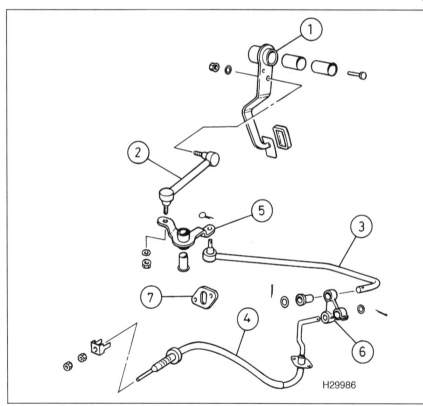

H29986

2.3 Unhook the inner cable from the top of the clutch pushrod pivot - right-hand drive model shown

1 Clutch pedal	3 Linkrod	6 Linkrod pivot
2 Pushrod	4 Clutch cable	7 Bulkhead flange
	5 Pushrod pivot	

1 General information

All models are fitted with a pedal operated, single dry plate clutch system. When the clutch pedal is depressed, effort is transmitted to the clutch release mechanism by means of a cable. The cable rotates the release shaft, which is mounted in the transmission casing on nylon bushes. A two pronged fork, mounted horizontally on the release shaft, slides a rotary release bearing along the sleeved transmission input shaft, and this transfers effort to the centre of the pressure plate diaphragm spring. The diaphragm spring withdraws the pressure plate from the flywheel and releases the driven plate, disconnecting drive to the transmission.

2 Clutch cable - removal and refitting

Note: *On right-hand drive models, effort from the clutch pedal is transferred across the inside of the engine bulkhead (behind the facia) via a system of pushrods and pivots, to the left-hand side of the vehicle. The clutch cable then transfers the effort from this point to the release mechanism. On left-hand drive models, the clutch cable is connected directly to the top of the clutch pedal.*

Removal

1 Refer to Chapter 4 and remove the air cleaner and its associated trunking.
2 At the transmission end of the clutch cable, unscrew the locknut and adjuster nut from the end of the cable fitting, then release the inner and outer cables from the bracket on the transmission housing. Note the position of the damper block **(see illustrations)**.
3 Working inside the vehicle, underneath the right-hand side of the facia, unhook the inner cable from the top of the clutch pushrod pivot **(see illustration)**.
4 Returning to the engine compartment, unscrew the nuts securing the outer cable flange to the bulkhead, then withdraw the cable assembly from the engine compartment.

Refitting

5 Apply a smear of multi-purpose grease to the cable end fittings, then pass the cable through the bulkhead. Refit and tighten the cable flange securing nuts.
6 Inside the vehicle hook the inner cable onto the top of the pushrod pivot.
7 In the engine compartment, attach the outer cable to the transmission housing and refit the damper block and nuts to the inner cable end.
8 Adjust the clutch cable as described in Chapter 1.
9 Refit the air cleaner with reference to Chapter 4.

3 Clutch assembly - removal, inspection and refitting

 Warning: Dust created by clutch wear and deposited on the clutch components may contain asbestos, which is a health hazard. DO NOT blow it out with compressed air, or inhale any of it. DO NOT use petrol or petroleum-based solvents to clean off the dust. Brake system cleaner or methylated spirit should be used to flush the dust into a suitable receptacle. After the clutch components are wiped clean with rags, dispose of the contaminated rags and cleaner in a sealed, marked container.

Note: *Although most clutch components no longer contain asbestos, if you are unsure of their origin, it is safest to assume that the dust may be harmful, and to take precautions accordingly.*

Removal

1 Unless the complete engine/transmission is to be removed from the car and separated for major overhaul (see Chapter 2C), the clutch can be reached by removing the transmission as described in Chapter 7.
2 Before disturbing the clutch, use chalk or a marker pen to mark the relationship of the pressure plate assembly to the flywheel.
3 Working in a diagonal sequence, slacken the pressure plate bolts by half a turn at a time, until spring pressure is released and the bolts can be unscrewed by hand **(see illustration)**.
4 Prise the pressure plate assembly off its locating dowels, and collect the friction plate, noting which way round the friction plate is fitted.

Inspection

Note: *Due to the amount of work necessary to remove and refit clutch components, it is usually considered good practice to renew the clutch friction plate, pressure plate assembly and release bearing as a matched set, even if only one of these is actually worn enough to require renewal. It is also worth considering the renewal of the clutch components on a preventative basis if the engine and/or transmission have been removed for some other reason.*

5 Separate the pressure plate and friction plate and place them on the bench.
6 When cleaning clutch components, read first the warning at the beginning of this Section; remove dust using a clean, dry cloth, and working in a well-ventilated atmosphere.
7 Check the friction plate facings for signs of wear, damage or oil contamination. If the friction material is cracked, burnt, scored or damaged, or if it is contaminated with oil or grease (shown by shiny black patches), the friction plate must be renewed.
8 If the friction material is still serviceable, check that the centre boss splines are unworn, that the torsion springs are in good

3.3 Working in a diagonal sequence, slacken the pressure plate bolts (arrowed) by half a turn at a time

condition and securely fastened, and that all the rivets are tight. If any wear or damage is found, the friction plate must be renewed.
9 If the friction material is fouled with oil, this must be due to an oil leak from the crankshaft rear (left-hand) oil seal, from the sump-to-cylinder block joint, or from the transmission input shaft. Renew the seal or repair the joint, as appropriate, before installing the new friction plate.
10 Check the pressure plate assembly for obvious signs of wear or damage; shake it to check for loose rivets or worn or damaged fulcrum rings, and check that the drive straps securing the pressure plate to the cover do not show signs (such as a deep yellow or blue discoloration) of overheating. If the diaphragm spring is worn or damaged, or if its pressure is in any way suspect, the pressure plate assembly should be renewed.
11 Examine the machined bearing surfaces of the pressure plate and of the flywheel; they should be clean, completely flat, and free from scratches or scoring. If either is discoloured from excessive heat, or shows signs of cracks, it should be renewed - although minor damage of this nature can sometimes be polished away using emery paper.
12 Check that the release bearing contact surface rotates smoothly and easily, with no sign of noise or roughness. Also check that the surface itself is smooth and unworn, with no signs of cracks, pitting or scoring. If there is any doubt about its condition, the bearing must be renewed.

3.17 Tightening the pressure plate bolts - use a clutch-aligning tool to keep the clutch friction plate centralised

Refitting

13 On reassembly, ensure that the bearing surfaces of the flywheel and pressure plate are completely clean, smooth, and free from oil or grease. Use solvent to remove any protective grease from new components.
14 Fit the friction plate so that its spring hub assembly faces away from the flywheel; there may also be a marking showing which way round the plate is to be refitted.
15 Refit the pressure plate assembly, aligning the marks made on dismantling (if the original pressure plate is re-used), and locating the pressure plate on its three locating dowels. Fit the pressure plate bolts, but tighten them only finger-tight, so that the friction plate can still be moved.
16 The friction plate must now be centralised, so that when the transmission is refitted, its input shaft will pass through the splines at the centre of the friction plate.
17 Centralisation can be achieved by passing a screwdriver or other long bar through the friction plate and into the hole in the crankshaft; the friction plate can then be moved around until it is centred on the crankshaft hole. Alternatively, a clutch-aligning -tool can be used to eliminate the guesswork; these can be obtained from most accessory shops **(see illustration)**.

 A home-made aligning tool can be fabricated from a length of metal rod or wooden dowel which fits closely inside the crankshaft hole, and has insulating tape wound around it to match the diameter of the friction plate splined hole.

18 When the friction plate is centralised, tighten the pressure plate bolts evenly and in a diagonal sequence to the specified torque setting.
19 Apply a thin smear of molybdenum disulphide grease to the splines of the friction plate, the transmission input shaft and release fork shaft. Do not use too much grease as this may risk contaminating the clutch friction material.
Caution: *Later 'Sporting' models are fitted with a pre-lubricated release bearing - do not apply grease to this type of bearing, or to the transmission input shaft sleeve, as it may affect the bearing's lubricant coating.*
20 Refit the transmission as described in Chapter 7.

4 Clutch release mechanism - removal, inspection and refitting

Removal

1 Unless the complete engine/transmission is to be removed from the car and separated for major overhaul (see Chapter 2C), the clutch

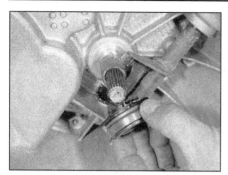

4.2 Unhook the release bearing from the fork and slide it off the transmission input shaft guide sleeve

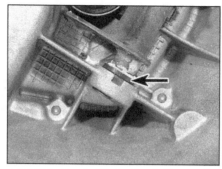

4.7 Release shaft lower bush (arrowed)

4.14 Release bearing correctly engaged with the release shaft fork

release mechanism can be reached by removing the transmission as described in Chapter 7.

2 Unhook the release bearing from the fork and slide it off the guide sleeve **(see illustration)**.

3 Using circlip pliers extract the circlip from the top of the release fork shaft.

4 Note the position of the arm then slide it off the splines.

5 Using a small drift, tap out the upper release shaft bush from the transmission casing.

6 Lift the release shaft from the lower bush then remove it from inside the transmission casing.

7 Extract the lower bush from the casing **(see illustration)**.

Inspection

8 Check the release mechanism, renewing any worn or damaged parts. Carefully check all bearing surfaces and points of contact.

9 When checking the release bearing itself, note that it is often considered worthwhile to renew it as a matter of course. Check that the contact surface rotates smoothly and easily, with no sign of roughness, and that the surface itself is smooth and unworn, with no signs of cracks, pitting or scoring. If there is any doubt about its condition, the bearing must be renewed.

Refitting

10 Apply a smear of molybdenum disulphide grease to the shaft pivot bushes and the contact surfaces of the release fork.

11 Tap the lower bush into the casing and refit the release fork and shaft.

12 Slide the upper bush down the shaft and tap it into the casing making sure that the ridge engages with the cut-out, then slide the arm on the splines the correct way round.

13 Refit the circlip in the shaft groove.

14 Slide the release bearing onto the guide sleeve and engage it with the fork **(see illustration)**.

15 Refit the transmission as described in Chapter 7.

Chapter 7
Manual transmission

Contents

Degrees of difficulty

Easy, suitable for novice with little experience	Fairly easy, suitable for beginner with some experience	Fairly difficult, suitable for competent DIY mechanic	Difficult, suitable for experienced DIY mechanic	Very difficult, suitable for expert DIY or professional

Specifications

General

Type . . . . Transverse mounted, front wheel drive layout with integral transaxle differential/final drive. 5 forward speeds, 1 reverse speed

Designation:
OHV engine C.501.5.10
OHC engine C.514.5.10
Lubricant capacity . . . . See Chapter 1

Torque wrench settings

	Nm	lbf ft
Roadwheel bolts	86	63
Transmission to engine bolt/nut	85	63

1 General information

The transmission is contained in a cast-aluminium alloy casing bolted to the engine's left-hand end, and consists of the gearbox and final drive differential.

Drive is transmitted from the crankshaft via the clutch to the input shaft, which has a splined extension to accept the clutch friction plate, and rotates in roller bearings at its right-hand end and ball bearings at its left-hand end. From the input shaft, drive is transmitted to the output shaft, which rotates in roller bearings at its right-hand end, and ball bearings at its left-hand end. From the output shaft, the drive is transmitted to the differential crownwheel, which rotates with the differential case and gears in taper roller bearings, thus driving the sun gears and driveshafts. The rotation of the differential gears on their shaft allows the inner roadwheel to rotate at a slower speed than the outer roadwheel when the car is cornering.

The input and output shafts are arranged side by side, parallel to the crankshaft and driveshafts, so that their gear pinion teeth are in constant mesh. In the neutral position, the relevant input shaft and output shaft gear pinions rotate freely, so that drive cannot be transmitted to the output shaft and crownwheel.

Gear selection is via a floor-mounted lever and two selector cables. The selector cables causes the appropriate selector fork to move its respective synchro-sleeve along the shaft, to lock the gear to the synchro-hub. Since the synchro-hubs are splined to the input and output shafts, this locks the gear to the shaft, so that drive can be transmitted. To ensure that gear-changing can be made quickly and quietly, a synchro-mesh system is fitted to all forward gears.

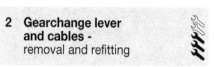

2.4a Improvised tool used for separating the gearchange cable balljoints on Sporting models

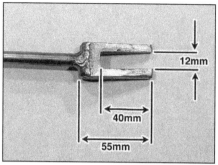

2.4b Fabricate the tapered, forked end to the dimensions shown

2.4c Insert the tool between the two halves of the balljoint and tap the end with a mallet to separate the joint

2 Gearchange lever and cables - removal and refitting

Removal

1 Jack up the front of the vehicle and support on axle stands (see *"Jacking and vehicle support"*).
2 Remove the exhaust system with reference to Chapter 4.
3 Unbolt the exhaust heatshield(s) and remove them from under the vehicle.
4 Working in the engine compartment, carefully prise the two gearchange cable balljoints from the selector levers on the transmission. To avoid damage to the balljoint assemblies, the fabrication of a special tool is recommended (see illustrations). Insert the forked tool under the balljoint head, then drive the balljoint off the selector levers by tapping the end of the tool with a mallet. The balljoints can also be separated by prising them apart with a pair of flat bladed screwdrivers, but this carries the risk of damaging the balljoints.
5 Using a pair of pliers, withdraw the metal retaining clips and release the gearchange cables from their support brackets (see illustrations).
6 Working inside the vehicle, remove the centre console (where applicable) and gearchange lever gaiter, as described in Chapter 11.

7 Remove the circlips and disconnect both gearchange cables from the base of the gearchange lever.
8 Working underneath the vehicle, unscrew the lower cover mounting bolts, then lower the assembly away from the underside of the vehicle (see illustration).
9 Using a pair of pliers, withdraw the metal retaining clips and release the gearchange cables from the lower cover.
10 Guide the gearchange cables out of the engine compartment and away from the underside of the vehicle.

Refitting

11 Refitting is a reversal of removal. Apply a little multi-purpose grease to all bearing surfaces, and tighten all nuts and bolts securely.

3 Manual transmission - removal and refitting

Removal

1 Select a solid, level surface to park the vehicle upon. Give yourself enough space to move around it easily. Disconnect the battery negative cable and position it away from the terminal.
2 Apply the handbrake firmly and chock both rear wheels. Jack up the front of the vehicle

and support securely on axle stands (see *"Jacking and vehicle support"*).
3 Remove the screws and detach the engine compartment lower cover(s).
4 Remove both front wheels, then undo the screws and remove the two-piece plastic liners from both front wheel arches.
5 Refer to Chapter 10 and separate both front suspension lower arms from their respective hub carriers. Remove the gaiter clips and disconnect the inner CV joints from the transmission plunge cups, with reference to Chapter 8. Secure the driveshafts away from the engine, to prevent them from obstructing the removal of the engine.
6 Unbolt the exhaust system front pipe from the exhaust manifold and the support bracket on the underside of the engine, with reference to Chapter 4. Remove the front pipe from the engine compartment.
7 Refer to Chapter 5A and remove the starter motor.
8 Remove the bolts and lower the flywheel protection plate away from the bottom of the bellhousing.
9 Remove the charcoal canister, together with its support bracket, from the front of the transmission casing with reference to Chapter 4. Secure the vacuum/vapour hoses away from the engine.
10 Remove the air cleaner and ducting as described in Chapter 4.
11 Disconnect the clutch cable from the transmission (refer to Chapter 6).

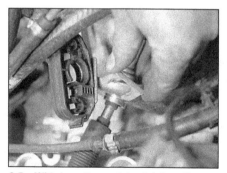

2.5a Withdraw the metal retaining clips . . .

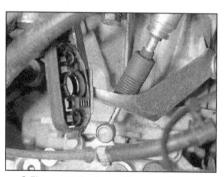

2.5b . . . and release the gearchange cables from their support brackets

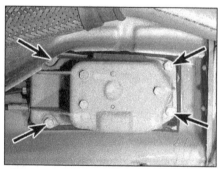

2.8 Unscrew the gearchange lever lower cover mounting bolts (arrowed)

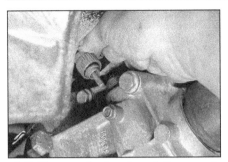

3.13 Unscrew the ferrule and disconnect the speedometer cable from the rear of the differential casing

3.14a Slacken and withdraw the clamp . . .

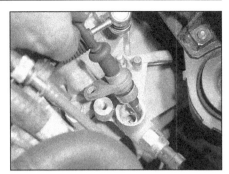

3.14b . . . then disconnect the reverse gear inhibitor cable

12 Refer to Section 2 and detach the gear-change and selector cables from the transmission.

13 Unscrew the ferrule and disconnect the speedometer cable from the rear of the differential casing **(see illustration)**.

14 Slacken and withdraw the clamp then disconnect the reverse gear inhibitor cable (where applicable) from the transmission casing **(see illustrations)**.

15 Unplug the wiring from the reversing lamp switch at the connector **(see illustration)**.

16 Unscrew the nut and disconnect the earth lead from the transmission **(see illustrations)**.

17 Release the plastic clips and free the main engine wiring harness from the top of the transmission casing.

18 Support the right-hand end of the engine using a lifting beam or engine hoist, then position a trolley jack with an interposed block of wood underneath the transmission casing.

Raise the jack so that it only just takes the weight of the transmission.

19 Working around the edge of the bellhousing, slacken and remove all **except** the uppermost bellhousing-to-engine block bolts **(see illustration)**.

20 With reference to Chapter 2A or 2B as applicable, unbolt the rear and left-hand engine mountings from the bodywork and transmission casing, and remove them from the engine compartment.

21 Unscrew the remaining bolt from the bellhousing and pull the transmission away from the engine. Lower it and remove it from under the vehicle **(see illustration)**.

Caution: Support the transmission to ensure that it remains steady on the jack head. Keep the transmission level until the input shaft is fully withdrawn from the clutch friction plate.

Refitting

22 Refitting is a reversal of the removal procedure, but note the following points:
a) *Apply a smear of high-melting-point grease to the clutch friction plate splines; take care to avoid contaminating the friction surfaces.*
b) *Tighten all bolts to the specified torque.*
c) *Fit new clips to secure the driveshaft gaiters to the transmission output shafts.*
d) *Adjust the clutch as described in Chapter 6.*

4 Manual transmission overhaul - general information

Overhauling a manual transmission is a difficult and involved job for the DIY home mechanic. In addition to dismantling and reassembling many small parts, clearances must be precisely measured and, if necessary, changed by selecting shims and spacers. Internal transmission components are also often difficult to obtain, and in many instances, extremely expensive. Because of this, if the transmission develops a fault or becomes noisy, the best course of action is to have the unit overhauled by a specialist repairer, or to obtain an exchange reconditioned unit.

Nevertheless, it is not impossible for the more experienced mechanic to overhaul the transmission, provided the special tools are available, and the job is done in a deliberate step-by-step manner, so that nothing is overlooked.

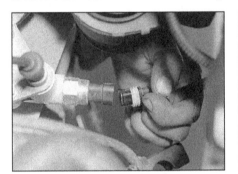

3.15 Unplug the wiring from the reversing lamp switch at the connector

3.16a Unscrew the nut . . .

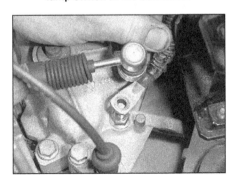

3.16b . . . and disconnect the earth lead from the transmission

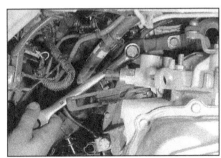

3.19 Work around the edge of the bellhousing and slacken the bellhousing-to-engine block bolts

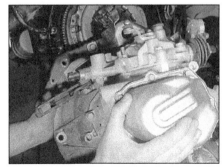

3.21 Removing the transmission from the engine compartment

The tools necessary for an overhaul include internal and external circlip pliers, bearing pullers, a slide hammer, a set of pin punches, a dial test indicator, and possibly a hydraulic press. In addition, a large, sturdy workbench and a vice will be required.

During dismantling of the transmission, make careful notes of how each component is fitted, to make reassembly easier and more accurate.

Before dismantling the transmission, it will help if you have some idea what area is malfunctioning. Certain problems can be closely related to specific areas in the transmission, which can make component examination and replacement easier. Refer to the *Fault Finding* Section at the end of this manual for more information.

5 Reversing light switch - testing, removal and refitting

Testing

1 The reversing light circuit is controlled by a plunger-type switch screwed into the front of the transmission casing. If a fault develops, first ensure that the circuit fuse has not blown.

2 To test the switch, disconnect the wiring connector, and use a multimeter (set to the resistance function) or a battery-and-bulb test circuit to check that there is continuity between the switch terminals only when reverse gear is selected. If this is not the case, and there are no obvious breaks or other damage to the wires, the switch is faulty and must be renewed.

Removal

3 Unplug the wiring connector from the switch.

4 Unscrew the switch body from the transmission casing.

Refitting

5 Refit the switch and tighten securely, then reconnect the wiring.

Chapter 8
Driveshafts

Contents

Degrees of difficulty

Easy, suitable for novice with little experience	Fairly easy, suitable for beginner with some experience	Fairly difficult, suitable for competent DIY mechanic	Difficult, suitable for experienced DIY mechanic	Very difficult, suitable for expert DIY or professional

Specifications

General

Driveshaft type	Solid steel shafts with inner and outer constant velocity (CV) joints, both outer joints are of the ball-and-cage type and the inner joints of the tripod type.

Torque wrench settings	Nm	lbf ft
Front hub nut	240	177
Lower arm balljoint nut	49	36
Track rod end balljoint-to-hub carrier nut	34	25

---

1 General information

Drive is transmitted from the differential to the front wheels by means of two, unequal-length driveshafts.

Each driveshaft is fitted with an inner and outer constant velocity (CV) joint. The inner constant velocity joint is of the tripod type and the outer joint is of the ball-and-cage type. Each outer joint is splined to engage with the wheel hub, and is threaded so that it can be fastened to the hub by a large nut. The inner joint tripod engages directly with the differential sungear.

On OHV engine models, the inboard end of the inner driveshaft gaiter is bolted directly to the differential casing, and so the gaiter remains stationary as the driveshaft rotates. To allow for this, a bearing is fitted to the driveshaft, and the outboard end of the gaiter is clamped to the bearing.

A vibration damper is fitted to the right-hand driveshaft, to reduce vibrations caused by the flexing of the long shaft.

2.2 Relieving the staking on the front hub nut

2 Driveshaft - removal and refitting

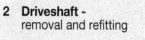

Removal

Note: *A balljoint separator tool will be required for this operation. A new hub nut must be used on refitting, and any Nyloc-type self-locking nuts must be renewed.*

Note: *The driveshaft outer joint splines may be a tight fit in the hub and it is possible that a puller/extractor will be required to draw the hub assembly off the driveshaft during removal.*

1 Chock the rear wheels, apply the handbrake, then jack up the front of the vehicle and support on axle stands (see *"Jacking and Vehicle Support"*). Remove the appropriate roadwheel.

2 Using a hammer and a suitable punch, relieve the staking on the front hub nut **(see illustration)**.

3 The front hub must be held stationary in order to loosen the hub nut. Ideally, the hub should be held by a suitable tool bolted into place using two of the roadwheel bolts **(see illustration)**. Alternatively, have an assistant firmly apply the brake pedal to prevent the hub from rotating. Using a socket and extension bar, slacken and remove the hub nut.

 Warning: The nut is extremely tight! Discard the nut - a new one must be used on refitting.

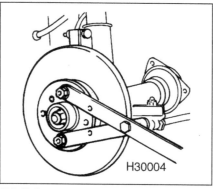

2.3 Using two lengths of metal bar to hold the front hub stationary when loosening the hub nut

4 Slacken the track-rod end balljoint nut, and unscrew it as far as the ends of the threads.

5 Disconnect the track-rod end balljoint from the hub carrier using a balljoint separator tool (leave the nut fitted to protect the threads), taking care not to damage the balljoint rubber seal **(see illustration)**. Once the balljoint has been released, remove the balljoint nut.

6 Counterhold the bolts, and unscrew the two nuts securing the hub carrier to the lower end of the suspension strut. Recover the washers. Withdraw the bolts, then separate the hub carrier from the strut, and remove the hub carrier **(see illustration)**.

7 The hub must now be freed from the end of the driveshaft. It should be possible to pull the hub carrier off the driveshaft, but if the end of the driveshaft is tight in the hub, temporarily refit the hub nut to protect the driveshaft threads, then tap the end of the driveshaft with a soft-faced hammer, or use a suitable puller to free it.

Caution: Do not allow the end of the driveshaft to hang down under its own weight, as this places strain on the CV joints; support the end of the shaft using wire or string.

8 Working at the inboard end of the driveshaft, release the clip securing the inboard driveshaft gaiter to the tripod housing on the transmission.

9 Release the tripod from the housing, then withdraw the driveshaft from under the vehicle **(see illustration)**.

2.5 Disconnecting the track-rod end balljoint using a balljoint separator tool

Refitting

10 Thoroughly clean the inboard driveshaft joint, the splines on the outboard driveshaft joint, and the apertures in the transmission and hub.

11 Apply a thin film of grease to the driveshaft splines and shoulder.

12 Offer up the driveshaft, and engage the tripod with the housing on the transmission. Push the joint fully into position, then fit the retaining clip to the gaiter (fit a new clip if necessary). Remove any slack in the gaiter retaining clip by carefully compressing the raised section of the clip. In the absence of the special tool, a pair of side cutters may be used.

13 Align the outer constant velocity joint splines with those of the hub, and slide the joint back into position in the hub.

14 Further refitting is a reversal of removal, bearing in mind the following points **(see illustration)**:

a) *Renew any Nyloc-type self-locking nuts on refitting.*

b) *Fit a new hub nut, and use the method used during removal to hold the hub stationary as the nut is tightened. Stake the nut in position once it has been tightened to the specified torque.*

c) *Tighten all fixings to the specified torque (where specified).*

2.6 Withdraw the bolts securing the hub carrier to the suspension strut

2.9 Withdrawing a driveshaft

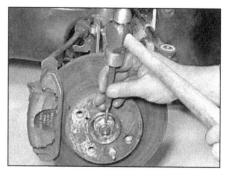

2.14 Staking a new hub nut into position

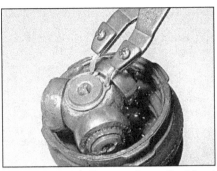

3.3a Use circlip pliers to release the tripod joint securing circlip . . .

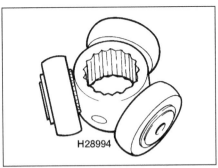

3.3b . . . then draw the tripod off the end of the driveshaft

3.8 Tapping the tripod joint onto the driveshaft splines

3 Driveshaft inner joint gaiter - renewal

1 With the driveshaft removed as described in Section 2, proceed as follows.
2 Fold the inner gaiter back from the tripod joint, then make alignment marks between the end of the shaft and the joint.
3 Using a pair of circlip pliers, remove the joint securing circlip then, using a puller if necessary, draw the tripod joint off the end of the driveshaft **(see illustrations)**. If a puller is used, ensure that the legs of the puller bear upon the cast centre section of the joint, not on the rollers.

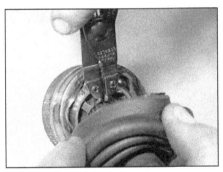

4.3a Using circlip pliers . . .

4 Release the clip securing the gaiter to the driveshaft, then slide the gaiter off the inner end of the driveshaft, and discard the gaiter.
5 Thoroughly clean the driveshaft splines, and CV joint components with paraffin or a suitable solvent, taking care not to remove the alignment marks made during removal.
6 Examine the CV joint components for wear and damage. Check that the rollers are free to rotate without resistance, and are not worn, damaged or corroded. The rollers are supported by arrays of needle bearings – wear or damage will show up as play in the rollers and/or roughness in rotation. If wear is discovered, the tripod joint must be renewed.
7 Fit a new gaiter to the inboard end of the driveshaft, and locate the smaller end of the gaiter on the driveshaft. Secure the smaller end of the gaiter with the retaining clip (fit a new clip if necessary).
8 Using the alignment marks made during removal, fit the tripod joint onto the driveshaft splines. Tap the joint into position, using a socket with an internal diameter slightly larger than that of the driveshaft as a drift **(see illustration)**. Secure the joint with the circlip (use a new circlip if the original shows any sign of wear or damage).
9 Slide the gaiter over the tripod joint, and pack the joint with grease from the gaiter kit.
10 Refit the driveshaft as described in Section 2.

4 Driveshaft outer joint gaiter - renewal

1 With the driveshaft removed as described in Section 2, proceed as follows.
2 Slacken the gaiter securing clips, and slide the gaiter back from the joint. Wipe away the old grease using a rag.
3 Mark the relationship between the joint and the driveshaft using a scriber or a dab of paint. Using a pair of circlip pliers, expand the circlip that secures the driveshaft in place, then withdraw the joint from the driveshaft **(see illustrations)**. Note that the circlip is captive in the joint, and need not be removed, unless it appears to be damaged or worn.
4 Slide the gaiter from the end of the driveshaft.
5 Fit a new rubber gaiter to the outboard end of the driveshaft, and locate the smaller end of the gaiter in the driveshaft groove **(see illustration)**. Secure the smaller end of the gaiter with the retaining clip (fit a new clip if necessary).
6 Pack the CV joint with grease from the gaiter kit.
7 Lubricate the splines of the driveshaft with a smear of grease, then push the driveshaft into the CV joint, aligning the marks made before removal, until the circlip snaps into

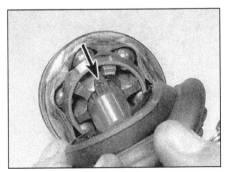

4.3b . . . expand the circlip (arrowed) . . .

4.3c . . . then withdraw the joint from the driveshaft

4.5 Fitting the new gaiter to the driveshaft

4.8 Pack the CV joint with the remainder of the grease from the gaiter kit

place. Pull on the driveshaft to ensure that the circlip has engaged securely locking the CV joint in position.

8 Pack the CV joint with the remainder of the grease from the gaiter kit, then slide the gaiter over the joint **(see illustration)**.

9 Lift the lip of the gaiter to expel any trapped air from the joint, then secure the gaiter in position with the larger securing clip (fit a new clip if necessary) **(see illustration)**.

10 Refit the driveshaft as described in Section 2.

5 Driveshaft inner joint gaiter bearing (OHV engines) - renewal

1 On OHV engine models, as the inboard end of the inner CV joint gaiter is secured directly to the differential housing, the outer end of the gaiter is secured to a bearing on the driveshaft, to prevent the gaiter from twisting as the driveshaft rotates.

Renewal

Note: *A suitable bearing puller will be required to draw the bearing off the driveshaft.*

2 With the driveshaft inner joint gaiter removed as described in Section 3, proceed as follows.

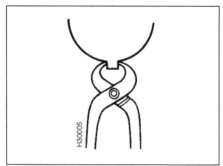

4.9 The gaiter clips can be secured using side cutters

3 Check that the bearing outer race rotates smoothly and easily, without any signs of roughness or undue free play between the inner and outer races. If necessary, renew the bearing as follows.

4 Using a long-reach universal bearing puller, carefully draw the bearing off the driveshaft inner end.

5 Apply a smear of grease to the inner race of the new bearing, then fit the bearing over the end of the driveshaft. Using a soft-faced hammer, and a suitable piece of tubing which bears only on the bearing inner race, tap the new bearing into position until it is located as shown **(see illustration)**.

6 Check that the bearing rotates freely, then refit the inner joint gaiter as described in Section 3.

7 Refit the driveshaft as described in Section 2.

6 Right-hand driveshaft damper - general information

1 Due to the long length of the right-hand driveshaft, a vibration damper is fitted towards the centre of the shaft.

2 Two types of damper may be fitted. The first type of damper consists of two metal halves secured to the driveshaft with clamp bolts. The second type of damper is a single piece of rubber, secured to the driveshaft using a clip – the driveshaft outer joint must be removed in order to remove this type of damper.

3 If the damper is removed for any reason, measure its original fitted position, and refit it in exactly the same position **(see illustration)**.

7 Driveshaft overhaul - general information

If any of the checks described in Chapter 1 reveal wear in any driveshaft joint, first remove the roadwheel trim or the roadwheel (as appropriate), for access to the front hub nut.

Relieve the staking on the front hub nut, then unscrew the nut (refer to Section 2), and use a torque wrench to check that the nut is tightened to the specified torque. Repeat this check on the remaining front hub nut. Ensure that the hub nuts are staked into position on completion, ideally, new nuts should be fitted.

Road test the vehicle, and listen for a metallic clicking from the front as the vehicle is driven slowly in a circle on full-lock. If a clicking noise is heard, this indicates wear in the outer constant velocity joint. This means that the joint must be renewed; reconditioning is not possible.

If vibration, consistent with road speed, is felt through the car when accelerating, there is a possibility of wear in the inner constant velocity joints.

To check the joints for wear, remove the driveshafts, then dismantle them as described in Sections 3 and 4; if any wear or free play is found, the affected joint must be renewed. Refer to your Fiat dealer for information on the availability of driveshaft components.

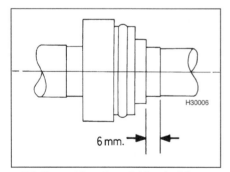

5.5 Correct location of driveshaft inner joint gaiter bearing – OHV engine models

6 mm.

6.3 Single-piece rubber driveshaft damper (arrowed)

Chapter 9
Braking system

Contents

Degrees of difficulty

Easy, suitable for novice with little experience		Fairly easy, suitable for beginner with some experience		Fairly difficult, suitable for competent DIY mechanic		Difficult, suitable for experienced DIY mechanic		Very difficult, suitable for expert DIY or professional	

Specifications

Front brakes
Disc diameter . . . . 240.0 mm
Disc thickness:
  New . . . . 10.8 to 11.1 mm
  Minimum thickness after refinishing . . . . 9.55 mm
  Minimum (wear limit) . . . . 9.2 mm
Maximum disc run-out (typical figure) . . . . 0.15 mm
Brake pad friction material minimum thickness . . . . 1.5 mm

Rear brakes
Drum internal diameter:
  New . . . . 185.24 to 185.53 mm
  Maximum diameter after refinishing . . . . 186.33 mm
  Minimum (wear limit) . . . . 186.83 mm
Brake shoe friction material minimum thickness . . . . 1.5 mm

Torque wrench settings	Nm	lbf ft
Brake disc securing bolt	12	9
Brake hose-to-front caliper union nut	15	11
Brake pedal securing nut (left-hand-drive models)	32	24
Brake pipe union nuts:		
M10	11	8
M12	18	13
Front caliper mounting bracket bolts	53	39
Handbrake lever securing nuts	15	11
Master cylinder securing nuts	20	15
Rear brake backplate bolts	24	18
Rear brake drum securing bolt	12	9
Rear brake pressure-regulating valve bolt/nut	24	18
Rear wheel cylinder securing bolts	10	7
Roadwheel bolts	86	63
Vacuum servo mounting nuts	25	18

1 General information

The braking system is of the vacuum servo-assisted, dual-circuit hydraulic type. The arrangement of the hydraulic system is such that each circuit operates one front and one rear brake from a tandem master cylinder. Under normal circumstances, both circuits operate in unison. However, in the event of hydraulic failure in one circuit, full braking force will still be available at two diagonally-opposite wheels.

All models covered in this manual are fitted with front disc brakes and rear drum brakes.

The front disc brakes are actuated by single-piston sliding type calipers, which ensure that equal pressure is applied to each disc pad.

The rear drum brakes incorporate leading and trailing shoes, which are actuated by twin-piston wheel cylinders. A friction self-adjust mechanism is incorporated, to automatically compensate for brake shoe wear. As the brake shoe linings wear, the footbrake operation automatically operates the adjuster mechanism, which effectively repositions the brake shoes, to remove the lining-to-drum clearance.

The mechanical handbrake linkage operates the brake shoes via levers attached to the trailing brake shoes.

Load sensitive proportioning valves operate on the rear brake hydraulic circuits, to prevent the possibility of the rear wheels locking before the front wheels under heavy braking.

 Warning: When servicing any part of the system, work carefully and methodically; also observe scrupulous cleanliness when overhauling any part of the hydraulic system. Always renew components (in axle sets, where applicable) if in doubt about their condition, and use only genuine Fiat replacement parts, or at least those of known good quality. Note the warnings given in "Safety first" and at relevant points in this Chapter concerning the dangers of asbestos dust and hydraulic fluid.

2.13a Removing the dust cap from a front brake caliper bleed screw

2 Hydraulic system - bleeding

 Warning: Hydraulic fluid is poisonous; wash off immediately and thoroughly in the case of skin contact, and seek immediate medical advice if any fluid is swallowed, or gets into the eyes. Certain types of hydraulic fluid are inflammable, and may ignite when allowed into contact with hot components. When servicing any hydraulic system, it is safest to assume that the fluid IS inflammable, and to take precautions against the risk of fire as though it is petrol that is being handled. Hydraulic fluid is also an effective paint stripper, and will attack plastics; if any is spilt, it should be washed off immediately, using copious quantities of fresh water. Finally, it is hygroscopic (it absorbs moisture from the air) - old fluid may be contaminated and unfit for further use. When topping-up or renewing the fluid, always use the recommended type, and ensure that it comes from a freshly-opened sealed container.

General

1 The correct operation of any hydraulic system is only possible after removing all air from the components and circuit; and this is achieved by bleeding the system.

2 During the bleeding procedure, add only clean, unused hydraulic fluid of the recommended type; never re-use fluid that has already been bled from the system. Ensure that sufficient fluid is available before starting work.

3 If there is any possibility of incorrect fluid being already in the system, the brake components and circuit must be flushed completely with uncontaminated, correct fluid, and new seals should be fitted throughout the system.

4 If hydraulic fluid has been lost from the system, or air has entered because of a leak, ensure that the fault is cured before proceeding further.

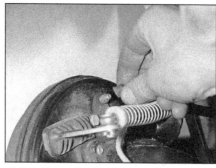

2.13b Removing the dust cap from a rear wheel cylinder bleed screw

5 Check that all pipes and hoses are secure, unions tight and bleed screws closed. Remove the dust caps (where applicable), and clean any dirt from around the bleed screws.

6 Unscrew the master cylinder reservoir cap, and top the master cylinder reservoir up to the "MAX" level line; refit the cap loosely. Remember to maintain the fluid level at least above the "MIN" level line throughout the procedure, otherwise there is a risk of further air entering the system.

7 There are a number of one-man, do-it-yourself brake bleeding kits currently available from motor accessory shops. It is recommended that one of these kits is used whenever possible, as they greatly simplify the bleeding operation, and also reduce the risk of expelled air and fluid being drawn back into the system. If such a kit is not available, the basic (two-man) method must be used, which is described in detail below.

8 If a kit is to be used, prepare the vehicle as described previously, and follow the kit manufacturer's instructions, as the procedure may vary slightly according to the type being used; generally, they are as outlined below in the relevant sub-section.

9 Whichever method is used, the same sequence must be followed (paragraphs 10 and 11) to ensure removal of all air from the system.

Bleeding sequence

10 If the system has been only partially disconnected, and suitable precautions were taken to minimise fluid loss, it should be necessary to bleed only that part of the system (ie the primary or secondary circuit).

11 If the complete system is to be bled, then it should be done working in the following sequence:
   a) *Left-hand rear wheel.*
   b) *Right-hand front wheel.*
   c) *Right-hand rear wheel.*
   d) *Left-hand front wheel.*

Bleeding - basic (two-man) method

12 Collect a clean glass jar, a suitable length of plastic or rubber tubing which is a tight fit over the bleed screw, and a ring spanner to fit the screw. The help of an assistant will also be required.

13 Remove the dust cap from the first screw in the sequence if not already done (see illustrations). Fit a suitable spanner and tube to the screw, place the other end of the tube in the jar, and pour in sufficient fluid to cover the end of the tube.

14 Ensure that the master cylinder reservoir fluid level is maintained at least above the "MIN" level line throughout the procedure.

15 Have the assistant fully depress the brake pedal several times to build up pressure, then maintain it on the final downstroke.

16 While pedal pressure is maintained, unscrew the bleed screw (approximately one turn) and allow the compressed fluid and air to

flow into the jar. The assistant should maintain pedal pressure, following the pedal down to the floor if necessary, and should not release the pedal until instructed to do so. When the flow stops, tighten the bleed screw again, have the assistant release the pedal slowly, and recheck the reservoir fluid level.

17 Repeat the steps given in paragraphs 15 and 16 until the fluid emerging from the bleed screw is free from air bubbles. If the master cylinder has been drained and refilled, and air is being bled from the first screw in the sequence, allow approximately five seconds between cycles for the master cylinder passages to refill.

18 When no more air bubbles appear, tighten the bleed screw securely, remove the tube and spanner, and refit the dust cap (where applicable). Do not overtighten the bleed screw.

19 Repeat the procedure on the remaining screws in the sequence, until all air is removed from the system, and the brake pedal feels firm again.

Bleeding - using a one-way valve kit

20 As their name implies, these kits consist of a length of tubing with a one-way valve fitted, to prevent expelled air and fluid being drawn back into the system; some kits include a translucent container, which can be positioned so that the air bubbles can be more easily seen flowing from the end of the tube.

21 The kit is connected to the bleed screw, which is then opened. The user returns to the driver's seat, depresses the brake pedal with a smooth, steady stroke, and slowly releases it; this is repeated until the expelled fluid is clear of air bubbles.

22 Note that these kits simplify work so much that it is easy to forget the master cylinder reservoir fluid level; ensure that this is maintained at least above the "MIN" level line at all times.

Bleeding - using a pressure-bleeding kit

23 These kits are usually operated by the reservoir of pressurised air contained in the spare tyre. However, note that it will probably be necessary to reduce the pressure to a lower level than normal; refer to the instructions supplied with the kit.

24 By connecting a pressurised, fluid-filled container to the master cylinder reservoir, bleeding can be carried out simply by opening each screw in turn (in the specified sequence), and allowing the fluid to flow out until no more air bubbles can be seen in the expelled fluid.

25 This method has the advantage that the large reservoir of fluid provides an additional safeguard against air being drawn into the system during bleeding.

26 Pressure-bleeding is particularly effective when bleeding "difficult" systems, or when bleeding the complete system at the time of routine fluid renewal.

All methods

27 When bleeding is complete, and firm pedal feel is restored, wash off any spilt fluid, tighten the bleed screws securely, and refit their dust caps (where applicable).

28 Check the hydraulic fluid level in the master cylinder reservoir, and top-up if necessary (see "Weekly checks").

29 Discard any hydraulic fluid that has been bled from the system; it will not be fit for re-use.

30 Check the feel of the brake pedal. If it feels at all spongy, air must still be present in the system, and further bleeding is required. Failure to bleed satisfactorily after a reasonable repetition of the bleeding procedure may be due to worn master cylinder seals.

3 Hydraulic pipes and hoses – renewal

Note: *Before starting work, refer to the note at the beginning of Section 2 concerning the dangers of hydraulic fluid.*

1 If any pipe or hose is to be renewed, minimise fluid loss by first removing the master cylinder reservoir cap, then tighten the cap down onto a piece of polythene to obtain an airtight seal. Alternatively, flexible hoses can be sealed, if required, using a proprietary brake hose clamp; metal brake pipe unions can be plugged (if care is taken not to allow dirt into the system) or capped immediately they are disconnected. Place a wad of rag under any union that is to be disconnected, to catch any spilt fluid.

2 If a flexible hose is to be disconnected, unscrew the brake pipe union nut before removing the spring clip which secures the hose to its mounting bracket **(see illustration).**

3 To unscrew the union nuts, it is preferable to obtain a brake pipe spanner of the correct size; these are available from most large motor accessory shops. Failing this, a close-fitting open-ended spanner will be required, though if the nuts are tight or corroded, their flats may be rounded-off if the spanner slips. In such a case, a self-locking wrench is often the only way to unscrew a stubborn union, but it follows that the pipe and the damaged nuts must be renewed on reassembly. Always clean a union and surrounding area before disconnecting it. If disconnecting a component with more than one union, make a careful note of the connections before disturbing any of them.

4 If a brake pipe is to be renewed, it can be obtained, cut to length and with the union nuts and end flares in place, from Fiat dealers. All that is then necessary is to bend it to shape, following the line of the original, before fitting it to the vehicle. Alternatively, most motor accessory shops can make up brake

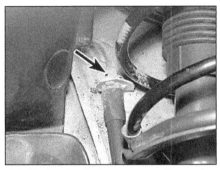

3.2 Brake pipe-to-hose connection under front wing. Spring clip arrowed

pipes from kits, but this requires very careful measurement of the original, to ensure that the replacement is of the correct length. The safest answer is usually to take the original to the shop as a pattern.

5 On refitting, do not overtighten the union nuts. It is not necessary to exercise brute force to obtain a sound joint.

6 Ensure that the pipes and hoses are correctly routed, with no kinks, and that they are secured in the clips or brackets provided. After fitting, remove the polythene from the reservoir, and bleed the hydraulic system as described in Section 2. Wash off any spilt fluid, and check carefully for fluid leaks.

4 Front brake pads – renewal

⚠️ *Warning: Renew BOTH sets of front brake pads at the same time - NEVER renew the pads on only one wheel, as uneven braking may result.*

⚠️ *Warning: Note that the dust created by wear of the pads may contain asbestos, which is a health hazard. Never blow it out with compressed air, and don't inhale any of it. An approved filtering mask should be worn when working on the brakes. DO NOT use petrol or petroleum-based solvents to clean brake parts; use proprietary brake cleaner or methylated spirit only.*

1 Chock the rear wheels, apply the handbrake, then jack up the front of the vehicle and support it on axle stands (see "Jacking and Vehicle Support"). Remove the front roadwheels.

2 Working on one side of the vehicle, push the caliper piston into its bore by pulling the caliper outwards. Keep a careful eye on the level of brake fluid in the reservoir as you do this - ensure that the level does not rise above the "MAX" level marking.

3 Release the caliper brake fluid hose from the bracket at the base of the suspension strut **(see illustration).**

4 Remove the locking clip and extract the lower slide pin from the caliper **(see illustrations).**

4.3 Release the fluid hose from the bracket on the suspension strut

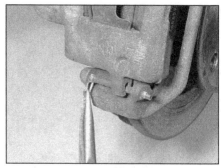

4.4a Remove the locking clip . . .

4.4b . . . and the lower slide pin . . .

5 Pivot the caliper body upwards and support in position with a length of wire or a cable-tie **(see illustration)**. Avoid straining the hydraulic hose.

Caution: Do not depress the brake pedal until the caliper is refitted, or the piston will be pushed out of its bore.

6 Withdraw the brake pads from the caliper mounting bracket **(see illustration)**.

7 Measure the thickness of each brake pad's friction material **(see illustration)**. If either pad is worn at any point to the specified minimum thickness or less, all four pads must be renewed. Also, the pads should be renewed if any are fouled with oil or grease; there is no satisfactory way of degreasing friction material, once contaminated. If any of the brake pads are worn unevenly, or are fouled with oil or grease, trace and rectify the cause before reassembly.

 Warning: Do not be tempted to swap brake pads over to compensate for uneven wear.

8 If the brake pads are still serviceable, carefully clean them using a clean, fine wire brush or similar and brake cleaning fluid. Pay particular attention to the sides and back of the metal backing. Where applicable, clean out the grooves in the friction material, and pick out any large embedded particles of dirt or debris.

9 Clean the surfaces of the brake pad contact points in the caliper body and caliper mounting bracket.

10 Prior to fitting the pads, check that the guide pin can slide freely in the caliper body, and check that the rubber guide pin seal is undamaged. Brush the dust and dirt from the caliper and piston, but *do not* inhale it, as it may contain asbestos.

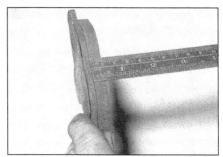

4.7 Measure the thickness of the brake pad friction material

4.5 . . . then pivot the caliper body upwards . . .

11 Inspect the dust seal and the area around the piston for signs of damage, corrosion or brake fluid leaks. If evident, refer to Section 8 and overhaul the caliper assembly.

12 If new brake pads are to be fitted, the caliper piston must be pushed back into the cylinder, to allow for the extra depth of the friction material. Either use a G-clamp or similar tool, or use suitable pieces of wood as levers **(see illustration)**. Provided that the master cylinder reservoir has not been overfilled with hydraulic fluid, there should be no spillage, but keep a careful watch on the fluid level while retracting the piston. If the fluid level rises above the "MAX" level mark at any time, the surplus should be siphoned off, or ejected via a plastic tube connected to the bleed screw (see Section 2).

 Warning: Do not syphon the fluid by mouth, as it is poisonous; use a syringe or an old poultry baster.

13 Apply a little high temperature brake grease to the contact surfaces of the pad backing plates; take great care not to allow any grease onto the pad friction linings. Similarly, apply brake grease to the pad contact points on the caliper mounting bracket - again take care not to apply excess grease, which may contaminate the pads.

14 Place the brake pads in position on the caliper mounting bracket, with the friction material facing the surfaces of the brake disc.

15 Pivot the caliper body down over the brake pads, then refit the slide pin and locking clip.

16 Check that the caliper body can slide freely on the guide pin. Ensure that the flexible

4.6 . . . and withdraw the brake pads

hydraulic hose is not twisted or kinked in any way. Turn the steering from lock to lock and check that the hose does not chafe against the suspension or steering gear.

17 Repeat the procedure to renew the pads on the remaining front caliper.

18 With both sets of front brake pads fitted, depress the brake pedal repeatedly until the pads are pressed into firm contact with the brake disc, and normal pedal pressure is restored. Any "sponginess" felt when depressing the pedal is most probably due to air trapped inside the hydraulic system - refer to Section 2 and bleed the hydraulic system before progressing any further.

19 Refit the roadwheels, and lower the vehicle to the ground.

20 Check the brake fluid level as described in "*Weekly checks*".

21 Check the operation of the braking system thoroughly using the vehicle on the road.

4.12 Using a G-clamp and a block of wood to push the caliper piston into the cylinder

5.5a Detach the lower . . .

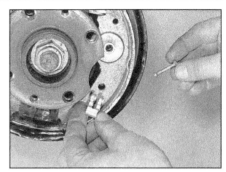

5.5b . . . and then the upper return springs

5.6 Remove the shoe hold-down clips and recover the pins

5.7 Fitting a cable-tie to hold the wheel cylinder pistons in the retracted position

5.8 Removing the trailing shoe. Note cut-out (1) in hub aligned with friction adjuster (2) on brake shoe

5 Rear brake shoes – renewal

 Warning: Renew BOTH sets of rear brake shoes at the same time - NEVER renew the shoes on only one wheel, as uneven braking may result.

 Warning: Before starting work, refer to the warning given at the beginning of Section 4, concerning the dangers of asbestos dust.

Note: *A new handbrake cable-to-handbrake operating lever split-pin should be used on refitting.*

1 Remove the rear brake drum, as described in Section 7.

2 Working on one side of the vehicle, brush the dirt and dust from the brake backplate and drum. Avoid inhaling the dust, as it may contain asbestos, which is a health hazard.

3 Measure that thickness of friction material remaining on each brake shoe, and renew all four shoes as a set if any are worn down to the minimum thickness or less.

4 Note the position of each shoe, and the location of the return springs.

5 Detach the lower and then the upper return springs from both brake shoes, using a suitable pair of pliers, and a large screwdriver as a lever **(see illustrations)**.

 Warning: It is advisable to wear eye protection during this procedure.

6 Again using a pair of pliers, remove the shoe hold-down clips, and recover the pins from the rear of the brake backplate **(see illustration)**.

7 Carefully push the wheel cylinder pistons into the wheel cylinder, until the brake shoes are clear of the slots in the pistons, then hold

the pistons retracted using a cable-tie or a large rubber band **(see illustration)**.

8 Turn the hub until the one of the cut-outs in its edge aligns with the friction adjuster on the trailing shoe, then lever the bottom of the shoe out from the lower anchor, and withdraw the leading shoe from the backplate and the handbrake operating strut **(see illustration)**.

9 Similarly, turn the hub until one of the cut-outs in its edge aligns with the friction adjuster on the leading shoe, then lever the bottom of the shoe out from the lower anchor, and withdraw the trailing shoe from the backplate and the handbrake operating strut **(see illustrations)**.

5.9a Lever the bottom of the leading shoe from the lower anchor . . .

5.9b . . . then withdraw the leading shoe

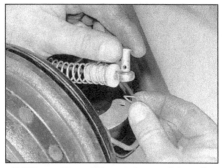

5.10a Remove the split-pin . . .

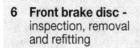

5.10b . . . then slide out the retaining pin and disconnect the handbrake cable from the lever

5.11 Manipulate the handbrake operating strut assembly out from the backplate

10 Working at the rear of the backplate, remove the split-pin, then slide out the retaining pin, and disconnect the handbrake cable from the handbrake operating lever. Recover the washers, noting their locations **(see illustrations)**.
11 Manipulate the handbrake operating strut assembly out from the front of the backplate, turning the hub as necessary to allow the strut assembly to pass out **(see illustration)**.
12 If there is any evidence of fluid leakage from the wheel cylinder, it should be renewed, as described in Section 9.
13 Thoroughly clean the surface of the backplate using brake component cleaner to remove all traces of dust and old lubricant. Examine all components for signs of corrosion, wear and damage.
14 Apply brake grease sparingly to the shoe contact surfaces on the brake backplate.
15 Manipulate the handbrake operating strut assembly back into position, ensuring that the lever passes through the hole in the brake backplate.
16 Reconnect the handbrake cable to the handbrake operating lever, and secure the retaining pin with a new split-pin. Ensure that the washers are positioned as noted before removal.
17 Turn the hub as necessary to align one of the cut-outs with the friction adjuster on the leading shoe, then fit the new leading shoe, ensuring that the shoe engages with the handbrake operating lever strut and the lower anchor, and that the friction adjuster locates over the lug on the brake backplate.

18 Repeat the procedure to fit the new trailing shoe.
19 Refit the shoe hold-down pins and secure with the clips **(see illustration)**.
20 Refit the upper and lower return springs, making sure that they are correctly fitted as noted before removal **(see illustration)**.
Caution: Take care, as the springs have a very high tension – refitting is a tricky procedure!
21 Refit the brake drum as described in Section 7.
22 Repeat the procedure on the remaining side of the vehicle.
23 Depress the brake pedal several times to bring the shoes into contact with the drums, then check and if necessary adjust the operation of the handbrake mechanism, as described in Section 13.
24 Lower the vehicle to the ground, and thoroughly check the operation of the braking system before using the vehicle on the road.

6 Front brake disc - inspection, removal and refitting

Note: Before starting work, refer to the note at the beginning of Section 4 concerning the dangers of asbestos dust.

Inspection

Note: If either disc requires renewal, BOTH should be renewed at the same time, to ensure even and consistent braking. New

brake pads should also be fitted.
1 Apply the handbrake, then jack up the front of the vehicle and support it on axle stands (see *"Jacking and Vehicle Support"*). Remove the appropriate front roadwheel.
2 Slowly rotate the brake disc so that the full area of both sides can be checked. Remove the brake pads if better access is required to the inboard surface. Light scoring is normal in the area swept by the brake pads, but if heavy scoring or cracks are found, the disc must be renewed. If light scoring is found, it may be possible to have the disc refinished, provided that the minimum refinishing thickness is not exceeded (see *"Specifications"*).
3 It is normal to find a lip of rust and brake dust around the disc's perimeter - this can be scraped off if required. If, however, a lip has formed due to excessive wear of the brake pad swept area, then the disc's thickness must be measured using a micrometer **(see illustration)**. Take measurements at several places around the disc, at the inside and outside of the pad swept area. If the disc has worn at any point to the specified minimum thickness or less, the disc must be renewed.
4 If the disc is thought to be warped, it can be checked for run-out. Ensure that the disc securing bolt and wheel locating pin are tight. Either use a dial gauge mounted on any convenient fixed point, while the disc is slowly rotated, or use feeler blades to measure (at several points all around the disc) the clearance between the disc and a fixed point, such as the caliper mounting bracket **(see illustration)**. If the measurements obtained

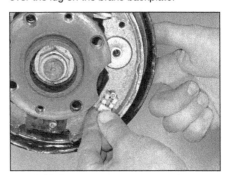

5.19 Refit the shoe hold-down pins and secure with the clips

5.20 Brake shoe components correctly reassembled

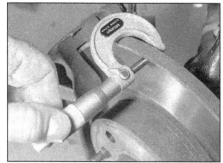

6.3 Measuring brake disc thickness using a micrometer

6.4 Checking for brake disc run-out using a dial gauge

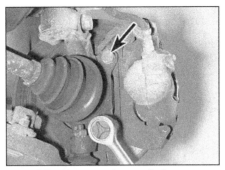

6.7a Unscrew the two bolts . . .

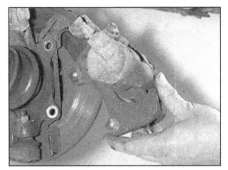

6.7b . . . and slide the caliper assembly off the disc

6.8a Removing the wheel locating pin. Note alignment marks on disc, wheel spacer and hub

6.8b Remove the wheel spacer . . .

6.8c . . . and the disc

are excessive, the disc must be renewed, however, it is worth checking first that the hub bearing is in good condition (see Chapter 1 and/or 10).

5 Check the disc for cracks, especially around the wheel bolt holes, and any other wear or damage, and renew if necessary.

Removal

6 With the front of the vehicle raised and the wheel removed, where applicable, release the caliper brake fluid hose from the bracket at the base of the suspension strut.

7 Slacken and remove the two bolts securing the brake caliper mounting bracket to the hub carrier. Slide the caliper assembly (complete with the brake pads) off the disc, and suspend the assembly from the suspension strut coil spring, using a piece of wire or string, to avoid placing any strain on the brake fluid hose **(see illustrations)**.

8 Use chalk or paint to mark the relationship of the disc and, where applicable, the wheel spacer, to the hub, then unscrew the disc securing screw and the wheel locating pin, and remove the wheel spacer (where applicable) and disc **(see illustrations)**. If the disc is tight, lightly tap its rear face with a soft-faced mallet.

Refitting

9 Refitting is the reverse of the removal procedure, noting the following points:

a) *Ensure that the mating surfaces of the disc, wheel spacer (where applicable) and hub are clean and flat.*

b) *If a new disc has been fitted, use a suitable solvent to wipe any preservative coating from the disc, before refitting the caliper.*

c) *Make sure that the marks made on the disc, wheel spacer (where applicable) and hub before removal are aligned.*

d) *Slide the caliper into position, making sure the pads pass either side of the disc, and tighten the caliper mounting bracket bolts to the specified torque setting.*

e) *Refit the roadwheel then lower the vehicle to the ground and tighten the wheel bolts to the specified torque. Apply the footbrake several times to force the pads back into contact with the disc before driving the vehicle.*

7.3a Unscrew the drum securing screw (arrowed) and the wheel locating pin . . .

7 Rear brake drum - removal, inspection and refitting

Note: *Before starting work, refer to the note at the beginning of Section 4 concerning the dangers of asbestos dust.*

Removal

1 Chock the front wheels and select 1st gear, then jack up the rear of the vehicle and support securely on axle stands (see *"Jacking and Vehicle Support"*). Remove the relevant rear roadwheel.

2 Working under the vehicle, back off the handbrake cable adjustment as described in Section 13.

3 Use chalk or paint to mark the relationship of the drum to the hub, then unscrew the drum securing screw and the wheel locating pin, and remove the drum. If the drum is tight, two suitable bolts can be screwed into the holes provided in the drum – tighten the bolts to force off the drum, then unscrew the bolts once the drum has been removed **(see illustrations)**.

Inspection

4 Working carefully, remove all traces of brake dust from the drum, but *avoid inhaling the dust, as it is injurious to health.*

5 Scrub clean the outside of the drum, and check it for obvious signs of wear or damage such as cracks around the roadwheel bolt holes; renew the drum if necessary.

7.3b ... and remove the drum

7.3c If the drum is tight, it can be forced off using two bolts

6 Examine carefully the inside of the drum. Light scoring of the friction surface is normal, but if heavy scoring is found, the drum must be renewed. It is usual to find a lip on the drum's inboard edge which consists of a mixture of rust and brake dust; this should be scraped away to leave a smooth surface which can be polished with fine (120 to 150 grade) emery paper. If the lip is due to the friction surface being recessed by wear, then the drum must be refinished (within the specified limits) or renewed.

7 If the drum is thought to be excessively worn or oval, its internal diameter must be measured at several points using an internal micrometer. Take measurements in pairs, the second at right-angles to the first, and compare the two to check for signs of ovality. Minor ovality can be corrected by machining; otherwise, renew the brake drum.

Refitting

8 If a new brake drum is to be fitted, use a suitable solvent to remove any preservative coating that may have been applied to its interior.

9 Ensure that the mating faces of the hub and drum are clean, then slide the drum into position on the hub, and refit and tighten the securing screw and the wheel locating pin.

10 Depress the footbrake several times to bring the shoes into contact with the drum.

11 Check the operation of the handbrake, and adjust if necessary as described in Section 13.

12 Refit the roadwheel then lower the vehicle to the ground and tighten the wheel bolts to the specified torque.

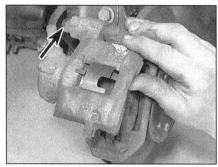

8.5 Unscrew the upper caliper guide pin bolt (arrowed)

8 Front brake caliper - removal, overhaul and refitting

Note: *Before starting work, refer to the note at the beginning of Section 2 concerning the dangers of hydraulic fluid, and to the warning at the beginning of Section 4 concerning the dangers of asbestos dust.*

Removal

1 Chock the rear wheels, apply the handbrake, then jack up the front of the vehicle and support it securely on axle stands (see *"Jacking and vehicle support"*). Remove the appropriate front roadwheel.

2 Remove the brake pads as described in Section 4.

3 To minimise fluid loss during the following operations, remove the master cylinder reservoir cap, then tighten it down onto a piece of polythene, to obtain an airtight seal. Alternatively, use a brake hose clamp to seal off the flexible hose running to the caliper.

⚠️ **Warning: Do not use an ordinary G-clamp or mole grips for this purpose, as these can easily damage the hydraulic hose internally, possibly leading to failure.**

4 Clean the area surrounding the brake hose union on the caliper, then slacken the union using a ring spanner. It won't be possible to separate the union completely without twisting the hose at this stage.

5 Unscrew the caliper upper guide pin bolt using a hexagon bit or Allen key, and remove the caliper body from the mounting bracket **(see illustration)**.

6 Hold the brake hose and rotate the caliper to unscrew the hose union from the caliper body. Recover the sealing washer(s). Cover the open ends of the hose union and the caliper fluid inlet, to prevent dirt entry. Alternatively, the flexible brake hose may be disconnected from the rigid brake pipe, at the bracket mounted on the inner wheel arch.

7 If desired, the caliper mounting bracket can be removed from the hub carrier after unscrewing the two securing bolts.

Overhaul

Note: *Before commencing work, ensure that the appropriate caliper overhaul kit is obtained.*

8 With the caliper on the bench, wipe away all traces of dust and dirt, but *avoid inhaling the dust, as it is a health hazard.*

9 Place a small block of wood between the caliper body and the piston, to act as padding. Remove the piston by applying a jet of compressed air (such as that produced by a tyre foot pump) to the fluid inlet port.

⚠️ **Warning: Protect your hands and eyes when using compressed air in this manner - brake fluid may be ejected under pressure when the piston is popped out of its bore.**

10 Peel the dust seal from the piston, then use a soft, blunt instrument (ie, **not** a screwdriver) to extract the piston seal from the caliper bore **(see illustration)**.

11 Thoroughly clean all components, using only methylated spirit or clean hydraulic fluid. Never use mineral-based solvents such as petrol or paraffin, which will attack the hydraulic system rubber components.

12 The caliper piston seal, the dust seal and the bleed nipple dust cap, are only available as part of a seal kit. Since the manufacturers recommend that the piston seal and dust seal are renewed whenever they are disturbed, all of these components should be discarded on disassembly and new ones fitted on reassembly as a matter of course.

13 Carefully examine all parts of the caliper assembly, looking for signs of wear or damage. In particular, the cylinder bore and piston must be free from any signs of scratches, corrosion or wear. If there is any doubt about the condition of any part of the caliper, the relevant part should be renewed. Note that the piston surface is plated, and **must not** be polished with emery or similar abrasives to remove corrosion or scratches. In addition, the pistons are matched to the caliper bores and can only be renewed as part of a complete caliper assembly.

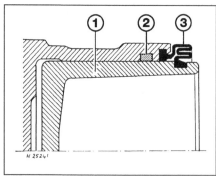

8.10 Sectional view of piston, caliper body and seals

1 Piston

2 Piston (fluid) seal

3 Dust seal

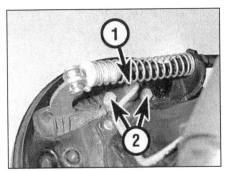

9.3 Rear wheel cylinder hydraulic pipe union (1) and securing bolts (2)

14 Check that the threads in the caliper body and the mounting bracket are in good condition. Check that the guide pin is undamaged, and (when cleaned) a reasonably tight sliding fit in the mounting bracket bore.

15 Use compressed air to blow clear the fluid passages.

 Warning: Wear eye protection when using compressed air.

16 Before commencing reassembly, ensure that all components are spotlessly-clean and dry.

17 Soak the new piston seal in clean hydraulic fluid, and fit it to the groove in the cylinder bore, using your fingers only (no tools) to manipulate it into place.

18 Fit the new dust seal inner lip to the cylinder groove, smear clean hydraulic fluid over the piston and caliper cylinder bore, and twist the piston into the dust seal. Press the piston squarely into the cylinder, then slide the dust seal outer lip into the groove in the piston.

Refitting

19 Where applicable, refit the caliper mounting bracket to the hub carrier. Coat the threads of the mounting bolts with locking compound, then tighten them to the specified torque.

20 Place the caliper in position on the mounting bracket, then refit the caliper upper guide pin bolt, and tighten to the specified torque.

21 Refit the brake pads as described in Section 4.

22 Check that the caliper slides smoothly on the guide pin.

23 Check that the brake fluid hose is correctly routed, without being twisted or kinked, then reconnect the union to the caliper, using new sealing washer(s).

24 Reposition the brake fluid hose in the bracket at the base of the suspension strut.

25 Remove the polythene from the master cylinder reservoir cap, or remove the clamp from the fluid hose, as applicable.

26 Bleed the hydraulic fluid circuit as described in Section 2. Note that if no other part of the system has been disturbed, it should only be necessary to bleed the relevant front circuit.

27 Depress the brake pedal repeatedly to bring the pads into contact with the brake disc, and ensure that normal pedal pressure is restored.

28 Refit the roadwheel, lower the vehicle to the ground and tighten the wheel bolts to the specified torque.

9 Rear wheel cylinder – removal, overhaul and refitting

⚠ *Warning: Before starting work, refer to the note at the beginning of Section 2 concerning the dangers of hydraulic fluid, and to the warning at the beginning of Section 4 concerning the dangers of asbestos dust.*

Removal

1 Remove the relevant rear brake shoes as described in Section 5.

2 To minimise fluid loss during the following operations, remove the master cylinder reservoir cap, then tighten it down onto a piece of polythene, to obtain an airtight seal.

3 Clean the brake backplate around the wheel cylinder mounting bolts and the hydraulic pipe union, then unscrew the union nut and disconnect the hydraulic pipe **(see illustration)** from the wheel cylinder. Plug or cover the open ends of the pipe and the master cylinder to prevent dirt ingress.

4 Unscrew the securing bolts, then withdraw the wheel cylinder from the backplate.

Overhaul

Note: *Before commencing work, ensure that the appropriate wheel cylinder overhaul kit is obtained.*

5 Clean the assembly thoroughly, using only methylated spirit or clean brake fluid.

6 Peel off both rubber dust covers, then use paint or similar to mark one of the pistons so that the pistons are not interchanged on reassembly **(see illustration)**.

7 Withdraw both pistons and the spring/washer assembly.

8 Discard the rubber piston seals and the dust covers. These components should be renewed as a matter of course, and are available as part of an overhaul kit, which also includes the bleed nipple dust cap.

9 Check the condition of the cylinder bore and the piston - the surfaces must be perfect and free from scratches, scoring and corrosion. It is advisable to renew the complete wheel cylinder if there is any doubt as to the condition of the cylinder bore or piston.

10 Ensure that all components are clean and dry. The pistons, spring and seals should be fitted wet, using hydraulic fluid as a lubricant - soak them in clean fluid before installation.

11 Fit the seals to the pistons, ensuring that they are the correct way round. Use only your fingers (no tools) to manipulate the seals into position.

12 Fit the first piston to the cylinder, taking care not to distort the seal. If the original pistons are being re-used, the marks made on dismantling should be used to ensure that the pistons are refitted to their original bores.

13 Refit the spring/washer assembly and the second piston.

14 Apply a smear of rubber grease to the exposed end of each piston and to the dust cover sealing lips, then fit the dust covers to each end of the wheel cylinder.

Refitting

15 Refitting is a reversal of removal, bearing in mind the following points:
a) Tighten the mounting bolts to the specified torque.
b) Refit the brake shoes as described in Section 5, and refit the brake drum as described in Section 7.
c) Before refitting the roadwheel and lowering the vehicle to the ground, remove the polythene from the fluid reservoir, and bleed the hydraulic system as described in Section 2. Note that if no other part of the system has been disturbed, it should only be necessary to bleed the relevant rear circuit.

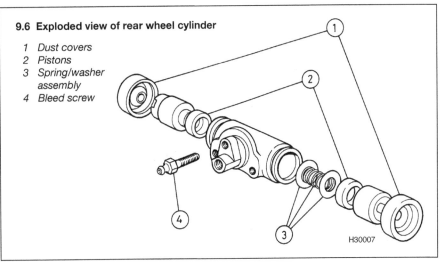

9.6 Exploded view of rear wheel cylinder

1 Dust covers
2 Pistons
3 Spring/washer assembly
4 Bleed screw

H30007

10.3 Disconnect the brake pipes (arrowed) from the master cylinder

10 Master cylinder -
removal, overhaul and refitting

Note: *Before starting work, refer to the warning at the beginning of Section 2 concerning the dangers of hydraulic fluid.*

Removal

1 Remove the master cylinder fluid reservoir cap, and syphon the hydraulic fluid from the reservoir. Alternatively, open any convenient bleed screw in the system, and gently pump the brake pedal to expel the fluid through a tube connected to the screw (see Section 2). Disconnect the wiring connector from the brake fluid level sender unit incorporated in the reservoir cap.

⚠️ *Warning: Do not syphon the fluid by mouth, as it is poisonous; use a syringe or an old poultry baster.*

10.4 Master cylinder securing nut (arrowed)

2 Carefully prise the fluid reservoir from the seals and release it from the top of the master cylinder.

3 Wipe clean the area around the brake pipe unions on the top of the master cylinder, and place absorbent rags beneath the pipe unions to catch any surplus fluid. Make a note of the correct fitted positions of the unions, then unscrew the union nuts and carefully withdraw the four pipes **(see illustration)**. Plug or tape over the pipe ends and master cylinder openings, to minimise the loss of brake fluid, and to prevent the entry of dirt into the system. Wash off any spilt fluid immediately with cold water.

> **HAYNES HiNT** *Cut the finger tips from an old rubber glove and secure them over the open ends of the brake pipes with elastic bands - this will help to minimise fluid loss and prevent the entry of dirt.*

4 Slacken and remove the nuts securing the master cylinder to the vacuum servo unit (note that the nuts also secure the pressure-regulating valve bracket), then withdraw the master cylinder from the engine compartment **(see illustration)**.

5 Where applicable, recover the seals from the rear of the master cylinder, and discard them - new seals should be used on refitting.

Overhaul

6 No spare parts are available for the master cylinder assembly, and if faulty, the complete assembly must be renewed.

Refitting

7 With the master cylinder removed, check that the distance between the end of the vacuum servo unit pushrod and the master cylinder mating surface is as shown **(see illustration)**. If necessary, the distance may be adjusted by turning the nut at the end of the servo unit pushrod.

8 Remove all traces of dirt from the master cylinder and servo unit mating surfaces, and where applicable, fit a new seal between the master cylinder body and the servo.

9 Fit the master cylinder to the servo unit, ensuring that the servo unit pushrod enters the master cylinder bore centrally.

10 Refit the master cylinder mounting nuts, and tighten them to the specified torque setting.

11 Wipe clean the brake pipe unions, then reconnect them to the correct master cylinder ports, as noted before removal, and tighten the union nuts to the specified torque setting.

12 Fit new rubber seals and then press the fluid reservoir into the ports at the top of the master cylinder.

13 Refill the master cylinder reservoir with new fluid, and bleed the complete hydraulic system as described in Section 2.

14 Check the operation of the braking system thoroughly before using the vehicle on the road.

11 Vacuum servo unit -
testing, removal and refitting

Testing

1 To test the operation of the servo unit, depress the footbrake several times to exhaust the vacuum, then start the engine whilst keeping the pedal firmly depressed. As the engine starts, there should be a noticeable "give" in the brake pedal as the vacuum builds up. Allow the engine to run for at least two minutes, then switch it off. If the brake pedal is now depressed it should feel normal, but further applications should result in the pedal feeling firmer, with the pedal stroke decreasing with each application.

2 If the servo does not operate as described, first inspect the servo unit check valve as described in Section 12.

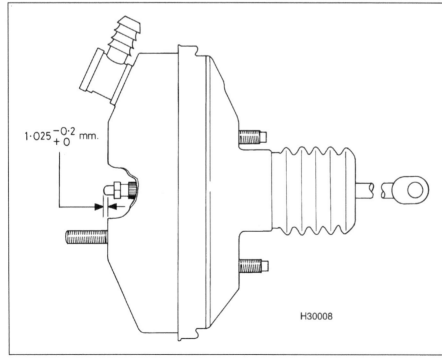

$1.025 ^{-0.2}_{+0}$ mm.

H30008

10.7 Check the distance between the end of the pushrod and the master cylinder mating surface

3 If the servo unit still fails to operate satisfactorily, the fault lies within the unit itself. Repairs to the unit are not possible - if faulty, the servo unit must be renewed.

Removal

Note: *A new servo pushrod-to-brake pedal split-pin should be used on refitting.*
4 Remove the master cylinder as described in Section 10.
5 Working in the engine compartment, slide the rear brake pressure regulator support bracket from the servo studs.
6 Working inside the car, in the footwell, unbolt the servo cover **(see illustration)**.
7 Remove the split-pin and pull out the clevis pin, and disconnect the servo pushrod from the pedal linkage. Recover the washer(s).
8 Unscrew the four nuts securing the brake servo to the engine compartment bulkhead **(see illustration)**.
9 Working in the engine compartment, carefully pull the check valve from the grommet in the servo casing.
10 Carefully manipulate the servo out from the engine compartment.

Refitting

11 Refitting is a reversal of removal, but use a new split-pin to secure the servo pushrod to the brake pedal, and refit the master cylinder as described in Section 10.

12 Vacuum servo unit check valve - removal, testing and refitting

Removal

1 The check valve is a push-fit in the grommet at the front of the brake vacuum servo **(see illustration)**.
2 Release the securing clip, and disconnect the vacuum hose from the check valve.
3 Withdraw the valve from its rubber sealing grommet, using a pulling and twisting motion. Remove the grommet from the servo.

Testing

4 Examine the check valve and hose for signs of damage, and renew if necessary. The valve may be tested by blowing through the hose in both directions. Air should flow through the valve in one direction only - when blown through from the servo unit end of the hose. Renew the valve and hose assembly if this is not the case.
5 Examine the servo unit rubber sealing grommet for signs of damage or deterioration, and renew as necessary.

Refitting

6 Fit the grommet into position in the servo unit.

11.6 Unbolt the servo cover – right-hand-drive model shown

7 Carefully ease the check valve into position, taking care not to displace or damage the grommet. Reconnect the vacuum hose to the valve, and refit the retaining clip.
8 On completion, start the engine and check the check valve-to-servo unit connection for signs of air leaks.

13 Handbrake – adjustment

1 Jack up the vehicle, and support it securely on axle stands (see *"Jacking and Vehicle Support"*).
2 Working inside the vehicle, pull up the handbrake lever to the third click of the ratchet.
3 Working under the vehicle floor, locate the handbrake adjuster, and slacken the adjuster locknut whilst counterholding the adjuster nut with a second spanner **(see illustration)**.
4 Turn the adjuster nut until the cable running forwards to the handbrake lever is taught, then tighten the locknut.
5 Release the handbrake, and check that the rear wheels are free to turn without binding, then pull the handbrake lever up three to four clicks, and check that the rear wheels are locked.
6 On completion, apply a little grease to the handbrake adjuster mechanism to prevent corrosion, then lower the vehicle to the ground.

12.1 Vacuum servo check valve location (arrowed)

11.8 Unscrew the four servo securing nuts (arrowed) – right-hand-drive model shown

14 Handbrake lever - removal and refitting

Removal

1 Jack up the vehicle, and support it securely on axle stands (see *"Jacking and Vehicle Support"*).
2 Disconnect the handbrake cable from the lever assembly as described in Section 15.
3 Working inside the vehicle, lift up the carpet for access to the handbrake lever securing bolts, as follows. Alternatively, the carpet can be slit with a sharp knife or scissors to enable access to the bolts.
  a) *Remove the front seats as described in Chapter 11.*
  b) *Unscrew and remove the front seat belt lower anchor bolts.*
  c) *Release the rear carpet panel securing clips.*
  d) *Fold the carpet panel forwards for access to the handbrake lever securing bolts.*
4 Unscrew the four bolts, and lift out the handbrake lever and withdraw it from the vehicle.

Refitting

5 Refitting is a reversal of removal, but reconnect the handbrake cable to the lever as described in Section 15, then adjust the handbrake mechanism as described in Section 13. Where applicable, tighten the front seat belt lower anchor bolts to the specified torque (see Chapter 11 Specifications).

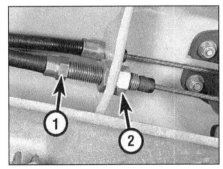

13.3 Handbrake adjuster nut (1) and locknut (2)

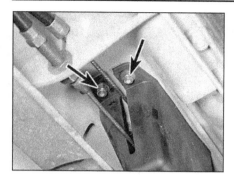

15.2a Unscrew the securing nuts – rear nuts arrowed . . .

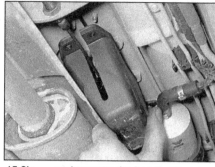

15.2b . . . and remove the handbrake lever cover

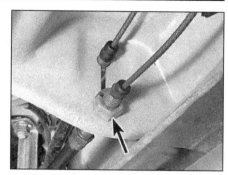

15.3 Slacken the handbrake adjuster locknut (arrowed)

15.4a Remove the split-pin . . .

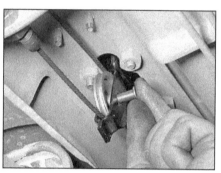

15.4b . . . pull out the pin . . .

15.4c . . . and remove the pulley

15 Handbrake cable - removal and refitting

Removal

1 Jack up the vehicle, and support it securely on axle stands (see *"Jacking and Vehicle Support"*).

2 Fully release the handbrake then, working under the vehicle, unscrew the securing nuts, and remove the handbrake lever cover **(see illustrations)**. Recover the washers.

3 Slacken the handbrake adjuster locknut **(see illustration)**.

4 Remove the split-pin and recover the washer, then pull out the pin securing the handbrake cable equaliser pulley to the lever assembly. Remove the pulley **(see illustrations)**.

5 Fully unscrew the handbrake adjuster locknut from the adjuster rod, then pass the slotted nut over the cable to remove it **(see illustration)**.

6 Working at each rear brake assembly in turn, remove the split-pin, then slide out the retaining pin, and disconnect the handbrake

cable from the handbrake operating lever. Recover the washers, noting their locations **(see illustration)**.

7 Working along the length of the cable, release the cable from the clips and brackets underneath the vehicle, noting the cable routing to aid refitting, then feed the cable through the slot in the bracket under the vehicle, and withdraw the cable assembly **(see illustrations)**.

Refitting

8 Refitting is a reversal of removal, bearing in mind the following points:

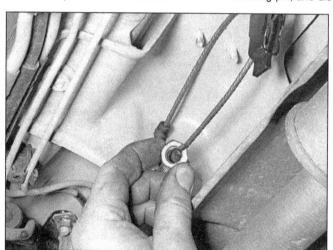

15.5 Withdraw the adjuster nut over the cable

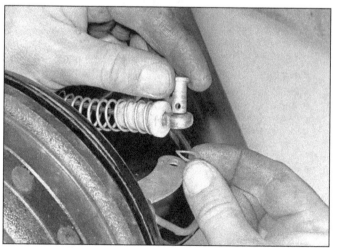

15.6 Slide out the retaining pin and disconnect the cable from the handbrake operating lever

15.7a Release the cable from the brackets on the rear suspension trailing arms . . .

a) Ensure that the cable is routed as noted before removal.
b) Use new split-pins to secure the handbrake cable ends to the operating levers, and make sure that the washers are located as noted before removal.
c) On completion, adjust the handbrake cable mechanism as described in Section 13.

16 Rear brake pressure-regulating valves - removal and refitting

Removal

1 Two rear brake pressure-regulating valves are fitted, mounted on a bracket secured by the master cylinder-to-vacuum servo nuts, in the engine compartment **(see illustration)**.
2 Remove the brake fluid master cylinder fluid reservoir cap, and syphon the hydraulic fluid from the reservoir. Alternatively, open any convenient bleed screw in the system, and gently pump the brake pedal to expel the fluid through a tube connected to the screw (see Section 2). Disconnect the wiring connector from the brake fluid level sender unit incorporated in the reservoir cap.

 Warning: Do not syphon the fluid by mouth, as it is poisonous; use a syringe or an old poultry baster.

3 Wipe clean the area around the brake pipe unions on the relevant pressure-regulating

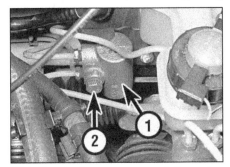

16.1 Rear brake pressure-regulating valve (1) and securing bolt (2)

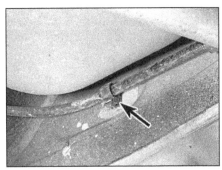

15.7b . . . and from the clips under the vehicle

valve, and place absorbent rags beneath the pipe unions to catch any surplus fluid. Make a note of the correct fitted positions of the unions, then unscrew the union nuts and carefully withdraw the two pipes. Plug or tape over the pipe ends and valve openings, to minimise the loss of brake fluid, and to prevent the entry of dirt into the system. Wash off any spilt fluid immediately with cold water.

 HAYNES HiNT *Cut the finger tips from an old rubber glove and secure them over the open ends of the brake pipes with elastic bands - this will help to minimise fluid loss and prevent the entry of dirt.*

4 Unscrew the nut or bolt, as applicable, securing the valve to the mounting bracket, then withdraw the valve.

Refitting

5 Refit the valve securing nut or bolt, and tighten it securely.
6 Wipe clean the brake pipe unions, then reconnect them to the correct valve ports, as noted before removal, and tighten the union nuts securely.
7 Refill the master cylinder reservoir with new fluid, and bleed the complete hydraulic system as described in Section 2.
8 Check the operation of the braking system thoroughly before using the vehicle on the road.

17.3 Stop-light switch locknut (arrowed) – viewed from under facia

17 Stop-light switch - removal, refitting and adjustment

Removal

1 Disconnect the battery negative lead.
2 Reach up under the fascia, and disconnect the wiring plug from the switch, which is located above the brake pedal.
3 Slacken the switch locknut, then unscrew the switch and withdraw it from the top of the mounting bracket **(see illustration)**. Note that the rubber cover over the end of the switch will be left in position between the pedal and the mounting bracket as the switch is removed.

Refitting

4 Refitting is a reversal of removal, but make sure that the rubber cover engages correctly with the switch and, before tightening the switch locknut, adjust the switch as follows.

Adjustment

5 Working under the fascia, above the brake pedal, slacken the switch locknut.
6 Turn the switch to adjust its position in the mounting bracket, until the stop-lights come on as soon as light pressure is applied to the brake pedal. If a large adjustment is required, temporarily disconnect the switch wiring plug to avoid twisting the wiring.

18 Handbrake "on" warning light switch – removal and refitting

Removal

1 Disconnect the battery negative lead.
2 Working below the handbrake lever, unscrew the handbrake "on" warning light switch securing screw **(see illustration)**. Note that it may be necessary to back-off the handbrake adjustment so that the handbrake lever can be pulled up sufficiently to use a screwdriver on the switch securing screw.
3 Lift the switch from the floor, and disconnect the wiring connector.

Refitting

4 Refitting is a reversal of removal.

18.2 Unscrewing the handbrake "on" warning light switch securing screw (arrowed)

Notes

Chapter 10
Suspension and steering

Contents

Degrees of difficulty

Easy, suitable for novice with little experience	Fairly easy, suitable for beginner with some experience	Fairly difficult, suitable for competent DIY mechanic	Difficult, suitable for experienced DIY mechanic	Very difficult, suitable for expert DIY or professional

Specifications

Wheel alignment and steering angles*

Front wheel castor:	
All except "Sporting" models	1°40' ± 30'
"Sporting" models	1°36' ± 30'
Front wheel camber:	
All except "Sporting" models	0°30' ± 30'
"Sporting" models	0°5' ± 30'
Front wheel toe-setting (all models)	0 ± 1.0 mm toe-in
Rear wheel camber:	
All except "Sporting" models	0°30' ± 30'
"Sporting" models	0°1' ± 30'
Rear wheel toe-setting:	
All except "Sporting" models	0 ± 3 mm toe-in
"Sporting" models	1.0 ± 3.0 mm toe-out

*Measured with tyres inflated to correct pressures, and fuel tank empty (5 litres of fuel).

Torque wrench settings	Nm	lbf ft
Front suspension		
Front hub nut	240	177
Lower arm balljoint nut	49	36
Lower arm front mounting nut	88	65
Lower arm rear mounting bolts	88	65
Suspension strut piston rod nut	88	65
Suspension strut-to-body nuts	25	18
Suspension strut-to-hub carrier nuts	108	78
Rear suspension		
Rear hub nut	216	159
Rear suspension crossmember mounting bolts	88	65
Shock absorber securing bolts	49	36
Trailing arm pivot nuts	88	65
Steering		
Lower steering column securing nuts	25	18
Steering column/intermediate shaft pinch-bolt nut	20	15
Steering gear securing bolts	49	36
Steering wheel nut	50	37
Track-rod end balljoint-to-hub carrier nut	34	25
Roadwheels		
Wheel bolts	86	63

2.2 Relieving the staking on a front hub nut

1 General information

Front suspension

The front suspension is independent, comprising transverse lower wishbones, coil spring-over-damper (McPherson) strut units and, on "Sporting" models, an anti-roll bar. The hub carriers are bolted to the base of the strut units and are linked to the lower arms by means of balljoints. The front suspension components are bolted directly to the body shell.

Rear suspension

The rear suspension incorporates a torsion beam axle, trailing arms, coil springs and separate telescopic shock absorbers. The components form a separate sub-assembly which can be unbolted from the underside of the vehicle as a complete unit, or the components can be removed individually.

Steering

The steering is of conventional rack-and-pinion type, incorporating a collapsible safety column. The column is joined to the steering gear via an intermediate shaft and universal joints. The steering gear is bolted directly to the bodyshell. The steering gear track-rods are attached via the track-rod ends to the steering arms on the hub carriers.

Certain later models are fitted with a driver's airbag system. Sensors built into the vehicle body are triggered in the event of a front end collision and prompt an Electronic Control Unit (ECU) to activate the airbag, mounted in the centre of the steering wheel. This reduces the risk of the driver striking the steering wheel during an accident.

⚠️ **Warning: Refer to the appropriate warnings given in Chapter 12 when working on a vehicle equipped with an air bag.**

2 Front hub carrier – removal and refitting

Note: *A balljoint separator tool will be required for this operation. A new hub nut must be used on refitting, and any Nyloc-type self-locking nuts must be renewed.*
Note: *The driveshaft outer joint splines may be a tight fit in the hub and it is possible that a puller/extractor will be required to draw the hub assembly off the driveshaft during removal.*

Removal

1 Chock the rear wheels, apply the handbrake, then jack up the front of the vehicle and support on axle stands (see "Jacking and Vehicle Support"). Remove the appropriate roadwheel.
2 Using a hammer and a suitable punch, relieve the staking on the front hub nut **(see illustration)**.
3 The front hub must be held stationary in order to loosen the hub nut. Ideally, the hub should be held by a suitable tool bolted into place using two of the roadwheel bolts **(see illustration)**. Alternatively, have an assistant firmly apply the brake pedal to prevent the hub from rotating. Using a socket and extension bar, slacken and remove the hub nut.

⚠️ **Warning: The nut is extremely tight! Discard the nut - a new one must be used on refitting.**

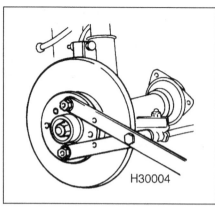

H30004

2.3 Using two lengths of metal bar to hold the front hub stationary when loosening the hub nut

4 Remove the brake disc as described in Chapter 9.
5 Slacken the track-rod end balljoint nut, and unscrew it as far as the ends of the threads.
6 Disconnect the track-rod end balljoint from the hub carrier using a balljoint separator tool (leave the nut fitted to protect the threads), taking care not to damage the balljoint rubber seal **(see illustration)**. Once the balljoint has been released, remove the balljoint nut.
7 Counterhold the bolts, and unscrew the two nuts securing the hub carrier to the lower end of the suspension strut **(see illustration)**. Recover the washers. Withdraw the bolts, then separate the hub carrier from the strut, and remove the hub carrier.
8 The hub must now be freed from the end of the driveshaft. It should be possible to pull the hub carrier off the driveshaft, but if the end of the driveshaft is tight in the hub, temporarily refit the hub nut to protect the driveshaft threads, then tap the end of the driveshaft with a soft-faced hammer, or use a suitable puller to free it **(see illustration)**.
Caution: Do not allow the end of the driveshaft to hang down under its own weight, as this places strain on the CV joints; support the end of the shaft using wire or string.

2.6 Disconnecting the track-rod end balljoint using a balljoint separator tool

2.7 Counterhold the bolts and unscrew the nuts securing the hub carrier to the suspension strut

2.8 Free the hub from the end of the driveshaft

5

9 Repeat the procedure in paragraphs 5 and 6 to disconnect the lower arm-to-hub carrier balljoint, then withdraw the hub carrier **(see illustrations)**.

Refitting

10 Refitting is a reversal of removal, bearing in mind the following points.
  a) *Renew any Nyloc-type self-locking nuts on refitting.*
  b) *Refit the brake disc with reference to Chapter 9.*
  c) *Fit a new hub nut, and use the method used during removal to hold the hub stationary as the nut is tightened. Stake the new nut in position.*
  d) *Tighten all fixings to the specified torque.*

3 Front hub bearings – renewal

Note: *A press, a suitable puller, or similar improvised tools will be required for this operation. Obtain a bearing overhaul kit before proceeding. A new bearing retaining circlip should be used on refitting.*

1 With the hub carrier removed as described in Section 2, proceed as follows.
2 The hub must now be removed from the bearing/hub carrier assembly. It is preferable to use a press to do this, but it is possible to drive out the hub using a metal tube of suitable diameter. Alternatively a suitable puller can be used.

3.5 Removing a front wheel bearing retaining circlip

3.10 Drawing the hub into the hub bearing using improvised tools

2.9a Use a balljoint separator tool to disconnect the lower arm-to-hub carrier balljoint . . .

3 Securely support the hub carrier, on two metal bars for instance, with the inner face uppermost then, using a metal bar or tube of suitable diameter, press or drive the hub from the hub bearing. Alternatively, use the puller to separate the hub from the bearing. Note that the bearing outer race will remain on the hub.
4 Using a suitable puller, pull the outer bearing race from the hub. Alternatively, support the bearing race on suitably thin metal bars, and press or drive the hub from the bearing race.
5 Remove the bearing retaining circlip from the inner face of the hub carrier – discard the circlip, a new one must be used on refitting **(see illustration)**.
6 Temporarily refit the outer bearing race to the bearing, then support the inner face of the hub carrier, and press or drive out the bearing.

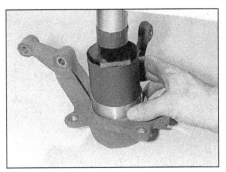

3.8 Pressing a front wheel bearing into position using a metal tube on the outer race

4.1a Removing the rubber cover from the top of the suspension strut

2.9b . . . then withdraw the hub carrier

7 Before fitting the new bearing, thoroughly clean the bearing location in the hub carrier.
8 Support the outer face of the hub carrier then, using a suitable metal bar or tube on the bearing outer race, press the new bearing into position **(see illustration)**. The outer face of the bearing should contact the shoulder in the hub carrier. It may be possible to pull the bearing into position using a suitable puller. A puller can be improvised using a socket, nut, washers and a length of threaded bar.
9 Fit a new bearing retaining circlip to the inner face of the hub carrier.
10 Press or draw the hub into the bearing. The bearing inner track must be supported during this operation. This can be achieved using a socket, nut, washers and a length of threaded bar **(see illustration)**.
11 Refit the hub carrier as described in Section 2.

4 Front suspension strut – removal, overhaul and refitting

Removal

Note: *Any Nyloc-type self-locking nuts must be renewed on refitting.*

1 If the strut is to be dismantled, the piston rod nut must be initially slackened before the strut is removed, with the vehicle resting on its wheels, as follows **(see illustrations)**.
  a) *Working in the engine compartment, pull the rubber cover from the top of the strut.*

4.1b Slackening the suspension strut piston rod nut. Strut top mounting locking plate arrowed

4.5 Release the brake caliper fluid hose
from the bracket on the strut

4.6 Withdraw the bolts securing the hub
carrier to the suspension strut

b) *Using a socket and a long extension bar,
slacken, but do not remove, the strut
piston rod nut. Note that it may be
necessary to counterhold the strut top
mounting locking plate. Fiat use a special
tool (No 1857510000) for this purpose,
but it should be possible to achieve the
same effect using a large pair of grips.*

2 Chock the rear wheels and apply the
handbrake, then jack up the front of the
vehicle and support securely on axle stands
(see *"Jacking and Vehicle Support"*). Remove
the appropriate roadwheel.

3 Slacken the track-rod end balljoint nut, and
unscrew it as far as the ends of the threads.

4 Disconnect the track-rod end balljoint from
the hub carrier using a balljoint separator tool
(leave the nut fitted to protect the threads),
taking care not to damage the balljoint rubber
seal. Once the balljoint has been released,
remove the balljoint nut.

5 Release the brake caliper fluid hose from
the bracket on the strut **(see illustration)**.

6 Counterhold the bolts, and unscrew the two
nuts securing the hub carrier to the lower end
of the suspension strut. Recover the washers.
Withdraw the bolts, then separate the hub
carrier from the strut **(see illustration)**.

7 If the left-hand suspension strut is being
removed, unscrew the three securing nuts,
and move the engine management electronic
control unit (ECU), complete with its mounting
bracket, to one side, for access to the
suspension strut top mounting nuts **(see
illustrations)**.

8 If not already done, pull the rubber cover
from the top of the strut in the engine
compartment.

9 Have an assistant support the strut from
under the wheel arch then, working in the
engine compartment, unscrew the three
suspension strut-to-body nuts – **do not**

remove the strut piston rod nut **(see
illustration)**. Recover the washers, noting
their locations. If the right-hand strut is being
removed, note that two of the strut mounting
nuts also secure the coolant reservoir.

10 Lower the strut assembly from under the
wheel arch **(see illustration)**.

Overhaul

Note: *Suitable spring compressor tools will be
required for this operation.*

11 With the suspension strut resting on a
bench, or clamped in a vice, fit suitable spring
compressor tools, and compress the coil spring
to relieve the pressure on the spring seats **(see
illustration)**. Ensure that the compressor tool is
securely located on the spring, in accordance
with the tool manufacturer's instructions. Take
care, as the spring is offset – some conventional
spring compressor tools cannot be used safely
for this operation.

12 Unscrew the piston rod nut. It may be
necessary to counterhold the strut top
mounting locking plate (Fiat use a special tool,
No 1857510000, for this purpose, but it
should be possible to achieve the same effect
using a large pair of grips).

13 Remove the piston rod nut, followed by
the top mounting locking plate, the bush and
top mounting assembly, the upper spring seat
assembly (metal plate and rubber), the spring,
the washer, the rubber bump stop and the
gaiter.

14 With the strut assembly now completely
dismantled, examine all the components for
wear, damage or deformation, and check the
thrust bearing in the top mounting plate for
smoothness of operation. Renew any of the
components as necessary.

15 Examine the strut for signs of fluid
leakage. Check the strut piston for signs of
pitting along its entire length, and check the
strut body for signs of damage. While holding
it in an upright position, test the operation of
the strut by moving the piston through a full
stroke, and then through short strokes of 50
to 100 mm. In both cases, the resistance felt
should be smooth and continuous. If the
resistance is jerky or uneven or if there is any
visible sign of wear or damage to the strut,
renewal is necessary.

16 If any doubt exists as to the condition of
the coil spring, carefully remove the spring

4.7a Unscrew the three securing nuts
(arrowed) . . .

4.7b . . . and move the ECU/bracket
assembly to one side – left-hand strut

4.9 Unscrew the suspension strut-to-body
nuts . . .

4.10 . . . then lower the strut from under
the wheel arch

4.11 Spring compressor tools fitted to
suspension strut coil spring

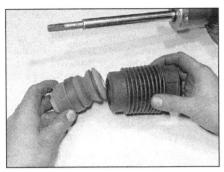

4.18a Clip the gaiter into position on the bump stop . . .

4.18b . . . then slide the gaiter/bump stop assembly onto the strut piston rod . . .

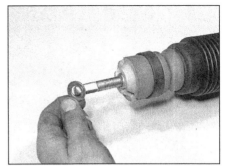

4.18c . . . and refit the washer

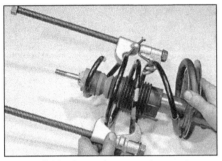

4.20 Slide the spring over the strut . . .

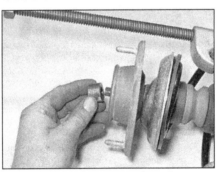

4.21 . . . then refit the upper spring seat assembly

compressors and check the spring for distortion and signs of cracking. Renew the spring if it is damaged or distorted, or if there is any doubt as to its condition.

17 Inspect all other components for damage or deterioration, and renew any that are suspect.

18 Clip the gaiter into position on the bump stop, then slide the gaiter/bump stop assembly, onto the strut piston rod, and refit the washer **(see illustrations)**.

19 If the spring compressor tool has been removed from the spring, refit it and compress the spring sufficiently to enable it to be refitted to the strut.

20 Slide the spring over the strut, and position it so that the lower end of the spring is resting against the stop on the lower seat **(see illustration)**.

21 Refit the upper spring seat assembly, and rotate it as necessary to position the stop against the upper end of the spring **(see illustration)**.

22 Refit the top mounting plate, then refit the bush, the top mounting locking plate, and the piston rod nut **(see illustrations)**. When refitting the piston rod nut, if necessary counterhold the top mounting locking plate as during removal – do not fully tighten the nut until the vehicle is resting on its wheels.

23 Slowly slacken the spring compressor tools to relieve the tension in the spring. Check that the ends of the spring locate correctly against the stops on the spring seats. If necessary, turn the spring and the upper seat so that the components locate correctly before the compressor tools are removed. Remove the compressor tools when the spring is fully seated.

Refitting

24 Refitting is a reversal of removal, bearing in mind the following points **(see illustration)**.
  a) *Renew any Nyloc-type self-locking nuts on refitting.*
  b) *Tighten all fixings to the specified torque.*
  c) *Where applicable, tighten the strut piston rod nut to the specified torque with the vehicle resting on its wheels. Counterhold the strut top mounting locking plate as during removal.*

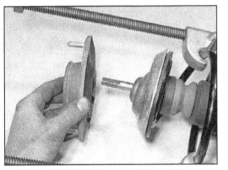

4.22a Refit the top mounting plate . . .

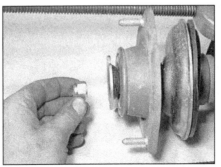

4.22b . . . the bush . . .

4.22c . . . the top mounting locking plate . . .

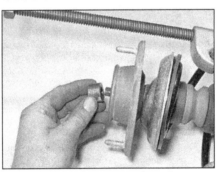

4.22d . . . and the piston rod nut

4.24 Counterholding the strut top mounting locking plate with a pair of grips whilst tightening the piston rod nut

5.4 Disconnecting the track-rod end balljoint using a balljoint separator tool

5.5 Unscrew the two nuts securing the hub carrier to the suspension strut

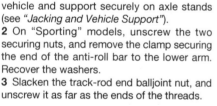

5.7 Counterhold the through-bolt (1) and unscrew the nut (2) securing the front of the lower arm to the body

5 Front suspension lower arm and balljoint – removal and refitting

Removal

Note: *Any Nyloc-type self-locking nuts must be renewed on refitting.*

1 Chock the rear wheels and apply the handbrake, then jack up the front of the vehicle and support securely on axle stands (see *"Jacking and Vehicle Support"*).

2 On "Sporting" models, unscrew the two securing nuts, and remove the clamp securing the end of the anti-roll bar to the lower arm. Recover the washers.

3 Slacken the track-rod end balljoint nut, and unscrew it as far as the ends of the threads.

6.2 Unscrewing an anti-roll bar-to-lower arm clamp nut – "Sporting" model

5.9 Unscrew the anti-roll bar clamp nut (1) and the lower arm rear mounting clamp bolts (2) – "Sporting" model

4 Disconnect the track-rod end balljoint from the hub carrier using a balljoint separator tool (leave the nut fitted to protect the threads), taking care not to damage the balljoint rubber seal **(see illustration)**. Once the balljoint has been released, remove the balljoint nut.

5 Counterhold the bolts, and unscrew the two nuts securing the hub carrier to the lower end of the suspension strut **(see illustration)**. Recover the washers. Withdraw the bolts, then separate the hub carrier from the strut.

6 Tilt the hub carrier until it is possible to fit a balljoint separator tool to the lower arm balljoint, then repeat the procedure in paragraphs 3 and 4 to disconnect the lower arm-to-hub carrier balljoint.

7 Counterhold the through-bolt, and unscrew the nut securing the front of the lower arm to the body **(see illustration)**. Withdraw the through-bolt.

6.3 Unscrew the bolt and the nut (arrowed) securing the anti-roll bar clamp to the vehicle floor

8 On "Sporting" models, unscrew the nut securing the rear of the anti-roll bar clamp to the body.

9 Unscrew the two bolts securing the lower arm rear mounting clamp to the body, and withdraw the clamp and lower arm (note that on "Sporting" models, the inboard lower arm mounting clamp bolt also secures the anti-roll bar clamp – remove the anti-roll bar clamp) **(see illustration)**. Recover the washers.

10 The lower arm balljoint is not available separately, and if the balljoint is worn or damaged, the complete lower arm assembly must be renewed.

Refitting

11 Refitting is a reversal of removal, bearing in mind the following points.
   a) *Renew any Nyloc-type self-locking nuts on refitting.*
   b) *Tighten all fixings to the specified torque.*

6 Front suspension anti-roll bar ("Sporting" models) – removal and refitting

Removal

Note: *Any Nyloc-type self-locking nuts must be renewed on refitting.*

1 Chock the rear wheels and apply the handbrake, then jack up the front of the vehicle and support securely on axle stands (see *"Jacking and Vehicle Support"*).

2 Working on each side of the vehicle in turn, unscrew the two securing nuts, and remove the clamp securing the end of the anti-roll bar to the lower arm **(see illustration)**. Recover the washers.

3 Similarly, working on each side of the vehicle in turn, unscrew the bolt and nut securing each anti-roll bar clamp to the vehicle floor, noting that the bolt also secures the lower arm clamp **(see illustration)**.

4 Withdraw the anti-roll bar from under the vehicle.

Refitting

5 Refitting is a reversal of removal, but renew any Nyloc-type self-locking nuts, and securely tighten all fixings.

7 Rear hub bearings – renewal

Note: *A new rear hub nut must be used on refitting. A slide hammer may be required for this operation.*

1 The rear hub bearings are integral with the hubs, and cannot be renewed independently. If a bearing is worn or damaged, the complete hub must be renewed as follows.

2 Chock the front wheels and select 1st gear, then jack up the rear of the vehicle and

7.4a Unscrew the rear hub nut . . .

7.4b . . . and recover the washer

7.5 Lifting the rear hub from the stub axle

support securely on axle stands (see *"Jacking and Vehicle Support"*). Remove the relevant rear roadwheel.

3 Remove the brake drum as described in Chapter 9.

4 Unscrew and remove the rear hub nut, using a suitable socket and extension bar. Recover the washer **(see illustrations)**. Discard the hub nut – a new one must be used on refitting.

 Warning: Take care as the rear hub nut is extremely tight!

5 Lift the hub from the stub axle. It should be possible to remove the hub easily, but if the hub is stuck on the stub axle, it can be freed using a slide hammer and adapter **(see illustration)**. The adapter can be bolted in place using the roadwheel bolts.

6 Thoroughly clean the mating faces of the stub axle, and the inner face of the new hub bearing.

7 Position the hub/bearing assembly on the end of the stub axle, then push the assembly into position, until the bearing rests against the shoulder on the stub axle.

8 Refit the washer, then fit a new rear hub nut, and tighten to the specified torque.

9 Refit the brake drum as described in Chapter 9, then refit the roadwheel, lower the vehicle to the ground and tighten the wheel bolts to the specified torque.

8 Rear suspension shock absorber – removal, testing and refitting

Removal

1 Chock the front wheels and select 1st gear, then jack up the rear of the vehicle and support securely on axle stands (see *"Jacking and Vehicle Support"*). Remove the relevant rear roadwheel.

2 Place a trolley jack under the trailing arm on the side of the vehicle from which the shock absorber is to be removed, and raise the jack to compress the shock absorber and coil spring. Ensure that the coil spring is compressed sufficiently so that it cannot fly out from its seats.

3 Unscrew the shock absorber upper and lower mounting bolts **(see illustration)**. Recover the washers.

4 Withdraw the shock absorber from under the rear of the vehicle.

Testing

5 Examine the shock absorber for signs of fluid leakage. Check the shock absorber piston for signs of pitting along its entire length, and check the shock absorber body for signs of damage. While holding it in an upright position, test the operation of the shock absorber by moving the piston through a full stroke, and then through short strokes of 50 to 100 mm. In both cases, the resistance felt should be smooth and continuous. If the resistance is jerky or uneven or if there is any visible sign of wear or damage to the shock absorber, renewal is necessary.

Refitting

6 Refitting is a reversal of removal, but do not fully tighten the shock absorber securing bolts to the specified torque until the vehicle is resting on its wheels.

9 Rear suspension coil spring – removal and refitting

Removal

1 Remove the relevant rear shock absorber, as described in Section 8. Note that if desired, the shock absorber can be left attached to its

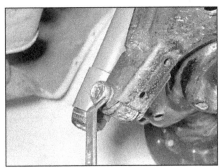

8.3 Unscrewing a rear shock absorber lower mounting bolt

upper mounting, provided that the upper mounting bolt is slackened.

2 Gently lower the trolley jack used to compress the coil spring during the shock absorber removal procedure, until the coil spring is fully extended and can be withdrawn from its location. Take care not to allow the spring to fly out.

Refitting

3 Refitting is a reversal of removal, but ensure that the coil spring is correctly located on its upper and lower seats, and refit the shock absorber with reference to Section 8.

10 Rear suspension trailing arm – removal and refitting

Removal

Note: *A new handbrake cable-to-handbrake operating lever split-pin should be used on refitting.*

1 Remove the relevant rear hub/bearing assembly, as described in Section 7.

2 Working at the rear of the brake backplate, remove the split-pin, then slide out the retaining pin (recover the washers), and disconnect the handbrake cable from the handbrake operating lever **(see illustration)**.

3 To minimise brake fluid loss during the following operations remove the brake master cylinder reservoir cap, then tighten it down onto a piece of polythene, to obtain an airtight seal.

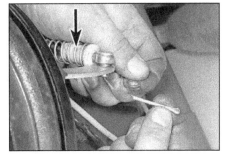

10.2 Remove the split-pin and the retaining pin and disconnect the handbrake cable (arrowed) from the operating lever

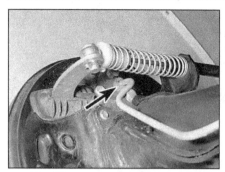

10.4 Disconnect the hydraulic pipe (arrowed) from the wheel cylinder

4 Clean the brake backplate around the brake wheel cylinder hydraulic pipe union, then unscrew the union nut and disconnect the hydraulic pipe from the wheel cylinder **(see illustration)**. Plug or cover the open ends of the pipe and the wheel cylinder to prevent dirt ingress.

5 Working at the bracket on the lower arm, pull out the metal clip securing the brake hydraulic pipe-to-flexible hose union to the bracket.

6 Unscrew the union, and disconnect the flexible hose from the brake pipe, with reference to Chapter 9.

7 Remove the relevant rear coil spring, as described in Section 9.

8 Working at the outboard end of the trailing arm, counterhold the securing bolt, and unscrew the nut securing the trailing arm to the bracket on the rear suspension crossmember **(see illustration)**. Recover the washer.

9 Repeat the procedure given in paragraph 8 to disconnect the inboard end of the trailing arm from the suspension crossmember, then withdraw the trailing arm from under the vehicle.

Refitting

10 Before refitting the trailing arm, examine it for damage and wear. Check for cracks or distortion to the trailing arm itself and signs of wear in the stub axle. Also check the condition of the rubber pivot bushes. If any wear or damage is found, the complete trailing arm must be renewed.

11.6 Pull out the metal clip (arrowed) securing the hydraulic pipe-to-hose union to the bracket

10.8 Counterhold the bolt and unscrew the nut securing the outboard end of the trailing arm to the bracket on the rear suspension

11 Refitting is a reversal of removal, bearing in mind the following points.
a) Do not fully tighten the trailing arm pivot nuts and bolts until the vehicle is resting on its wheels.
b) Refit the rear coil spring as described in Section 9.
c) Use a new split-pin to secure the handbrake cable to the handbrake operating lever.
d) Refit the rear hub/bearing assembly as described in Section 7.
e) Tighten all fixings to the specified torque.
f) Before refitting the roadwheel and lowering the vehicle to the ground, remove the polythene from the fluid reservoir, and bleed the hydraulic system as described in Chapter 9. Note that if no other part of the system has been disturbed, it should only be necessary to bleed the relevant rear circuit.

11 Rear suspension crossmember – removal and refitting

Removal

Note: During this procedure, it is necessary to partially lower the fuel tank. It is advisable to run the fuel tank as near to empty as possible before carrying out this procedure.

1 Remove the trailing arms as described in Section 10. Note that if desired, the trailing

11.7a Unscrew the front . . .

arms can be left bolted to the crossmember, provided all the other steps given in the trailing arm removal procedure are carried out.

2 Remove the exhaust rear section as described in Chapter 4.

3 Ensure that the fuel tank is almost empty. Place a trolley jack, or an axle stand and a block of wood under the rear of the fuel tank (note that if a jack is used, a second jack will be required later in the procedure), then unscrew and remove the two fuel tank rear securing bolts, and lower the tank sufficiently to enable the suspension crossmember to be removed.

4 Position a hydraulic jack under the centre of the suspension crossmember.

5 To minimise brake fluid loss during the following operation remove the brake master cylinder reservoir cap, then tighten it down onto a piece of polythene, to obtain an airtight seal.

6 Working at each end of the crossmember in turn, pull out the metal clip securing the brake hydraulic pipe-to-flexible hose union to the crossmember bracket **(see illustration)**. Unscrew the union, and disconnect the flexible hose from the brake pipe, with reference to Chapter 9.

7 Unscrew the two bolts on each side, securing the crossmember to the body, then carefully lower the jack, and withdraw the crossmember from under the vehicle **(see illustrations)**.

Refitting

8 Refitting is a reversal of removal, bearing in mind the following points.
a) Tighten all fixings to the specified torque.
b) Refit the exhaust rear section with reference to Chapter 4.
c) Refit the trailing arms as described in Section 10.
d) Before refitting the roadwheels and lowering the vehicle to the ground, remove the polythene from the fluid reservoir, and bleed the hydraulic system as described in Chapter 9. Note that if no other part of the system has been disturbed, it should only be necessary to bleed the rear circuits.

11.7b . . . and rear bolts (arrowed) securing the crossmember to the body

12.2a Prise the rubber cover from the horn push

12.2b Release the horn push securing lugs (arrowed)

12.2c Lift out the horn push springs

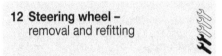

12 Steering wheel –
removal and refitting

Models without air bag

Removal

Note: *A suitable three-legged puller may be required to remove the steering wheel.*

1 Disconnect the battery negative lead.

2 Prise the rubber cover from the horn push then, using a screwdriver, release the three horn push ring securing lugs, and remove the horn push ring from the steering wheel. Lift out the horn push springs **(see illustrations)**.

3 Turn the steering wheel to its centre position so that the roadwheels are pointing straight-ahead.

4 Make alignment marks between the steering wheel and the end of the column shaft to aid refitting.

5 Unscrew and remove the steering wheel securing nut, noting that the nut is peened to the end of the steering column shaft **(see illustration)**. Recover the washer.

6 Grip the steering wheel on each side, then pull and withdraw it from the splines on the end of the column. If it is tight, tap it near its centre, using the palm of your hand, or twist it from side-to-side, whilst pulling upwards to release it from the shaft splines. If the wheel is particularly tight, a suitable three-legged puller should be used **(see illustration)**.

12.7a The direction indicator self-cancelling lug (1) must engage with the hole (2) in the indicator switch wiper

12.5 Remove the steering wheel securing nut and the washer

Refitting

7 Refitting is a reversal of removal, bearing in mind the following points **(see illustrations)**:

a) *Align the marks made on the wheel and the steering column shaft before removal.*

b) *As the steering wheel is refitted, make sure that the direction indicator self-cancelling lug on the steering wheel engages with the hole in the indicator switch wiper.*

c) *Tighten the steering wheel securing nut to the specified torque, and carefully peen the nut to the end of the column shaft on each side to lock it in position.*

d) *Before refitting the horn push components, refit the rubber cover to the horn push, making sure that the lug on the horn push ring engages with the slot in the rubber cover, then push the assembly into place on the steering wheel until the securing lugs engage.*

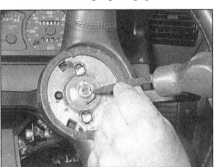

12.7b Peen the nut to the end of the column shaft

12.6 Using a three-legged puller to remove the steering wheel

Models with air bag

> ⚠ **Warning: Refer to the precautions given in Chapter 12 for models fitted with an air bag before starting work.**

Removal

8 With the air bag unit removed (see Chapter 12), proceed as described in paragraphs 3 to 6 inclusive.

Refitting

9 Refitting is a reversal of removal, bearing in mind the following points.

a) *Align the marks made on the wheel and the steering column shaft before removal.*

b) *As the steering wheel is refitted, make sure that the direction indicator self-cancelling lug on the steering wheel engages with the hole in the indicator switch wiper.*

12.7c Make sure that the lug on the horn push ring engages with the slot in the rubber cover

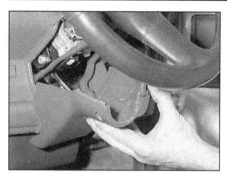

13.1a Remove the lower . . .

13.1b . . . and upper steering column shrouds

13.3 Steering intermediate shaft-to-steering gear pinion pinch-nut (arrowed)

c) Tighten the steering wheel securing nut to the specified torque, and carefully peen the nut to the end of the column shaft on each side to lock it in position.
d) Refit the air bag as described in Chapter 12.

13 Steering column – removal and refitting

Removal

Note: *Any Nyloc-type self-locking nuts must be renewed on refitting.*

1 Remove the steering column shrouds, with reference to Chapter 11 if necessary **(see illustrations)**.
2 Remove the steering wheel as described in Section 12.
3 Working in the driver's footwell, make alignment marks between the lower end of the steering intermediate shaft and the steering gear pinion to aid refitting, then unscrew the pinch-nut and bolt securing the intermediate shaft to the pinion **(see illustration)**.
4 Working at the upper end of the column, disconnect the wiring from the ignition switch and the column-mounted stalk switches. Where applicable, trace the wiring back from the relevant switch and separate the two halves of the wiring connector(s) **(see illustration)**.

5 Unscrew the through-bolt and nut securing the upper end of the column to the upper mounting bracket **(see illustration)**. Recover the washers.
6 Make a final check and release any remaining wiring harnesses or cables from the clips on the steering column.
7 Working at the lower end of the column, unscrew the two nuts securing the column to the lower mounting bracket **(see illustration)**. Recover any washers and spacers, noting their locations.
8 Withdraw the steering column from the vehicle.

Refitting

9 Refitting is a reversal of removal, bearing in mind the following points.
a) Tighten all fixings to the specified torque.
b) Renew any Nyloc-type self-locking nuts.
c) Align the marks made before removal on the steering intermediate shaft and the steering gear pinion.
d) Refit the steering wheel as described in Section 12.

14 Steering gear rubber gaiters – renewal

1 Remove the relevant track-rod end as described in Section 16.

2 Remove the inboard and outboard securing clips, then slide the gaiter off the end of the track-rod.
3 Thoroughly clean the track-rod, then slide the new gaiter into position.
4 Fit the gaiter securing clips, using new clips if necessary, making sure that the gaiter is not twisted.
5 Refit the track-rod end as described in Section 16.

15 Steering gear – removal and refitting

Removal

Note: *Any Nyloc-type self-locking nuts must be renewed on refitting.*

1 Turn the steering wheel to its centre position so that the roadwheels are pointing straight-ahead.
2 Working in the driver's footwell, make alignment marks between the lower end of the steering intermediate shaft and the steering gear pinion to aid refitting, then unscrew the pinch nut and bolt securing the intermediate shaft to the pinion.
3 Chock the rear wheels and apply the handbrake, then jack up the front of the vehicle and support securely on axle stands (see *"Jacking and Vehicle Support"*). Remove the front roadwheels.

13.4 Column-mounted stalk switch wiring connectors (arrowed)

13.5 Unscrewing the steering column upper through-bolt and nut

13.7 Lower steering column securing nut (arrowed)

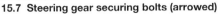

15.7 Steering gear securing bolts (arrowed)

16.3 Disconnecting the track-rod end balljoint using a balljoint separator tool

4 Working on one side of the vehicle, slacken the track-rod end balljoint nut, and unscrew it as far as the ends of the threads.

5 Disconnect the track-rod end balljoint from the hub carrier using a balljoint separator tool (leave the nut fitted to protect the threads), taking care not to damage the balljoint rubber seal. Once the balljoint has been released, remove the balljoint nut.

6 Repeat the procedure given in paragraphs 3 and 4 to disconnect the remaining track-rod end balljoint.

7 Unscrew the two bolts securing the steering gear to the body, then manipulate the steering gear out from under the vehicle **(see illustration)**.

Refitting

8 Refitting is a reversal of removal, bearing in mind the following points.
 a) *Tighten all fixings to the specified torque.*
 b) *Renew any Nyloc-type self-locking nuts.*
 c) *Align the marks made before removal on the steering intermediate shaft and the steering gear pinion.*
 d) *On completion, check the front wheel alignment at the earliest opportunity, with reference to Section 17.*

16 Track-rod end – removal and refitting

Note: *A balljoint separator tool will be required for this operation. Where applicable, Nyloc-type self-locking nuts must be renewed on refitting.*

Removal

1 Chock the rear wheels and apply the handbrake, then jack up the front of the vehicle and support securely on axle stands (see *"Jacking and Vehicle Support"*). Remove the roadwheel.

2 Slacken the track-rod end balljoint nut, and unscrew it as far as the ends of the threads.

3 Disconnect the track-rod end balljoint from the hub carrier using a balljoint separator tool (leave the nut fitted to protect the threads), taking care not to damage the balljoint rubber seal **(see illustration)**. Once the balljoint has been released, remove the balljoint nut.

4 Slacken the track-rod end locknut (counterhold the track-rod using a spanner on the flats provided), then unscrew the track-rod end from the track-rod, counting the number of turns necessary to remove it.

Refitting

5 Screw the track-rod end onto the track-rod the number of turns noted during removal, then tighten the locknut while holding the balljoint in position.

6 Engage the track-rod end balljoint pin with the hub carrier, then fit a new securing nut. Tighten the nut to the specified torque.

7 Refit the roadwheel, lower the vehicle to the ground and tighten the bolts to the specified torque setting.

8 Check the front wheel alignment at the earliest opportunity, with reference to Section 17.

17 Wheel alignment and steering angles – general information

Front wheel alignment

1 Accurate front wheel alignment is essential to good steering and for even tyre wear. Before considering the steering angles, check that the tyres are correctly inflated, that the front wheels are not buckled, the hub bearings are not worn and that the steering linkage is in good order, without slackness or wear at the joints.

2 Wheel alignment consists of four factors:

Camber is the angle at which the roadwheels are set from the vertical when viewed from the front or rear of the vehicle. Positive camber is the angle (in degrees) that the wheels are tilted outwards at the top from the vertical. The camber angle is given for reference only and cannot be adjusted.

Castor is the angle between the steering axis and a vertical line when viewed from each side of the vehicle. Positive castor is indicated when the steering axis is inclined towards the rear of the vehicle at its upper end. This angle is not adjustable.

Steering axis inclination (kingpin inclination) is the angle, when viewed from the front or rear of the vehicle, between the vertical and an imaginary line drawn between the upper and lower front suspension strut mountings. This angle is not adjustable.

Toe is the amount by which the distance between the front inside edges of the roadwheel rim differs from that between the rear inside edges. If the distance between the front edges is less than that at the rear, the wheels are said to toe-in. If the distance between the front inside edges is greater than that at the rear, the wheels toe-out.

3 Owing to the need for precision gauges to measure the small angles of the steering and suspension settings, it is preferable that checking of camber and castor is left to a service station having the necessary equipment. Camber and castor is set during production of the vehicle, and any deviation from the specified angle will be due to accident damage or gross wear in the suspension mountings.

4 To check the front wheel alignment, first make sure that the lengths of both track-rods are equal when the steering is in the straight-ahead position. The track-rod lengths can be adjusted if necessary by releasing the locknuts from the track-rod ends and rotating the track-rods. If necessary, self-locking grips can be used to rotate the track-rods.

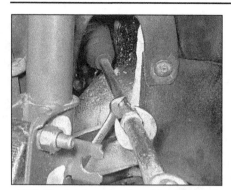

17.7 Slackening a track-rod end locknut whilst counterholding the track-rod on the flats

5 Obtain a tracking gauge. These are available in various forms from accessory stores, or one can be fabricated from a length of steel tubing suitably cranked to clear the sump and transmission, and having a setscrew and locknut at one end.

6 With the gauge, measure the distances between the two wheel inner rims (at hub height) at the rear of the wheel. Push the vehicle forward to rotate the wheel through 180° (half a turn) and measure the distance between the wheel inner rims, again at hub height, at the front of the wheel. This last measurement should differ from the first by the appropriate toe-in which is given in the Specifications. The vehicle must be on level ground.

7 If the toe-in is found to be incorrect, release the track-rod end locknuts (counterhold the track-rods using a spanner on the flats provided) and turn both track-rods equally **(see illustration)**. Only turn them a quarter-of-a-turn at a time before re-checking the alignment. Turn the track rods using a spanner on the flats provided. It is important not to allow the track-rods to become unequal in length during adjustment, otherwise the alignment of the steering wheel will become incorrect and tyre scrubbing will occur on turns.

8 On completion tighten the locknuts without disturbing the setting. Check that the balljoint is at the centre of its arc of travel.

Rear wheel alignment

9 Figures are provided in the Specifications for rear wheel camber and toe-setting for reference only. No adjustment is possible. Refer to paragraph 2 for a description of the settings.

Chapter 11
Bodywork and fittings

Contents

Degrees of difficulty

Easy, suitable for novice with little experience	**Fairly easy,** suitable for beginner with some experience	**Fairly difficult,** suitable for competent DIY mechanic	**Difficult,** suitable for experienced DIY mechanic	**Very difficult,** suitable for expert DIY or professional

Specifications

Torque wrench settings	Nm	lbf ft
Front seat belt pre-tensioner safety bracket nut	4	3
Seat belt anchor bolts	40	30

1 General information

The bodyshell is of three-door Hatchback configuration, and is made of pressed steel sections. Most components are welded together, but some use is made of structural adhesives. The front wings are bolted on.

The bonnet, doors and some other vulnerable panels are made of zinc-coated metal, and are further protected by being coated with an anti-chip primer prior to being sprayed.

Extensive use is made of plastic materials, mainly in the interior, but also in exterior components. The front and rear bumpers are injection-moulded from a synthetic material which is very strong, and yet light. Plastic components such as wheel arch liners are fitted to the underside of the vehicle, to improve the body's resistance to corrosion.

2 Maintenance - bodywork and underframe

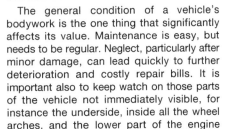

The general condition of a vehicle's bodywork is the one thing that significantly affects its value. Maintenance is easy, but needs to be regular. Neglect, particularly after minor damage, can lead quickly to further deterioration and costly repair bills. It is important also to keep watch on those parts of the vehicle not immediately visible, for instance the underside, inside all the wheel arches, and the lower part of the engine compartment.

The basic maintenance routine for the bodywork is washing - preferably with a lot of water, from a hose. This will remove all the loose solids which may have stuck to the vehicle. It is important to flush these off in such a way as to prevent grit from scratching the finish. The wheel arches and underframe need washing in the same way, to remove any accumulated mud which will retain moisture and tend to encourage rust. Paradoxically enough, the best time to clean the underframe and wheel arches is in wet weather, when the mud is thoroughly wet and soft. In very wet weather, the underframe is usually cleaned of large accumulations automatically, and this is a good time for inspection.

Periodically, except on vehicles with a wax-based underbody protective coating, it is a good idea to have the whole of the underframe of the vehicle steam-cleaned, engine compartment included, so that a thorough inspection can be carried out to see what minor repairs and renovations are necessary. Steam-cleaning is available at many garages, and is necessary for the removal of the accumulation of oily grime, which sometimes is allowed to become thick in certain areas. If steam-cleaning facilities are not available, there are one or two excellent grease solvents available, which can be brush-applied; the dirt can then be simply hosed off. Note that these methods should not be used on vehicles with wax-based underbody protective coating, or the coating will be removed. Such vehicles should be inspected annually, preferably just prior to Winter, when the underbody should be washed down, and any damage to the wax coating repaired. Ideally, a completely fresh coat should be applied. It would also be worth considering the use of such wax-based protection for injection into door panels, sills, box sections, etc, as an additional safeguard against rust damage, where such protection is not provided by the vehicle manufacturer.

After washing paintwork, wipe off with a chamois leather to give an unspotted clear finish. A coat of clear protective wax polish will give added protection against chemical pollutants in the air. If the paintwork sheen has dulled or oxidised, use a cleaner/polisher combination to restore the brilliance of the shine. This requires a little effort, but such dulling is usually caused because regular washing has been neglected. Care needs to be taken with metallic paintwork, as special non-abrasive cleaner/polisher is required to avoid damage to the finish. Always check that the door and ventilator opening drain holes and pipes are completely clear, so that water can be drained out. Brightwork should be treated in the same way as paintwork. Windscreens and windows can be kept clear of the smeary film which often appears, by the use of proprietary glass cleaner. Never use any form of wax or other body or chromium polish on glass.

3 Maintenance - upholstery and carpets

Mats and carpets should be brushed or vacuum-cleaned regularly, to keep them free of grit. If they are badly stained, remove them from the vehicle for scrubbing or sponging, and make quite sure they are dry before refitting. Seats and interior trim panels can be kept clean by wiping with a damp cloth. If they do become stained (which can be more apparent on light-coloured upholstery), use a little liquid detergent and a soft nail brush to scour the grime out of the grain of the material. Do not forget to keep the headlining clean in the same way as the upholstery. When using liquid cleaners inside the vehicle, do not over-wet the surfaces being cleaned. Excessive damp could get into the seams and padded interior, causing stains, offensive odours or even rot. If the inside of the vehicle gets wet accidentally, it is worthwhile taking some trouble to dry it out properly, particularly where carpets are involved.

Caution: Do not leave oil or electric heaters inside the vehicle for this purpose.

4 Minor body damage - repair

Note: *For more detailed information about bodywork repair, Haynes Publishing produce a book called "The Car Bodywork Repair Manual". This incorporates information on such aspects as rust treatment, painting and glass-fibre repairs, as well as details on more ambitious repairs involving welding and panel beating.*

Repairs of minor scratches in bodywork

If the scratch is very superficial, and does not penetrate to the metal of the bodywork, repair is very simple. Lightly rub the area of the scratch with a paintwork renovator, or a very fine cutting paste, to remove loose paint from the scratch, and to clear the surrounding bodywork of wax polish. Rinse the area with clean water.

Apply touch-up paint to the scratch using a fine paint brush; continue to apply fine layers of paint until the surface of the paint in the scratch is level with the surrounding paintwork. Allow the new paint at least two weeks to harden, then blend it into the surrounding paintwork by rubbing the scratch area with a paintwork renovator or a very fine cutting paste. Finally, apply wax polish.

Where the scratch has penetrated right through to the metal of the bodywork, causing the metal to rust, a different repair technique is required. Remove any loose rust from the bottom of the scratch with a penknife, then apply rust-inhibiting paint, to prevent the formation of rust in the future. Using a rubber or nylon applicator, fill the scratch with bodystopper paste. If required, this paste can be mixed with cellulose thinners, to provide a very thin paste which is ideal for filling narrow scratches. Before the stopper-paste in the scratch hardens, wrap a piece of smooth cotton rag around the top of a finger. Dip the finger in cellulose thinners, and quickly sweep it across the surface of the stopper-paste in the scratch; this will ensure that the surface of the stopper-paste is slightly hollowed. The scratch can now be painted over as described earlier in this Section.

Repairs of dents in bodywork

When deep denting of the vehicle's bodywork has taken place, the first task is to pull the dent out, until the affected bodywork almost attains its original shape. There is little point in trying to restore the original shape completely, as the metal in the damaged area will have stretched on impact, and cannot be reshaped fully to its original contour. It is better to bring the level of the dent up to a point which is about 3 mm below the level of the surrounding bodywork. In cases where the dent is very shallow anyway, it is not worth trying to pull it out at all. If the underside of the

dent is accessible, it can be hammered out gently from behind, using a mallet with a wooden or plastic head. Whilst doing this, hold a suitable block of wood firmly against the outside of the panel, to absorb the impact from the hammer blows and thus prevent a large area of the bodywork from being "belled-out".

Should the dent be in a section of the bodywork which has a double skin, or some other factor making it inaccessible from behind, a different technique is called for. Drill several small holes through the metal inside the area - particularly in the deeper section. Then screw long self-tapping screws into the holes, just sufficiently for them to gain a good purchase in the metal. Now the dent can be pulled out by pulling on the protruding heads of the screws with a pair of pliers.

The next stage of the repair is the removal of the paint from the damaged area, and from an inch or so of the surrounding "sound" bodywork. This is accomplished most easily by using a wire brush or abrasive pad on a power drill, although it can be done just as effectively by hand, using sheets of abrasive paper. To complete the preparation for filling, score the surface of the bare metal with a screwdriver or the tang of a file, or alternatively, drill small holes in the affected area. This will provide a really good "key" for the filler paste.

To complete the repair, see the Section on filling and respraying.

Repairs of rust holes or gashes in bodywork

Remove all paint from the affected area, and from an inch or so of the surrounding "sound" bodywork, using an abrasive pad or a wire brush on a power drill. If these are not available, a few sheets of abrasive paper will do the job most effectively. With the paint removed, you will be able to judge the severity of the corrosion, and therefore decide whether to renew the whole panel (if this is possible) or to repair the affected area. New body panels are not as expensive as most people think, and it is often quicker and more satisfactory to fit a new panel than to attempt to repair large areas of corrosion.

Remove all fittings from the affected area, except those which will act as a guide to the original shape of the damaged bodywork (eg headlamp shells etc). Then, using tin snips or a hacksaw blade, remove all loose metal and any other metal badly affected by corrosion. Hammer the edges of the hole inwards, in order to create a slight depression for the filler paste.

Wire-brush the affected area to remove the powdery rust from the surface of the remaining metal. Paint the affected area with rust-inhibiting paint; if the back of the rusted area is accessible, treat this also.

Before filling can take place, it will be necessary to block the hole in some way. This can be achieved by the use of aluminium or plastic mesh, or aluminium tape.

Aluminium or plastic mesh, or glass-fibre matting is probably the best material to use for a large hole. Cut a piece to the approximate size and shape of the hole to be filled, then position it in the hole so that its edges are below the level of the surrounding bodywork. It can be retained in position by several blobs of filler paste around its periphery.

Aluminium tape should be used for small or very narrow holes. Pull a piece off the roll, trim it to the approximate size and shape required, then pull off the backing paper (if used) and stick the tape over the hole; it can be overlapped if the thickness of one piece is insufficient. Burnish down the edges of the tape with the handle of a screwdriver or similar, to ensure that the tape is securely attached to the metal underneath.

Bodywork repairs - filling and respraying

Before using this Section, see the Sections on dent, deep scratch, rust holes and gash repairs.

Many types of bodyfiller are available, but generally speaking, those proprietary kits which contain a tin of filler paste and a tube of resin hardener are best for this type of repair. A wide, flexible plastic or nylon applicator will be found invaluable for imparting a smooth and well-contoured finish to the surface of the filler.

Mix up a little filler on a clean piece of card or board - measure the hardener carefully (follow the maker's instructions on the pack), otherwise the filler will set too rapidly or too slowly. Using the applicator, apply the filler paste to the prepared area; draw the applicator across the surface of the filler to achieve the correct contour and to level the surface. As soon as a contour that approximates to the correct one is achieved, stop working the paste - if you carry on too long, the paste will become sticky and begin to "pick-up" on the applicator. Continue to add thin layers of filler paste at 20-minute intervals, until the level of the filler is just proud of the surrounding bodywork.

Once the filler has hardened, the excess can be removed using a metal plane or file. From then on, progressively-finer grades of abrasive paper should be used, starting with a 40-grade production paper, and finishing with a 400-grade wet-and-dry paper. Always wrap the abrasive paper around a flat rubber, cork, or wooden block - otherwise the surface of the filler will not be completely flat. During the smoothing of the filler surface, the wet-and-dry paper should be periodically rinsed in water. This will ensure that a very smooth finish is imparted to the filler at the final stage.

At this stage, the "dent" should be surrounded by a ring of bare metal, which in turn should be encircled by the finely "feathered" edge of the good paintwork. Rinse the repair area with clean water, until all of the dust produced by the rubbing-down operation has gone.

Spray the whole area with a light coat of primer - this will show up any imperfections in the surface of the filler. Repair these imperfections with fresh filler paste or bodystopper, and once more smooth the surface with abrasive paper. If bodystopper is used, it can be mixed with cellulose thinners, to form a really thin paste which is ideal for filling small holes. Repeat this spray-and-repair procedure until you are satisfied that the surface of the filler, and the feathered edge of the paintwork, are perfect. Clean the repair area with clean water, and allow to dry fully.

The repair area is now ready for final spraying. Paint spraying must be carried out in a warm, dry, windless and dust-free atmosphere. This condition can be created artificially if you have access to a large indoor working area, but if you are forced to work in the open, you will have to pick your day very carefully. If you are working indoors, dousing the floor in the work area with water will help to settle the dust which would otherwise be in the atmosphere. If the repair area is confined to one body panel, mask off the surrounding panels; this will help to minimise the effects of a slight mis-match in paint colours. Bodywork fittings (eg chrome strips, door handles etc) will also need to be masked off. Use genuine masking tape, and several thicknesses of newspaper, for the masking operations.

Before commencing to spray, agitate the aerosol can thoroughly, then spray a test area (an old tin, or similar) until the technique is mastered. Cover the repair area with a thick coat of primer; the thickness should be built up using several thin layers of paint, rather than one thick one. Using 400 grade wet-and-dry paper, rub down the surface of the primer until it is really smooth. While doing this, the work area should be thoroughly doused with water, and the wet-and-dry paper periodically rinsed in water. Allow to dry before spraying on more paint.

Spray on the top coat, again building up the thickness by using several thin layers of paint. Start spraying in the centre of the repair area, and then, using a circular motion, work outwards until the whole repair area and about 2 inches of the surrounding original paintwork is covered. Remove all masking material 10 to 15 minutes after spraying on the final coat of paint.

Allow the new paint at least two weeks to harden, then, using a paintwork renovator or a very fine cutting paste, blend the edges of the paint into the existing paintwork. Finally, apply wax polish.

Plastic components

With the use of more and more plastic body components by the vehicle manufacturers (eg bumpers. spoilers, and in some cases major body panels), rectification of more serious damage to such items has become a matter of either entrusting repair work to a specialist in this field, or renewing complete components. Repair of such damage by the DIY owner is not really feasible, owing to the cost of the equipment and materials required for effecting such repairs. The basic technique involves making a groove along the line of the crack in the plastic, using a rotary burr in a power drill. The damaged part is then welded back together, using a hot air gun to heat up and fuse a plastic filler rod into the groove. Any excess plastic is then removed, and the area rubbed down to a smooth finish. It is important that a filler rod of the correct plastic is used, as body components can be made of a variety of different types (eg polycarbonate, ABS, polypropylene).

Damage of a less serious nature (abrasions, minor cracks etc) can be repaired by the DIY owner using a two-part epoxy filler repair. Once mixed in equal, this is used in similar fashion to the bodywork filler used on metal panels. The filler is usually cured in twenty to thirty minutes, ready for sanding and painting.

If the owner is renewing a complete component himself, or if he has repaired it with epoxy filler, he will be left with the problem of finding a suitable paint for finishing which is compatible with the type of plastic used. At one time, the use of a universal paint was not possible, owing to the complex range of plastics encountered in body component applications. Standard paints, generally speaking, will not bond to plastic or rubber satisfactorily, but suitable paints to match any plastic or rubber finish, can be obtained from dealers. However, it is now possible to obtain a plastic body parts finishing kit which consists of a pre-primer treatment, a primer and coloured top coat. Full instructions are normally supplied with a kit, but basically, the method of use is to first apply the pre-primer to the component concerned, and allow it to dry for up to 30 minutes. Then the primer is applied, and left to dry for about an hour before finally applying the special-coloured top coat. The result is a correctly-coloured component, where the paint will flex with the plastic or rubber, a property that standard paint does not normally posses.

5 Major body damage - repair

Where serious damage has occurred, or large areas need renewal due to neglect, it means that complete new panels will need welding-in, and this is best left to professionals. If the damage is due to impact, it will also be necessary to check completely the alignment of the bodyshell, and this can only be carried out accurately by a Fiat dealer using special jigs. If the body is left misaligned, it is primarily dangerous, as the car will not handle properly, and secondly, uneven stresses will be imposed on the steering, suspension and possibly transmission, causing abnormal wear, or complete failure, particularly to such items as the tyres.

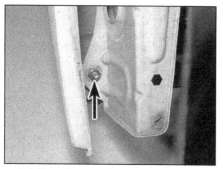

6.4 Front bumper lower securing bolt (arrowed)

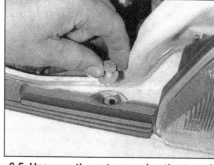

6.5 Unscrew the nuts securing the top of the front bumper to the body

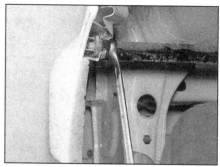

6.6a Slacken the screws securing the sides of the front bumper to the body . . .

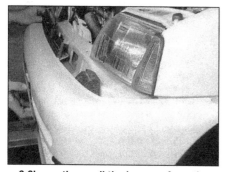

6.6b . . . then pull the bumper from the front of the vehicle

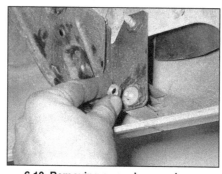

6.10 Removing a rear bumper lower securing nut

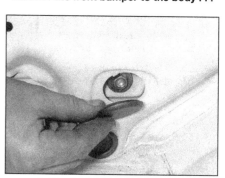

6.11a Prise out the covers . . .

6 Bumpers - removal and refitting

Front bumper

Removal

1 If desired, for improved access, chock the rear wheels and apply the handbrake, then jack up the front of the vehicle and support securely on axle stands (see *"Jacking and Vehicle Support"*).

2 Working at each side of the bumper in turn, carefully prise the wheel arch liner from the rear edge of the bumper.

3 Working under the front of the vehicle, remove the securing screws and withdraw the radiator splash shield.

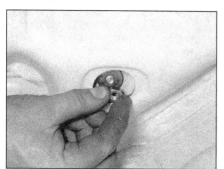

6.11b . . . then unscrew the three rear bumper upper securing nuts

4 Working at each lower corner of the bumper in turn, unscrew the nut securing the lower corner of the bumper to the body **(see illustration)**.

5 Working in the engine compartment, unscrew the two nuts securing the top of the bumper assembly to the body **(see illustration)**.

6 Working at the top rear corners of the bumper, slacken the screws securing the sides of the bumper to the body then, with the aid of an assistant, carefully pull the bumper from the front of the vehicle, noting that the corners of the bumper must be released from the guides on the body **(see illustrations)**.

Refitting

7 Refitting is a reversal of removal, but make sure that the corners of the bumper are correctly engaged with the guides on the body.

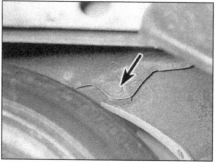

6.12 Slacken the screws (arrowed) securing the sides of the rear bumper to the body

Rear bumper

Removal

8 Disconnect the battery negative lead.

9 If desired, for improved access, chock the front wheels and select 1st gear, then jack up the rear of the vehicle and support securely on axle stands (see *"Jacking and Vehicle Support"*).

10 Working at each lower corner of the bumper in turn, unscrew the nut securing the lower corner of the bumper to the body **(see illustration)**. Recover the washers.

11 Working in the luggage compartment, prise out the covers, then unscrew the three bumper securing nuts **(see illustrations)**. Recover the metal and rubber washers.

12 Working at the top corners of the bumper, slacken the screws securing the sides of the bumper to the body **(see illustration)**.

13 With the aid of an assistant, carefully pull the bumper from the rear of the vehicle, noting that the corners of the bumper must be released from the guides on the body. Carefully lower the bumper, taking care not to strain the number plate wiring, then disconnect the number plate wiring connectors, and withdraw the bumper **(see illustrations)**.

Refitting

14 Refitting is a reversal of removal, but make sure that the corners of the bumper are correctly engaged with the guides on the body.

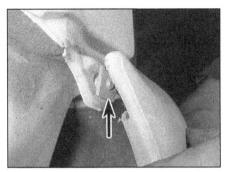

6.13a Pull the bumper forwards to release its corners from the guides (arrowed) on the body

7 Bonnet -
removal, refitting and adjustment

Removal

1 Open the bonnet, and support it using the bonnet support strut.

2 Disconnect the windscreen washer fluid hose from the washer nozzle under the bonnet (be prepared for fluid spillage), then tie a length of string to the end of the hose, and pull the hose down through the hole in the right-hand corner of the bonnet **(see illustrations)**. Untie the string, and leave it in position in the bonnet to aid refitting.

3 Using a pencil or felt tip pen, mark the outline position of each bonnet hinge relative to the bonnet, to use as a guide on refitting.

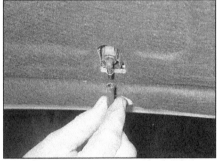

7.2a Disconnect the windscreen washer fluid hose from the washer nozzle . . .

7.4 Unscrewing a bonnet securing bolt

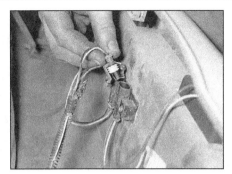

6.13b Disconnect the number plate wiring connectors

4 With the aid of an assistant, support the bonnet (disengage the support strut), then unscrew the bolts securing the bonnet to the hinges, and carefully lift the bonnet from the vehicle **(see illustration)**.

Refitting and adjustment

5 With the aid of an assistant, offer up the bonnet to the hinges, and loosely fit the retaining bolts. Align the hinges with the marks made on removal, then tighten the retaining bolts securely.

6 Close the bonnet, and check for alignment with the adjacent panels. If necessary, slacken the hinge bolts and re-align the bonnet to suit. Once the bonnet is correctly aligned, tighten the hinge bolts.

7 Once the bonnet is correctly aligned, check that the bonnet fastens and releases in a satisfactory manner. If adjustment is necessary, slacken the bonnet lock retaining

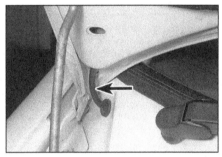

7.2b . . . then pull the hose down through the hole in the right-hand corner of the bonnet

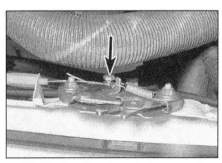

8.1 Slacken the clamp bolt (arrowed) securing the bonnet release cable to the lock operating lever

nuts, and adjust the position of the lock to suit. The rubber bonnet stops at the corners of the front body panel and can be rotated to adjust the closed height of the front of the bonnet. Once the lock operation is satisfactory, securely tighten the retaining nuts.

8 Bonnet release cable -
removal and refitting

Removal

1 Open the bonnet, then slacken the clamp bolt securing the bonnet release cable to the lock operating lever **(see illustration)**. Disconnect the release cable from the lock.

2 Release the outer cable from the bracket on the body.

3 Trace the cable run in the engine compartment, and release the cable from any locating clips and brackets.

4 Working inside the vehicle, reach behind the bonnet release lever, then squeeze the two lugs securing the release lever to its mounting bracket, and pull the lever from the bracket **(see illustration)**.

5 Again working in the engine compartment, tie a length of string to the end of the release cable.

6 Working inside the vehicle, pull the cable through the bulkhead into the interior. Untie the string from the end of the cable and leave it in position to aid refitting. Withdraw the cable assembly from the vehicle.

Refitting

7 Check that the cable grommet is securely located in the bulkhead, then tie the string to the end of the cable in the interior, and use the string to pull the cable through into the engine compartment.

8 Push the bonnet release lever back into the bracket under the facia.

9 Untie the string from the cable, then reconnect the cable to the lock, ensuring that it is located in any clips and brackets as noted before removal.

10 Check the operation of the bonnet release mechanism. If desired, the cable can be adjusted by altering the position of the end of the cable in the lock operating lever. Ensure that the clamp bolt is tight on completion of adjustment.

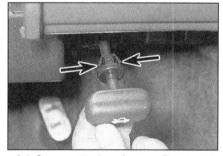

8.4 Squeeze the lugs (arrowed) and pull the bonnet release lever from its mounting bracket

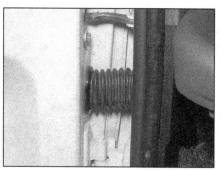

10.1 Pull the wiring grommet from the front edge of the door

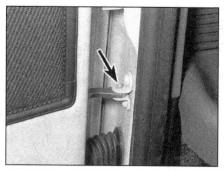

10.2 Drive out the door check strap pivot pin (arrowed)

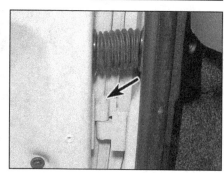

10.3 Unscrew the bolts (arrowed) securing the door hinge pins

9 Bonnet lock -
removal, refitting and adjustment

Removal

1 Open the bonnet, then slacken the clamp bolt securing the bonnet release cable to the lock operating lever. Disconnect the release cable from the lock.
2 Using a pencil or felt tip pen, mark the outline position of the bonnet lock relative to the body panel, to use as a guide on refitting.
3 Unscrew the two securing nuts and withdraw the lock.

Refitting and adjustment

4 Offer the lock into position, aligning the lock with the marks made on removal, then tighten the retaining nuts securely.
5 Reconnect the bonnet release cable, and tighten the clamp bolt.
6 Close the bonnet and check that it fastens and releases in a satisfactory manner. If adjustment is necessary, slacken the bonnet lock retaining nuts, and adjust the position of the lock to suit. The rubber bonnet stops at the corners of the front body panel and can be rotated to adjust the closed height of the front of the bonnet. Once the lock operation is satisfactory, securely tighten the retaining nuts.
7 If necessary, adjust the position of the bonnet release cable in the clamp to achieve satisfactory operation.

10 Door -
removal, refitting and adjustment

Removal

1 On models fitted with central locking and/or electric windows, proceed as follows **(see illustration)**.
 a) *Disconnect the battery negative lead.*
 b) *Remove the door inner trim panel as described in Section 11.*
 c) *Working through the rear aperture in the door, disconnect the two door lock wiring connectors, and/or the electric window regulator motor wiring plug.*
 d) *Release the wiring from any clips inside the door, then carefully pull the wiring grommet from the front edge of the door, and feed the wiring through the hole in the door.*
2 Fully open the door then, using a suitable punch, carefully drive out the door check strap pivot pin, taking care not to damage the paintwork **(see illustration)**.
3 Unscrew the bolts securing the two door hinge pins – the upper hinge bolt is accessible from below, and the lower hinge bolt is accessible from above **(see illustration)**.
4 Lift the door to release the tapered hinge pins from their housings, and withdraw the door.

Refitting

5 Refitting is a reversal of removal, bearing in mind the following points.

 a) *Do not fully tighten the door hinge pin securing bolts until the door check strap pivot pin has been refitted.*
 b) *Refitting of the door check strap pivot pin will be greatly eased if an assistant holds the door so that the pivot pin holes are exactly aligned.*
 c) *On completion check the alignment of the door with the surrounding body panels, and adjust if necessary as described in the following paragraphs.*

Adjustment

6 Using a suitable cranked spanner, slacken the bolts securing the door hinges to the body.
7 Move the door as required within the elongated bolt holes, then tighten the hinge securing bolts.
8 Check that the door lock operation is satisfactory. If adjustment is required, slacken the bolts securing the door lock striker to the body pillar, and move the striker as necessary within the elongated holes. Tighten the striker securing bolts on completion.

11 Door inner trim panel -
removal and refitting

Removal

Note: *If the door sealing sheet is removed, new door trim panel securing clips will be required on refitting – see text, and double-sided adhesive tape will be required to stick the sealing sheet in position.*
1 On models with manually-operated windows, release the securing clip and remove the window regulator handle. To release the securing clip, insert a length of wire with a hooked end between the handle and the trim plate on the door trim panel, and manipulate it to free the securing clip from the handle. Withdraw the handle and the trim plate.
2 Working at the front edge of the door release handle trim plate, remove the securing screw, then slide the trim plate towards the front of the door, and withdraw it over the release handle **(see illustrations)**.
3 Unscrew the two securing screws, and remove the door handle/armrest from the door **(see illustrations)**.

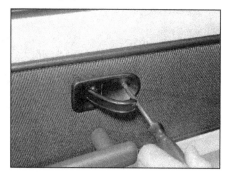

11.2a Remove the securing screw . . .

11.2b . . . and withdraw the door release handle trim plate

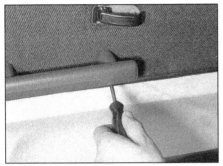

11.3a Unscrew the securing screws . . .

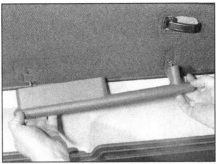

11.3b . . . and remove the door handle/armrest

11.4 Use a forked tool to release the door trim panel securing clips

4 Using a forked tool, or a large flat-bladed screwdriver (care must be taken not to cause damage if this method is used), release the clips around the edge of the door trim panel, then withdraw the panel from the door **(see illustration)**.

5 If work is to be carried out on any of the components inside the door, the door sealing sheet must be removed as follows **(see illustrations)**.

a) *Prise the female halves of the door trim panel securing clips from the door – the clips will be broken as they are removed (the tops of the clips must be broken off) – take care not to allow the clips to fall down inside the door.*

b) *Carefully peel the sealing sheet from the door – it should be possible to remove it intact.*

c) *If any of the sealing sheet adhesive is left on the door, clean it off.*

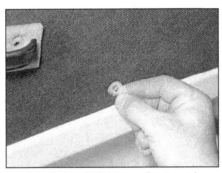

11.5a Prise off the tops of a door trim panel retaining clips . . .

Refitting

6 Refitting is a reversal of removal, but if the door sealing sheet has been removed, stick the sealing sheet to the door using double-sided adhesive tape, then fit the new female halves of the trim panel securing clips to the door.

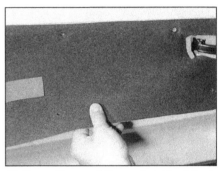

11.5b . . . then peel the sealing sheet from the door

12 Door handles and lock components - removal and refitting

Door interior handle

Removal

1 Remove the door inner trim panel and the sealing sheet, as described in Section 11.

2 Pull the foam pad from the interior handle, then unscrew the securing screw, and unclip the handle from the door **(see illustrations)**.

3 Unclip the interior handle lock operating rod from the lock at the rear edge of the door, and from the clip inside the door, then withdraw the interior handle, complete with the operating rod **(see illustrations)**.

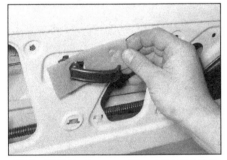

12.2a Pull the foam pad from the interior handle . . .

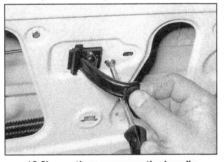

12.2b . . . then unscrew the handle securing screw

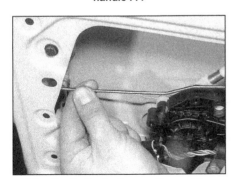

12.3a Unclip the lock operating rod from the lock . . .

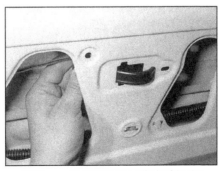

12.3b . . . and from the clip inside the door . . .

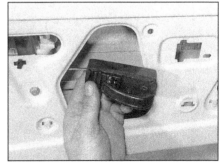

12.3c . . . then withdraw the interior handle

12.5 Unscrew the exterior handle retaining screw . . .

12.6a . . . then pull the handle from the door . . .

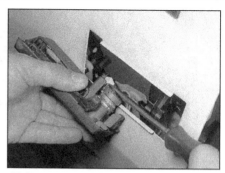

12.6b . . . and prise the lock operating rod from the lever on the lock cylinder

Refitting

4 Refitting is a reversal of removal, bearing in mind the following points.

a) *Make sure that the lock operating rod is correctly reconnected.*

b) *If necessary, adjust the position of the interior handle (the securing screw hole in the handle is elongated) to achieve satisfactory lock operation.*

c) *Refit the door sealing sheet and the inner trim panel with reference to Section 11.*

Door exterior handle

Removal

5 Working at the rear edge of door, unscrew the exterior handle retaining screw **(see illustration)**.

6 Slide the handle towards the front of the door, then pull the handle out from the door, and carefully prise the lock operating rod from the lever on the lock cylinder **(see illustrations)**. Withdraw the handle assembly.

Refitting

7 Refitting is a reversal of removal, but make sure that the lock operating rod is securely reconnected to the lever on the lock cylinder, and make sure that the window guide rail inside the door does not foul the handle/lock operating mechanism (it is easy for the guide rail to slot in between the lock operating rod and its surround).

Door lock cylinder

8 The door lock cylinder is integral with the exterior handle, and cannot be removed separately.

Door lock

Removal

9 Make sure that the window is fully raised.

10 Remove the door inner trim panel and the sealing sheet, as described in Section 11.

11 Unscrew the securing screws, and remove the door pocket from the bottom of the door **(see illustration)**.

12 Working at the rear edge of the door, unscrew the two window glass rear guide rail securing bolts, and withdraw the guide rail through the aperture in the door **(see illustrations)**.

13 Reach in through the aperture in the door, and disconnect the lock operating rods from the lock, noting their locations to aid refitting **(see illustration)**.

14 Working at the rear edge of the door, unscrew the three securing screws, then withdraw the lock from inside the door **(see illustrations)**.

Refitting

15 Refitting is a reversal of removal, but make

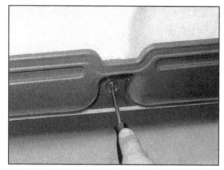

12.11 Unscrewing a door pocket securing screw

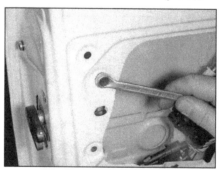

12.12a Unscrew the upper . . .

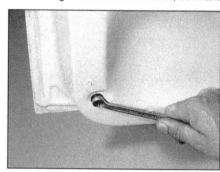

12.12b . . . and lower securing screws . . .

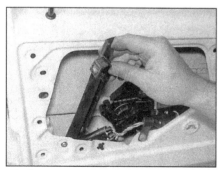

12.12c . . . and withdraw the window glass rear guide rail

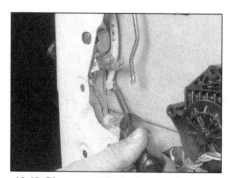

12.13 Disconnect the lock operating rods from the lock

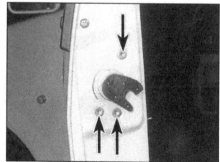

12.14a Unscrew the three securing screws (arrowed) . . .

12.14b ... and withdraw the lock

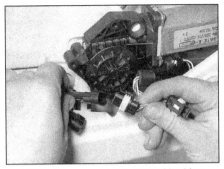

12.18 Disconnect the central locking motor wiring connectors

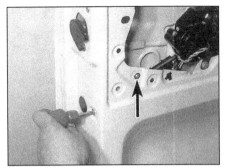

12.19a Unscrew the two securing screws ...

sure that the lock operating rods are correctly reconnected as noted before removal, and refit the door sealing sheet and the inner trim panel with reference to Section 11.

Central door-locking motor

Removal

16 Disconnect the battery negative lead.
17 Remove the door inner trim panel and the sealing sheet, as described in Section 11.
18 Working at the lower edge of the rear aperture in the door, unclip the two central locking motor wiring connectors from the door, then separate the two halves of each connector **(see illustration)**.
19 Unscrew the two securing screws, one at the rear edge of the door, and one at the lower edge of the rear door aperture, then manipulate the motor out through the door aperture, and unhook the lock operating rod from the lever on the motor **(see illustrations)**.

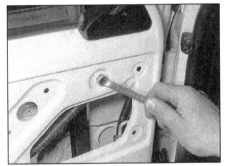

13.2a Unscrew the upper ...

Refitting

20 Refitting is a reversal of removal, but refit the door sealing sheet and the inner trim panel with reference to Section 11.

13 Door window glass and regulator - removal and refitting

Window glass

Removal

Note: *The manufacturers recommend that the lower window aperture weatherstrips are removed to ease removal of the window glass. In practise, it is impossible to remove the weatherstrips without breaking them (in this case new weatherstrips must be used on refitting) – provided that care is taken, the weatherstrips can be left in place, and the glass (and the bracket on the bottom of the glass panel) will pass through between the weatherstrips.*
1 Ensure that the window glass is fully raised, then remove the door inner trim panel and the sealing sheet, as described in Section 11 (note that on models fitted with electric windows, the battery negative lead should not be disconnected).
2 Working at the front edge of the door, unscrew the two securing bolts, then withdraw the window front guide rail through the aperture in the door **(see illustrations)**.

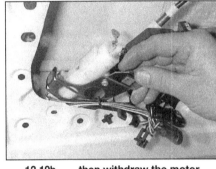

12.19b ... then withdraw the motor through the door aperture

3 Lower the window glass until the two glass panel-to-regulator bolts are visible through the aperture towards the top of the door **(see illustration)** then, on models with electric windows, disconnect the battery negative lead.
4 Ensure that the glass panel is supported (either with the aid of an assistant, or by securing it to the top of the door using strong adhesive tape), then unscrew the glass panel-to-regulator bolts.
5 Tilt the glass panel forwards, then carefully lift it out from the outside of the door **(see illustration)**. Take care not to damage the weatherstrips at the lower edge of the window aperture as the glass is removed – ideally, have an assistant spread the weatherstrips apart slightly to allow the glass to pass through.

13.2b ... and lower securing bolts ...

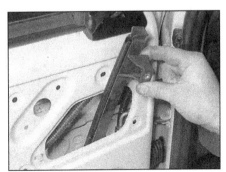

13.2c ... then withdraw the window front guide rail

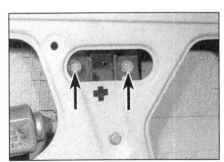

13.3 Lower the window until the glass panel-to-regulator bolts (arrowed) are visible

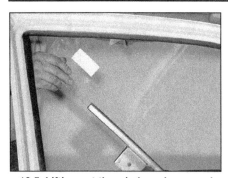

13.5 Lifting out the window glass panel

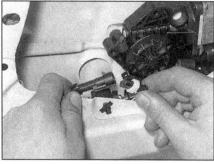

13.16a Disconnect the wiring plugs from the central locking motor . . .

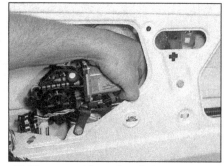

13.16b . . . and from the window regulator motor

Refitting

6 Refitting is a reversal of removal, but check the operation of the window before refitting the door sealing sheet, and refit the sealing sheet and the door inner trim panel with reference to Section 11.

Manual window regulator assembly

Removal

7 Ensure that the window glass is fully raised, then remove the door inner trim panel and the sealing sheet as described in Section 11.

8 Remove the door interior handle assembly as described in Section 12.

9 Raise or lower the window glass, as necessary, until the two glass panel-to-regulator bolts are visible through the aperture towards the top of the door (see illustration 13.3).

10 Ensure that the glass panel is supported (either with the aid of an assistant, or by securing it to the top of the door using strong adhesive tape), then unscrew the glass panel-to-regulator bolts.

11 Lift the glass panel upwards to the top of the window aperture, and secure it in position using strong adhesive tape – ensure that the glass cannot fall down into the door.

12 Unscrew the securing screws, and remove the door pocket from the bottom of the door.

13 Unscrew the four bolts securing the regulator mechanism to the door, then manipulate the mechanism out through the rear door aperture.

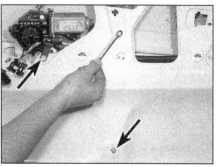

13.17a Unscrew the three regulator mechanism securing bolts (arrowed) . . .

Refitting

14 Refitting is a reversal of removal, bearing in mind the following points.

a) Check the operation of the regulator mechanism before refitting the door sealing sheet.

b) Refit the door interior handle assembly with reference to Section 12.

c) Refit the door sealing sheet and the inner trim panel with reference to Section 11.

Electric window regulator assembly

Removal

15 Proceed as described in paragraphs 7

13.17b . . . then manipulate the assembly out through the door aperture

to 12, but do not disconnect the battery until the window has been lowered for access to the glass panel-to-regulator bolts.

16 Disconnect the wiring plugs from the central locking motor, and move the wiring harness clear of the regulator assembly, then disconnect the wiring plug from the window regulator motor (see illustrations).

17 Unscrew the three bolts securing the regulator mechanism to the door, then manipulate the assembly out through the rear door aperture (see illustrations).

Refitting

18 Refer to paragraph 14.

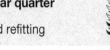

14 Opening rear quarter windows - removal and refitting

Removal

1 Fully open the window, then remove the three screws securing the window catch to the body (see illustration).

2 Support the window, then remove the screw securing the window hinges to the body, and lift out the window (see illustration).

Refitting

3 Refitting is a reversal of removal.

14.1 Unscrew the rear quarter window catch-to-body screws . . .

14.2 . . . and the hinge-to-body screw (arrowed)

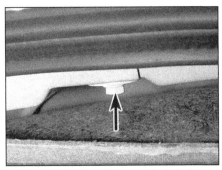

15.2 Disconnect the washer fluid hose from the connector in the body pillar

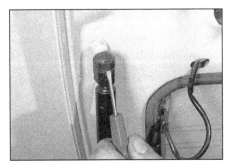

15.10 Tailgate hinge-to-body bolt (arrowed)

15.12 Slacken the bolts (arrowed) to adjust the tailgate anti-rattle stops

15 Tailgate and support struts - removal, refitting and adjustment

Tailgate

Removal

1 Disconnect the battery negative lead.
2 Working at the upper left-hand corner of the tailgate aperture, disconnect the washer fluid hose from the connector pushed into the grommet in the body pillar **(see illustration)**. Be prepared for fluid spillage.
3 Support the tailgate in the open position using a wooden prop or similar tool, or with the aid of an assistant.
4 Using a flat-bladed screwdriver, prise out the securing clips, then carefully prise the upper ends of the tailgate support struts from the studs on the tailgate.
5 Unscrew the tailgate hinge bolts then, with the aid of an assistant, carefully lift the tailgate from the hinges.

Refitting

6 With the aid of an assistant, offer up the tailgate to the hinges, then refit the securing bolts, and tighten them securely.
7 Close the tailgate, and check for alignment with the adjacent panels. If necessary, adjust the position of the tailgate as described in the following paragraphs.

Adjustment

8 Carefully prise the weatherstrip from the top edge of the tailgate aperture.
9 Using a suitable forked tool, or a large flat-bladed screwdriver (care must be taken not to cause damage if this method is used), prise out the securing clips, and release the rear edge of the headlining from the vehicle roof.
10 Slacken the bolts (one bolt on each side) securing the tailgate hinges to the body, then adjust the position of the tailgate within the elongated holes until it aligns with the surrounding body panels **(see illustration)**. When the adjustment is satisfactory, tighten the hinge bolts.
11 Refit the headlining, and secure it in position with the clips, then refit the weatherstrip.

12 Note that the rubber buffers at the lower corners of the tailgate can be moved, by screwing them in or out, to adjust the closed height of the tailgate lower edge. Tailgate anti-rattle stops are also fitted, at the lower corners of the tailgate aperture in the body, and these can be adjusted after slackening the securing screws **(see illustration)**.
13 Check the operation of the tailgate lock, and if necessary adjust it as described in Section 17.

Support struts

Removal

14 Support the tailgate in the open position, with the help of an assistant or using a suitable wooden prop.
15 Using a flat-bladed screwdriver, prise out the locking clip, then pull the support strut from its balljoint on the tailgate **(see illustrations)**.
16 Similarly, release the strut from the

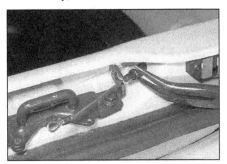

16.1 Unhook the tailgate release cable from the lock

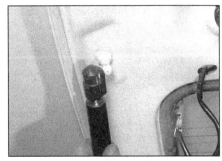

15.15a Prise out the locking clip . . .

balljoint on the body, and withdraw the strut from the vehicle.

Refitting

17 Refitting is a reversal of removal, but ensure that the locking clips are securely engaged.

16 Tailgate release cable - removal and refitting

Removal

1 Open the tailgate, and unhook the end of the release cable from the lock operating lever at the bottom of the tailgate aperture. Release the outer cable from the bracket on the lock **(see illustration)**.
2 Working inside the vehicle, remove the driver's seat, as described in Section 24.
3 Unclip the driver's side sill trim panel **(see illustration)**.

15.15b . . . then pull the tailgate support strut from the balljoint

16.3 Unclip the driver's side sill trim panel

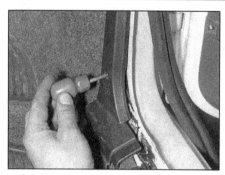

16.5 Unscrewing a driver's side footwell trim panel securing screw

16.6 Prise out the carpet trim panel securing clips

16.7 Disconnecting the tailgate release cable from the release lever

4 Prise off the trim cover, and unscrew the front seat belt lower anchor bolt, then remove the securing screw, and withdraw the trim panel from above the seat belt lower anchor.
5 Prise the weatherstrip from the edge of the driver's side footwell trim panel, then unscrew the securing screws, and remove panel **(see illustration)**.
6 Prise out the carpet trim panel securing clips, then pull the carpet panel away from the sill, and over the top of the tailgate release lever **(see illustration)**.
7 Unhook the cable end fitting from the release lever, then unhook the cable sheath from the bracket, and move the cable clear of the lever **(see illustration)**.
8 Working in the luggage compartment, tie a length of string to the end of the release cable.
9 Working inside the vehicle, pull the cable through from the luggage compartment,

noting its routing. Once all of the cable has been pulled through, untie the string from the end of the cable, and leave it in position to aid refitting. Withdraw the cable from the vehicle.
10 If desired, the release lever can be removed after unscrewing the two securing bolts **(see illustration)**.

Refitting

11 Refitting is a reversal of removal, bearing in mind the following points.
  a) *Use the string to pull the cable into position, ensuring that it is routed as noted before removal.*
  b) *Before refitting the carpet panel, check the operation of the release mechanism, and if necessary adjust the cable by altering the position of the adjuster nut at the release lever end of the cable.*
  c) *Refit the driver's seat with reference to Section 24, and tighten the securing bolts to the specified torque.*

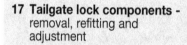

17 Tailgate lock components - removal, refitting and adjustment

Lock

Removal

1 Open the tailgate then, using a pencil or felt tip pen, mark the outline position of the catch relative to the tailgate, to use as a guide on refitting.

16.10 Unscrewing a tailgate release lever securing bolt

2 Unscrew the two securing nuts, then lift out the catch, followed by the lock cylinder assembly. Where applicable twist the lock cylinder assembly round to disconnect the lock operating rod from the central locking motor **(see illustrations)**.
3 If desired, the lock barrel can be separated from the housing, after driving out the retaining pin using a suitable drift. Recover the spring **(see illustration)**.

Refitting

4 Where applicable, refit the lock barrel to the housing, noting that the spring fits with its smaller diameter away from the lock barrel. Tap the retaining pin back into position to secure the barrel.
5 Offer the lock cylinder assembly into position, then refit the catch, aligning the catch with the marks made on removal, and tighten the securing nuts securely.

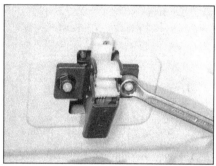

17.2a Unscrew the two securing nuts . . .

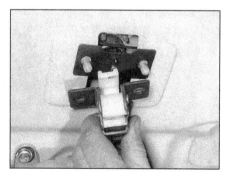

17.2b . . . and lift out the catch . . .

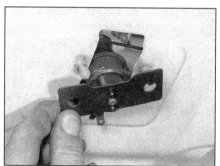

17.2c . . . followed by the lock cylinder assembly

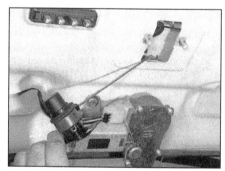

17.2d Twist the lock cylinder assembly round to disconnect the lock operating rod from the central locking motor

6 Close the tailgate, and check for satisfactory operation of the lock. If adjustment is necessary, the positions of the lock and the lock striker can be adjusted by slackening the nuts or bolts, as applicable, and moving the lock or striker within the elongated holes.

Exterior handle

Removal

7 Remove the tailgate lock as described previously in this Section.
8 Working inside the tailgate, unscrew the two securing nuts, then withdraw the exterior handle from outside the tailgate **(see illustration)**.

Refitting

9 Refitting is a reversal of removal, but refit the tailgate lock as described previously in this Section.

Lock striker

Removal

10 Open the tailgate then, using a pencil or felt tip pen, mark the outline position of the lock striker relative to the body, to use as a guide on refitting.
11 Where applicable, unhook the end of the tailgate lock release cable from the lock release lever on the striker assembly, then slide the cable sheath from the bracket on the striker.
12 Unscrew the two securing bolts and withdraw the striker **(see illustration)**.

Refitting

13 Refitting is a reversal of removal, but align the lock with the marks made on removal, before tightening the retaining bolts.
14 Close the tailgate, and check for satisfactory operation of the lock. If adjustment is necessary, the positions of the lock and the lock striker can be adjusted by slackening the nuts or bolts, as applicable, and moving the lock or striker within the elongated holes.

Central locking motor

Removal

15 Disconnect the battery negative lead.
16 Remove the two securing screws, then manipulate the lock out from the tailgate, and disconnect the lock operating rod and the wiring plug **(see illustrations)**.

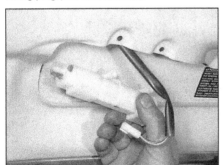

17.16b ... then withdraw the tailgate central locking motor

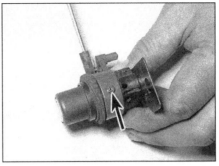

17.3 Lock barrel-to-housing retaining pin (arrowed)

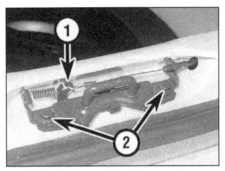

17.12 Disconnect the tailgate release cable (1) and unscrew the lock striker securing bolts (2)

Refitting

17 Refitting is a reversal of removal, but ensure that the lock operating rod is correctly reconnected.

Tailgate electrical contact assemblies

Removal

18 Disconnect the battery negative lead.
19 Working at the bottom of the tailgate, or the tailgate aperture, as applicable, unscrew the securing screw(s) and withdraw the contact unit **(see illustrations)**.
20 Trace the wiring back from the contact unit, and separate the two halves of the connector. Note that the contact units in the tailgate connect directly to the wiper motor and the central locking motor (where applicable).

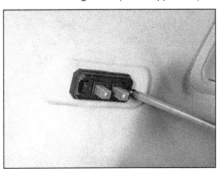

17.19a Unscrew the securing screws ...

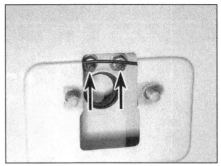

17.8 Tailgate exterior handle securing nuts (arrowed)

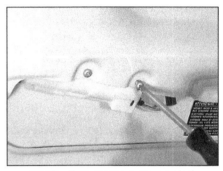

17.16a Remove the two securing screws ...

21 Pull the wiring through, and withdraw the contact assembly.

Refitting

22 Refitting is a reversal of removal.

18 Central locking system components - general information

Door lock motors

1 The procedure for removal and refitting of the door lock motors is described in Section 12.

Tailgate lock motor

2 The procedure for removal and refitting of the tailgate lock motor is described in Section 17.

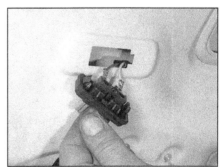

17.19b ... and withdraw the tailgate contact unit

18.3 Central locking control unit location (arrowed) – viewed from passenger's footwell

Central locking control unit

Removal

3 The control unit is located under the passenger's side of the facia (see illustration). To remove the unit, reach up under the facia and pull the unit from its socket.

Refitting

4 Refitting is a reversal of removal, but make sure that the pins on the unit engage correctly with the socket.

Remote control receiver

Removal

5 Certain models are fitted with a remote-controlled central locking system. The receiver unit for this system is mounted in the roof console.
6 To remove the receiver, carefully prise the

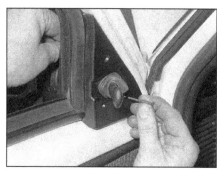

20.1 Unscrew the three mirror securing screws . . .

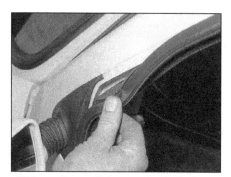

20.2 . . . then pull the weatherstrips from the edge of the mirror

unit from the roof panel, and disconnect the wiring plug(s).

Refitting

7 Refitting is a reversal of removal.

19 Electric window components - removal and refitting

Electric window switches

1 The removal and refitting procedure for the electric window switches is given in Chapter 12.

Electric window motors

2 The electric window motors are integral with the regulator assemblies. Removal and refitting details for the regulator assemblies are given in Section 13.

Electric windows control relay

3 The relay is located under the passenger's side of the facia, to the left of the central locking control unit (see Section 18). To remove the relay, reach up under the facia and pull the relay from its socket.
4 Refitting is a reversal of removal, but make sure that the pins on the unit engage correctly with the socket.

20 Rear view mirrors and mirror glass - removal and refitting

Exterior mirror

Removal

1 Working at the inside front corner of the door, unscrew the three mirror securing screws (see illustration).
2 Lower the door window, then carefully pull the weatherstrips from the edge of the mirror and the mirror trim panel, and from the front lower corner of the window aperture – take care, as the weatherstrips are easily damaged (see illustration).
3 Support the mirror, then pull off the mirror trim panel from inside the door, and withdraw it over the mirror adjustment lever (see illustration).

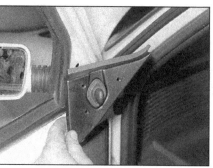

20.3 Pull the mirror trim panel from inside the door . . .

4 Carefully withdraw the mirror from the door (see illustration).

Refitting

5 Refitting is a reversal of removal.

Exterior mirror glass

6 The glass is integral with the mirror, and cannot be renewed separately. If the glass is broken, the complete mirror must be renewed.

Interior mirror

Removal

7 Disconnect the battery negative lead.
8 Carefully prise off the courtesy light lens.
9 Unscrew the two screws securing the mirror/courtesy light assembly to the roof, then lower the assembly, and disconnect the wiring plugs from the courtesy light.

Refitting

10 Refitting is a reversal of removal.

21 Windscreen, tailgate and fixed window glass - general information

These areas of glass are bonded in position with a special adhesive. Renewal of such fixed glass is a difficult, messy and time-consuming task, which is considered beyond the scope of the home mechanic. It is difficult, unless one has plenty of practice, to obtain a secure, waterproof fit. Furthermore, the task carries a high risk of breakage; this applies especially to the laminated glass windscreen. In view of this, owners are strongly advised to have this sort of work carried out by one of the many specialist windscreen fitters.

22 Sunroof - general information, removal and refitting

General information

1 Two different types of sunroof may be fitted, depending on model. A manually-operated tilting glass panel may be fitted, or an electric sliding canvas roof may be fitted.

20.4 . . . then withdraw the mirror from the door

Tilting glass sunroof panel

Removal

2 Working inside the vehicle, unscrew the two securing screws, and remove the glass panel cover **(see illustration)**.
3 Turn the sunroof control knob to open the glass panel slightly.
4 Unscrew the bolt securing the glass panel to the control knob **(see illustration)**.
5 Working outside the vehicle, tilt the glass panel forwards, until the hinges can be released from the roof, then lift out the panel.

Refitting

6 Refitting is a reversal of removal.

Electric sliding canvas sunroof

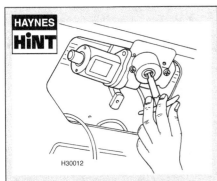

If the sunroof mechanism is faulty, and the roof panel is stuck in the open position, the panel can be closed manually as follows:

a) *Remove the securing screw, and lower the roof console panel. Disconnect the wiring plug from the sunroof switch.*

b) *Insert the handle supplied with the car in the hole provided in the sunroof motor spindle, then use the handle to turn the motor and close the roof panel.*

Roof assembly

7 Due to the complexity of the sliding canvas sunroof mechanism, considerable expertise is required to repair, replace or adjust the

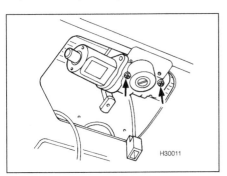

22.10 Sunroof motor securing bolts (arrowed)

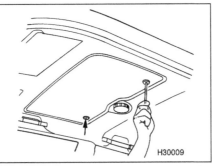

22.2 Unscrew the two screws securing the sunroof glass cover panel

sunroof components successfully. Removal of the roof first requires the headlining to be removed. Therefore, any problems with this type of sunroof should be referred to a Fiat dealer.

Roof motor

8 Disconnect the battery negative lead.
9 Remove the securing screw, and lower the roof console panel. Disconnect the wiring plug from the sunroof switch.
10 Unscrew the two securing bolts, and withdraw the motor from the roof **(see illustration)**.
11 In order to obtain satisfactory operation of the roof, before refitting the motor, slide the roof back to the fully open position, then refit the motor using a reversal of the removal procedure.

Roof switch

12 Refer to Chapter 12.

23 Body exterior fittings -
removal and refitting

Bumpers

1 Refer to Section 6.

Wheel arch liners and engine undershield

2 The wheel arch liners and engine undershield (where applicable) are secured by a combination of self-tapping screws and

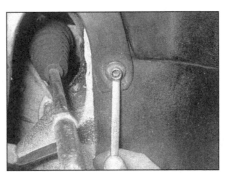

23.2a Unscrew the securing screws . . .

push-fit clips. Removal is self-evident, and normally the clips can be released by pulling the liner or undershield away from its mountings **(see illustrations)**.

Body trim strips and badges

3 The various body trim strips and badges are held in position with a special adhesive. Removal requires the trim/badge to be heated, to soften the adhesive, and then cut away from the surface. Due to the high risk of damage to the vehicle paintwork during this operation, it is recommended that this task should be entrusted to a Fiat dealer.

24 Seats -
removal and refitting

Front seats

Removal

1 Slide the seat fully forwards then, working at the rear of the seat rails, unscrew the bolts (one on each side) securing the rear of the seat rails to the floor **(see illustration)**.
2 Slide the seat fully rearwards.
3 Working at the front of the seat, unscrew the bolts (one on each side) securing the front of the seat rails to the floor.
4 Withdraw the seat from the vehicle.

Refitting

5 Refitting is a reversal of removal.

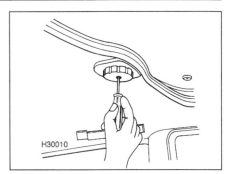

22.4 Unscrew the bolt securing the glass panel to the control knob

23.2b . . . to remove the wheel arch liners

24.1 Unscrewing a front seat rail rear securing bolt

Rear seat cushion

Removal

6 Tilt the relevant cushion forwards, then remove the bolt(s) securing the cushion hinges to the floor (see illustration).
7 Lift the seat cushion from the vehicle.

Refitting

8 Refitting is a reversal of removal.

Rear seat back

Removal

9 Fold the seat back down then, using a forked tool, or a large flat-bladed screwdriver (take care not to cause damage if this method is used), prise out the plastic clips securing the luggage compartment carpet trim panel to the rear of the seat back. If desired, the carpet trim panel can be left attached to the seat, and removed complete with the seat back.

24.6 Rear seat cushion securing bolt (arrowed)

10 Unscrew the bolts securing the seat back to the body then, on models with split seats, release the seat back from the centre hinge, and lift the seat back from the vehicle (see illustration).

Refitting

11 Refitting is a reversal of removal.

25 Seat belt components – removal and refitting

Front seat belt – models without seat belt pre-tensioners

Removal

1 Unclip the trim plate from the seat belt upper anchor by sliding it upwards, then unscrew the seat belt upper anchor bolt (see illustration).

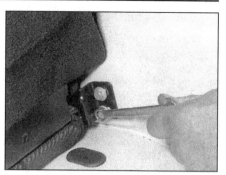

24.10 Unscrewing a rear seat back securing bolt

2 Prise the trim from the lower seat belt anchor bolt, then unscrew the lower anchor bolt (see illustration).
3 Using a forked tool, or a larger flat-bladed screwdriver (care must be taken not to cause damage if this method is used), work around the edge of the rear passenger compartment side trim panel, and release the trim panel securing clips. Remove the trim panel (see illustration).
4 Carefully prise the seat belt surround from the aperture in the body panel (see illustration).
5 Prise off the trim cover, then unscrew the inertia reel securing bolt. Withdraw the inertia reel through the aperture in the body panel, feeding the seat belt webbing and upper and lower anchor brackets through the small aperture in the body as the assembly is withdrawn (see illustrations).

25.1 Unclipping the trim plate from the front seat belt upper anchor

25.2 Unscrewing the front seat belt lower anchor bolt

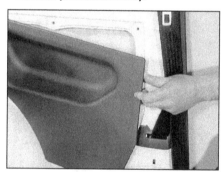

25.3 Removing the rear passenger compartment side trim panel

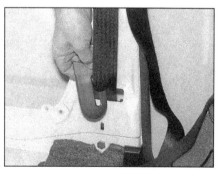

25.4 Prise the seat belt surround from the body panel

25.5a Prising the trim cover from the front seat belt inertia reel securing bolt

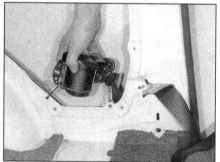

25.5b Removing the front seat belt assembly

Refitting

6 Refitting is a reversal of removal, but tighten the inertia reel securing bolt securely and the seat belt anchor bolts to the specified torque setting, and renew any passenger compartment side trim panel securing clips which were broken during removal.

Front seat belt – models with seat belt pre-tensioners

 Warning: DO NOT attempt to remove a front seat belt on a model fitted with pre-tensioners without first reading the precautions given in Section 26.

7 Refer to Sections 26 and 27.

Rear side seat belt

Removal

8 Remove the rear seat back, as described in Section 24.

9 Prise the trim from the lower seat belt anchor bolt, then unscrew the lower anchor bolt **(see illustration)**.

10 Unclip the trim plate from the seat belt upper anchor by sliding it upwards, then unscrew the seat belt upper anchor bolt **(see illustration)**.

11 Lift out the rear parcel shelf, then remove the two screws securing the parcel shelf side trim panel, and remove the panel **(see illustrations)**. Pass the seat belt webbing through the slot in the panel as the panel is withdrawn.

12 Working in the luggage compartment, remove the two securing screws, and

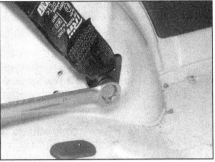

25.9 Unscrewing a rear side seat belt lower anchor bolt

withdraw the cover panel from the seat belt inertia reel **(see illustrations)**.

13 Unscrew the inertia reel securing bolt, then withdraw the seat belt assembly **(see illustration)**.

Refitting

14 Refitting is a reversal of removal, but tighten the inertia reel securing bolt securely and the seat belt anchor bolts to the specified torque setting.

Rear centre seat belt

Removal

15 Fold the relevant seat back down then, lift up the luggage compartment carpet trim panel for access to the seat belt anchor bolts.

16 Prise the trim from the relevant seat belt anchor bolt, then unscrew the anchor bolt and withdraw the seat belt or buckle assemblies, as applicable.

25.10 Unclip the trim plate from the seat belt upper anchor bolt

Refitting

17 Refitting is a reversal of removal, but tighten the seat belt anchor bolts to the specified torque setting.

---

26 Seat belt pre-tensioners - general information and precautions

General information

On models fitted with front seat belt tensioners, the pre-tensioner mechanism is incorporated in the seat belt inertia reel.

The pre-tensioners are mechanically-operated pyrotechnic devices, which operate instantaneously in the event of an impact, to remove all slack from the seat belt, therefore holding the driver or passenger (as applicable) firmly in their seat.

When the pre-tensioner mechanism is triggered, a striker is activated, puncturing a gas canister (containing mainly Nitrogen, and therefore harmless). The gas is released into a cylinder (attached to the inertia reel assembly), pushing a piston up the cylinder. The piston is attached, via a steel cable, to the seat belt inertia reel winding unit, therefore as the piston moves up the cylinder, the seat belt is retracted into the inertia reel.

Once a pre-tensioner unit has been activated, the seat belt winding mechanism will remain locked, and the complete seat belt assembly must be renewed.

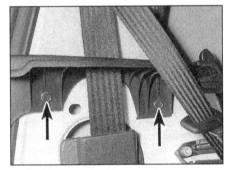

25.11a Remove the securing screws (arrowed) . . .

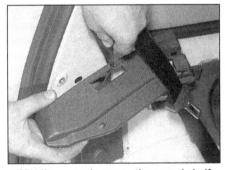

25.11b . . . and remove the parcel shelf side trim panel

25.12a Remove the two securing screws . . .

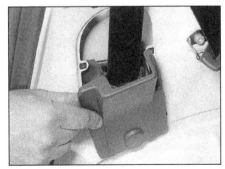

25.12b . . . and withdraw the cover panel from the inertia reel

25.13 Unscrewing the inertia reel securing bolt

A safety bracket, secured to the mechanism by a nut, effectively "arms" the mechanism. When the bracket is removed, the mechanism is in a "safe" condition, and cannot normally be activated unless mishandled.

The following precautions **must** be observed when working on models equipped with seat belt pre-tensioners.

Precautions

Removal and refitting of the seat belt assembly is potentially dangerous if the components are mishandled – the following precautions must be observed implicitly to prevent the possibility of injury:

 Warning: It is strongly recommended that eye protection is worn when working in the vicinity of the seat belt mechanism, and Fiat also advise the use of ear defenders and protective gloves to provide additional protection.

The system is armed until the safety bracket is removed (see Section 27) – DO NOT attempt to remove the seat belt assembly with the safety bracket fitted.

NEVER refit the safety bracket with the seat belt assembly removed from the vehicle – the safety bracket must only be refitted with the seat belt assembly refitted to the vehicle.

When handling the inertia reel/pre-tensioner assembly, always hold the assembly by the inertia reel – NEVER hold the assembly by the pre-tensioner cylinder.

DO NOT drop the assembly or subject it to impacts.

DO NOT attempt to carry out any dismantling of the assembly.

Once the assembly has been removed, according to legislation, it should be stored in a lockable metal cupboard meeting the appropriate legal requirements.

Keep the assembly away from naked flames, fluids, solvents, and lubricants.

If an assembly which has been activated is being handled, wear protective gloves and eye protection.

If the assembly has been activated, ALWAYS wait for 30 minutes after activation before carrying out any work in the vicinity of the seat belt assembly.

Wash your hands thoroughly after handling the assembly.

If any bodywork repairs are to be carried out which involve panel-beating, any type of impact, or high heat (welding, paint-curing operations, etc), the front seat belt assemblies MUST be removed from the vehicle to prevent the risk of inadvertent activation.

The pre-tensioner mechanisms are designed for use with a specific model of vehicle – DO NOT attempt to fit them to any other vehicle, even any other model of Cinquecento.

27 Front seat belts (models with seat belt pre-tensioners) - removal and refitting

 Warning: The precautions given in Section 26 MUST be read before proceeding.

Removal

1 The pre-tensioner mechanism is incorporated in the inertia reel assembly.
2 Unclip the trim plate from the seat belt

upper anchor by sliding it upwards, then unscrew the seat belt upper anchor bolt.
3 Prise the trim from the lower seat belt anchor bolt, then unscrew the lower anchor bolt.
4 Using a forked tool, or a larger flat-bladed screwdriver (care must be taken not to cause damage if this method is used), work around the edge of the rear passenger compartment side trim panel, and release the trim panel securing clips. Remove the trim panel (**see illustration 25.3**).
5 Working at the rear of the seat belt webbing slot in the body panel, unscrew the nut securing the pre-tensioner safety bracket to the stud on the pre-tensioner assembly. Remove the safety bracket (**see illustration**). *Caution: DO NOT refit the safety bracket until after the seat belt assembly has been refitted to the vehicle.*
6 Where applicable, carefully prise the seat belt surround from the aperture in the body panel.
7 Unscrew the inertia reel securing bolt, then withdraw the inertia reel/pre-tensioner through the aperture in the body panel, feeding the seat belt webbing and upper and lower anchor brackets through the small aperture in the body as the assembly is withdrawn.
8 Observe the precautions given in Section 26 when handling the assembly.

Refitting

9 Feed the seat belt webbing and the upper and lower anchor brackets through the body aperture, then offer the inertia reel/pre-tensioner assembly into position in the body pillar. Refit the inertia reel securing bolt, and tighten it securely.
10 Offer the safety bracket into position on the stud, ensuring that the lug on the bracket enters the slot in the body pillar (**see illustration 27.5**).
11 Refit the safety bracket securing nut, and tighten it to the specified torque.
12 Further refitting is a reversal of removal, but tighten the seat belt upper and lower anchor bolts to the specified torque setting.

28 Interior trim - removal and refitting

The interior trim panels are secured by a combination of clips and screws. Removal and refitting is generally self-explanatory, noting that it may be necessary to remove or loosen surrounding components to allow a particular panel to be removed.

When removing plastic push-fit type clips, if possible use a forked tool, as the clips are easily broken. Renew any broken clips on refitting.

Removal and refitting details for the centre console and facia assembly are given in Sections 29 and 30 respectively.

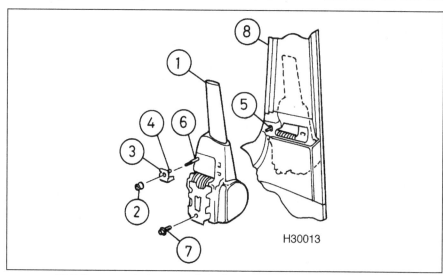

H30013

27.5 Front seat belt pre-tensioner/inertia reel assembly fitting details

1 Pre-tensioner/inertia reel assembly
2 Safety bracket securing nut
3 Safety bracket
4 Safety bracket lug
5 Safety bracket lug slot in body pillar
6 Safety bracket stud
7 Inertia reel securing bolt
8 Body pillar

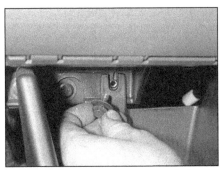

29.1 Removing the centre console front securing screw

29.2 Removing the gear lever gaiter

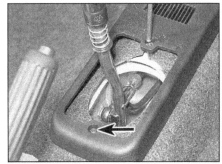

29.3a Remove the two rear securing screws . . .

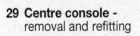

29 Centre console -
removal and refitting

Removal

1 Working at the front of the console, unscrew the centre console front securing screw **(see illustration)**.
2 Release the clip and the velcro from the top of the gear lever gaiter, then unclip the gaiter from the centre console, and pull the gaiter up over the gear lever **(see illustration)**.
3 Unscrew the two rear securing screws, then withdraw the centre console over the gear lever, and remove it from the vehicle **(see illustrations)**.

Refitting

4 Refitting is a reversal of removal.

30 Facia assembly -
removal and refitting

Removal

1 Disconnect the battery negative lead.
2 Where applicable, remove the centre console as described in Section 29.
3 Remove the instrument panel as described in Chapter 12.
4 Carefully prise out the centre facia-mounted switches, and disconnect the wiring connectors from the switches **(see illustration)**. Once the upper switches have been removed, the lower switches can be pushed out by reaching in behind the facia.
5 Unscrew the two clock securing screws, then withdraw the clock and disconnect the wiring plug **(see illustration)**.

29.3b . . . then withdraw the centre console

6 Remove the four heater control panel securing screws **(see illustration)**.
7 On models fitted with a headlight beam adjustment switch, proceed as follows.

a) Carefully pull the knob from the headlight beam adjustment switch.
b) Carefully prise the switch trim plate from the facia.
c) Remove the two screws securing the switch assembly to the facia.

8 Working on each side of the facia in turn, carefully prise out the ventilation nozzle, using a small flat-bladed screwdriver, then unscrew the facia securing screw from the ventilation nozzle housing **(see illustrations)**.
9 Working under the lower steering column shroud, unscrew the three securing screws, then withdraw the upper and lower steering column shrouds.

30.4 Prising out a switch from the facia

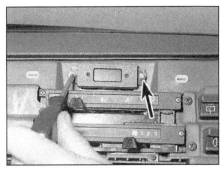

30.5 Unscrew the two clock securing screws

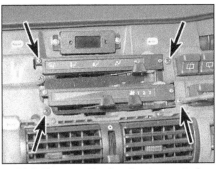

30.6 Unscrew the four heater control panel securing screws (arrowed)

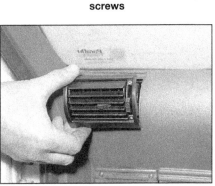

30.8a Prise out the ventilation nozzle . . .

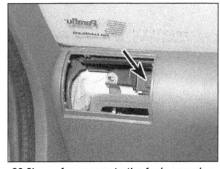

30.8b . . . for access to the facia securing screw (arrowed)

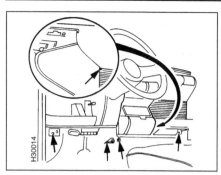

30.11 Facia securing screw locations (arrowed) – left-hand drive model shown

10 Unscrew the steering column upper through-bolt and nut, and the lower securing nuts, with reference to Chapter 10 if necessary, then lower the steering column from the facia, taking care not to strain the steering column-mounted switch wiring.

11 Unscrew and remove the remaining facia securing screws, then carefully pull the facia back from the bulkhead for access to the wiring looms **(see illustration)**. Note the routing of the wiring looms to aid refitting.

12 Reach down behind the rear of the facia, and remove the screws securing the wiring harnesses to the facia.

13 Make a final check to ensure than all relevant wiring has been released from the facia, then pull the facia back, and withdraw it through one of the door apertures.

Refitting

14 Refitting is a reversal of removal, bearing in mind the following points.

a) *Ensure that the wiring looms are routed as noted before removal.*

b) *Tighten the steering column securing nuts to the specified torque (see Chapter 10).*

c) *Refit the instrument panel with reference to Chapter 12.*

Chapter 12
Body electrical system

Contents

Degrees of difficulty

Easy, suitable for novice with little experience		Fairly easy, suitable for beginner with some experience		Fairly difficult, suitable for competent DIY mechanic		Difficult, suitable for experienced DIY mechanic		Very difficult, suitable for expert DIY or professional	

Specifications

General
System type . . . . 12-volt negative earth

Fuses
Refer to symbols stamped on fusebox for circuit identification

Bulbs

	Type	Wattage
Courtesy light	Festoon	5
Front direction indicator side repeater	Push-fit	5
Front direction indicator	Bayonet-fit	21
Front sidelight	Push-fit	5
Headlight	H4	60/55
Rear direction indicator light	Bayonet-fit	21
Rear foglight	Bayonet-fit	21
Rear number plate light	Festoon	5
Reversing light	Bayonet-fit	21
Stop/tail light	Bayonet-fit	21/5

1 General information and precautions

 Warning: Before carrying out any work on the electrical system, read through the precautions given in "Safety first!" at the beginning of this manual and in Chapter 5A.

The electrical system is of 12-volt negative earth type. Power for the lights and all electrical accessories is supplied by a lead/acid type battery, which is charged by the alternator.

This Chapter covers repair and service procedures for the various electrical components not associated with the engine. Information on the battery, alternator and starter motor can be found in Chapter 5A.

It should be noted that, prior to working on any component in the electrical system, the battery negative terminal should first be disconnected, to prevent the possibility of electrical short-circuits and/or fires.

Caution: Before disconnecting the battery, refer to the information given in the Reference section of this manual.

2 Electrical fault-finding - general information

Note: *Refer to the precautions given in "Safety first!" and at the beginning of Chapter 5A before starting work. The following tests relate to testing of the main electrical circuits, and should not be used to test delicate electronic circuits (such as anti-lock braking systems), particularly where an electronic control module is used.*

General

A typical electrical circuit consists of an electrical component, any switches, relays, motors, fuses, fusible links, or circuit breakers related to that component, and the wiring and connectors which link the component to both the battery and the chassis. To help to pinpoint a problem in an electrical circuit, wiring diagrams are included at the end of this Chapter.

Before attempting to diagnose an electrical fault, first study the appropriate wiring diagram, to obtain a more complete understanding of the components included in the particular circuit concerned. The possible sources of a fault can be narrowed down by noting whether other components related to the circuit are operating properly. If several components or circuits fail at one time, the problem is likely to be related to a shared fuse or earth connection.

Electrical problems usually stem from simple causes, such as loose or corroded connections, a faulty earth connection, a blown fuse, a melted fusible link, or a faulty relay (refer to Section 3 for details of testing relays). Visually inspect the condition of all fuses, wires and connections in a problem circuit before testing the components. Use the wiring diagrams to determine which terminal connections will need to be checked, in order to pinpoint the trouble-spot.

The basic tools required for electrical fault-finding include a circuit tester or voltmeter (a 12-volt bulb with a set of test leads can also be used for certain tests); a self-powered test light (sometimes known as a continuity tester); an ohmmeter (to measure resistance); a battery and set of test leads; and a jumper wire, preferably with a circuit breaker or fuse incorporated, which can be used to bypass suspect wires or electrical components. Before attempting to locate a problem with test instruments, use the wiring diagram to determine where to make the connections.

To find the source of an intermittent wiring fault (usually due to a poor or dirty connection, or damaged wiring insulation), a "wiggle" test can be performed on the wiring. This involves wiggling the wiring by hand, to see if the fault occurs as the wiring is moved. It should be possible to narrow down the source of the fault to a particular section of wiring. This method of testing can be used in conjunction with any of the tests described in the following sub-Sections.

Apart from problems due to poor connections, two basic types of fault can occur in an electrical circuit - open-circuit, or short-circuit.

Open-circuit faults are caused by a break somewhere in the circuit, which prevents current from flowing. An open-circuit fault will prevent a component from working, but will not cause the relevant circuit fuse to blow.

Short-circuit faults are caused by a "short" somewhere in the circuit, which allows the current flowing in the circuit to "escape" along an alternative route, usually to earth. Short-circuit faults are normally caused by a breakdown in wiring insulation, which allows a feed wire to touch either another wire, or an earthed component such as the bodyshell. A short-circuit fault will normally cause the relevant circuit fuse to blow.

Finding an open-circuit

To check for an open-circuit, connect one lead of a circuit tester or voltmeter to either the negative battery terminal or a known good earth.

Connect the other lead to a connector in the circuit being tested, preferably nearest to the battery or fuse.

Switch on the circuit, bearing in mind that some circuits are live only when the ignition switch is moved to a particular position.

If voltage is present (indicated either by the tester bulb lighting or a voltmeter reading, as applicable), this means that the section of the circuit between the relevant connector and the battery is problem-free.

Continue to check the remainder of the circuit in the same fashion.

When a point is reached at which no voltage is present, the problem must lie between that point and the previous test point with voltage. Most problems can be traced to a broken, corroded or loose connection

Finding a short-circuit

To check for a short-circuit, first disconnect the load(s) from the circuit (loads are the components which draw current from a circuit, such as bulbs, motors, heating elements, etc).

Remove the relevant fuse from the circuit, and connect a circuit tester or voltmeter to the fuse connections.

Switch on the circuit, bearing in mind that some circuits are live only when the ignition switch is moved to a particular position.

If voltage is present (indicated either by the tester bulb lighting or a voltmeter reading, as applicable), this means that there is a short-circuit.

If no voltage is present, but the fuse still blows with the load(s) connected, this indicates an internal fault in the load(s).

Finding an earth fault

The battery negative terminal is connected to "earth" - the metal of the engine/transmission unit and the car body - and most systems are wired so that they only receive a positive feed, the current returning via the metal of the car body. This means that the component mounting and the body form part of that circuit. Loose or corroded mountings can therefore cause a range of electrical faults, ranging from total failure of a circuit, to a puzzling partial fault. In particular, lights may shine dimly (especially when another circuit sharing the same earth point is in operation), motors (eg wiper motors or the radiator cooling fan motor) may run slowly, and the operation of one circuit may have an apparently-unrelated effect on another. Note that on many vehicles, earth straps are used between certain components, such as the engine/transmission and the body, usually where there is no metal-to-metal contact between components, due to flexible rubber mountings, etc.

To check whether a component is properly earthed, disconnect the battery, and connect one lead of an ohmmeter to a known good earth point. Connect the other lead to the wire or earth connection being tested. The resistance reading should be zero; if not, check the connection as follows.

If an earth connection is thought to be faulty, dismantle the connection, and clean back to bare metal both the bodyshell and the wire terminal or the component earth connection mating surface. Be careful to remove all traces of dirt and corrosion, then use a knife to trim away any paint, so that a clean metal-to-metal joint is made. On reassembly, tighten the joint fasteners securely; if a wire terminal is being refitted, use serrated washers between the terminal and the bodyshell, to ensure a clean and secure connection. When the connection is remade, prevent the onset of corrosion in the future by applying a coat of petroleum jelly or silicone-based grease, or by spraying on (at regular intervals) a proprietary ignition sealer.

3 Fuses and relays - general information

Fuses

1 Fuses are designed to break a circuit when a predetermined current is reached, in order to protect the components and wiring which could be damaged by excessive current flow. Any excessive current flow will be due to a fault in the circuit, usually a short-circuit (see Section 2).

2 The main fuses are located in the fusebox, below the driver's side of the facia.

3 For access to the fuses, depress the securing clip and lower the fusebox cover **(see illustration)**.

4 A blown fuse can be recognised from its melted or broken wire.

3.3 Depress the securing clip and lower the fusebox cover

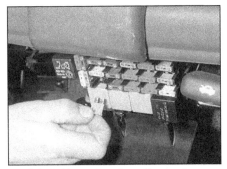

3.5 Pulling a fuse from the fusebox

3.14 Direction indicator/hazard flasher relay location (arrowed)

5 To remove a fuse, first ensure that the relevant circuit is switched off, then pull the fuse from its location **(see illustration)**.

6 Before renewing a blown fuse, trace and rectify the cause, and always use a fuse of the correct rating. Never substitute a fuse of a higher rating, or make temporary repairs using wire or metal foil; more serious damage, or even fire, could result.

7 Note that the fuses are colour-coded as follows. A symbol stamped next to each fuse indicates the main circuit protected.

Colour	Rating
Orange	5A
Red	10A
Blue	15A
Yellow	20A
Clear or white	25A
Green	30A

8 On certain models (eg, models with air conditioning and "Sporting" models), additional fuses are located in a fusebox on the left-hand side of the engine compartment, behind the engine electronic control unit.

Relays

9 A relay is an electrically-operated switch, which is used for the following reasons:
 a) A relay can switch a heavy current remotely from the circuit in which the current is flowing, allowing the use of lighter-gauge wiring and switch contacts.
 b) A relay can receive more than one control input, unlike a mechanical switch.
 c) A relay can have a timer function - for example, the intermittent wiper relay.

10 Most of the relays are located in the main fusebox, below the fuses.

11 Access to the relays can be obtained after removing the fusebox cover.

12 If a circuit or system controlled by a relay develops a fault, and the relay is suspect, operate the system. If the relay is functioning, it should be possible to hear it "click" as it is energised. If this is the case, the fault lies with the components or wiring of the system. If the relay is not being energised, then either the relay is not receiving a main supply or a switching voltage, or the relay itself is faulty. Testing is by the substitution of a known good unit, but be careful - while some relays are identical in appearance and in operation, others look similar but perform different functions.

13 To remove a relay, first ensure that the relevant circuit is switched off. The relay can then simply be pulled out from the socket, and pushed back into position.

14 The direction indicator/hazard flasher relay is on the right-hand side of the four relays in the main fusebox **(see illustration)**.

4 Switches - removal and refitting

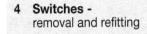

Note: *Disconnect the battery negative lead, with reference to "Disconnecting the battery" before removing any switch, and reconnect the lead after refitting the switch.*

Ignition switch/steering column lock

1 Working under the steering column, unscrew the three securing screws, then withdraw the lower and upper steering column shrouds.

2 To remove the lock barrel, insert the ignition key, and turn it to position "MAR" then, working through the slot in the lock housing, depress the lock barrel retaining lug, and pull out the lock barrel using the key **(see illustration)**.

3 To remove the ignition switch, make sure that the lock barrel is fitted, then unscrew the upper steering column securing through-bolt and nut, slacken the lower securing nuts, and lower the steering column.

4 Disconnect the wiring plug from the ignition switch, then carefully depress the two securing lugs, and withdraw the switch from the housing **(see illustrations)**.

5 Refitting is a reversal of removal, but make sure that the ignition switch and steering column lock securing lugs are securely engaged and, where applicable, tighten the steering column securing nuts and bolt to the specified torque (see Chapter 10).

Steering column-mounted stalk switches

6 Remove the steering wheel as described in Chapter 10.

7 Working under the steering column, unscrew the three securing screws and remove the lower and then the upper steering column shrouds.

4.2 Removing the ignition switch/steering column lock barrel

4.4a Depress the two securing lugs . . .

4.4b . . . and withdraw the ignition switch from the housing

4.8a Locate the stalk switch wiring connectors (arrowed) . . .

4.8b . . . then separate the two halves of each connector

4.9a Slacken the switch clamp bolt . . .

4.9b . . . then withdraw the switch assembly

4.11 Prise out the switch . . .

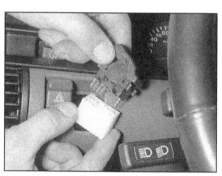

4.12 . . . and disconnect the wiring plug

8 Trace the wiring back from the stalk switches, and locate the switch wiring connectors. Remove the insulating foam, then disconnect the wiring connectors (see illustrations).

4.16 Pull the knob from the blower motor switch lever

9 Working at the lower left-hand side of the switch assembly, slacken the switch clamp bolt, then withdraw the switch assembly from the steering column (see illustrations).
10 Refitting is a reversal of removal, but refit the steering wheel as described in Chapter 10.

Facia-mounted pushbutton switches

11 Using a small flat-bladed screwdriver, carefully prise the relevant switch from the facia, taking care not to damage the facia panel (see illustration). Note that to remove the hazard warning light switch, it is necessary to prise out the lighting switch, then push the hazard warning light switch out from behind.
12 Disconnect the wiring plug and remove the switch (see illustration).

13 To refit a switch, reconnect the wiring plug, then push the switch into position in the facia until the securing clips engage.

Headlight adjustment switch

14 Refer to Section 8.

Heater blower motor switch

15 Remove the complete heater assembly as described in Chapter 3.
16 Pull the knob from the blower motor switch lever (see illustration).
17 Unscrew the two screws securing the switch to the heater control panel, then pull out the switch and disconnect the wiring plug (see illustrations).
18 Refitting is a reversal of removal, but refit the heater assembly as described in Chapter 3.

4.17a Unscrew the two securing screws . . .

4.17b . . . then disconnect the wiring plug . . .

4.17c . . . and pull the blower motor switch from the control panel

4.20 Reach up behind the facia and push out the electric window switch . . .

Stop light switch and handbrake "on" warning light switch

19 Refer to Chapter 9.

Electric window switches

20 Reach up behind the facia and push out the relevant switch (see illustration).
21 Disconnect the wiring plug and withdraw the switch (see illustration).
22 To refit, reconnect the wiring connector, then push the switch into position until the locking clips engage.

Courtesy light switches

23 Open the relevant door, then pull the rubber grommet from the courtesy light switch.
24 Unscrew the securing screw, then pull the switch from the door pillar and disconnect the wiring plug (see illustration). Tape the wiring to the door pillar to prevent it from falling into the hole in the body.

5.1a Disconnect the wiring plug . . .

5.2a Release the spring clip . . .

4.21 . . . then disconnect the wiring plug

25 Refitting is a reversal of removal.

5 Bulbs (exterior lights) – renewal

General

Whenever a bulb is renewed, note the following points.
a) Disconnect the battery negative lead, with reference to "Disconnecting the battery" before starting work.
b) Remember that, if the light has just been in use, the bulb may be extremely hot.
c) Always check the bulb contacts and holder, ensuring that there is clean metal-to metal contact between the bulb and its live(s) and earth. Clean off any corrosion or dirt before fitting a new bulb.

5.1b . . . then pull the cover from the rear of the headlight unit

5.2b . . . then withdraw the bulb

4.24 Removing the courtesy light switch

d) Wherever bayonet-type bulbs are fitted (see Specifications), ensure that the live contact(s) bear firmly against the bulb contact.
e) Always ensure that the new bulb is of the correct rating, and that it is completely clean before fitting it; this applies particularly to halogen headlight bulbs (see below).

Headlights

1 Working in the engine compartment, disconnect the wiring plug from the rear of the headlight unit, then pull the rubber cover from the rear of the light unit (see illustrations).
2 Release the spring clip by compressing its ends, then withdraw the bulb (see illustrations).
3 When handling a new halogen-type bulb, use a tissue or clean cloth, to avoid touching the glass with the fingers; moisture and grease from the skin can cause blackening and rapid failure of this type of bulb. If the glass is accidentally touched, wipe it clean using methylated spirit.
4 Install the new bulb, ensuring that its locating tabs are correctly seated in the light cut-outs. Secure the bulb in position with the spring clip, refit the rubber cover and reconnect the wiring plug.

Front sidelight

5 Working in the engine compartment, at the rear inboard corner of the headlight unit, twist the sidelight bulbholder anti-clockwise, then withdraw the bulbholder from the light unit (see illustration).

5.5 Withdraw the sidelight bulbholder . . .

5.6 . . . then pull the bulb from the bulbholder

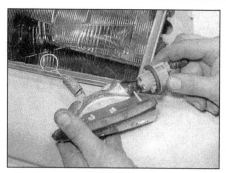

5.9a Twist the bulbholder anti-clockwise to remove it from the light unit . . .

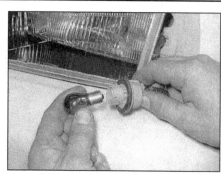

5.9b . . . then remove the bulb

6 The bulb is a push-fit in the bulbholder (see illustration).
7 Fit the new bulb using a reversal of the removal procedure.

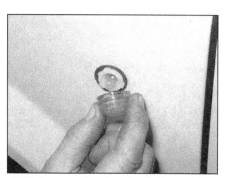

5.11 Remove the direction indicator side repeater lens . . .

Front direction indicators

8 Remove the light unit as described in Section 7.
9 Twist the bulbholder anti-clockwise to release it from the light unit. The bulb is a bayonet-fit in the bulbholder (see illustrations).
10 Fit the new bulb using a reversal of the removal procedure. Refit the light unit as described in Section 7.

Front direction indicator side repeater light

11 Carefully twist the lens anti-clockwise to remove it from the light unit (see illustration).
12 The bulb is a push-fit in the bulbholder (see illustration).
13 Fit the new bulb using a reversal of the removal procedure.

Rear lights

14 Remove the light unit as described in Section 7.
15 Working at the rear of the light unit, remove the two securing screws, then withdraw the bulbholder. The bulbs are a bayonet-fit in the bulbholder (see illustrations).
16 Fit the new bulb using a reversal of the removal procedure.

Rear number plate light

17 Unscrew the two securing screws, then withdraw the relevant light unit from the bumper (see illustrations).
18 Unclip the lens for access to the festoon bulb (see illustrations).
19 Fit the new bulb using a reversal of the removal procedure.

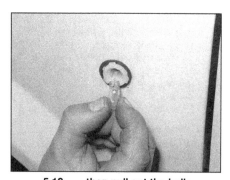

5.12 . . . then pull out the bulb

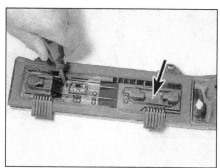

5.15a Remove the securing screws . . .

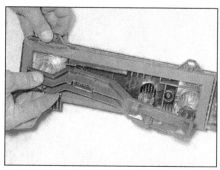

5.15b . . . then withdraw the rear light bulbholder . . .

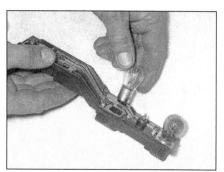

5.15c . . . and remove the bulb

5.17a Unscrew the securing screws . . .

5.17b . . . and withdraw the number plate light unit from the bumper . . .

5.18a ... then unclip the lens ...

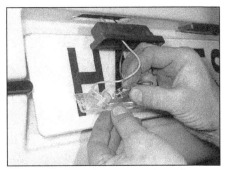

5.18b ... and pull out the bulb

6.2 Prise the lens from the courtesy light unit ...

6 Bulbs (interior lights) – renewal

General

1 Refer to Section 5, paragraph 1.

Courtesy light

2 Carefully prise the lens from the light unit **(see illustration)**.
3 Pull the bulb from the sprung contacts **(see illustration)**.
4 Fit the new bulb using a reversal of the removal procedure.

Instrument panel illumination lights

5 Refer to Section 11.

Heater control panel illumination bulbs

6 Working inside the vehicle, unscrew the three lower instrument panel surround securing screws.
7 Prise out the covers and unscrew the two upper instrument panel surround securing screws from either side of the clock housing, then withdraw the instrument panel surround.
8 Unscrew the two securing screws, and remove the relevant heater control cover panel **(see illustrations)**.
9 Pull the relevant bulb from the bulbholder **(see illustration)**.
10 Fit the new bulb using a reversal of the removal procedure.

Clock illumination bulb

11 Remove the clock as described in Section 12.

12 Twist the bulbholder anti-clockwise to remove it from the rear of the clock **(see illustration)**. The bulb is integral with the bulbholder.
13 Fit the new bulb using a reversal of the removal procedure.

Facia pushbutton switch illumination bulbs

Note: *Not all of the pushbutton switches have renewable illumination bulbs.*
14 Remove the relevant switch as described in Section 4.
15 Pull the bulbholder from the rear of the switch – if no bulbholder is visible, it is not possible to renew the bulb. The bulbs may be integral with the bulbholders, or may be a push-fit in the bulbholders **(see illustrations)**.
16 Fit the new bulb using a reversal of the removal procedure.

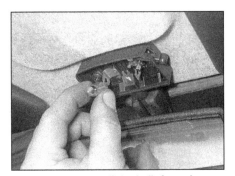

6.3 ... then pull the bulb from the contacts

6.8a Unscrew the securing screws ...

6.8b ... and remove the relevant heater control cover panel

6.9 Pull the bulb from the bulbholder

6.12 Removing the clock illumination bulb

6.15a The heated rear window switch illumination bulb is integral with the bulbholder

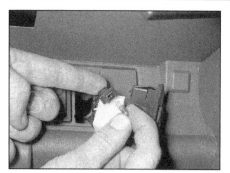

6.15b The electric window switch illumination bulbs are a push-fit in the bulbholders

7.1a Release the spring (arrowed) from the lug on the rear of the headlight unit . . .

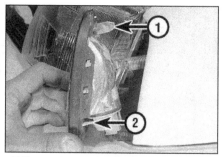

7.1b . . . then pull the direction indicator light unit forwards. Lug (1) which engages with headlight and pin (2) which engages with wing panel

7 Exterior light units - removal and refitting

Note: *Disconnect the battery negative lead, with reference to "Disconnecting the battery" before removing any light unit, and reconnect the lead after refitting the unit.*

Front direction indicator lights

1 Working in the engine compartment, release the direction indicator light unit retaining spring from the lug on the rear of the headlight unit, then pull the direction indicator assembly forwards to release the locating tabs from the headlight unit, and withdraw the indicator assembly from the front wing panel **(see illustrations)**.

2 Disconnect the wiring plug from the rear of the bulbholder, and withdraw the assembly.
3 Refitting is a reversal of removal, bearing in mind the following points.
   a) Make sure that the two lugs on the rear of the light unit engage with the headlight.
   b) Make sure that the pin engages with the hole in the wing panel.
   c) Make sure that the light unit retaining spring engages securely with the lug on the headlight.

Headlights

4 Working in the engine compartment, at the inboard rear corner of the headlight, unscrew the securing nut, then pull the headlight/direction indicator light unit forwards **(see illustration)**.
5 Disconnect the wiring plugs from the

headlight and the direction indicator light, then withdraw the assembly **(see illustration)**.
6 The direction indicator light unit can be separated from the headlight after releasing the retaining spring from the lug on the rear of the headlight.
7 Refitting is a reversal of removal but, where applicable, make sure that the light unit retaining spring engages securely with the lug on the headlight, and make sure that the locating lugs at the outboard edge of the headlight engage with the holes in the wing panel **(see illustration)**.

Front direction indicator side repeater lights

8 Remove the relevant front wheel arch liner, with reference to Chapter 11 if necessary.
9 Reach in behind the wing panel, and squeeze the side repeater light retaining lugs, then push the light unit out through the wing **(see illustration)**.
10 Disconnect the wiring plug and remove the light unit.
11 Refitting is a reversal of removal.

Rear light cluster

12 Open the tailgate, then unscrew the two light unit securing screws from the top edge of the light unit **(see illustration)**.
13 Withdraw the light unit and disconnect the wiring plug from the rear of the bulbholder **(see illustrations)**.
14 Refitting is a reversal of removal.

7.4 Unscrew the securing nut . . .

7.5 . . . then pull the light unit forwards and disconnect the wiring plugs

7.7 Make sure that the locating lugs (1) engage with the holes (2) in the wing panel

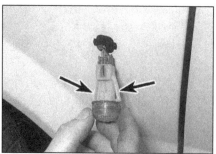

7.9 Squeeze the side repeater light retaining lugs (arrowed) then push out the light

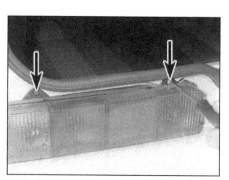

7.12 Unscrew the two securing screws . . .

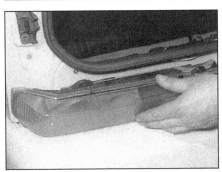

7.13a ... then withdraw the rear light unit ...

Rear number plate light

15 Unscrew the two securing screws, then withdraw the relevant light unit from the bumper and disconnect the wiring connectors.
16 Refitting is a reversal of removal.

8 Headlight beam adjustment components – removal and refitting

1 On certain models, a vertical headlight beam adjustment switch is provided on the facia. The switch operates two actuators, one fitted to each headlight unit. Hollow tubes filled with fluid (antifreeze) connect the adjustment switch to each actuator. Moving the adjustment switch varies the pressure of the fluid in the tubes, which moves the adjusters accordingly. The components are sealed, and no individual spare parts are available. If any of the system components are faulty, the complete adjuster/tube/switch assembly must be renewed.

Removal

2 Carefully pull the control knob from the switch.

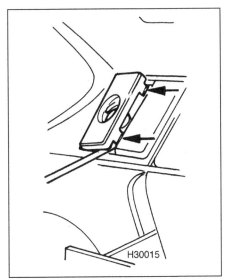

8.3 Prise off the headlight beam adjuster switch trim panel ...

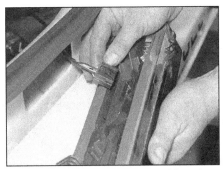

7.13b ... and disconnect the wiring plug

3 Using a small flat-bladed screwdriver, carefully prise the trim panel from the switch (see illustration).
4 Unscrew the two switch securing screws (see illustration).
5 Working in the engine compartment, carefully twist each of the headlight actuators to release the actuator body from the headlight housing, then pull the actuating rod from the balljoint on the headlight.
6 Trace the tubes back from the actuators, and release them from any clips and brackets in the engine compartment, noting their routing. Similarly, reach up behind the facia, and release the tubes from any remaining clips and/or brackets.
7 Release the actuator tubing grommet from the engine compartment bulkhead (push the grommet through into the passenger compartment), then carefully pull the tubing and the actuators through into the passenger compartment, taking care not to strain or bend the tubing excessively, and withdraw the assembly from behind the facia.

Refitting

8 Refitting is a reversal of removal, but on completion, have the headlight beam alignment checked at the earliest opportunity.

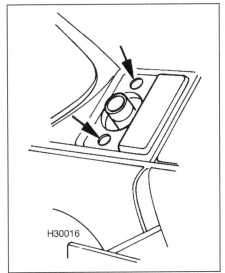

8.4 ... then unscrew the switch securing screws (arrowed)

9 Headlight beam alignment - general information

Certain vehicles are equipped with a four-position hydraulic vertical beam adjuster unit - this can be used to adjust the headlight beam, to compensate for the load which the vehicle is carrying. An adjuster switch is provided on the facia. The adjuster switch should be positioned as follows, according to the load being carried in the vehicle. Refer to the vehicle handbook for further information.

Position "0"	Driver only, or driver and 1 front seat passenger
Position "1"	Driver and three passengers
Position "2"	Driver and three passengers plus 50kg of luggage in luggage compartment
Position "3"	Driver plus fully-loaded luggage compartment

Accurate adjustment of the headlight beam is only possible using optical beam-setting equipment, and this work should therefore be carried out by a Fiat dealer or suitably-equipped workshop.

For reference, the headlights can be finely adjusted by rotating the adjuster screws fitted to the rear of each light unit. The vertical adjustment screw is mounted at the inner end of the headlight. The horizontal adjustment screw is mounted at the outer end of the headlight. Note that if the vertical adjustment is altered, this will affect the horizontal adjustment, which will have to be adjusted also.

10 Instrument panel - removal and refitting

Removal

1 Disconnect the battery negative lead (see "Disconnecting the battery").
2 Unscrew the three lower instrument panel surround securing screws (see illustration).

10.2 Unscrew the lower instrument panel surround securing screws ...

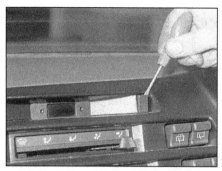

10.3a ... then prise out the covers ...

10.3b ... unscrew the upper screws ...

10.3c ... and withdraw the instrument panel surround

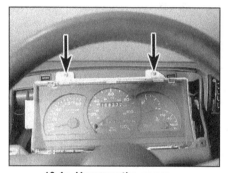

10.4a Unscrew the upper ...

10.4b ... and lower instrument panel securing screws (arrowed)

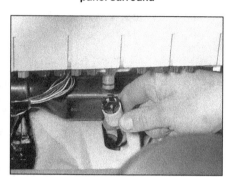

10.5 Disconnect the speedometer cable ...

3 Prise out the covers and unscrew the two upper instrument panel surround securing screws, then withdraw the instrument panel surround **(see illustrations)**.

4 Unscrew the four securing screws, and withdraw the instrument panel from the facia for access to the speedometer cable and wiring connections **(see illustrations)**.

5 Pull the securing sleeve back, and disconnect the speedometer cable from the rear of the speedometer **(see illustration)**.

6 Disconnect the instrument panel wiring plugs, noting their locations to ensure correct refitting, then remove the instrument panel **(see illustration)**.

Refitting

7 Refitting is a reversal of removal, but make sure that the speedometer cable and wiring

plugs are securely reconnected. To reconnect the speedometer cable, reach up from behind the steering column, and push the end of the cable onto the speedometer.

---

11 Instrument panel components - removal and refitting

Illumination bulbs

Removal

1 With the instrument panel removed as described in Section 10, twist the relevant bulbholder anti-clockwise and withdraw it from the rear of the instrument panel. The bulbs are a push-fit in the bulbholders **(see illustrations)**.

Refitting

2 Fit the new bulb and twist it clockwise to lock it in position. Refit the instrument panel as described in Section 10.

Speedometer

Removal

3 With the instrument panel removed as described in Section 10, proceed as follows.

4 Carefully prise the lens out from the front of the instrument panel **(see illustration)**.

5 Release the securing clips, and remove the instrument panel front panel **(see illustration)**.

6 Working at the rear of the instrument panel, unscrew the two securing screws, then withdraw the speedometer from the front of the panel **(see illustrations)**.

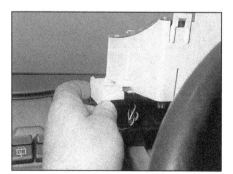

10.6 ... then disconnect the wiring plugs

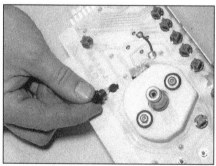

11.1a Remove the bulbholder from the instrument panel ...

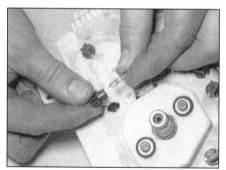

11.1b ... then pull the bulb from the bulbholder

11.4 Prise the lens from the front of the instrument panel . . .

11.5 . . . then release the securing clips and remove the front panel

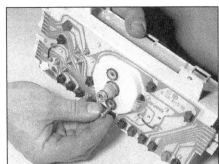

11.6a Unscrew the two securing screws . . .

Refitting

7 Refitting is a reversal of removal, but refit the instrument panel as described in Section 10.

Tachometer

Removal

8 Remove the speedometer as described previously in this Section.
9 Working at the front of the tachometer, unscrew the two securing screws (see illustration).

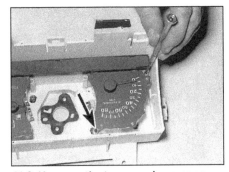

11.9 Unscrew the two securing screws . . .

10 Lift the tachometer from the front of the instrument panel, then reach behind the tachometer and carefully disconnect the wiring plug (see illustration).

Refitting

11 Refitting is a reversal of removal, but take care not to damage the circuit board when reconnecting the wiring plug, and refit the instrument panel as described in Section 10.

Fuel and coolant temperature gauges

Removal

12 Proceed as described in paragraphs 3 to 5.
13 Working at the rear of the instrument panel, unscrew the three securing nuts, then withdraw the relevant gauge from the front of the panel (see illustration).

Refitting

14 Refitting is a reversal of removal, but refit the instrument panel as described in Section 10.

11.6b . . . and withdraw the speedometer

12 Clock – removal and refitting

Removal

1 Disconnect the battery negative lead (see "Disconnecting the battery").
2 Unscrew the three lower instrument panel surround securing screws.
3 Prise out the covers and unscrew the two upper instrument panel surround securing screws, then withdraw the instrument panel surround.

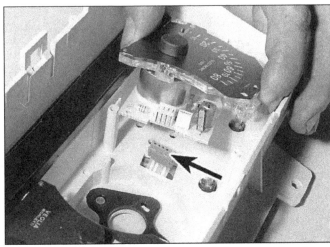

11.10 . . . then lift out the tachometer and disconnect the wiring plug (arrowed)

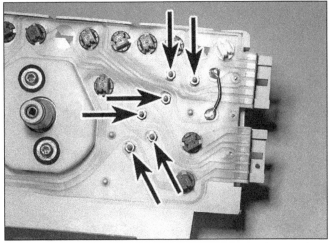

11.13 Fuel and temperature gauge securing nuts (arrowed)

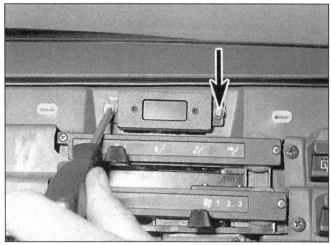

12.4a Unscrew the two securing screws . . .

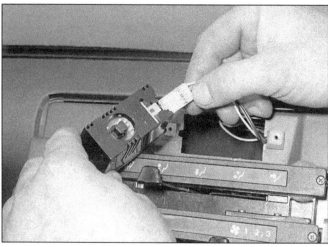

12.4b . . . then pull out the clock and disconnect the wiring plug

4 Unscrew the two securing screws, noting the locations of the washers (take care not to allow the washers to drop down behind the facia), where applicable, then pull out the clock and disconnect the wiring plug **(see illustrations)**.

Refitting

5 Refitting is a reversal of removal but, where applicable, ensure that the washers are located as noted before removal.

13 Horn -
removal and refitting

Removal

1 The horn is located on a bracket behind the left-hand side of the front bumper **(see illustration)**. If desired, to improve access, apply the handbrake then jack up the front of the vehicle and support securely on axle stands (see *"Jacking and Vehicle Support"*).
2 Disconnect the battery negative lead (see *"Disconnecting the battery"*).
3 Disconnect the horn wiring plug, then unscrew the securing nut, and withdraw the horn from the bracket.

Refitting

4 Refitting is a reversal of removal.

14 Speedometer cable -
removal and refitting

Removal

1 Remove the instrument panel as described in Section 10.
2 Working in the engine compartment, locate the end of the speedometer cable at the transmission. Unscrew the securing collar, then pull the end of the cable from the transmission.
3 Pull the weatherstrip from the front edge of the scuttle panel.
4 Unscrew the six screws securing the heater coolant pipe support plate to the engine compartment bulkhead.
5 On left-hand drive models, release the speedometer cable from the clip on the edge of the sound insulating shield on the left-hand side of the bulkhead.
6 Unscrew the four securing screws and withdraw the left-hand sound insulating shield from the bulkhead **(see illustrations)**.

13.1 Horn location (arrowed) – viewed with front bumper removed

7 Locate the speedometer cable grommet, and pull it out from the bulkhead **(see illustration)**.
8 Pull the end of the cable through the bulkhead from the passenger compartment into the engine compartment.
9 Release the cable from any clips and/or brackets, noting its routing, then withdraw the cable from the engine compartment.

Refitting

10 Refitting is a reversal of removal, but make sure that the cable is routed as noted before removal, and refit the instrument panel as described in Section 10.

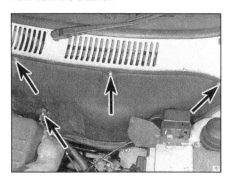

14.6a Unscrew the securing screws (arrowed) . . .

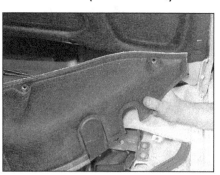

14.6b . . . and withdraw the left-hand sound insulating shield

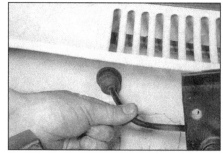

14.7 Pull the speedometer cable grommet from the bulkhead (left-hand sound insulating panel removed)

15 Wiper arm -
removal and refitting

Removal

1 Operate the wiper motor, then switch it off so that the wiper arm returns to the at-rest position.

 HAYNES HiNT *Stick a piece of masking tape along the edge of the wiper blade, to use as an alignment aid on refitting.*

2 Prise up the wiper arm spindle nut cover, then slacken and remove the spindle nut. Recover the washer, where applicable **(see illustrations)**.
3 Lift the blade off the glass, and pull the wiper arm off its spindle. Note that on some models, the wiper arms may be very tight on the spindle splines - it should be possible to lever the arm off the spindle, using a flat-bladed screwdriver (take care not to damage the scuttle cover panel) **(see illustration)**.

Refitting

4 Ensure that the wiper arm and spindle splines are clean and dry, then refit the arm to the spindle. Where applicable, align the wiper blade with the tape fitted on removal.
5 Refit the spindle nut, tightening it securely, and clip the nut cover back into position.

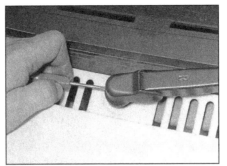

15.2a Prise up the wiper arm spindle nut cover . . .

16 Windscreen wiper motor and linkage -
removal and refitting

Right-hand drive models

Removal

1 Working in the engine compartment, carefully pull the weatherstrip from the front edge of the scuttle panel.
2 Unscrew the six screws securing the heater coolant pipe support plate to the engine compartment bulkhead **(see illustrations)**.
3 Unscrew the four securing screws, and withdraw the left-hand sound insulating shield from the bulkhead **(see illustrations 14.6a and 14.6b)**.

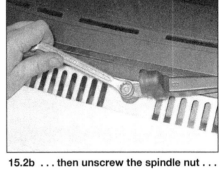

15.2b . . . then unscrew the spindle nut . . .

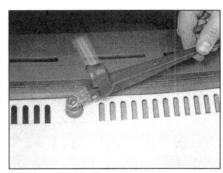

15.3 . . . and remove the wiper arm

4 Remove the windscreen wiper arms as described in Section 15.
5 Unscrew the two wiper arm spindle securing nuts from the top of the scuttle, and recover the plastic washers **(see illustration)**.
6 Unscrew the three securing screws, and remove the plastic shield panel from above the heater assembly **(see illustrations)**.
7 Unscrew the two bolts securing the wiper motor bracket **(see illustration)**.
8 Where applicable, to allow clearance for the wiper motor bracket to pass out from the scuttle, unclip the cover from the fuse assembly to the rear of the engine management electronic control unit bracket **(see illustration)**.
9 Manipulate the motor/linkage assembly out from the scuttle, and disconnect the motor wiring plug **(see illustrations)**.

16.2a Unscrew the six securing screws . . .

16.2b . . . and pull the coolant pipe support plate forward from the bulkhead

16.5 Unscrew the wiper arm spindle securing nuts

16.6a Unscrew the three securing screws . . .

16.6b . . . and remove the plastic shield from above the heater assembly

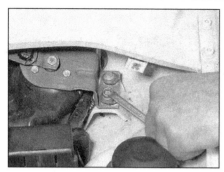

16.7 Unscrew the two bolts securing the wiper motor bracket

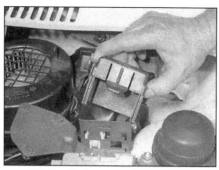

16.8 Unclip the cover from the fuse assembly

16.9a Manipulate the motor/linkage assembly out from the scuttle . . .

Refitting

10 Refitting is a reversal of removal, but refit the wiper arms with reference to Section 15.

Left-hand drive models

Removal

11 Remove the battery, as described in Chapter 5A.
12 Proceed as described in paragraphs 1 to 3.
13 Unscrew the securing bolt, and remove the sound insulating shield from the right-hand side of the bulkhead.
14 Release the speedometer cable from the clip on the edge of the sound insulating shield on the left-hand side of the bulkhead.
15 Proceed as described in paragraphs 4 to 9.

Refitting

16 Refitting is a reversal of removal, but refit the wiper arms with reference to Section 15.

17 Tailgate wiper motor - removal and refitting

Removal

1 Remove the wiper arm as described in Section 15.
2 Disconnect the battery negative lead (see *"Disconnecting the battery"*).
3 Open the tailgate, and disconnect the tailgate wiper motor wiring plug **(see illustration)**.
4 Unscrew the three securing bolts, and withdraw the wiper motor from the tailgate **(see illustrations)**.

Refitting

5 Refitting is a reversal of removal, but refit the wiper arm with reference to Section 15.

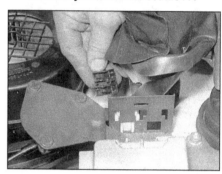

16.9b . . . and disconnect the motor wiring plug

18 Windscreen/tailgate washer system components - removal and refitting

Washer fluid reservoir

Removal

1 Disconnect the battery negative lead (see *"Disconnecting the battery"*).
2 Apply the handbrake, then jack up the front of the vehicle and support securely on axle stands (see *"Jacking and Vehicle Support"*).
3 Remove the front right-hand wheel arch liner.
4 Working in the engine compartment, remove the washer fluid reservoir filler cap.
5 Working under the wheel arch, unscrew the two bolts securing the front wing bracing bracket to the wing and the inner body panel, and remove the bracing bracket **(see illustrations)**.

17.3 Disconnect the tailgate wiper motor wiring plug

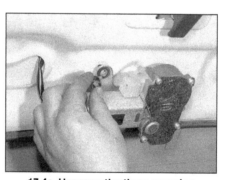

17.4a Unscrew the three securing bolts . . .

17.4b . . . and withdraw the wiper motor from the tailgate

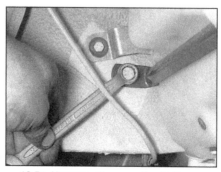

18.5a Unscrew the securing bolts . . .

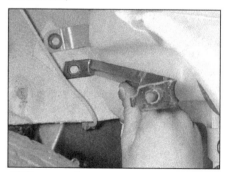

18.5b . . . and remove the bracing bracket

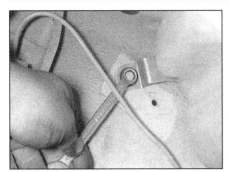

18.6a Unscrew the upper . . .

18.6b . . . and lower reservoir securing
bolts . . .

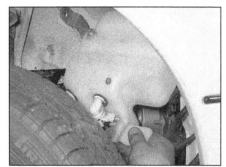

18.7 . . . then lower the reservoir

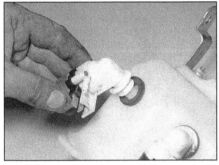

18.10 Removing a washer fluid pump from
the reservoir – reservoir removed for clarity

18.13 Disconnect the washer fluid hose
from the washer nozzle

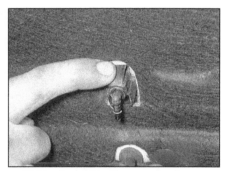

18.14a Compress the securing lug . . .

6 Unscrew the two bolts securing the fluid reservoir to the body **(see illustrations)**.
7 Carefully lower the reservoir, and disconnect the washer fluid hoses and wiring plugs from the fluid pumps, noting their locations to ensure correct refitting **(see illustration)**. Be prepared for fluid spillage, and have a suitable container ready to catch the fluid as it drains from the reservoir. Withdraw the reservoir.

Refitting

8 Refitting is a reversal of removal, but make sure that the washer fluid hoses and wiring plugs are correctly reconnected to the fluid pumps as noted before removal.

Washer fluid pump

Removal

9 Proceed as described in paragraphs 1 to 3.
10 Reach up under the wheel arch, then twist

and pull the pump from the fluid reservoir **(see illustration)**. Be prepared for fluid spillage, and have a suitable container ready to catch the fluid as it drains from the reservoir.
11 Disconnect the wiring plug and the fluid hose, and withdraw the pump.

Refitting

12 Refitting is a reversal of removal, but make sure that the pump is firmly engaged with the grommet in the reservoir.

Windscreen washer nozzle

Removal

13 Open the bonnet, and disconnect the washer fluid hose from the washer nozzle. Be prepared for fluid spillage **(see illustration)**.
14 Compress the securing lug, and carefully pull the washer nozzle from the outside of the bonnet **(see illustrations)**.

Refitting

15 Refitting is a reversal of removal, but make sure that the washer fluid hose is securely reconnected.

Tailgate washer nozzle

Removal

16 Open the tailgate then, working at the upper left-hand corner of the tailgate aperture, disconnect the washer fluid hose from the connector pushed into the grommet in the body pillar **(see illustration)**. Be prepared for fluid spillage.
17 Working at the top of the tailgate, prise the plastic blanking plug from the hole below the washer nozzle **(see illustration)**.
18 Reach in through the hole in the tailgate, and depress the washer nozzle securing tabs,

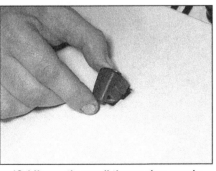

18.14b . . . then pull the washer nozzle
from the bonnet

18.16 Disconnect the washer fluid hose
from the connector

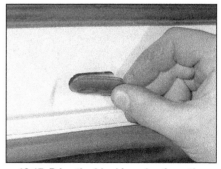

18.17 Prise the blanking plug from the
tailgate . . .

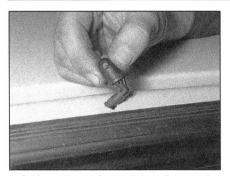

18.18 ... then release the washer nozzle

19.4 Removing the radio/cassette player using DIN removal tools

19.5 Disconnecting the radio/cassette player wiring plug

then pull the nozzle from the outside of the tailgate, and disconnect the fluid hose **(see illustration)**.

Refitting

19 Refitting is a reversal of removal, but ensure that the fluid hose is securely reconnected to the nozzle and the connector.

19 Radio/cassette player - removal and refitting

Note: On models with a security-coded radio/cassette player, once the battery has been disconnected, the unit cannot be re-activated until the appropriate security code has been entered. Do not remove the unit unless the appropriate code is known. The following information applies to radio/cassette players having standard DIN fixings. Two DIN removal tools will be required for this operation.

Removal

1 Disconnect the battery negative lead, with reference to *"Disconnecting the battery"*.
2 Insert the DIN removal tools into the holes on each side of the radio/cassette player, and push them until they click into place.

3 Pull the tools gently to the left and right to release the locking tangs.
4 Gently pull the radio/cassette player from the facia, using the removal tools **(see illustration)**.
5 Disconnect the wiring plug(s) and the aerial lead, and withdraw the unit **(see illustration)**.

Refitting

6 Reconnect the wiring plug(s) and the aerial lead, then push the unit into its housing until the securing clips engage.
7 On completion, reconnect the battery negative lead and, where applicable, enter the security code.

20 Loudspeakers - removal and refitting

Removal

1 Disconnect the battery negative lead (see "Disconnecting the battery").
2 Unscrew the two securing screws, and withdraw the relevant loudspeaker cover panel from the facia **(see illustration)**.
3 Unscrew the remaining two securing screws (two of the loudspeaker securing

screws also secure the cover panel), then lift the loudspeaker out from the facia, and disconnect the wiring plug **(see illustrations)**.

Refitting

4 Refitting is a reversal of removal.

21 Radio aerial - removal and refitting

Aerial mast

1 The aerial mast can simply be unscrewed from the base.

Complete aerial

Removal

2 Tilt the aerial mast fully downwards (towards the rear of the vehicle), then pull out the now-exposed cover plug to reveal the aerial securing screw.
3 Unscrew the securing screw, then lift the aerial from the roof. Recover the surround moulding.

Refitting

4 Refitting is a reversal of removal.

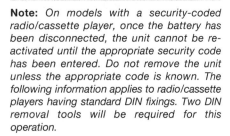

20.2 Withdraw the loudspeaker cover panel ...

20.3a ... then unscrew the two securing screws ...

20.3b ... lift out the loudspeaker and disconnect the wiring plug

22 Anti-theft alarm system and engine immobiliser -
general information

Certain vehicles are equipped with an anti-theft alarm system and/or and engine immobiliser system. Various types of system may be fitted depending on vehicle specification, and market.

The anti-theft alarm system, is automatically activated by the central locking system (manually, or via the remote control, where applicable), or via a remote control transmitter incorporated in the ignition key. The engine immobiliser system is operated by a coded unit in the ignition key – the engine can only be started using one of the ignition keys originally supplied with the car when new.

The alarm system has switches on the bonnet, tailgate and each of the doors.

Any faults with the system should be referred to a Fiat dealer.

23 Air bag system -
general information and precautions

General information

A driver's side air bag is fitted as standard equipment on some models, and is available as an option on others. The air bag is fitted to the steering wheel centre pad.

The system is mechanically-operated, via an impact sensor fitted to the steering wheel. This means that there is no effective way of disarming the air bag.

The air bag is inflated by a gas generator, which forces the bag out from its housing in the steering wheel.

Once activated, the airbag unit must be renewed – this work should be carried out by a Fiat dealer.

Precautions

 Warning: Do not attempt to tamper with, or remove any of the airbag components.

The following precautions **must** be observed when carrying out work on a vehicle equipped with an air bag.

Do not use tools such as hammers or impact screwdrivers in any area of the vehicle which could transmit impact or jolts to the steering wheel or air bag.

Do not expose the steering wheel or air bag to excessively high temperatures (above 90°C).

The removal and refitting of the air bag components should be entrusted to a Fiat dealer.

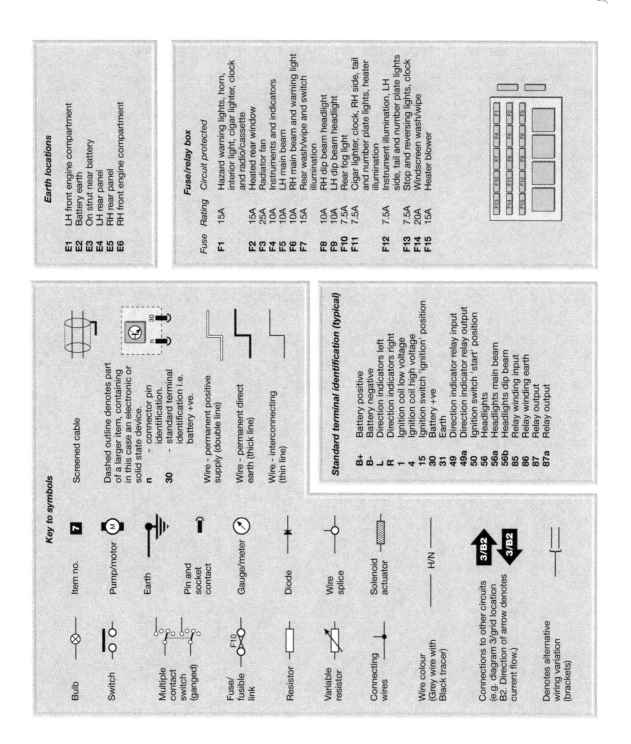

Earth locations

E1	LH front engine compartment
E2	Battery earth
E3	On strut near battery
E4	LH rear panel
E5	RH rear panel
E6	RH front engine compartment

Fuse/relay box

Fuse	Rating	Circuit protected
F1	15A	Hazard warning lights, horn, interior light, cigar lighter, clock and radio/cassette
F2	15A	Heated rear window
F3	25A	Radiator fan
F4	10A	Instruments and indicators
F5	10A	LH main beam
F6	10A	RH main beam and warning light
F7	15A	Rear wash/wipe and switch illumination
F8	10A	RH dip beam headlight
F9	10A	LH dip beam headlight
F10	7.5A	Rear fog light
F11	7.5A	Cigar lighter, clock, RH side, tail and number plate lights, heater illumination
F12	7.5A	Instrument illumination, LH side, tail and number plate lights
F13	7.5A	Stop and reversing lights, clock
F14	20A	Windscreen wash/wipe
F15	15A	Heater blower

Key to symbols

Bulb	
Switch	
Multiple contact switch (ganged)	
Fuse/ fusible link	F10
Resistor	
Variable resistor	
Connecting wires	
Wire colour (Grey wire with Black tracer)	H/N
Connections to other circuits (e.g. diagram 3/grid location B2. Direction of arrow denotes current flow.)	3/B2
Denotes alternative wiring variation (brackets)	
Screened cable	
Dashed outline denotes part of a larger item, containing in this case an electronic or solid state device.	
n	- connector pin identification.
30	- standard terminal identification i.e. battery +ve.
Wire - permanent positive supply (double line)	
Wire - permanent direct earth (thick line)	
Wire - interconnecting (thin line)	
Item no.	7
Pump/motor	M
Earth	
Pin and socket contact	
Gauge/meter	
Diode	
Wire splice	
Solenoid actuator	

Standard terminal identification (typical)

B+	Battery positive
B-	Battery negative
L	Direction indicators left
R	Direction indicators right
1	Ignition coil low voltage
4	Ignition coil high voltage
15	Ignition switch 'ignition' position
30	Battery +ve
31	Earth
49	Direction indicator relay input
49a	Direction indicator relay output
50	Ignition switch 'start' position
56	Headlights
56a	Headlights main beam
56b	Headlights dip beam
85	Relay winding input
86	Relay winding earth
87	Relay output
87a	Relay output

Diagram 1 : Information for wiring diagrams

H31016

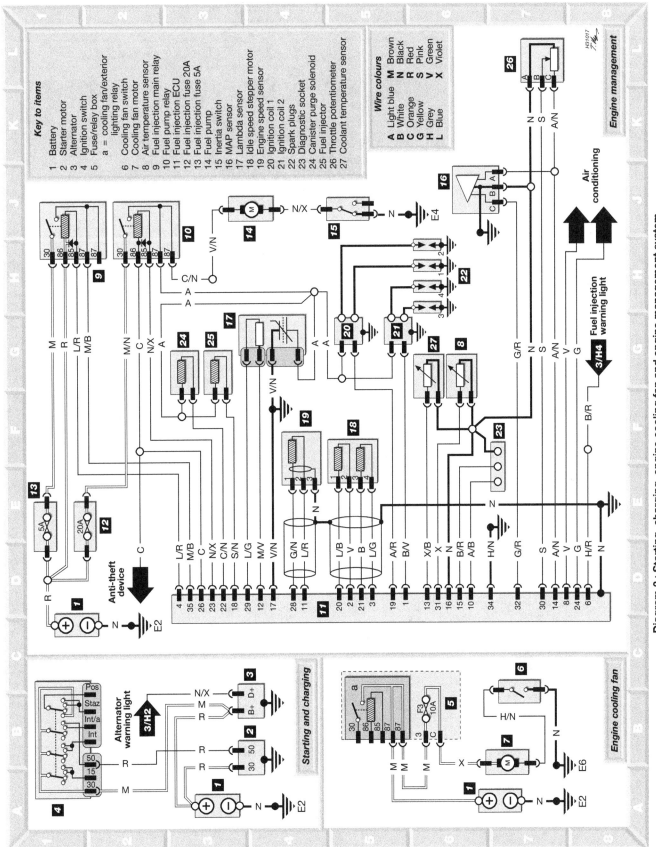

Diagram 2 : Starting, charging, engine cooling fan and engine management system

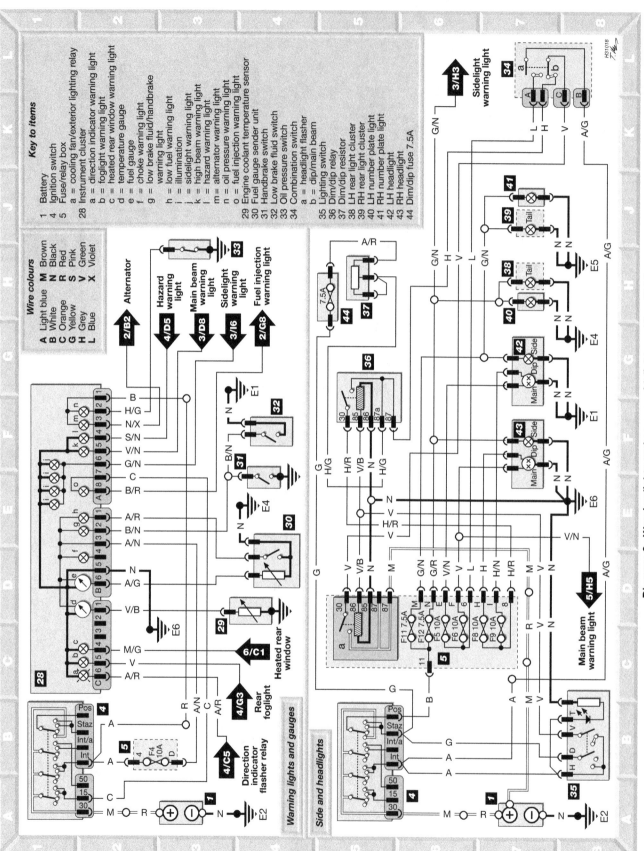

Key to items

1 Battery
4 Ignition switch
5 Fuse/relay box
  a = cooling fan/exterior lighting relay
28 Instrument cluster
  a = direction indicator warning light
  b = foglight warning light
  c = heated rear window warning light
  d = temperature gauge
  e = fuel gauge
  f = choke warning light
  g = low brake fluid/handbrake warning light
  h = low fuel warning light
  i = illumination
  j = sidelight warning light
  k = high beam warning light
  l = hazard warning light
  m = alternator warning light
  n = oil pressure warning light
  o = fuel injection warning light
29 Engine coolant temperature sensor
30 Fuel gauge sender unit
31 Handbrake switch
32 Low brake fluid switch
33 Oil pressure switch
34 Combination switch
  a = headlight flasher
  b = dip/main beam
35 Lighting switch
36 Dim/dip relay
37 Dim/dip resistor
38 LH rear light cluster
39 RH rear light cluster
40 LH number plate light
41 RH number plate light
42 LH headlight
43 RH headlight
44 Dim/dip fuse 7.5A

Wire colours

A Light blue   M Brown
B White   N Black
C Orange   R Red
G Yellow   S Pink
H Grey   V Green
L Blue   X Violet

Alternator   2/B2

Hazard warning light   4/D5

Main beam warning light   3/D8

Sidelight warning light   3/I6

Fuel injection warning light   2/G8

Heated rear window   6/C1

Rear foglight   4/C3

Direction indicator flasher relay   4/C5

Sidelight warning light   3/H3

Main beam warning light   5/H5

Warning lights and gauges

Side and headlights

Diagram 3 : Warning lights and gauges, sidelights and headlights

H31018

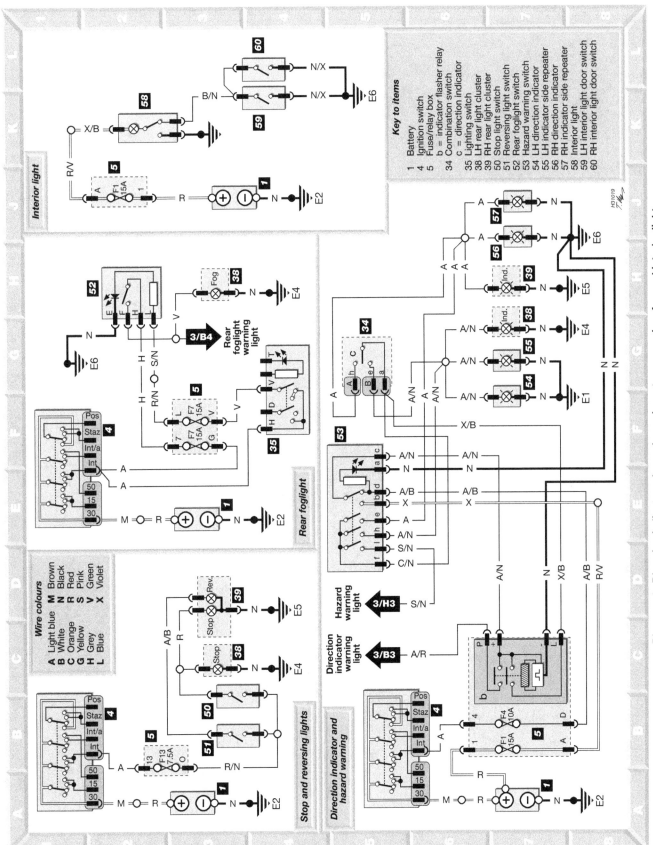

Diagram 4 : Direction indicators, hazard warning, stop, reversing, fog and interior lights

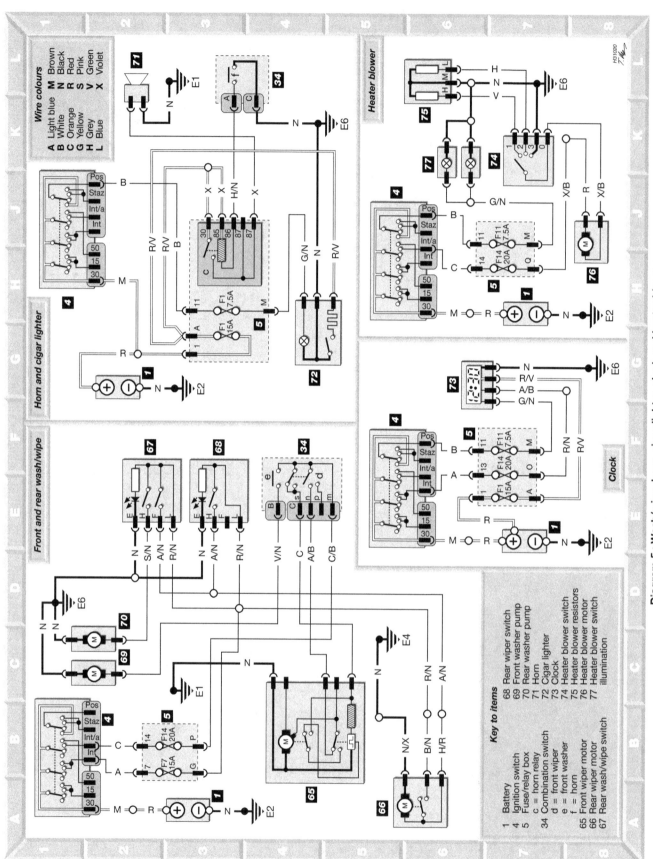

Wire colours
A Light blue
B White
C Orange
G Yellow
H Grey
L Blue
M Brown
N Black
R Red
S Pink
V Green
X Violet

Horn and cigar lighter

Front and rear wash/wipe

Heater blower

Clock

H31020

Key to items
1 Battery
4 Ignition switch
5 Fuse/relay box
34 Combination switch
 c = horn relay
 d = front wiper
 e = front washer
 f = horn
65 Front wiper motor
66 Rear wiper motor
67 Rear wash/wipe switch
68 Rear wiper switch
69 Front washer pump
70 Rear washer pump
71 Horn
72 Cigar lighter
73 Clock
74 Heater blower switch
75 Heater blower resistors
76 Heater blower motor
77 Heater blower switch
 illumination

Diagram 5 : Wash/wipe, horn, cigar lighter, clock and heater blower

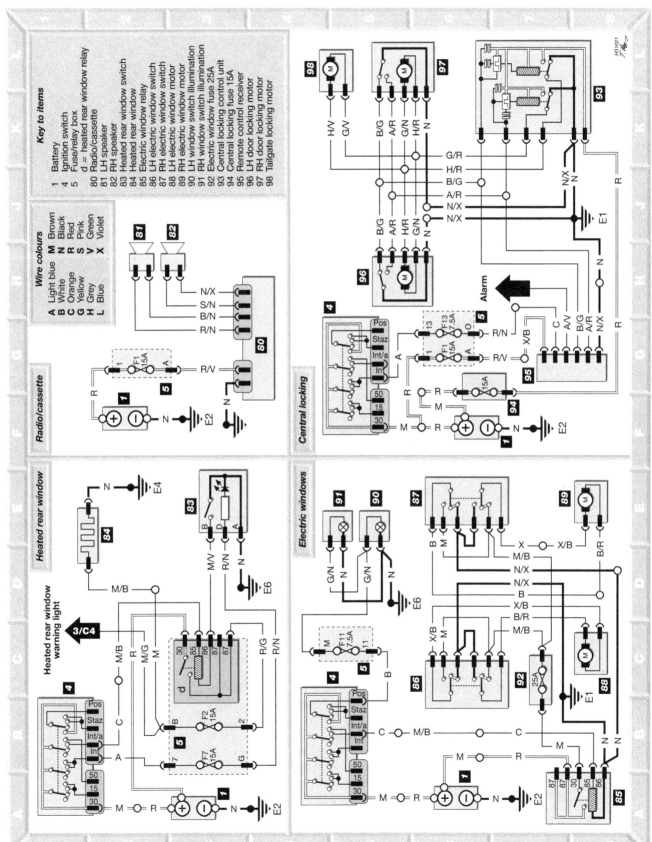

Key to items

1   Battery
4   Ignition switch
5   Fuse/relay box
    d = heated rear window relay
80 Radio/cassette
81 LH speaker
82 RH speaker
83 Heated rear window switch
84 Heated rear window
85 Electric window relay
86 LH electric window switch
87 RH electric window switch
88 LH electric window motor
89 RH electric window motor
90 LH window switch illumination
91 RH window switch illumination
92 Electric window fuse 25A
93 Central locking control unit
94 Central locking fuse 15A
95 Remote control receiver
96 LH door locking motor
97 RH door locking motor
98 Tailgate locking motor

Wire colours

A Light blue   M Brown
B White   N Black
C Orange   R Red
G Yellow   S Pink
H Grey   V Green
L Blue   X Violet

Radio/cassette

Heated rear window

Heated rear window warning light

Central locking

Electric windows

Alarm

Diagram 6 : Heated rear window, radio/cassette, central locking and electric windows

Dimensions and Weights

Note: *All figures are approximate, and may vary according to model. Refer to manufacturer's data for exact figures.*

Dimensions
Overall length . . . . 3227 mm
Overall width (excluding mirrors) . . . . 1487 mm
Overall height (unladen) . . . . 1435 mm
Wheelbase . . . . 2200 mm
Front track . . . . 1264 mm
Rear track . . . . 1257 mm

Weights
Kerb weight:
  OHV engine models:
    Without air conditioning . . . . 710 kg
    With air conditioning . . . . 750 kg
  OHC engine models:
    Without air conditioning . . . . 735 kg
    With air conditioning . . . . 750 kg
Maximum gross vehicle weight (all models) . . . . 1150 kg
Maximum towing weights:
  Trailer with brakes . . . . 400 kg
  Trailer without brakes . . . . 350 kg
Trailer nose weight . . . . 20 to 35 kg
Maximum roof rack load . . . . 50 kg

Conversion factors

Length (distance)
Inches (in)	x 25.4	= Millimetres (mm)	x 0.0394	= Inches (in)
Feet (ft)	x 0.305	= Metres (m)	x 3.281	= Feet (ft)
Miles	x 1.609	= Kilometres (km)	x 0.621	= Miles

Volume (capacity)
Cubic inches (cu in; in³)	x 16.387	= Cubic centimetres (cc; cm³)	x 0.061	= Cubic inches (cu in; in³)
Imperial pints (Imp pt)	x 0.568	= Litres (l)	x 1.76	= Imperial pints (Imp pt)
Imperial quarts (Imp qt)	x 1.137	= Litres (l)	x 0.88	= Imperial quarts (Imp qt)
Imperial quarts (Imp qt)	x 1.201	= US quarts (US qt)	x 0.833	= Imperial quarts (Imp qt)
US quarts (US qt)	x 0.946	= Litres (l)	x 1.057	= US quarts (US qt)
Imperial gallons (Imp gal)	x 4.546	= Litres (l)	x 0.22	= Imperial gallons (Imp gal)
Imperial gallons (Imp gal)	x 1.201	= US gallons (US gal)	x 0.833	= Imperial gallons (Imp gal)
US gallons (US gal)	x 3.785	= Litres (l)	x 0.264	= US gallons (US gal)

Mass (weight)
Ounces (oz)	x 28.35	= Grams (g)	x 0.035	= Ounces (oz)
Pounds (lb)	x 0.454	= Kilograms (kg)	x 2.205	= Pounds (lb)

Force
Ounces-force (ozf; oz)	x 0.278	= Newtons (N)	x 3.6	= Ounces-force (ozf; oz)
Pounds-force (lbf; lb)	x 4.448	= Newtons (N)	x 0.225	= Pounds-force (lbf; lb)
Newtons (N)	x 0.1	= Kilograms-force (kgf; kg)	x 9.81	= Newtons (N)

Pressure
Pounds-force per square inch (psi; lbf/in²; lb/in²)	x 0.070	= Kilograms-force per square centimetre (kgf/cm²; kg/cm²)	x 14.223	= Pounds-force per square inch (psi; lbf/in²; lb/in²)
Pounds-force per square inch (psi; lbf/in²; lb/in²)	x 0.068	= Atmospheres (atm)	x 14.696	= Pounds-force per square inch (psi; lbf/in²; lb/in²)
Pounds-force per square inch (psi; lbf/in²; lb/in²)	x 0.069	= Bars	x 14.5	= Pounds-force per square inch (psi; lbf/in²; lb/in²)
Pounds-force per square inch (psi; lbf/in²; lb/in²)	x 6.895	= Kilopascals (kPa)	x 0.145	= Pounds-force per square inch (psi; lbf/in²; lb/in²)
Kilopascals (kPa)	x 0.01	= Kilograms-force per square centimetre (kgf/cm²; kg/cm²)	x 98.1	= Kilopascals (kPa)
Millibar (mbar)	x 100	= Pascals (Pa)	x 0.01	= Millibar (mbar)
Millibar (mbar)	x 0.0145	= Pounds-force per square inch (psi; lbf/in²; lb/in²)	x 68.947	= Millibar (mbar)
Millibar (mbar)	x 0.75	= Millimetres of mercury (mmHg)	x 1.333	= Millibar (mbar)
Millibar (mbar)	x 0.401	= Inches of water (inH₂O)	x 2.491	= Millibar (mbar)
Millimetres of mercury (mmHg)	x 0.535	= Inches of water (inH₂O)	x 1.868	= Millimetres of mercury (mmHg)
Inches of water (inH₂O)	x 0.036	= Pounds-force per square inch (psi; lbf/in²; lb/in²)	x 27.68	= Inches of water (inH₂O)

Torque (moment of force)
Pounds-force inches (lbf in; lb in)	x 1.152	= Kilograms-force centimetre (kgf cm; kg cm)	x 0.868	= Pounds-force inches (lbf in; lb in)
Pounds-force inches (lbf in; lb in)	x 0.113	= Newton metres (Nm)	x 8.85	= Pounds-force inches (lbf in; lb in)
Pounds-force inches (lbf in; lb in)	x 0.083	= Pounds-force feet (lbf ft; lb ft)	x 12	= Pounds-force inches (lbf in; lb in)
Pounds-force feet (lbf ft; lb ft)	x 0.138	= Kilograms-force metres (kgf m; kg m)	x 7.233	= Pounds-force feet (lbf ft; lb ft)
Pounds-force feet (lbf ft; lb ft)	x 1.356	= Newton metres (Nm)	x 0.738	= Pounds-force feet (lbf ft; lb ft)
Newton metres (Nm)	x 0.102	= Kilograms-force metres (kgf m; kg m)	x 9.804	= Newton metres (Nm)

Power
Horsepower (hp)	x 745.7	= Watts (W)	x 0.0013	= Horsepower (hp)

Velocity (speed)
Miles per hour (miles/hr; mph)	x 1.609	= Kilometres per hour (km/hr; kph)	x 0.621	= Miles per hour (miles/hr; mph)

Fuel consumption*
Miles per gallon (mpg)	x 0.354	= Kilometres per litre (km/l)	x 2.825	= Miles per gallon (mpg)

Temperature
Degrees Fahrenheit = (°C x 1.8) + 32   Degrees Celsius (Degrees Centigrade; °C) = (°F - 32) x 0.56

It is common practice to convert from miles per gallon (mpg) to litres/100 kilometres (l/100km), where mpg x l/100 km = 282

Buying spare parts REF•3

Spare parts are available from many sources, including maker's appointed garages, accessory shops, and motor factors. To be sure of obtaining the correct parts, it will sometimes be necessary to quote the vehicle identification number. If possible, it can also be useful to take the old parts along for positive identification. Items such as starter motors and alternators may be available under a service exchange scheme - any parts returned should be clean.

Our advice regarding spare parts is as follows.

Officially appointed garages

This is the best source of parts which are peculiar to your car, and which are not otherwise generally available (eg, badges, interior trim, certain body panels, etc). It is also the only place at which you should buy parts if the vehicle is still under warranty.

Accessory shops

These are very good places to buy materials and components needed for the maintenance of your car (oil, air and fuel filters, light bulbs, drivebelts, greases, brake pads, touch-up paint, etc). Components of this nature sold by a reputable shop are usually of the same standard as those used by the car manufacturer.

Besides components, these shops also sell tools and general accessories, usually have convenient opening hours, charge lower prices, and can often be found close to home. Some accessory shops have parts counters where components needed for almost any repair job can be purchased or ordered.

Motor factors

Good factors will stock all the more important components which wear out comparatively quickly, and can sometimes supply individual components needed for the overhaul of a larger assembly (eg, brake seals and hydraulic parts, bearing shells, pistons, valves). They may also handle work such as cylinder block reboring, crankshaft regrinding, etc.

Tyre and exhaust specialists

These outlets may be independent, or members of a local or national chain. They frequently offer competitive prices when compared with a main dealer or local garage, but it will pay to obtain several quotes before making a decision. When researching prices, also ask what "extras" may be added - for instance fitting a new valve and balancing the wheel are both commonly charged on top of the price of a new tyre.

Other sources

Beware of parts or materials obtained from market stalls, car boot sales or similar outlets. Such items are not invariably sub-standard, but there is little chance of compensation if they do prove unsatisfactory. in the case of safety-critical components such as brake pads, there is the risk not only of financial loss, but also of an accident causing injury or death.

Second-hand components or assemblies obtained from a car breaker can be a good buy in some circumstances, but this sort of purchase is best made by the experienced DIY mechanic.

Vehicle Identification

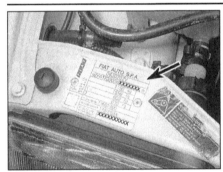
VIN plate on body front panel

Modifications are a continuing and unpublicised process in vehicle manufacture, quite apart from major model changes. Spare parts manuals and lists are compiled upon a numerical basis, the individual vehicle identification numbers being essential to correct identification of the component concerned.

When ordering spare parts, always give as much information as possible. Quote the car model, year of manufacture and registration, chassis and engine numbers as appropriate.

The *Vehicle Identification Number (VIN)* plate is located either on the body front panel, above the right-hand headlight, or on the left-hand side of the luggage compartment floor **(see illustration)**.

The *chassis number* is stamped into the right-hand side of the luggage compartment floor **(see illustration)**.

The *engine number* is stamped into the cylinder block, usually on the right-hand end of the block on OHV engines, and on the left-hand end of the block on OHC engines **(see illustration)**.

The *paint code* plate is located on the inside of the tailgate **(see illustration)**.

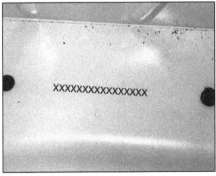
Chassis number stamped into luggage compartment floor

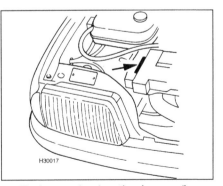
Engine number location (arrowed) – OHC engine models

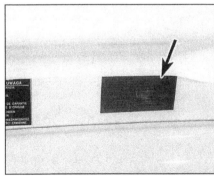
Paint code plate location (arrowed) on lower edge of tailgate

Whenever servicing, repair or overhaul work is carried out on the car or its components, observe the following procedures and instructions. This will assist in carrying out the operation efficiently and to a professional standard of workmanship.

Joint mating faces and gaskets

When separating components at their mating faces, never insert screwdrivers or similar implements into the joint between the faces in order to prise them apart. This can cause severe damage which results in oil leaks, coolant leaks, etc upon reassembly. Separation is usually achieved by tapping along the joint with a soft-faced hammer in order to break the seal. However, note that this method may not be suitable where dowels are used for component location.

Where a gasket is used between the mating faces of two components, a new one must be fitted on reassembly; fit it dry unless otherwise stated in the repair procedure. Make sure that the mating faces are clean and dry, with all traces of old gasket removed. When cleaning a joint face, use a tool which is unlikely to score or damage the face, and remove any burrs or nicks with an oilstone or fine file.

Make sure that tapped holes are cleaned with a pipe cleaner, and keep them free of jointing compound, if this is being used, unless specifically instructed otherwise.

Ensure that all orifices, channels or pipes are clear, and blow through them, preferably using compressed air.

Oil seals

Oil seals can be removed by levering them out with a wide flat-bladed screwdriver or similar implement. Alternatively, a number of self-tapping screws may be screwed into the seal, and these used as a purchase for pliers or some similar device in order to pull the seal free.

Whenever an oil seal is removed from its working location, either individually or as part of an assembly, it should be renewed.

The very fine sealing lip of the seal is easily damaged, and will not seal if the surface it contacts is not completely clean and free from scratches, nicks or grooves. If the original sealing surface of the component cannot be restored, and the manufacturer has not made provision for slight relocation of the seal relative to the sealing surface, the component should be renewed.

Protect the lips of the seal from any surface which may damage them in the course of fitting. Use tape or a conical sleeve where possible. Lubricate the seal lips with oil before fitting and, on dual-lipped seals, fill the space between the lips with grease.

Unless otherwise stated, oil seals must be fitted with their sealing lips toward the lubricant to be sealed.

Use a tubular drift or block of wood of the appropriate size to install the seal and, if the seal housing is shouldered, drive the seal down to the shoulder. If the seal housing is unshouldered, the seal should be fitted with its face flush with the housing top face (unless otherwise instructed).

Screw threads and fastenings

Seized nuts, bolts and screws are quite a common occurrence where corrosion has set in, and the use of penetrating oil or releasing fluid will often overcome this problem if the offending item is soaked for a while before attempting to release it. The use of an impact driver may also provide a means of releasing such stubborn fastening devices, when used in conjunction with the appropriate screwdriver bit or socket. If none of these methods works, it may be necessary to resort to the careful application of heat, or the use of a hacksaw or nut splitter device.

Studs are usually removed by locking two nuts together on the threaded part, and then using a spanner on the lower nut to unscrew the stud. Studs or bolts which have broken off below the surface of the component in which they are mounted can sometimes be removed using a stud extractor. Always ensure that a blind tapped hole is completely free from oil, grease, water or other fluid before installing the bolt or stud. Failure to do this could cause the housing to crack due to the hydraulic action of the bolt or stud as it is screwed in.

When tightening a castellated nut to accept a split pin, tighten the nut to the specified torque, where applicable, and then tighten further to the next split pin hole. Never slacken the nut to align the split pin hole, unless stated in the repair procedure.

When checking or retightening a nut or bolt to a specified torque setting, slacken the nut or bolt by a quarter of a turn, and then retighten to the specified setting. However, this should not be attempted where angular tightening has been used.

For some screw fastenings, notably cylinder head bolts or nuts, torque wrench settings are no longer specified for the latter stages of tightening, "angle-tightening" being called up instead. Typically, a fairly low torque wrench setting will be applied to the bolts/nuts in the correct sequence, followed by one or more stages of tightening through specified angles.

Locknuts, locktabs and washers

Any fastening which will rotate against a component or housing during tightening should always have a washer between it and the relevant component or housing.

Spring or split washers should always be renewed when they are used to lock a critical component such as a big-end bearing retaining bolt or nut. Locktabs which are folded over to retain a nut or bolt should always be renewed.

Self-locking nuts can be re-used in non-critical areas, providing resistance can be felt when the locking portion passes over the bolt or stud thread. However, it should be noted that self-locking stiffnuts tend to lose their effectiveness after long periods of use, and should then be renewed as a matter of course.

Split pins must always be replaced with new ones of the correct size for the hole.

When thread-locking compound is found on the threads of a fastener which is to be re-used, it should be cleaned off with a wire brush and solvent, and fresh compound applied on reassembly.

Special tools

Some repair procedures in this manual entail the use of special tools such as a press, two or three-legged pullers, spring compressors, etc. Wherever possible, suitable readily-available alternatives to the manufacturer's special tools are described, and are shown in use. In some instances, where no alternative is possible, it has been necessary to resort to the use of a manufacturer's tool, and this has been done for reasons of safety as well as the efficient completion of the repair operation. Unless you are highly-skilled and have a thorough understanding of the procedures described, never attempt to bypass the use of any special tool when the procedure described specifies its use. Not only is there a very great risk of personal injury, but expensive damage could be caused to the components involved.

Environmental considerations

When disposing of used engine oil, brake fluid, antifreeze, etc, give due consideration to any detrimental environmental effects. Do not, for instance, pour any of the above liquids down drains into the general sewage system, or onto the ground to soak away. Many local council refuse tips provide a facility for waste oil disposal, as do some garages. If none of these facilities are available, consult your local Environmental Health Department, or the National Rivers Authority, for further advice.

With the universal tightening-up of legislation regarding the emission of environmentally-harmful substances from motor vehicles, most vehicles have tamperproof devices fitted to the main adjustment points of the fuel system. These devices are primarily designed to prevent unqualified persons from adjusting the fuel/air mixture, with the chance of a consequent increase in toxic emissions. If such devices are found during servicing or overhaul, they should, wherever possible, be renewed or refitted in accordance with the manufacturer's requirements or current legislation.

OIL CARE
FOLLOW THE CODE

OIL BANK LINE
0800 66 33 66
www.oilbankline.org.uk

Note: It is antisocial and illegal to dump oil down the drain. To find the location of your local oil recycling bank, call this number free.

The jack supplied with the vehicle tool kit should only be used for changing the roadwheels - see *"Wheel changing"* at the front of this manual. When carrying out any other kind of work, raise the vehicle using a hydraulic (or "trolley") jack, and always supplement the jack with axle stands positioned under the vehicle jacking points.

To raise one side of the front of the vehicle, position the jack head underneath the suspension lower arm front mounting.

Support the vehicle with an axle stand located under the reinforced point at the front of the vehicle floor – place a block of wood between the axle stand and the floor **(see illustrations)**. If the whole of the front of the vehicle is to be raised, jack up each side in turn, as described previously.

To raise one side of the rear of the vehicle, position the jack under the rear shock absorber lower mounting. Support the vehicle with an axle stand located under one of the

reinforced points on the rear vehicle floor – place a block of wood between the axle stand and the floor **(see illustrations)**.

The jack supplied with the vehicle locates with the jacking points on the sills. Ensure that the jack head is correctly engaged before attempting to raise the vehicle.

Never work under, around, or near a raised vehicle, unless it is adequately supported in at least two places with axle stands.

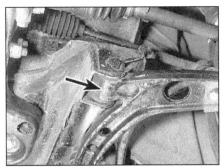

Jack up the front of the vehicle under the lower arm front mountings (arrowed)

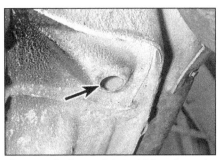

Support the front of the vehicle using axle stands positioned under the reinforced points (arrowed) under the vehicle floor

Jack up the rear of the vehicle under the rear shock absorber lower mountings (arrowed)

Support the rear of the vehicle using axle stands positioned under the reinforced points (arrowed) under the vehicle floor

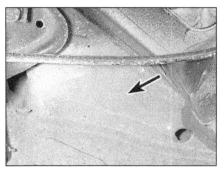

Alternative position (arrowed) for rear axle stands

Disconnecting the battery

Several systems fitted to the vehicle require battery power to be available at all times, either to ensure their continued operation (such as the clock) or to maintain control unit memories which would be wiped if the battery were to be disconnected. Whenever the battery is to be disconnected therefore, first note the following, to ensure that there are no unforeseen consequences of this action:

a) *First, on any vehicle with central locking, it is a wise precaution to remove the key from the ignition, and to keep it with you, so that it does not get locked in if the central locking should engage accidentally when the battery is reconnected.*

b) *If the battery is disconnected while the alarm system is armed or activated, the alarm may be activated when the battery is reconnected. To switch the factory-option alarm system off (to prevent the siren from sounding when the battery is*

reconnected), before disconnecting the battery, insert the special key provided into the alarm switch, located beneath the engine management ECU in the engine compartment. Turn the switch clockwise to de-activate the alarm system, and clockwise to re-activate the system after reconnecting the battery.

c) *If a security-coded audio unit is fitted, and the unit and/or the battery is disconnected, the unit will not function again on reconnection until the correct security code is entered. Details of this procedure, which varies according to the unit fitted, are given in the vehicle owner's handbook. Ensure you have the correct code before you disconnect the battery. If you do not have the code or details of the correct procedure, but can supply proof of ownership and a legitimate reason for wanting this information, a Fiat dealer may be able to help.*

Devices known as "memory-savers" (or "code-savers") can be used to avoid some of the above problems. Precise details vary according to the device used. Typically, it is plugged into the cigarette lighter, and is connected by its own wires to a spare battery; the vehicle's own battery is then disconnected from the electrical system, leaving the "memory-saver" to pass sufficient current to maintain audio unit security codes and any other memory values, and also to run permanently-live circuits such as the clock.

 Warning: Some of these devices allow a considerable amount of current to pass, which can mean that many of the vehicle's systems are still operational when the main battery is disconnected. If a "memory-saver" is used, ensure that the circuit concerned is actually "dead" before carrying out any work on it!

Introduction

A selection of good tools is a fundamental requirement for anyone contemplating the maintenance and repair of a motor vehicle. For the owner who does not possess any, their purchase will prove a considerable expense, offsetting some of the savings made by doing-it-yourself. However, provided that the tools purchased meet the relevant national safety standards and are of good quality, they will last for many years and prove an extremely worthwhile investment.

To help the average owner to decide which tools are needed to carry out the various tasks detailed in this manual, we have compiled three lists of tools under the following headings: *Maintenance and minor repair, Repair and overhaul,* and *Special.* Newcomers to practical mechanics should start off with the *Maintenance and minor repair* tool kit, and confine themselves to the simpler jobs around the vehicle. Then, as confidence and experience grow, more difficult tasks can be undertaken, with extra tools being purchased as, and when, they are needed. In this way, a *Maintenance and minor repair* tool kit can be built up into a *Repair and overhaul* tool kit over a considerable period of time, without any major cash outlays. The experienced do-it-yourselfer will have a tool kit good enough for most repair and overhaul procedures, and will add tools from the *Special* category when it is felt that the expense is justified by the amount of use to which these tools will be put.

Maintenance and minor repair tool kit

The tools given in this list should be considered as a minimum requirement if routine maintenance, servicing and minor repair operations are to be undertaken. We recommend the purchase of combination spanners (ring one end, open-ended the other); although more expensive than open-ended ones, they do give the advantages of both types of spanner.

☐ *Combination spanners:*
Metric - 8 to 19 mm inclusive
☐ *Adjustable spanner - 35 mm jaw (approx.)*
☐ *Spark plug spanner (with rubber insert) - petrol models*
☐ *Spark plug gap adjustment tool - petrol models*
☐ *Set of feeler gauges*
☐ *Brake bleed nipple spanner*
☐ *Screwdrivers:*
Flat blade - 100 mm long x 6 mm dia
Cross blade - 100 mm long x 6 mm dia
Torx - various sizes (not all vehicles)
☐ *Combination pliers*
☐ *Hacksaw (junior)*
☐ *Tyre pump*
☐ *Tyre pressure gauge*
☐ *Oil can*
☐ *Oil filter removal tool*
☐ *Fine emery cloth*
☐ *Wire brush (small)*
☐ *Funnel (medium size)*
☐ *Sump drain plug key (not all vehicles)*

Repair and overhaul tool kit

These tools are virtually essential for anyone undertaking any major repairs to a motor vehicle, and are additional to those given in the *Maintenance and minor repair* list. Included in this list is a comprehensive set of sockets. Although these are expensive, they will be found invaluable as they are so versatile - particularly if various drives are included in the set. We recommend the half-inch square-drive type, as this can be used with most proprietary torque wrenches.

The tools in this list will sometimes need to be supplemented by tools from the *Special* list.

☐ *Sockets (or box spanners) to cover range in previous list (including Torx sockets)*
☐ *Reversible ratchet drive (for use with sockets)*
☐ *Extension piece, 250 mm (for use with sockets)*
☐ *Universal joint (for use with sockets)*
☐ *Flexible handle or sliding T "breaker bar" (for use with sockets)*
☐ *Torque wrench (for use with sockets)*
☐ *Self-locking grips*
☐ *Ball pein hammer*
☐ *Soft-faced mallet (plastic or rubber)*
☐ *Screwdrivers:*
Flat blade - long & sturdy, short (chubby), and narrow (electrician's) types
Cross blade - long & sturdy, and short (chubby) types
☐ *Pliers:*
Long-nosed
Side cutters (electrician's)
Circlip (internal and external)
☐ *Cold chisel - 25 mm*
☐ *Scriber*
☐ *Scraper*
☐ *Centre-punch*
☐ *Pin punch*
☐ *Hacksaw*
☐ *Brake hose clamp*
☐ *Brake/clutch bleeding kit*
☐ *Selection of twist drills*
☐ *Steel rule/straight-edge*
☐ *Allen keys (inc. splined/Torx type)*
☐ *Selection of files*
☐ *Wire brush*
☐ *Axle stands*
☐ *Jack (strong trolley or hydraulic type)*
☐ *Light with extension lead*
☐ *Universal electrical multi-meter*

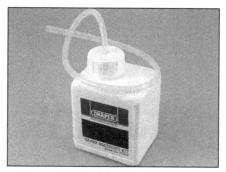
Brake bleeding kit

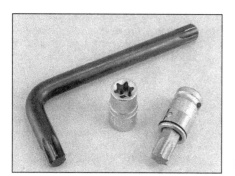
Sockets and reversible ratchet drive

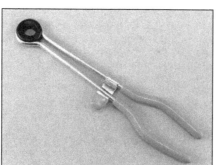
Hose clamp

Angular-tightening gauge

Torx key, socket and bit

Special tools

The tools in this list are those which are not used regularly, are expensive to buy, or which need to be used in accordance with their manufacturers' instructions. Unless relatively difficult mechanical jobs are undertaken frequently, it will not be economic to buy many of these tools. Where this is the case, you could consider clubbing together with friends (or joining a motorists' club) to make a joint purchase, or borrowing the tools against a deposit from a local garage or tool hire specialist. It is worth noting that many of the larger DIY superstores now carry a large range of special tools for hire at modest rates.

The following list contains only those tools and instruments freely available to the public, and not those special tools produced by the vehicle manufacturer specifically for its dealer network. You will find occasional references to these manufacturers' special tools in the text of this manual. Generally, an alternative method of doing the job without the vehicle manufacturers' special tool is given. However, sometimes there is no alternative to using them. Where this is the case and the relevant tool cannot be bought or borrowed, you will have to entrust the work to a dealer.

☐ Angular-tightening gauge
☐ Valve spring compressor
☐ Valve grinding tool
☐ Piston ring compressor
☐ Piston ring removal/installation tool
☐ Cylinder bore hone
☐ Balljoint separator
☐ Coil spring compressors (where applicable)
☐ Two/three-legged hub and bearing puller
☐ Impact screwdriver
☐ Micrometer and/or vernier calipers
☐ Dial gauge
☐ Stroboscopic timing light
☐ Dwell angle meter/tachometer
☐ Fault code reader
☐ Cylinder compression gauge
☐ Hand-operated vacuum pump and gauge
☐ Clutch plate alignment set
☐ Brake shoe steady spring cup removal tool
☐ Bush and bearing removal/installation set
☐ Stud extractors
☐ Tap and die set
☐ Lifting tackle
☐ Trolley jack

Buying tools

Reputable motor accessory shops and superstores often offer excellent quality tools at discount prices, so it pays to shop around.

Remember, you don't have to buy the most expensive items on the shelf, but it is always advisable to steer clear of the very cheap tools. Beware of 'bargains' offered on market stalls or at car boot sales. There are plenty of good tools around at reasonable prices, but always aim to purchase items which meet the relevant national safety standards. If in doubt, ask the proprietor or manager of the shop for advice before making a purchase.

Care and maintenance of tools

Having purchased a reasonable tool kit, it is necessary to keep the tools in a clean and serviceable condition. After use, always wipe off any dirt, grease and metal particles using a clean, dry cloth, before putting the tools away. Never leave them lying around after they have been used. A simple tool rack on the garage or workshop wall for items such as screwdrivers and pliers is a good idea. Store all normal spanners and sockets in a metal box. Any measuring instruments, gauges, meters, etc, must be carefully stored where they cannot be damaged or become rusty.

Take a little care when tools are used. Hammer heads inevitably become marked, and screwdrivers lose the keen edge on their blades from time to time. A little timely attention with emery cloth or a file will soon restore items like this to a good finish.

Working facilities

Not to be forgotten when discussing tools is the workshop itself. If anything more than routine maintenance is to be carried out, a suitable working area becomes essential.

It is appreciated that many an owner-mechanic is forced by circumstances to remove an engine or similar item without the benefit of a garage or workshop. Having done this, any repairs should always be done under the cover of a roof.

Wherever possible, any dismantling should be done on a clean, flat workbench or table at a suitable working height.

Any workbench needs a vice; one with a jaw opening of 100 mm is suitable for most jobs. As mentioned previously, some clean dry storage space is also required for tools, as well as for any lubricants, cleaning fluids, touch-up paints etc, which become necessary.

Another item which may be required, and which has a much more general usage, is an electric drill with a chuck capacity of at least 8 mm. This, together with a good range of twist drills, is virtually essential for fitting accessories.

Last, but not least, always keep a supply of old newspapers and clean, lint-free rags available, and try to keep any working area as clean as possible.

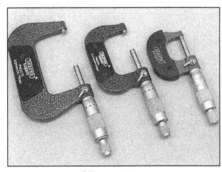
Micrometers

Dial test indicator ("dial gauge")

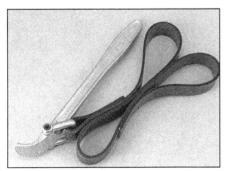
Strap wrench

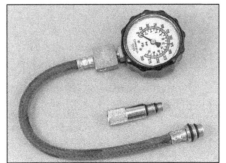
Compression tester

Fault code reader

This is a guide to getting your vehicle through the MOT test. Obviously it will not be possible to examine the vehicle to the same standard as the professional MOT tester. However, working through the following checks will enable you to identify any problem areas before submitting the vehicle for the test.

Where a testable component is in borderline condition, the tester has discretion in deciding whether to pass or fail it. The basis of such discretion is whether the tester would be happy for a close relative or friend to use the vehicle with the component in that condition. If the vehicle presented is clean and evidently well cared for, the tester may be more inclined to pass a borderline component than if the vehicle is scruffy and apparently neglected.

It has only been possible to summarise the test requirements here, based on the regulations in force at the time of printing. Test standards are becoming increasingly stringent, although there are some exemptions for older vehicles.

An assistant will be needed to help carry out some of these checks.

The checks have been sub-divided into four categories, as follows:

1 Checks carried out **FROM THE DRIVER'S SEAT**

2 Checks carried out **WITH THE VEHICLE ON THE GROUND**

3 Checks carried out **WITH THE VEHICLE RAISED AND THE WHEELS FREE TO TURN**

4 Checks carried out on **YOUR VEHICLE'S EXHAUST EMISSION SYSTEM**

1 Checks carried out **FROM THE DRIVER'S SEAT**

Handbrake

☐ Test the operation of the handbrake. Excessive travel (too many clicks) indicates incorrect brake or cable adjustment.

☐ Check that the handbrake cannot be released by tapping the lever sideways. Check the security of the lever mountings.

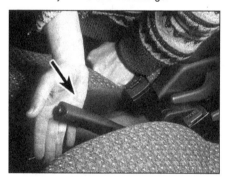

Footbrake

☐ Depress the brake pedal and check that it does not creep down to the floor, indicating a master cylinder fault. Release the pedal, wait a few seconds, then depress it again. If the pedal travels nearly to the floor before firm resistance is felt, brake adjustment or repair is necessary. If the pedal feels spongy, there is air in the hydraulic system which must be removed by bleeding.

☐ Check that the brake pedal is secure and in good condition. Check also for signs of fluid leaks on the pedal, floor or carpets, which would indicate failed seals in the brake master cylinder.

☐ Check the servo unit (when applicable) by operating the brake pedal several times, then keeping the pedal depressed and starting the engine. As the engine starts, the pedal will move down slightly. If not, the vacuum hose or the servo itself may be faulty.

Steering wheel and column

☐ Examine the steering wheel for fractures or looseness of the hub, spokes or rim.

☐ Move the steering wheel from side to side and then up and down. Check that the steering wheel is not loose on the column, indicating wear or a loose retaining nut. Continue moving the steering wheel as before, but also turn it slightly from left to right.

☐ Check that the steering wheel is not loose on the column, and that there is no abnormal

movement of the steering wheel, indicating wear in the column support bearings or couplings.

Windscreen, mirrors and sunvisor

☐ The windscreen must be free of cracks or other significant damage within the driver's field of view. (Small stone chips are acceptable.) Rear view mirrors must be secure, intact, and capable of being adjusted.

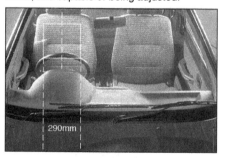

☐ The driver's sunvisor must be capable of being stored in the "up" position.

Seat belts and seats

Note: *The following checks are applicable to all seat belts, front and rear.*

☐ Examine the webbing of all the belts (including rear belts if fitted) for cuts, serious fraying or deterioration. Fasten and unfasten each belt to check the buckles. If applicable, check the retracting mechanism. Check the security of all seat belt mountings accessible from inside the vehicle.

☐ Seat belts with pre-tensioners, once activated, have a "flag" or similar showing on the seat belt stalk. This, in itself, is not a reason for test failure.

☐ The front seats themselves must be securely attached and the backrests must lock in the upright position.

Doors

☐ Both front doors must be able to be opened and closed from outside and inside, and must latch securely when closed.

2 Checks carried out
WITH THE VEHICLE ON THE GROUND

Vehicle identification

☐ Number plates must be in good condition, secure and legible, with letters and numbers correctly spaced – spacing at (A) should be at least twice that at (B).

☐ The VIN plate and/or homologation plate must be legible.

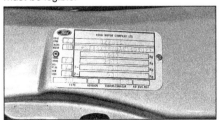

Electrical equipment

☐ Switch on the ignition and check the operation of the horn.

☐ Check the windscreen washers and wipers, examining the wiper blades; renew damaged or perished blades. Also check the operation of the stop-lights.

☐ Check the operation of the sidelights and number plate lights. The lenses and reflectors must be secure, clean and undamaged.

☐ Check the operation and alignment of the headlights. The headlight reflectors must not be tarnished and the lenses must be undamaged.

☐ Switch on the ignition and check the operation of the direction indicators (including the instrument panel tell-tale) and the hazard warning lights. Operation of the sidelights and stop-lights must not affect the indicators - if it does, the cause is usually a bad earth at the rear light cluster.

☐ Check the operation of the rear foglight(s), including the warning light on the instrument panel or in the switch.

☐ The ABS warning light must illuminate in accordance with the manufacturers' design. For most vehicles, the ABS warning light should illuminate when the ignition is switched on, and (if the system is operating properly) extinguish after a few seconds. Refer to the owner's handbook.

Footbrake

☐ Examine the master cylinder, brake pipes and servo unit for leaks, loose mountings, corrosion or other damage.

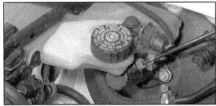

☐ The fluid reservoir must be secure and the fluid level must be between the upper (**A**) and lower (**B**) markings.

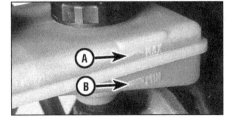

☐ Inspect both front brake flexible hoses for cracks or deterioration of the rubber. Turn the steering from lock to lock, and ensure that the hoses do not contact the wheel, tyre, or any part of the steering or suspension mechanism. With the brake pedal firmly depressed, check the hoses for bulges or leaks under pressure.

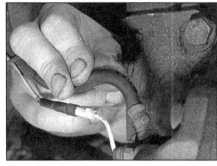

Steering and suspension

☐ Have your assistant turn the steering wheel from side to side slightly, up to the point where the steering gear just begins to transmit this movement to the roadwheels. Check for excessive free play between the steering wheel and the steering gear, indicating wear or insecurity of the steering column joints, the column-to-steering gear coupling, or the steering gear itself.

☐ Have your assistant turn the steering wheel more vigorously in each direction, so that the roadwheels just begin to turn. As this is done, examine all the steering joints, linkages, fittings and attachments. Renew any component that shows signs of wear or damage. On vehicles with power steering, check the security and condition of the steering pump, drivebelt and hoses.

☐ Check that the vehicle is standing level, and at approximately the correct ride height.

Shock absorbers

☐ Depress each corner of the vehicle in turn, then release it. The vehicle should rise and then settle in its normal position. If the vehicle continues to rise and fall, the shock absorber is defective. A shock absorber which has seized will also cause the vehicle to fail.

Exhaust system

☐ Start the engine. With your assistant holding a rag over the tailpipe, check the entire system for leaks. Repair or renew leaking sections.

3 Checks carried out
WITH THE VEHICLE RAISED AND THE WHEELS FREE TO TURN

Jack up the front and rear of the vehicle, and securely support it on axle stands. Position the stands clear of the suspension assemblies. Ensure that the wheels are clear of the ground and that the steering can be turned from lock to lock.

Steering mechanism

☐ Have your assistant turn the steering from lock to lock. Check that the steering turns smoothly, and that no part of the steering mechanism, including a wheel or tyre, fouls any brake hose or pipe or any part of the body structure.
☐ Examine the steering rack rubber gaiters for damage or insecurity of the retaining clips. If power steering is fitted, check for signs of damage or leakage of the fluid hoses, pipes or connections. Also check for excessive stiffness or binding of the steering, a missing split pin or locking device, or severe corrosion of the body structure within 30 cm of any steering component attachment point.

Front and rear suspension and wheel bearings

☐ Starting at the front right-hand side, grasp the roadwheel at the 3 o'clock and 9 o'clock positions and rock gently but firmly. Check for free play or insecurity at the wheel bearings, suspension balljoints, or suspension mountings, pivots and attachments.
☐ Now grasp the wheel at the 12 o'clock and 6 o'clock positions and repeat the previous inspection. Spin the wheel, and check for roughness or tightness of the front wheel bearing.

☐ If excess free play is suspected at a component pivot point, this can be confirmed by using a large screwdriver or similar tool and levering between the mounting and the component attachment. This will confirm whether the wear is in the pivot bush, its retaining bolt, or in the mounting itself (the bolt holes can often become elongated).

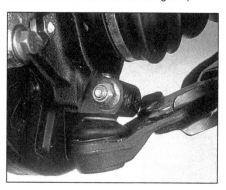

☐ Carry out all the above checks at the other front wheel, and then at both rear wheels.

Springs and shock absorbers

☐ Examine the suspension struts (when applicable) for serious fluid leakage, corrosion, or damage to the casing. Also check the security of the mounting points.
☐ If coil springs are fitted, check that the spring ends locate in their seats, and that the spring is not corroded, cracked or broken.
☐ If leaf springs are fitted, check that all leaves are intact, that the axle is securely attached to each spring, and that there is no deterioration of the spring eye mountings, bushes, and shackles.

☐ The same general checks apply to vehicles fitted with other suspension types, such as torsion bars, hydraulic displacer units, etc. Ensure that all mountings and attachments are secure, that there are no signs of excessive wear, corrosion or damage, and (on hydraulic types) that there are no fluid leaks or damaged pipes.
☐ Inspect the shock absorbers for signs of serious fluid leakage. Check for wear of the mounting bushes or attachments, or damage to the body of the unit.

Driveshafts (fwd vehicles only)

☐ Rotate each front wheel in turn and inspect the constant velocity joint gaiters for splits or damage. Also check that each driveshaft is straight and undamaged.

Braking system

☐ If possible without dismantling, check brake pad wear and disc condition. Ensure that the friction lining material has not worn excessively, (A) and that the discs are not fractured, pitted, scored or badly worn (B).

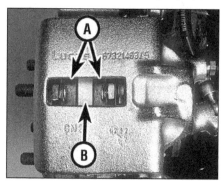

☐ Examine all the rigid brake pipes underneath the vehicle, and the flexible hose(s) at the rear. Look for corrosion, chafing or insecurity of the pipes, and for signs of bulging under pressure, chafing, splits or deterioration of the flexible hoses.
☐ Look for signs of fluid leaks at the brake calipers or on the brake backplates. Repair or renew leaking components.
☐ Slowly spin each wheel, while your assistant depresses and releases the footbrake. Ensure that each brake is operating and does not bind when the pedal is released.

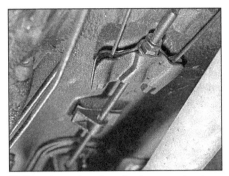

□ Examine the handbrake mechanism, checking for frayed or broken cables, excessive corrosion, or wear or insecurity of the linkage. Check that the mechanism works on each relevant wheel, and releases fully, without binding.

□ It is not possible to test brake efficiency without special equipment, but a road test can be carried out later to check that the vehicle pulls up in a straight line.

Fuel and exhaust systems

□ Inspect the fuel tank (including the filler cap), fuel pipes, hoses and unions. All components must be secure and free from leaks.

□ Examine the exhaust system over its entire length, checking for any damaged, broken or missing mountings, security of the retaining clamps and rust or corrosion.

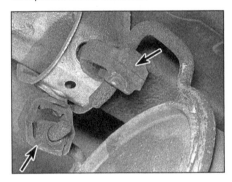

Wheels and tyres

□ Examine the sidewalls and tread area of each tyre in turn. Check for cuts, tears, lumps, bulges, separation of the tread, and exposure of the ply or cord due to wear or damage. Check that the tyre bead is correctly seated on the wheel rim, that the valve is sound and properly seated, and that the wheel is not distorted or damaged.

□ Check that the tyres are of the correct size for the vehicle, that they are of the same size and type on each axle, and that the pressures are correct.

□ Check the tyre tread depth. The legal minimum at the time of writing is 1.6 mm over at least three-quarters of the tread width. Abnormal tread wear may indicate incorrect front wheel alignment.

Body corrosion

□ Check the condition of the entire vehicle structure for signs of corrosion in load-bearing areas. (These include chassis box sections, side sills, cross-members, pillars, and all suspension, steering, braking system and seat belt mountings and anchorages.) Any corrosion which has seriously reduced the thickness of a load-bearing area is likely to cause the vehicle to fail. In this case professional repairs are likely to be needed.

□ Damage or corrosion which causes sharp or otherwise dangerous edges to be exposed will also cause the vehicle to fail.

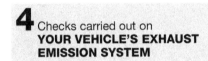

4 Checks carried out on **YOUR VEHICLE'S EXHAUST EMISSION SYSTEM**

Petrol models

□ Have the engine at normal operating temperature, and make sure that it is in good tune (ignition system in good order, air filter element clean, etc).

□ Before any measurements are carried out, raise the engine speed to around 2500 rpm, and hold it at this speed for 20 seconds. Allow the engine speed to return to idle, and watch for smoke emissions from the exhaust tailpipe. If the idle speed is obviously much too high, or if dense blue or clearly-visible black smoke comes from the tailpipe for more than 5 seconds, the vehicle will fail. As a rule of thumb, blue smoke signifies oil being burnt (engine wear) while black smoke signifies unburnt fuel (dirty air cleaner element, or other carburettor or fuel system fault).

□ An exhaust gas analyser capable of measuring carbon monoxide (CO) and hydrocarbons (HC) is now needed. If such an instrument cannot be hired or borrowed, a local garage may agree to perform the check for a small fee.

CO emissions (mixture)

□ At the time of writing, for vehicles first used between 1st August 1975 and 31st July 1986 (P to C registration), the CO level must not exceed 4.5% by volume. For vehicles first used between 1st August 1986 and 31st July 1992 (D to J registration), the CO level must not exceed 3.5% by volume. Vehicles first

used after 1st August 1992 (K registration) must conform to the manufacturer's specification. The MOT tester has access to a DOT database or emissions handbook, which lists the CO and HC limits for each make and model of vehicle. The CO level is measured with the engine at idle speed, and at "fast idle". The following limits are given as a general guide:

At idle speed -
    CO level no more than 0.5%
At "fast idle" (2500 to 3000 rpm) -
    CO level no more than 0.3%
    (Minimum oil temperature 60°C)

□ If the CO level cannot be reduced far enough to pass the test (and the fuel and ignition systems are otherwise in good condition) then the carburettor is badly worn, or there is some problem in the fuel injection system or catalytic converter (as applicable).

HC emissions

□ With the CO within limits, HC emissions for vehicles first used between 1st August 1975 and 31st July 1992 (P to J registration) must not exceed 1200 ppm. Vehicles first used after 1st August 1992 (K registration) must conform to the manufacturer's specification. The MOT tester has access to a DOT database or emissions handbook, which lists the CO and HC limits for each make and model of vehicle. The HC level is measured with the engine at "fast idle". The following is given as a general guide:

At "fast idle" (2500 to 3000 rpm) -
    HC level no more than 200 ppm
    (Minimum oil temperature 60°C)

□ Excessive HC emissions are caused by incomplete combustion, the causes of which can include oil being burnt, mechanical wear and ignition/fuel system malfunction.

Diesel models

□ The only emission test applicable to Diesel engines is the measuring of exhaust smoke density. The test involves accelerating the engine several times to its maximum unloaded speed.

Note: *It is of the utmost importance that the engine timing belt is in good condition before the test is carried out.*

□ The limits for Diesel engine exhaust smoke, introduced in September 1995 are:
Vehicles first used before 1st August 1979:
    Exempt from metered smoke testing, but must not emit "dense blue or clearly visible black smoke for a period of more than 5 seconds at idle" or "dense blue or clearly visible black smoke during acceleration which would obscure the view of other road users".
Non-turbocharged vehicles first used after 1st August 1979: 2.5m-1
Turbocharged vehicles first used after 1st August 1979: 3.0m-1

□ Excessive smoke can be caused by a dirty air cleaner element. Otherwise, professional advice may be needed to find the cause.

Engine 1
- ☐ Engine fails to rotate when attempting to start
- ☐ Engine rotates, but will not start
- ☐ Engine difficult to start when cold
- ☐ Engine difficult to start when hot
- ☐ Starter motor noisy or excessively-rough in engagement
- ☐ Engine starts, but stops immediately
- ☐ Engine idles erratically
- ☐ Engine misfires at idle speed
- ☐ Engine misfires throughout the driving speed range
- ☐ Engine hesitates on acceleration
- ☐ Engine stalls
- ☐ Engine lacks power
- ☐ Engine backfires
- ☐ Oil pressure warning light illuminated with engine running
- ☐ Engine runs-on after switching off
- ☐ Engine noises

Cooling system 2
- ☐ Overheating
- ☐ Overcooling
- ☐ External coolant leakage
- ☐ Internal coolant leakage
- ☐ Corrosion

Fuel and exhaust systems 3
- ☐ Excessive fuel consumption
- ☐ Fuel leakage and/or fuel odour
- ☐ Excessive noise or fumes from exhaust system

Clutch 4
- ☐ Pedal travels to floor - no pressure or very little resistance
- ☐ Clutch fails to disengage (unable to select gears)
- ☐ Clutch slips (engine speed increases, with no increase in vehicle speed)
- ☐ Judder as clutch is engaged
- ☐ Noise when depressing or releasing clutch pedal

Transmission 5
- ☐ Noisy in neutral with engine running
- ☐ Noisy in one particular gear
- ☐ Difficulty engaging gears
- ☐ Jumps out of gear
- ☐ Vibration
- ☐ Lubricant leaks

Driveshafts 6
- ☐ Vibration when accelerating or decelerating
- ☐ Clicking or knocking noise on turns (at slow speed on full-lock)

Braking system 7
- ☐ Vehicle pulls to one side under braking
- ☐ Noise (grinding or high-pitched squeal) when brakes applied
- ☐ Excessive brake pedal travel
- ☐ Brake pedal feels spongy when depressed
- ☐ Excessive brake pedal effort required to stop vehicle
- ☐ Judder felt through brake pedal or steering wheel when braking
- ☐ Brakes binding
- ☐ Rear wheels locking under normal braking

Suspension and steering 8
- ☐ Vehicle pulls to one side
- ☐ Wheel wobble and vibration
- ☐ Excessive pitching and/or rolling around corners, or during braking
- ☐ Wandering or general instability
- ☐ Excessively-stiff steering
- ☐ Excessive play in steering
- ☐ Tyre wear excessive

Electrical system 9
- ☐ Battery will not hold a charge for more than a few days
- ☐ Ignition/no-charge warning light remains illuminated with engine running
- ☐ Ignition/no-charge warning light fails to come on
- ☐ Lights inoperative
- ☐ Instrument readings inaccurate or erratic
- ☐ Horn inoperative, or unsatisfactory in operation
- ☐ Windscreen wipers inoperative, or unsatisfactory in operation
- ☐ Windscreen washers inoperative, or unsatisfactory in operation
- ☐ Electric windows inoperative, or unsatisfactory in operation
- ☐ Central locking system inoperative, or unsatisfactory in operation

Introduction

The vehicle owner who does his or her own maintenance according to the recommended service schedules should not have to use this section of the manual very often. Modern component reliability is such that, provided those items subject to wear or deterioration are inspected or renewed at the specified intervals, sudden failure is comparatively rare. Faults do not usually just happen as a result of sudden failure, but develop over a period of time. Major mechanical failures in particular are usually preceded by characteristic symptoms over hundreds or even thousands of miles. Those components which do occasionally fail without warning are often small and easily carried in the vehicle.

With any fault-finding, the first step is to decide where to begin investigations.

Sometimes this is obvious, but on other occasions, a little detective work will be necessary. The owner who makes half a dozen haphazard adjustments or replacements may be successful in curing a fault (or its symptoms), but will be none the wiser if the fault recurs, and ultimately may have spent more time and money than was necessary. A calm and logical approach will be found to be more satisfactory in the long run. Always take into account any warning signs or abnormalities that may have been noticed in the period preceding the fault - power loss, high or low gauge readings, unusual smells, etc - and remember that failure of components such as fuses or spark plugs may only be pointers to some underlying fault.

The pages which follow provide an easy-reference guide to the more common problems which may occur during the operation of the vehicle. These problems and their possible causes are grouped under headings denoting various components or systems, such as Engine, Cooling system, etc. The Chapter and/or Section which deals with the problem is also shown in brackets. Whatever the fault, certain basic principles apply. These are as follows:

☐ *Verify the fault*. This is simply a matter of being sure that you know what the symptoms are before starting work. This is particularly important if you are investigating a fault for someone else, who may not have described it very accurately.

☐ *Don't overlook the obvious.* For example, if the vehicle won't start, is there fuel in the tank? (Don't take anyone else's word on this particular point, and don't trust the fuel gauge either!) If an electrical fault is indicated, look for loose or broken wires before digging out the test gear.

☐ *Cure the disease, not the symptom.* Substituting a flat battery with a fully-charged one will get you off the hard shoulder, but if the underlying cause is not attended to, the new battery will go the same way. Similarly, changing oil-fouled spark plugs for a new set will get you moving again, but remember that the reason for the fouling (if it wasn't simply an incorrect grade of plug) will have to be established and corrected.

☐ *Don't take anything for granted.* Particularly, don't forget that a "new" component may itself be defective (especially if it's been rattling around in the boot for months), and don't leave components out of a fault diagnosis sequence just because they are new or recently-fitted. When you do finally diagnose a difficult fault, you'll probably realise that all the evidence was there from the start.

1 Engine

Engine fails to rotate when attempting to start

☐ Battery terminal connections loose or corroded (see *"Weekly checks"*)
☐ Battery discharged or faulty (Chapter 5A)
☐ Broken, loose or disconnected wiring in the starting circuit (Chapter 5A)
☐ Defective starter solenoid or switch (Chapter 5A)
☐ Defective starter motor (Chapter 5A)
☐ Starter pinion or flywheel ring gear teeth loose or broken (Chapters 2 and 5A)
☐ Engine earth strap broken or disconnected (Chapter 5A)

Engine rotates, but will not start

☐ Fuel cut-off switch energised (Chapter 4)
☐ Fuel tank empty
☐ Battery discharged (engine rotates slowly) (Chapter 5A)
☐ Battery terminal connections loose or corroded (see *"Weekly checks"*)
☐ Ignition components damp or damaged (Chapters 1 and 5B)
☐ Broken, loose or disconnected wiring in the ignition circuit (Chapters 1 and 5B)
☐ Worn, faulty or incorrectly-gapped spark plugs (Chapter 1)
☐ Fuel injection system fault (Chapter 4)
☐ Major mechanical failure (eg camshaft drive) (Chapter 2)

Engine difficult to start when cold

☐ Battery discharged (Chapter 5A)
☐ Battery terminal connections loose or corroded (see *"Weekly checks"*)
☐ Worn, faulty or incorrectly-gapped spark plugs (Chapter 1)
☐ Fuel injection system fault (Chapter 4)
☐ Other ignition system fault (Chapters 1 and 5B)
☐ Low cylinder compressions (Chapter 2)

Engine difficult to start when hot

☐ Air filter element dirty or clogged (Chapter 1)
☐ Fuel injection system fault (Chapter 4)
☐ Low cylinder compressions (Chapter 2)

Starter motor noisy or excessively-rough in engagement

☐ Starter pinion or flywheel ring gear teeth loose or broken (Chapters 2 and 5A)
☐ Starter motor mounting bolts loose or missing (Chapter 5A)
☐ Starter motor internal components worn or damaged (Chapter 5A)

Engine starts, but stops immediately

☐ Loose or faulty electrical connections in the ignition circuit (Chapters 1 and 5B)
☐ Vacuum leak at the throttle body or inlet manifold (Chapter 4)
☐ Blocked injector/fuel injection system fault (Chapter 4)

Engine idles erratically

☐ Air filter element clogged (Chapter 1)
☐ Vacuum leak at the throttle body, inlet manifold or associated hoses (Chapter 4)

Engine idles erratically (continued)

☐ Worn, faulty or incorrectly-gapped spark plugs (Chapter 1)
☐ Uneven or low cylinder compressions (Chapter 2)
☐ Camshaft lobes worn (Chapter 2)
☐ Timing belt/chain incorrectly fitted (Chapter 2)
☐ Blocked injector/fuel injection system fault (Chapter 4)

Engine misfires at idle speed

☐ Worn, faulty or incorrectly-gapped spark plugs (Chapter 1)
☐ Faulty spark plug HT leads (Chapter 1)
☐ Vacuum leak at the throttle body, inlet manifold or associated hoses (Chapter 4)
☐ Blocked injector/fuel injection system fault (Chapter 4)
☐ Uneven or low cylinder compressions (Chapter 2)
☐ Disconnected, leaking, or perished crankcase ventilation hoses (Chapter 4)

Engine misfires throughout the driving speed range

☐ Fuel filter choked (Chapter 1)
☐ Fuel pump faulty, or delivery pressure low (Chapter 4)
☐ Fuel tank vent blocked, or fuel pipes restricted (Chapter 4)
☐ Vacuum leak at the throttle body, inlet manifold or associated hoses (Chapter 4)
☐ Worn, faulty or incorrectly-gapped spark plugs (Chapter 1)
☐ Faulty spark plug HT leads (Chapter 1)
☐ Faulty ignition coil (Chapter 5B)
☐ Uneven or low cylinder compressions (Chapter 2)
☐ Blocked injector/fuel injection system fault (Chapter 4)

Engine hesitates on acceleration

☐ Worn, faulty or incorrectly-gapped spark plugs (Chapter 1)
☐ Vacuum leak at the throttle body, inlet manifold or associated hoses (Chapter 4)
☐ Blocked injector/fuel injection system fault (Chapter 4)

Engine stalls

☐ Vacuum leak at the throttle body, inlet manifold or associated hoses (Chapter 4)
☐ Fuel filter choked (Chapter 1)
☐ Fuel pump faulty, or delivery pressure low (Chapter 4)
☐ Fuel tank vent blocked, or fuel pipes restricted (Chapter 4)
☐ Blocked injector/fuel injection system fault (Chapter 4)

Engine lacks power

☐ Timing belt/chain incorrectly fitted (Chapter 2)
☐ Fuel filter choked (Chapter 1)
☐ Fuel pump faulty, or delivery pressure low (Chapter 4)
☐ Uneven or low cylinder compressions (Chapter 2)
☐ Worn, faulty or incorrectly-gapped spark plugs (Chapter 1)
☐ Vacuum leak at the throttle body, inlet manifold or associated hoses (Chapter 4)
☐ Blocked injector/fuel injection system fault (Chapter 4)
☐ Brakes binding (Chapters 1 and 9)
☐ Clutch slipping (Chapter 6)

Engine (continued)

Engine backfires

- ☐ Timing belt incorrectly fitted (Chapter 2)
- ☐ Vacuum leak at the throttle body, inlet manifold or associated hoses (Chapter 4)
- ☐ Blocked injector/fuel injection system fault (Chapter 4)

Oil pressure warning light illuminated with engine running

- ☐ Low oil level, or incorrect oil grade (see "Weekly checks")
- ☐ Faulty oil pressure sensor
- ☐ Worn engine bearings and/or oil pump (Chapter 2)
- ☐ High engine operating temperature (Chapter 3)
- ☐ Oil pressure relief valve defective (Chapter 2)
- ☐ Oil pick-up strainer clogged (Chapter 2)

Engine runs-on after switching off

- ☐ Excessive carbon build-up in engine (Chapter 2)
- ☐ High engine operating temperature (Chapter 3)
- ☐ Fuel injection system fault (Chapter 4)

Engine noises

Pre-ignition (pinking) or knocking during acceleration or under load

- ☐ Ignition timing incorrect/ignition system fault (Chapters 1 and 5B)
- ☐ Incorrect grade of spark plug (Chapter 1)
- ☐ Incorrect grade of fuel (Chapter 4)

Pre-ignition (pinking) or knocking during acceleration or under load (continued)

- ☐ Vacuum leak at the throttle body, inlet manifold or associated hoses (Chapter 4)
- ☐ Excessive carbon build-up in engine (Chapter 2)
- ☐ Blocked injector/fuel injection system fault (Chapter 4)

Whistling or wheezing noises

- ☐ Leaking inlet manifold or throttle body gasket (Chapter 4)
- ☐ Leaking exhaust manifold gasket or pipe-to-manifold joint (Chapter 4)
- ☐ Leaking vacuum hose (Chapters 4, 5 and 9)
- ☐ Blowing cylinder head gasket (Chapter 2)

Tapping or rattling noises

- ☐ Worn valve gear or camshaft (Chapter 2)
- ☐ Ancillary component fault (coolant pump, alternator, etc) (Chapters 3, 5, etc)

Knocking or thumping noises

- ☐ Worn big-end bearings (regular heavy knocking, perhaps less under load) (Chapter 2)
- ☐ Worn main bearings (rumbling and knocking, perhaps worsening under load) (Chapter 2)
- ☐ Piston slap (most noticeable when cold) (Chapter 2)
- ☐ Ancillary component fault (coolant pump, alternator, etc) (Chapters 3, 5A, etc)

2 Cooling system

Overheating

- ☐ Insufficient coolant in system (see "Weekly checks")
- ☐ Thermostat faulty (Chapter 3)
- ☐ Radiator core blocked, or grille restricted (Chapter 3)
- ☐ Cooling fan faulty (Chapter 3)
- ☐ Inaccurate temperature gauge sender unit (Chapter 3)
- ☐ Airlock in cooling system (Chapter 3)
- ☐ Pressure cap faulty (Chapter 3)

Overcooling

- ☐ Thermostat faulty (Chapter 3)
- ☐ Inaccurate temperature gauge sender unit (Chapter 3)
- ☐ Cooling fan faulty (Chapter 3)

External coolant leakage

- ☐ Deteriorated or damaged hoses or hose clips (Chapter 1)
- ☐ Radiator core or heater matrix leaking (Chapter 3)
- ☐ Pressure cap faulty (Chapter 3)
- ☐ Coolant pump internal seal leaking (Chapter 3)
- ☐ Coolant pump-to-block seal leaking (Chapter 3)
- ☐ Boiling due to overheating (Chapter 3)
- ☐ Core plug leaking (Chapter 2)

Internal coolant leakage

- ☐ Leaking cylinder head gasket (Chapter 2)
- ☐ Cracked cylinder head or cylinder block (Chapter 2)

Corrosion

- ☐ Infrequent draining and flushing (Chapter 1)
- ☐ Incorrect coolant mixture or inappropriate coolant type (Chapter 1 and "Weekly checks")

3 Fuel and exhaust systems

Excessive fuel consumption

- ☐ Air filter element dirty or clogged (Chapter 1)
- ☐ Fuel injection system fault (Chapter 4)
- ☐ Ignition timing incorrect/ignition system fault (Chapters 1 and 5B)
- ☐ Tyres under-inflated (see "Weekly checks")

Fuel leakage and/or fuel odour

- ☐ Damaged or corroded fuel tank, pipes or connections (Chapter 4)

Excessive noise or fumes from exhaust system

- ☐ Leaking exhaust system or manifold joints (Chapters 1 and 4)
- ☐ Leaking, corroded or damaged silencers or pipe (Chapters 1 and 4)
- ☐ Broken mountings causing body or suspension contact (Chapter 1)

4 Clutch

Pedal travels to floor - no pressure or very little resistance

- ☐ Broken clutch cable (Chapter 6)
- ☐ Incorrect clutch cable adjustment (Chapter 6)
- ☐ Broken clutch release bearing or fork (Chapter 6)
- ☐ Broken diaphragm spring in clutch pressure plate (Chapter 6)

Clutch fails to disengage (unable to select gears)

- ☐ Incorrect clutch cable adjustment (Chapter 6)
- ☐ Clutch disc sticking on gearbox input shaft splines (Chapter 6)
- ☐ Clutch disc sticking to flywheel or pressure plate (Chapter 6)
- ☐ Faulty pressure plate assembly (Chapter 6)
- ☐ Clutch release mechanism worn or incorrectly assembled (Chapter 6)

Clutch slips (engine speed increases, with no increase in vehicle speed)

- ☐ Incorrect clutch cable adjustment (Chapter 6)
- ☐ Clutch disc linings excessively worn (Chapter 6)
- ☐ Clutch disc linings contaminated with oil or grease (Chapter 6)
- ☐ Faulty pressure plate or weak diaphragm spring (Chapter 6)

Judder as clutch is engaged

- ☐ Clutch disc linings contaminated with oil or grease (Chapter 6)
- ☐ Clutch disc linings excessively worn (Chapter 6)
- ☐ Faulty or distorted pressure plate or diaphragm spring (Chapter 6)
- ☐ Worn or loose engine or gearbox mountings (Chapter 2)
- ☐ Clutch disc hub or gearbox input shaft splines worn (Chapter 6)

Noise when depressing or releasing clutch pedal

- ☐ Worn clutch release bearing (Chapter 6)
- ☐ Worn or dry clutch pedal bushes (Chapter 6)
- ☐ Faulty pressure plate assembly (Chapter 6)
- ☐ Pressure plate diaphragm spring broken (Chapter 6)
- ☐ Broken clutch disc cushioning springs (Chapter 6)

5 Transmission

Noisy in neutral with engine running

- ☐ Input shaft bearings worn (noise apparent with clutch pedal released, but not when depressed) (Chapter 7)*
- ☐ Clutch release bearing worn (noise apparent with clutch pedal depressed, possibly less when released) (Chapter 6)

Noisy in one particular gear

- ☐ Worn, damaged or chipped gear teeth (Chapter 7)*

Difficulty engaging gears

- ☐ Clutch faulty (Chapter 6)
- ☐ Worn or damaged gearchange linkage (Chapter 7)
- ☐ Worn synchroniser units (Chapter 7)*

Jumps out of gear

- ☐ Worn or damaged gearchange linkage (Chapter 7)
- ☐ Worn synchroniser units (Chapter 7)*
- ☐ Worn selector forks (Chapter 7)*

Vibration

- ☐ Lack of oil (Chapter 1)
- ☐ Worn bearings (Chapter 7)*

Lubricant leaks

- ☐ Leaking differential output oil seal (Chapter 7)
- ☐ Leaking housing joint (Chapter 7)*
- ☐ Leaking input shaft oil seal (Chapter 7)*

Although the corrective action necessary to remedy the symptoms described is beyond the scope of the home mechanic, the above information should be helpful in isolating the cause of the condition, so that the owner can communicate clearly with a professional mechanic.

6 Driveshafts

Vibration when accelerating or decelerating

- ☐ Worn inner constant velocity joint (Chapter 8)
- ☐ Bent or distorted driveshaft (Chapter 8)
- ☐ Worn intermediate bearing (Chapter 8)

Clicking or knocking noise on turns (at slow speed on full-lock)

- ☐ Worn outer constant velocity joint (Chapter 8)
- ☐ Lack of constant velocity joint lubricant, possibly due to damaged gaiter (Chapter 8)
- ☐ Worn intermediate bearing (Chapter 8)

7 Braking system

Note: *Before assuming that a brake problem exists, make sure that the tyres are in good condition and correctly inflated, that the front wheel alignment is correct, and that the vehicle is not loaded with weight in an unequal manner. Apart from checking the condition of all pipe and hose connections, any faults occurring on the anti-lock braking system should be referred to a Ford dealer for diagnosis.*

Vehicle pulls to one side under braking

☐ Worn, defective, damaged or contaminated brake pads/shoes on one side (Chapters 1 and 9)
☐ Seized or partially-seized brake caliper piston/wheel cylinder (Chapters 1 and 9)
☐ A mixture of brake pad/shoe lining materials fitted between sides (Chapters 1 and 9)
☐ Brake caliper/backplate mounting bolts loose (Chapter 9)
☐ Worn or damaged steering or suspension components (Chapters 1 and 10)

Noise (grinding or high-pitched squeal) when brakes applied

☐ Brake pad/shoe friction lining material worn down to metal backing (Chapters 1 and 9)
☐ Excessive corrosion of brake disc/drum (may be apparent after the vehicle has been standing for some time (Chapters 1 and 9)
☐ Foreign object (stone chipping, etc) trapped between brake disc and shield (Chapters 1 and 9)

Excessive brake pedal travel

☐ Faulty master cylinder (Chapter 9)
☐ Air in hydraulic system (Chapters 1 and 9)
☐ Faulty vacuum servo unit (Chapter 9)

Brake pedal feels spongy when depressed

☐ Air in hydraulic system (Chapters 1 and 9)
☐ Deteriorated flexible rubber brake hoses (Chapters 1 and 9)
☐ Master cylinder mounting nuts loose (Chapter 9)
☐ Faulty master cylinder (Chapter 9)

Excessive brake pedal effort required to stop vehicle

☐ Faulty vacuum servo unit (Chapter 9)
☐ Disconnected, damaged or insecure brake servo vacuum hose (Chapter 9)
☐ Primary or secondary hydraulic circuit failure (Chapter 9)
☐ Seized brake caliper/wheel cylinder piston (Chapter 9)
☐ Brake pads/shoes incorrectly fitted (Chapters 1 and 9)
☐ Incorrect grade of brake pads/shoes fitted (Chapters 1 and 9)
☐ Brake pad/shoe linings contaminated (Chapters 1 and 9)

Judder felt through brake pedal or steering wheel when braking

☐ Excessive run-out or distortion of discs/drums (Chapters 1 and 9)
☐ Brake pad/shoe linings worn (Chapters 1 and 9)
☐ Brake caliper/backplate mounting bolts loose (Chapter 9)
☐ Wear in suspension or steering components or mountings (Chapters 1 and 10)

Brakes binding

☐ Seized brake caliper/wheel cylinder piston (Chapter 9)
☐ Incorrectly-adjusted handbrake mechanism (Chapter 9)
☐ Faulty master cylinder (Chapter 9)

Rear wheels locking under normal braking

☐ Rear brake pad/shoe linings contaminated (Chapters 1 and 9)
☐ Rear brake discs/drums warped (Chapters 1 and 9)

8 Suspension and steering

Note: *Before diagnosing suspension or steering faults, be sure that the trouble is not due to incorrect tyre pressures, mixtures of tyre types, or binding brakes.*

Vehicle pulls to one side

☐ Defective tyre (see *"Weekly checks"*)
☐ Excessive wear in suspension or steering components (Chapters 1 and 10)
☐ Incorrect front wheel alignment (Chapter 10)
☐ Accident damage to steering or suspension components (Chapter 1)

Wheel wobble and vibration

☐ Front roadwheels out of balance (vibration felt mainly through the steering wheel) (Chapter 10)
☐ Rear roadwheels out of balance (vibration felt throughout the vehicle) (Chapter 10)
☐ Roadwheels damaged or distorted
☐ Faulty or damaged tyre (see *"Weekly checks"*)
☐ Worn steering or suspension joints, bushes or components (Chapters 1 and 10)
☐ Wheel bolts loose

Excessive pitching and/or rolling around corners, or during braking

☐ Defective shock absorbers (Chapters 1 and 10)
☐ Broken or weak spring and/or suspension component (Chapters 1 and 10)
☐ Worn or damaged anti-roll bar or mountings – "Sporting" models (Chapter 10)

Wandering or general instability

☐ Incorrect front wheel alignment (Chapter 10)
☐ Worn steering or suspension joints, bushes or components (Chapters 1 and 10)
☐ Roadwheels out of balance (Chapter 10)
☐ Faulty or damaged tyre (see *"Weekly checks"*)
☐ Wheel bolts loose
☐ Defective shock absorbers (Chapters 1 and 10)

Excessively-stiff steering

☐ Seized steering linkage balljoint or suspension balljoint (Chapters 1 and 10)
☐ Broken or incorrectly-adjusted auxiliary drivebelt (Chapter 1)
☐ Incorrect front wheel alignment (Chapter 10)
☐ Steering gear damaged (Chapter 10)

Excessive play in steering

☐ Worn steering column/intermediate shaft joints (Chapter 10)
☐ Worn track rod balljoints (Chapters 1 and 10)
☐ Worn steering gear (Chapter 10)
☐ Worn steering or suspension joints, bushes or components (Chapters 1 and 10)

Tyre wear excessive

Tyres worn on inside or outside edges

- [ ] Tyres under-inflated (wear on both edges) (see *"Weekly checks"*)
- [ ] Incorrect camber or castor angles (wear on one edge only) (Chapter 10)
- [ ] Worn steering or suspension joints, bushes or components (Chapters 1 and 10)
- [ ] Excessively-hard cornering
- [ ] Accident damage

Tyre treads exhibit feathered edges

- [ ] Incorrect toe-setting (Chapter 10)

Tyres worn in centre of tread

- [ ] Tyres over-inflated (see *"Weekly checks"*)

Tyres worn on inside and outside edges

- [ ] Tyres under-inflated (see *"Weekly checks"*)

Tyres worn unevenly

- [ ] Tyres/wheels out of balance (Chapter 10)
- [ ] Excessive wheel or tyre run-out (see *"Weekly checks"*)
- [ ] Worn shock absorbers (Chapters 1 and 10)
- [ ] Faulty tyre (see *"Weekly checks"*)

9 Electrical system

Note: *For problems associated with the starting system, refer to the faults listed under "Engine" earlier in this Section.*

Battery will not hold a charge for more than a few days

- [ ] Battery defective internally (Chapter 5A)
- [ ] Battery terminal connections loose or corroded (see *"Weekly checks"*)
- [ ] Auxiliary drivebelt worn or incorrectly adjusted (Chapter 1)
- [ ] Alternator not charging at correct output (Chapter 5A)
- [ ] Alternator or voltage regulator faulty (Chapter 5A)
- [ ] Short-circuit causing continual battery drain (Chapters 5A and 12)

Ignition/no-charge warning light remains illuminated with engine running

- [ ] Auxiliary drivebelt broken, worn, or incorrectly adjusted (Chapter 1)
- [ ] Internal fault in alternator or voltage regulator (Chapter 5A)
- [ ] Broken, disconnected, or loose wiring in charging circuit (Chapter 5A)

Ignition/no-charge warning light fails to come on

- [ ] Warning light bulb blown (Chapter 12)
- [ ] Broken, disconnected, or loose wiring in warning light circuit (Chapter 12)
- [ ] Alternator faulty (Chapter 5A)

Lights inoperative

- [ ] Bulb blown (Chapter 12)
- [ ] Corrosion of bulb or bulbholder contacts (Chapter 12)
- [ ] Blown fuse (Chapter 12)
- [ ] Faulty relay (Chapter 12)
- [ ] Broken, loose, or disconnected wiring (Chapter 12)
- [ ] Faulty switch (Chapter 12)

Instrument readings inaccurate or erratic

Instrument readings increase with engine speed

- [ ] Faulty voltage regulator (Chapter 12)

Fuel or temperature gauges give no reading

- [ ] Faulty gauge sender unit (Chapters 3 and 4)
- [ ] Wiring open-circuit (Chapter 12)
- [ ] Faulty gauge (Chapter 12)

Fuel or temperature gauges give continuous maximum reading

- [ ] Faulty gauge sender unit (Chapters 3 and 4)
- [ ] Wiring short-circuit (Chapter 12)
- [ ] Faulty gauge (Chapter 12)

Horn inoperative, or unsatisfactory in operation

Horn operates all the time

- [ ] Horn push either earthed or stuck down (Chapter 12)
- [ ] Horn cable-to-horn push earthed (Chapter 12)

Horn fails to operate

- [ ] Blown fuse (Chapter 12)
- [ ] Cable or cable connections loose, broken or disconnected (Chapter 12)
- [ ] Faulty horn (Chapter 12)

Horn emits intermittent or unsatisfactory sound

- [ ] Cable connections loose (Chapter 12)
- [ ] Horn mountings loose (Chapter 12)
- [ ] Faulty horn (Chapter 12)

Windscreen wipers inoperative, or unsatisfactory in operation

Wipers fail to operate, or operate very slowly

- [ ] Wiper blades stuck to screen, or linkage seized or binding (Chapters 1 and 12)
- [ ] Blown fuse (Chapter 12)
- [ ] Cable or cable connections loose, broken or disconnected (Chapter 12)
- [ ] Faulty relay (Chapter 12)
- [ ] Faulty wiper motor (Chapter 12)

Wiper blades sweep over too large or too small an area of the glass

- [ ] Wiper arms incorrectly positioned on spindles
- [ ] Excessive wear of wiper linkage (Chapter 12)
- [ ] Wiper motor or linkage mountings loose or insecure (Chapter 12)

Wiper blades fail to clean the glass effectively

- [ ] Wiper blade rubbers worn or perished (see *"Weekly checks"*)
- [ ] Wiper arm tension springs broken, or arm pivots seized (Chapter 12)
- [ ] Insufficient windscreen washer additive to adequately remove road film (see *"Weekly checks"*)

Windscreen washers inoperative, or unsatisfactory in operation

One or more washer jets inoperative

- [ ] Blocked washer jet
- [ ] Disconnected, kinked or restricted fluid hose (Chapter 12)
- [ ] Insufficient fluid in washer reservoir (see *"Weekly checks"*)

Electrical system (continued)

Washer pump fails to operate

- ☐ Broken or disconnected wiring or connections (Chapter 12)
- ☐ Blown fuse (Chapter 12)
- ☐ Faulty washer switch (Chapter 12)
- ☐ Faulty washer pump (Chapter 12)

Washer pump runs for some time before fluid is emitted from jets

- ☐ Faulty one-way valve in fluid supply hose (Chapter 12)

Electric windows inoperative, or unsatisfactory in operation

Window glass will only move in one direction

- ☐ Faulty switch (Chapter 12)

Window glass slow to move

- ☐ Regulator seized or damaged, or in need of lubrication (Chapter 11)
- ☐ Door internal components or trim fouling regulator (Chapter 11)
- ☐ Faulty motor (Chapter 11)

Window glass fails to move

- ☐ Blown fuse (Chapter 12)
- ☐ Faulty relay (Chapter 12)
- ☐ Broken or disconnected wiring or connections (Chapter 12)
- ☐ Faulty motor (Chapter 11)

Central locking system inoperative, or unsatisfactory in operation

Complete system failure

- ☐ Blown fuse (Chapter 12)
- ☐ Faulty relay (Chapter 12)
- ☐ Broken or disconnected wiring or connections (Chapter 12)
- ☐ Faulty motor (Chapter 11)

Latch locks but will not unlock, or unlocks but will not lock

- ☐ Faulty master switch (Chapter 12)
- ☐ Broken or disconnected latch operating rods or levers (Chapter 11)
- ☐ Faulty relay (Chapter 12)
- ☐ Faulty motor (Chapter 11)

One solenoid/motor fails to operate

- ☐ Broken or disconnected wiring or connections (Chapter 12)
- ☐ Faulty operating assembly (Chapter 11)
- ☐ Broken, binding or disconnected latch operating rods or levers (Chapter 11)
- ☐ Fault in door latch (Chapter 11)

A

ABS (Anti-lock brake system) A system, usually electronically controlled, that senses incipient wheel lockup during braking and relieves hydraulic pressure at wheels that are about to skid.

Air bag An inflatable bag hidden in the steering wheel (driver's side) or the dash or glovebox (passenger side). In a head-on collision, the bags inflate, preventing the driver and front passenger from being thrown forward into the steering wheel or windscreen.

Air cleaner A metal or plastic housing, containing a filter element, which removes dust and dirt from the air being drawn into the engine.

Air filter element The actual filter in an air cleaner system, usually manufactured from pleated paper and requiring renewal at regular intervals.

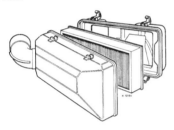

Air filter

Allen key A hexagonal wrench which fits into a recessed hexagonal hole.

Alligator clip A long-nosed spring-loaded metal clip with meshing teeth. Used to make temporary electrical connections.

Alternator A component in the electrical system which converts mechanical energy from a drivebelt into electrical energy to charge the battery and to operate the starting system, ignition system and electrical accessories.

Alternator (exploded view)

Ampere (amp) A unit of measurement for the flow of electric current. One amp is the amount of current produced by one volt acting through a resistance of one ohm.

Anaerobic sealer A substance used to prevent bolts and screws from loosening. Anaerobic means that it does not require oxygen for activation. The Loctite brand is widely used.

Antifreeze A substance (usually ethylene glycol) mixed with water, and added to a vehicle's cooling system, to prevent freezing of the coolant in winter. Antifreeze also contains chemicals to inhibit corrosion and the formation of rust and other deposits that would tend to clog the radiator and coolant passages and reduce cooling efficiency.

Anti-seize compound A coating that reduces the risk of seizing on fasteners that are subjected to high temperatures, such as exhaust manifold bolts and nuts.

Anti-seize compound

Asbestos A natural fibrous mineral with great heat resistance, commonly used in the composition of brake friction materials. Asbestos is a health hazard and the dust created by brake systems should never be inhaled or ingested.

Axle A shaft on which a wheel revolves, or which revolves with a wheel. Also, a solid beam that connects the two wheels at one end of the vehicle. An axle which also transmits power to the wheels is known as a live axle.

Axle assembly

Axleshaft A single rotating shaft, on either side of the differential, which delivers power from the final drive assembly to the drive wheels. Also called a driveshaft or a halfshaft.

B

Ball bearing An anti-friction bearing consisting of a hardened inner and outer race with hardened steel balls between two races.

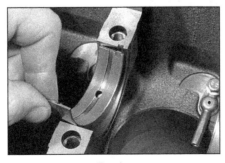

Bearing

Bearing The curved surface on a shaft or in a bore, or the part assembled into either, that permits relative motion between them with minimum wear and friction.

Big-end bearing The bearing in the end of the connecting rod that's attached to the crankshaft.

Bleed nipple A valve on a brake wheel cylinder, caliper or other hydraulic component that is opened to purge the hydraulic system of air. Also called a bleed screw.

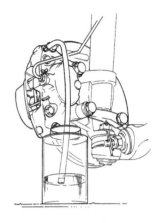

Brake bleeding

Brake bleeding Procedure for removing air from lines of a hydraulic brake system.

Brake disc The component of a disc brake that rotates with the wheels.

Brake drum The component of a drum brake that rotates with the wheels.

Brake linings The friction material which contacts the brake disc or drum to retard the vehicle's speed. The linings are bonded or riveted to the brake pads or shoes.

Brake pads The replaceable friction pads that pinch the brake disc when the brakes are applied. Brake pads consist of a friction material bonded or riveted to a rigid backing plate.

Brake shoe The crescent-shaped carrier to which the brake linings are mounted and which forces the lining against the rotating drum during braking.

Braking systems For more information on braking systems, consult the *Haynes Automotive Brake Manual*.

Breaker bar A long socket wrench handle providing greater leverage.

Bulkhead The insulated partition between the engine and the passenger compartment.

C

Caliper The non-rotating part of a disc-brake assembly that straddles the disc and carries the brake pads. The caliper also contains the hydraulic components that cause the pads to pinch the disc when the brakes are applied. A caliper is also a measuring tool that can be set to measure inside or outside dimensions of an object.

Camshaft A rotating shaft on which a series of cam lobes operate the valve mechanisms. The camshaft may be driven by gears, by sprockets and chain or by sprockets and a belt.

Canister A container in an evaporative emission control system; contains activated charcoal granules to trap vapours from the fuel system.

Canister

Carburettor A device which mixes fuel with air in the proper proportions to provide a desired power output from a spark ignition internal combustion engine.

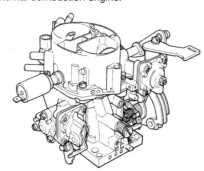

Carburettor

Castellated Resembling the parapets along the top of a castle wall. For example, a castellated balljoint stud nut.

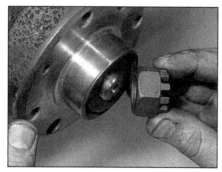

Castellated nut

Castor In wheel alignment, the backward or forward tilt of the steering axis. Castor is positive when the steering axis is inclined rearward at the top.

Catalytic converter A silencer-like device in the exhaust system which converts certain pollutants in the exhaust gases into less harmful substances.

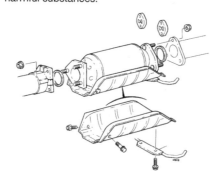

Catalytic converter

Circlip A ring-shaped clip used to prevent endwise movement of cylindrical parts and shafts. An internal circlip is installed in a groove in a housing; an external circlip fits into a groove on the outside of a cylindrical piece such as a shaft.

Clearance The amount of space between two parts. For example, between a piston and a cylinder, between a bearing and a journal, etc.

Coil spring A spiral of elastic steel found in various sizes throughout a vehicle, for example as a springing medium in the suspension and in the valve train.

Compression Reduction in volume, and increase in pressure and temperature, of a gas, caused by squeezing it into a smaller space.

Compression ratio The relationship between cylinder volume when the piston is at top dead centre and cylinder volume when the piston is at bottom dead centre.

Constant velocity (CV) joint A type of universal joint that cancels out vibrations caused by driving power being transmitted through an angle.

Core plug A disc or cup-shaped metal device inserted in a hole in a casting through which core was removed when the casting was formed. Also known as a freeze plug or expansion plug.

Crankcase The lower part of the engine block in which the crankshaft rotates.

Crankshaft The main rotating member, or shaft, running the length of the crankcase, with offset "throws" to which the connecting rods are attached.

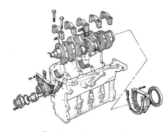

Crankshaft assembly

Crocodile clip See Alligator clip

D

Diagnostic code Code numbers obtained by accessing the diagnostic mode of an engine management computer. This code can be used to determine the area in the system where a malfunction may be located.

Disc brake A brake design incorporating a rotating disc onto which brake pads are squeezed. The resulting friction converts the energy of a moving vehicle into heat.

Double-overhead cam (DOHC) An engine that uses two overhead camshafts, usually one for the intake valves and one for the exhaust valves.

Drivebelt(s) The belt(s) used to drive accessories such as the alternator, water pump, power steering pump, air conditioning compressor, etc. off the crankshaft pulley.

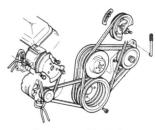

Accessory drivebelts

Driveshaft Any shaft used to transmit motion. Commonly used when referring to the axleshafts on a front wheel drive vehicle.

Driveshaft

Drum brake A type of brake using a drum-shaped metal cylinder attached to the inner surface of the wheel. When the brake pedal is pressed, curved brake shoes with friction linings press against the inside of the drum to slow or stop the vehicle.

Drum brake assembly

E

EGR valve A valve used to introduce exhaust gases into the intake air stream.

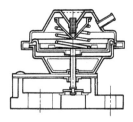

EGR valve

Electronic control unit (ECU) A computer which controls (for instance) ignition and fuel injection systems, or an anti-lock braking system. For more information refer to the *Haynes Automotive Electrical and Electronic Systems Manual.*

Electronic Fuel Injection (EFI) A computer controlled fuel system that distributes fuel through an injector located in each intake port of the engine.

Emergency brake A braking system, independent of the main hydraulic system, that can be used to slow or stop the vehicle if the primary brakes fail, or to hold the vehicle stationary even though the brake pedal isn't depressed. It usually consists of a hand lever that actuates either front or rear brakes mechanically through a series of cables and linkages. Also known as a handbrake or parking brake.

Endfloat The amount of lengthwise movement between two parts. As applied to a crankshaft, the distance that the crankshaft can move forward and back in the cylinder block.

Engine management system (EMS) A computer controlled system which manages the fuel injection and the ignition systems in an integrated fashion.

Exhaust manifold A part with several passages through which exhaust gases leave the engine combustion chambers and enter the exhaust pipe.

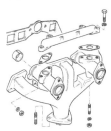

Exhaust manifold

F

Fan clutch A viscous (fluid) drive coupling device which permits variable engine fan speeds in relation to engine speeds.

Feeler blade A thin strip or blade of hardened steel, ground to an exact thickness, used to check or measure clearances between parts.

Feeler blade

Firing order The order in which the engine cylinders fire, or deliver their power strokes, beginning with the number one cylinder.

Flywheel A heavy spinning wheel in which energy is absorbed and stored by means of momentum. On cars, the flywheel is attached to the crankshaft to smooth out firing impulses.

Free play The amount of travel before any action takes place. The "looseness" in a linkage, or an assembly of parts, between the initial application of force and actual movement. For example, the distance the brake pedal moves before the pistons in the master cylinder are actuated.

Fuse An electrical device which protects a circuit against accidental overload. The typical fuse contains a soft piece of metal which is calibrated to melt at a predetermined current flow (expressed as amps) and break the circuit.

Fusible link A circuit protection device consisting of a conductor surrounded by heat-resistant insulation. The conductor is smaller than the wire it protects, so it acts as the weakest link in the circuit. Unlike a blown fuse, a failed fusible link must frequently be cut from the wire for replacement.

G

Gap The distance the spark must travel in jumping from the centre electrode to the side

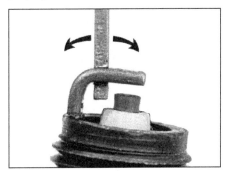

Adjusting spark plug gap

electrode in a spark plug. Also refers to the spacing between the points in a contact breaker assembly in a conventional points-type ignition, or to the distance between the reluctor or rotor and the pickup coil in an electronic ignition.

Gasket Any thin, soft material - usually cork, cardboard, asbestos or soft metal - installed between two metal surfaces to ensure a good seal. For instance, the cylinder head gasket seals the joint between the block and the cylinder head.

Gasket

Gauge An instrument panel display used to monitor engine conditions. A gauge with a movable pointer on a dial or a fixed scale is an analogue gauge. A gauge with a numerical readout is called a digital gauge.

H

Halfshaft A rotating shaft that transmits power from the final drive unit to a drive wheel, usually when referring to a live rear axle.

Harmonic balancer A device designed to reduce torsion or twisting vibration in the crankshaft. May be incorporated in the crankshaft pulley. Also known as a vibration damper.

Hone An abrasive tool for correcting small irregularities or differences in diameter in an engine cylinder, brake cylinder, etc.

Hydraulic tappet A tappet that utilises hydraulic pressure from the engine's lubrication system to maintain zero clearance (constant contact with both camshaft and valve stem). Automatically adjusts to variation in valve stem length. Hydraulic tappets also reduce valve noise.

I

Ignition timing The moment at which the spark plug fires, usually expressed in the number of crankshaft degrees before the piston reaches the top of its stroke.

Inlet manifold A tube or housing with passages through which flows the air-fuel mixture (carburettor vehicles and vehicles with throttle body injection) or air only (port fuel-injected vehicles) to the port openings in the cylinder head.

J

Jump start Starting the engine of a vehicle with a discharged or weak battery by attaching jump leads from the weak battery to a charged or helper battery.

L

Load Sensing Proportioning Valve (LSPV) A brake hydraulic system control valve that works like a proportioning valve, but also takes into consideration the amount of weight carried by the rear axle.

Locknut A nut used to lock an adjustment nut, or other threaded component, in place. For example, a locknut is employed to keep the adjusting nut on the rocker arm in position.

Lockwasher A form of washer designed to prevent an attaching nut from working loose.

M

MacPherson strut A type of front suspension system devised by Earle MacPherson at Ford of England. In its original form, a simple lateral link with the anti-roll bar creates the lower control arm. A long strut - an integral coil spring and shock absorber - is mounted between the body and the steering knuckle. Many modern so-called MacPherson strut systems use a conventional lower A-arm and don't rely on the anti-roll bar for location.

Multimeter An electrical test instrument with the capability to measure voltage, current and resistance.

N

NOx Oxides of Nitrogen. A common toxic pollutant emitted by petrol and diesel engines at higher temperatures.

O

Ohm The unit of electrical resistance. One volt applied to a resistance of one ohm will produce a current of one amp.

Ohmmeter An instrument for measuring electrical resistance.

O-ring A type of sealing ring made of a special rubber-like material; in use, the O-ring is compressed into a groove to provide the sealing action.

O-ring

Overhead cam (ohc) engine An engine with the camshaft(s) located on top of the cylinder head(s).

Overhead valve (ohv) engine An engine with the valves located in the cylinder head, but with the camshaft located in the engine block.

Oxygen sensor A device installed in the engine exhaust manifold, which senses the oxygen content in the exhaust and converts this information into an electric current. Also called a Lambda sensor.

P

Phillips screw A type of screw head having a cross instead of a slot for a corresponding type of screwdriver.

Plastigage A thin strip of plastic thread, available in different sizes, used for measuring clearances. For example, a strip of Plastigage is laid across a bearing journal. The parts are assembled and dismantled; the width of the crushed strip indicates the clearance between journal and bearing.

Plastigage

Propeller shaft The long hollow tube with universal joints at both ends that carries power from the transmission to the differential on front-engined rear wheel drive vehicles.

Proportioning valve A hydraulic control valve which limits the amount of pressure to the rear brakes during panic stops to prevent wheel lock-up.

R

Rack-and-pinion steering A steering system with a pinion gear on the end of the steering shaft that mates with a rack (think of a geared wheel opened up and laid flat). When the steering wheel is turned, the pinion turns, moving the rack to the left or right. This movement is transmitted through the track rods to the steering arms at the wheels.

Radiator A liquid-to-air heat transfer device designed to reduce the temperature of the coolant in an internal combustion engine cooling system.

Refrigerant Any substance used as a heat transfer agent in an air-conditioning system. R-12 has been the principle refrigerant for many years; recently, however, manufacturers have begun using R-134a, a non-CFC substance that is considered less harmful to the ozone in the upper atmosphere.

Rocker arm A lever arm that rocks on a shaft or pivots on a stud. In an overhead valve engine, the rocker arm converts the upward movement of the pushrod into a downward movement to open a valve.

Rotor In a distributor, the rotating device inside the cap that connects the centre electrode and the outer terminals as it turns, distributing the high voltage from the coil secondary winding to the proper spark plug. Also, that part of an alternator which rotates inside the stator. Also, the rotating assembly of a turbocharger, including the compressor wheel, shaft and turbine wheel.

Runout The amount of wobble (in-and-out movement) of a gear or wheel as it's rotated. The amount a shaft rotates "out-of-true." The out-of-round condition of a rotating part.

S

Sealant A liquid or paste used to prevent leakage at a joint. Sometimes used in conjunction with a gasket.

Sealed beam lamp An older headlight design which integrates the reflector, lens and filaments into a hermetically-sealed one-piece unit. When a filament burns out or the lens cracks, the entire unit is simply replaced.

Serpentine drivebelt A single, long, wide accessory drivebelt that's used on some newer vehicles to drive all the accessories, instead of a series of smaller, shorter belts. Serpentine drivebelts are usually tensioned by an automatic tensioner.

Serpentine drivebelt

Shim Thin spacer, commonly used to adjust the clearance or relative positions between two parts. For example, shims inserted into or under bucket tappets control valve clearances. Clearance is adjusted by changing the thickness of the shim.

Slide hammer A special puller that screws into or hooks onto a component such as a shaft or bearing; a heavy sliding handle on the shaft bottoms against the end of the shaft to knock the component free.

Sprocket A tooth or projection on the periphery of a wheel, shaped to engage with a chain or drivebelt. Commonly used to refer to the sprocket wheel itself.

Starter inhibitor switch On vehicles with an

automatic transmission, a switch that prevents starting if the vehicle is not in Neutral or Park.

Strut See MacPherson strut.

T

Tappet A cylindrical component which transmits motion from the cam to the valve stem, either directly or via a pushrod and rocker arm. Also called a cam follower.

Thermostat A heat-controlled valve that regulates the flow of coolant between the cylinder block and the radiator, so maintaining optimum engine operating temperature. A thermostat is also used in some air cleaners in which the temperature is regulated.

Thrust bearing The bearing in the clutch assembly that is moved in to the release levers by clutch pedal action to disengage the clutch. Also referred to as a release bearing.

Timing belt A toothed belt which drives the camshaft. Serious engine damage may result if it breaks in service.

Timing chain A chain which drives the camshaft.

Toe-in The amount the front wheels are closer together at the front than at the rear. On rear wheel drive vehicles, a slight amount of toe-in is usually specified to keep the front wheels running parallel on the road by offsetting other forces that tend to spread the wheels apart.

Toe-out The amount the front wheels are closer together at the rear than at the front. On

front wheel drive vehicles, a slight amount of toe-out is usually specified.

Tools For full information on choosing and using tools, refer to the *Haynes Automotive Tools Manual.*

Tracer A stripe of a second colour applied to a wire insulator to distinguish that wire from another one with the same colour insulator.

Tune-up A process of accurate and careful adjustments and parts replacement to obtain the best possible engine performance.

Turbocharger A centrifugal device, driven by exhaust gases, that pressurises the intake air. Normally used to increase the power output from a given engine displacement, but can also be used primarily to reduce exhaust emissions (as on VW's "Umwelt" Diesel engine).

U

Universal joint or U-joint A double-pivoted connection for transmitting power from a driving to a driven shaft through an angle. A U-joint consists of two Y-shaped yokes and a cross-shaped member called the spider.

V

Valve A device through which the flow of liquid, gas, vacuum, or loose material in bulk may be started, stopped, or regulated by a movable part that opens, shuts, or partially

obstructs one or more ports or passageways. A valve is also the movable part of such a device.

Valve clearance The clearance between the valve tip (the end of the valve stem) and the rocker arm or tappet. The valve clearance is measured when the valve is closed.

Vernier caliper A precision measuring instrument that measures inside and outside dimensions. Not quite as accurate as a micrometer, but more convenient.

Viscosity The thickness of a liquid or its resistance to flow.

Volt A unit for expressing electrical "pressure" in a circuit. One volt that will produce a current of one ampere through a resistance of one ohm.

W

Welding Various processes used to join metal items by heating the areas to be joined to a molten state and fusing them together. For more information refer to the *Haynes Automotive Welding Manual.*

Wiring diagram A drawing portraying the components and wires in a vehicle's electrical system, using standardised symbols. For more information refer to the *Haynes Automotive Electrical and Electronic Systems Manual.*

Note: *References throughout this index are in the form - "Chapter number" • "page number"*

Preserving Our Motoring Heritage

< The Model J Duesenberg Derham Tourster. Only eight of these magnificent cars were ever built – this is the only example to be found outside the United States of America

Almost every car you've ever loved, loathed or desired is gathered under one roof at the Haynes Motor Museum. Over 300 immaculately presented cars and motorbikes represent every aspect of our motoring heritage, from elegant reminders of bygone days, such as the superb Model J Duesenberg to curiosities like the bug-eyed BMW Isetta. There are also many old friends and flames. Perhaps you remember the 1959 Ford Popular that you did your courting in? The magnificent 'Red Collection' is a spectacle of classic sports cars including AC, Alfa Romeo, Austin Healey, Ferrari, Lamborghini, Maserati, MG, Riley, Porsche and Triumph.

A Perfect Day Out

Each and every vehicle at the Haynes Motor Museum has played its part in the history and culture of Motoring. Today, they make a wonderful spectacle and a great day out for all the family. Bring the kids, bring Mum and Dad, but above all bring your camera to capture those golden memories for ever. You will also find an impressive array of motoring memorabilia, a comfortable 70 seat video cinema and one of the most extensive transport book shops in Britain. The Pit Stop Cafe serves everything from a cup of tea to wholesome, home-made meals or, if you prefer, you can enjoy the large picnic area nestled in the beautiful rural surroundings of Somerset.

> John Haynes O.B.E., Founder and Chairman of the museum at the wheel of a Haynes Light 12.

< Graham Hill's Lola Cosworth Formula 1 car next to a 1934 Riley Sports.

The Museum is situated on the A359 Yeovil to Frome road at Sparkford, just off the A303 in Somerset. It is about 40 miles south of Bristol, and 25 minutes drive from the M5 intersection at Taunton.
Open 9.30am - 5.30pm (10.00am - 4.00pm Winter) 7 days a week, *except Christmas Day, Boxing Day and New Years Day*
Special rates available for schools, coach parties and outings Charitable Trust No. 292048